TRANSPORT CORRIDORS IN AFRICA

T0385743

RELATED JAMES CURREY TITLES ON CENTRAL & SOUTHERN AFRICA

Roots of Rural Poverty in South Central Africa
ROBIN PALMER & NEIL PARSONS (EDS)

Diamonds, Dispossession and Democracy in Botswana
KENNETH GOOD

Crossing the Zambezi: The Politics of Landscape on a Central African Frontier
JO-ANN MCGREGOR

Circular Migration in Zimbabwe and Contemporary Sub-Saharan Africa
DEBORAH POTTS

Remaking Mutirikwi: Landscape, Water and Belonging in Southern Zimbabwe
JOOST FONTEIN

The War Within: New Perspectives on the Civil War in Mozambique, 1976–1992
ERIC MORIER-GENOUD ET AL. (EDS)

Faith, Power and Family: Christianity and Social Change in French Cameroon
CHARLOTTE WALKER-SAID

Manhood, Morality & the Transformation of Angolan Society:
MPLA Veterans & Post-war Dynamics
JOHN SPALL

Protestant Missionaries & Humanitarianism in the DRC:
The Politics of Aid in Cold War Africa
JEREMY RICH

Across the Copperbelt: Urban & Social Change in Central Africa's
Borderland Communities
MILES LARMER ET AL. (EDS)

Namib: The Archaeology of an African Desert
JOHN KINAHAN

The Politics of the Dead in Zimbabwe 2000–2020: Bones, Rumours & Spirits
JOOST FONTEIN

Competing Catholicisms:
The Jesuits, the Vatican & the Making of Postcolonial French Africa
JEAN LUC ENYEGUE, SJ

Manufacturing in Colonial Zimbabwe, 1890–1979:
Interest Group Politics, Protectionism & the State
VICTOR MUCHINERIPI GWANDE*

Conservation, Markets & the Environment in Southern and Eastern Africa:
Commodifying the 'Wild'
MICHAEL BOLLIG ET AL. (EDS)*

* forthcoming

TRANSPORT CORRIDORS IN AFRICA

Edited by
Hugh Lamarque and Paul Nugent

 JAMES CURREY

James Currey is an imprint of
Boydell & Brewer Ltd
PO Box 9, Woodbridge, Suffolk IP 12 3DF (GB)
www.jamescurrey.com
and of
Boydell & Brewer Inc.,
668 Mt Hope Avenue, Rochester, NY 14620–2731 (US)
www.boydellandbrewer.com

This book is based on research from a European Research Council (ERC)
Advanced Grant for the project entitled African Governance and Space:
Transport Corridors, Border Towns and Port Cities in Transition (AFRIGOS)
[ADG-2014–670851]

A catalogue record for this book is available from the British Library

ISBN 978–1–84701–294–4 (James Currey paperback)

The publisher has no responsibility for the continued existence or accuracy
of URLs for external or third-party internet websites referred to in this book,
and does not guarantee that any content on such websites is, or will remain,
accurate or appropriate

Contents

Illustrations

Maps

Photographs

Figures

Tables

Full credit details are provided in the captions to the images in the text. The editors, contributors and publisher are grateful to all the institutions and persons for permission to reproduce the materials in which they hold copyright. Every effort has been made to trace the copyright holders; apologies are offered for any omission, and the publisher will be pleased to add any necessary acknowledgement in subsequent editions.

Notes on Contributors

Bruce Byiers is a development economist with a doctorate from the University of Sussex. He has headed the African Institutions and Regional Dynamics Programme at ECDPM since 2011. The main focus of his work is on regional organisations and broader regional co-operation and integration dynamics in Africa, seeking to link a political economy approach to understanding these dynamics with policy implications for regional policy-makers and international partners. He has also worked on issues related to enterprise development, informality and tax policies, all of which come into this work. He worked in the Mozambican Ministry of Planning and Development/Finance for five years, and has worked on multiple projects across the continent, working at both regional and national levels for a variety of international partners.

Yunnan Chen is a Senior Research Officer at the Overseas Development Institute, focusing on development finance institutions China's role in the global development finance architecture, and Chinese infrastructure projects (particularly rail) in Africa. She is a PhD candidate at Johns Hopkins School of Advanced International Studies and formerly a pre-doc fellow at the Global Development Policy Centre, Boston University, and at the Centre for Global Development. She has worked at the SAIS China Africa Research Initiative, where she was a research assistant, at the Institute of Development Studies, Sussex, and Chinadialogue, London. She holds an MA in Political Science from the University of British Columbia, and a BA in Politics, Philosophy and Economics from the University of Oxford.

Sidy Cissokho is a post-doctoral Research Fellow on the AFRIGOS project at the University of Edinburgh. For his PhD he has researched the Senegalese professional driver association and their relationship with the government and political parties of Senegal.

Elisa Gambino is a Fellow in the International Politics of China at the London School of Economics and Political Sciences. Prior to this, her PhD in African Studies at the University of Edinburgh contributed to the 'African Governance and Space: Transport Corridors, Border Towns and Port Cities in Transition' (AFRIGOS) project funded by the European Research Council. Elisa's research focuses on the analysis of power relations among Chinese and African state and non-state actors in the development of major infrastructure projects. She has a Master's in Chinese Studies from the University of Edinburgh and a Bachelor's in Applied Languages from the University of Turin.

Hugh Lamarque is a Leverhulme Research Fellow at the University of Edinburgh with a Doctorate in Politics from the School of Oriental and African Studies, University of London. Hugh has previously worked for the European Research Council AFRIGOS Project, the United Nations Development Programme, the World Bank, the Social Science in Humanitarian Action Platform, AKE Group, the British Institute in Eastern Africa, and as visiting Research Fellow at Lisbon University's Institute for Social Sciences.

Jerome Lombard is Doctor in Geography and Research Director at the French Research Institute for Development. His current research is on African transport systems and their relationship with territorial development. He focuses mainly on West Africa, especially on Senegal, Mauritania and Morocco.

Francesc Magrinyà is a civil engineer with a PhD in urban planning, and an expert in urban planning, transportation and resilience of metropolitan areas. He is Professor of Urban Planning at the Department of Civil and Environmental Engineering (Technical University of Catalonia, Barcelona Tech) and the Coordinator of the EXIT-UPC Research Group (Engineering, Networks, Infrastructures and Transport). He was previously Director of the Strategic Planning Area of the Barcelona Metropolitan Area.

José-María Muñoz is a social anthropologist who has conducted research in West–Central Africa since 2003. He is a Senior Lecturer in African Studies and International Development at the University of Edinburgh. His works include *Doing Business in Cameroon* (Cambridge University Press, 2018), a book monograph on economic governance in the city of Ngaoundéré.

Paul Nugent is a historian and political economist with a first postgraduate degree from the University of Cape Town and a doctorate from SOAS, University of London. He is Professor of Comparative African History at the University of Edinburgh and the Principal Investigator of the AFRIGOS project. In 2019, he published *Boundaries, Communities and State-Making in West Africa* (Cambridge University Press, 2019) which is a comparison of the ways in which border dynamics in Ghana/Togo and Senegal/Gambia have shaped states and understandings of community differently across two sub-regions. As part of the AFRIGOS project, he has also conducted research in East Africa. Paul is the founder/chair of the African Borderlands Research Network. He is also a member of the Africa–Europe Strategic Taskforce dealing with transport and connectivity, which is convened by the Africa Europe Foundation in support of African Union/European Union co-operation.

Sergio Oliete Josa is a civil engineer and urban planner specialising in transport and cities in Sub-Saharan Africa. He works for the European Commission as team leader for the transport sector in the Directorate-General for International Partnerships. He has been posted in several countries in West and Central Africa and has written a number of academic papers analysing the evolution and sustainability of the transport networks in the continent.

Isabella Soi is an associate professor in African History at the University of Cagliari. Her research interests focus on borders development and dynamics, particularly in relation to trade and population movements; refugee movements; national and religious minorities; and the relation between religion and politics in East Africa, particularly in Uganda. Her publications include *Minoranze religiose nel continente africano: Il caso delle comunità ebraiche di Tunisia e di Uganda* (with Filippo Petrucci; Aracne Editore, 2016.

Nina Sylvanus is a political and economic anthropologist whose work centres on capital and labour, value and aesthetics, infrastructure and technology, and, more broadly, critical transformations in the neoliberal global economy. Sylvanus is the author of *Patterns in Circulation: Cloth, Gender and Materiality in West Africa* (University of Chicago Press, 2016), a study of the dense materiality and rich signifying qualities of African print cloth.

Sean Woolfrey is a Senior Policy Advisor at the International Institute for Sustainable Development (IISD). He is responsible for developing and coordinating IISD's research on how trade, investment and equitable markets in food and agriculture can serve to promote food security, improve livelihoods, reduce inequality, and ensure more responsible use the planet's resources. Prior to joining IISD, Sean worked at the European Centre for Development Policy Management, where his work covered topics relating to African and European trade, the political economy of regional integration in Africa and the sustainability of African food systems.

Preface and Acknowledgements

This volume arises out of a European Research Council (ERC) Advanced Grant for the project entitled *African Governance and Space: Transport Corridors, Border Towns and Port Cities in Transition (AFRIGOS)* [ADG-2014–670851]. Paul Nugent was the principal investigator for the project hosted at the University of Edinburgh which has, at various times employed Sidy Cissokho, Elisa Gambino, Hugh Lamarque, José-María Muñoz, Wolfgang Zeller and Tim Zajontz, with Isabella Soi from the University of Cagliari participating as a research affiliate. Under the architecture of the project, Cissokho was mandated to research the role of international institutions, while the doctoral project of Gambino was focused on the Chinese involvement in corridor development. All the other researchers were mandated to deal with one or more sub-region and a specific corridor within it. When it came to compiling a book for the project, we wished to bring out the richness from each of these sets of case studies. But we were also conscious of the fact that we needed to offer a more rounded view and to address some case studies that were not part of the original project design. We are fortunate, therefore, to have been able to enrich the volume by including contributions from Sergio Oliete and Francesc Magrinyà, Bruce Byiers and Sean Woolfrey, Jérôme Lombard, Nina Sylvanus and Yunnan Chen.

The editors are grateful to all of the above. In addition, we would like to acknowledge three individuals who offered advice at various stages and facilitated the field research: Ziad Hamoui of the Borderless Alliance in West Africa, Michael Ojatum of TradeMark East Africa and Lovemore Bingandadi of the SADC Secretariat. Finally, we are indebted to our ethics advisor, Karine Bennafla and the other members of the advisory board, Mohamadou Abdoul, Gregor Dobler and Olivier Walther. Many thanks are also extended to Brooks Marmon and Simon Dix for outstanding editing work.

Hugh Lamarque and Paul Nugent

CHAPTER 1

Introduction
Transport Corridors in Africa:
Synergy, Slippage and Sustainability

PAUL NUGENT AND HUGH LAMARQUE

The critical attention and material resources that governments have devoted to transport infrastructure has fluctuated markedly over time. A hundred years ago, colonial regimes were investing in infrastructure to serve the incipient mining industry and the cash crop zones, in an effort to render their colonies economically viable – that is before the onset of the Great Depression forced them back into their shells. In the 1950s, the post-war commodity boom, and the imperative to win the compliance of African subjects, led to unprecedented investments in roads, railways and seaports across the British and French colonies – all in the name of something that came to be labelled as 'development'.[1] This provided the infrastructural foundations that post-colonial regimes continued to build upon over the ensuing decades. The one difference was that almost no railways were built after the 1960s, because they had come to be perceived as being prohibitively expensive – although certain key lines were maintained when they were needed by the mining industry or were regarded as an essential lifeline for landlocked countries.[2]

---

[1] Frederick Cooper, 'Modernising Bureaucrats, Backward Africans, and the Development Concept', in Frederick Cooper and Randall Packard (eds), *International Development and the Social Sciences: Essays in the History and Politics of Knowledge* (Berkeley & London, 1998), pp. 64–92; On seaports, see B.S. Hoyle and D. Hilling (eds), *Seaports and Development in Tropical Africa*, London, 1970.

[2] The Transcamerounais, which is dealt with by Muñoz in this volume, was one important exception. The other was the Chinese-constructed Tazara railway, running from Zambia to the Tanzanian port of Dar-es-Salaam. It was completed in 1975. Jamie Monson, *Africa's Freedom Railway: How a Chinese Development Project Changed Lives and Livelihoods in Tanzania*, Bloomington, 2011. The slow decay of the Bamako–Dakar railway exemplifies the continental pattern.

After the oil crisis of the mid-1970s, most cash-strapped African governments lacked the resources to do more than mark time. In the case of the Democratic Republic of Congo (DRC) and the Central African Republic (CAR) functional transport infrastructure may actually have halved.[3] Donors to heavily indebted countries became increasingly sceptical about the ability of large-scale and costly infrastructural investments to deliver economic transformation. Most donor funding went into supporting road networks, and much was channelled into feeder roads linked to agricultural development projects sponsored by the World Bank. During the heyday of structural adjustment in the 1980s, African governments were pressured to establish the right macroeconomic conditions, to get the agricultural prices right and to scale back on costly public investments. At the same time, they were encouraged to let the private sector take the lead in fostering transport links. The shift was most evident in ports and on the railways where international corporations like Bolloré and Maersk managed to cement their grip.[4] But this did not necessarily translate into significant fresh investment in the underpinning infrastructure, in a context where donor investment in the transport sector was miserly.[5] It is only since the turn of the millennium that the pendulum has swung back again – and with some force.[6] As we indicate below, African governments have been willing to take on new debts, and new types of debt, in order to achieve their own infrastructural ambitions. It also has had much to do with the willingness of China to finance and construct new infrastructure (Gambino, this volume), which has been matched by a paradigm shift within the World Bank, the European Union (EU) and the African Development Bank (AfDB). Given Africa's limited contribution to global trade, the revised wisdom is that Africa's economic potential needs to be 'unblocked', which involves tackling a number of geographical challenges and

---

3   Peer Schouten, 'Roadblock Politics in Central Africa', *Environmental Planning D: Society and Space*, 37:5, 2019, 924–41, at p. 933. Oil-rich states like Nigeria invested heavily in infrastructure during the boom, but much of it was centred on the cities. This was especially apparent in Lagos.

4   Jean Debrie, 'The West African Port System: Global Insertion and Regional Particularities', *EchoGéo*, 20, 2012, 1–11, at pp. 3–4.

5   Sergio Oliete Josa and Francesc Magrinyà, 'Patchwork in an Interconnected World: The Challenges of Transport Networks in Sub-Saharan Africa', *Transport Reviews*, 38:6, 2018, p. 720.

6   Paul Nugent, 'Africa's Re-Enchantment with Big Infrastructure: White Elephants Dancing in Virtuous Circles?', in Jon Schubert, Ulf Engel and Elisio Macamo (eds), *Extractive Industries and Changing State Dynamics in Africa: Beyond the Resource Curse*, Abingdon, 2018, pp. 22–40.

historical legacies that have served to fragment African economies.[7] In 2010, a
World Bank report, explicitly invoking the language of 'transformation' (and
jettisoning the logic of the once-hegemonic Berg Report), estimated that African
countries would need to spend US$93 billion per year (or 15 per cent of GDP)
to cover the infrastructure deficit.[8] Railways are back in vogue, multi-lane continental highways are planned, and large-scale investments are being made in port
developments across the continent. Indeed, such has been the infrastructural
feeding frenzy that doubts are emerging about the capacity of governments to
manage mountains of debt, which are often secured against the expectation of
windfalls from natural resources, in the coming years. At the time of writing –
as the COVID-19 pandemic pushes the global economy into recession – some
of the enthusiasm seems decidedly misplaced. What is abundantly clear is that
African governments have channelled resources into infrastructure – with the
active compliance of donors and the banks – on an impressive scale. This book
therefore comes at an important crossroads where it makes sense to take stock.

The topic of infrastructure in Africa is potentially vast. In this book, we have
chosen to narrow the focus to transport corridors – not merely because this is
where so much of the spending has been directed, but also because these are
precisely where the claims about the transformative potential of infrastructure
reside. In tackling this topic, it makes sense to avoid both African exception-
alism and methodological nationalism. There is a tradition of writing about
transport corridors in other parts of the world, very largely emanating from
the work of economic geographers.[9] Much of this has been concerned with
North America and Europe, but it has also reflected a more recent proliferation

---

7   Benno J. Ndulu, 'Infrastructure, Regional Integration and Growth in Sub-Saharan
    Africa: Dealing with the Disadvantages of Geography and Sovereign Fragmentation',
    Journal of African Economies, 15, AERC Supplement 2, 2006, 212–44, at pp. 214–15.

8   Vivien Foster and Cecilia Briceño-Garmendia (eds), *Africa's Infrastructure: A Time
    for Transformation*, Washington, D.C., 2010. Elliot Berg, who was the driving force
    behind the 1981 report, which provided the rationale for structural adjustment,
    had earlier critiqued the transformationist agenda in Ghana. See Elliot J. Berg,
    'Structural Transformation versus Gradualism: Recent Economic Development in
    Ghana', in Philip Foster and Aristide Zolberg (eds), *Ghana and the Ivory Coast:
    Perspectives on Modernisation*, Chicago & London, 1971, pp. 187–230.

9   Jean Debrie and Claude Comtois, 'Une Relecture du Concept de Corridors de
    Transport: Illustration Comparée Europe/Amerique du Nord', *Cahiers Scientifiques
    du Transport*, 58, 2010, pp. 127–44.

of corridors in Asia.[10] It is very noticeable, but not altogether surprising, that Africa has been marginal to most of these discussions. At the present time, much of what is currently available consists of official publications and grey literature generated by institutions involved in rolling out, or otherwise supporting, corridor development. On the academic side, the greater part of the literature has been generated by economists, often with an applied focus on transport and logistics, as well as by economic geographers.[11] The rest of the Social Sciences is drifting somewhat behind the infrastructural wave, with the exception of a body of anthropological literature that addresses what infrastructure means to those who are impacted by it and/or actively engage with it.[12] From a political economy perspective, there is also some work emerging on the logic that underpins decisions about what to invest in and where.[13] This provides the potential for a less positivist and much more critical approach to the topic. But clearly this is a subject that cannot properly be grasped from within narrow disciplinary silos. The offerings within this book often reflect a grounding within a specific discipline, but also range more widely. What also makes it distinctive is that it includes contributions from authors who have been directly engaged with the policy domain. While there are inevitably differences

[10]   Nathalie Fau, Sirivanh Khonthapane and Christian Taillard (eds), *Transnational Dynamics in Southeast Asia: The Greater Mekong Subregion and Malacca Straits Economic Corridor*, Singapore, 2014.

[11]   Ndulu, 'Infrastructure', pp. 212–44; César Caldéron and Luis Servén, 'Infrastructure and Economic Development in Sub-Saharan Africa', *Journal of African Economies*, 19, AERC Supplement 11, 2010, pp. i13–i87.

[12]   Adeline Masquelier, 'Road Mythographies: Space, Mobility and the Historical Imagination in Postcolonial Niger', *American Ethnologist*, 29:4, 2002, 829–56; Brian Larkin, 'The Politics and Poetics of Infrastructure', *Annual Review of Anthropology*, 42, 2013, 327–43; Penny Harvey and Hannah Knox, 'The Enchantments of Infrastructure', *Mobilities*, 7:4, 2012, 521–36; Kurt Beck, Gabriel Klaeger and Michael Stasik, "An Introduction to the African Road", and other contributions to Gabriel Klaeger and Michael Stasik (eds), *The Making of the African Road*, Leiden, 2017; and Dimitris Dalakoglou, *The Road: An Ethnography of (Im)mobility, Space and Cross-Border Infrastructure in the Balkans*, Manchester, 2017.

[13]   An early marker was laid down by contributions to Fredrik Söderbaum and Ian Taylor (eds), *Afro-Regions: The Dynamics of Cross-Border Micro-Regionalism in Africa*, Uppsala, 2008. For the political economy of ports, see Hugh Lamarque, 'Profitable Inefficiency: The Politics of Port Infrastructure in Mombasa, Kenya', *Journal of Modern African Studies*, 57:1, 2019, pp. 85–109; Jana Hönke and Iván Cuesta-Fernández, 'Mobilising Security and Logistics through an African Port: A Controversies Approach to Infrastructure', *Mobilities*, 13:2, 2018, pp. 246–60.

in register across the pieces, we believe that the advantages of a catholic approach outweigh the downsides. In this introduction, we seek to convey a sense of emerging themes in the study of transport corridors in Africa, while pointing to certain methodological challenges along the way.

What is a Transport Corridor?

Let us begin with a deceptively simple question: namely, what is a transport corridor? This is arguably more complex than addressing the question of what is a city, or even what is a pandemic, for the reason that the object of study has been so heavily shaped by a paradigm in flux. At the most basic level, a transport corridor may be defined as an infrastructural assemblage that connects two or more geographical points across international borders and provides a conduit for the movement of people and goods. Transport corridors do not simply exist in a straightforward empirical sense: there may be cranes, rail tracks and road surfaces to be sure, but even when bundled together these do not a corridor make. It is the level of connectivity that counts, which is why corridors are often described in terms of networks. The problem here is that corridors exist in large part because governments, funders and development experts either believe that they *do* or that they *should* exist. The reality is that the *should* very easily slips into the *do*, at the same time as what already exists is repeatedly rebranded. This accounts for the often stark contrast between corridors that are described on paper and what actually exists on the ground. Moreover, many of the corridors that are the object of vigorous boosting by national governments, regional economic communities (RECs), donors and investors are characterised less by effortless flows than recurring blockages. Containers pile up at seaports and trucks routinely find themselves stuck in queues at weigh stations and at border crossings. Meanwhile, efforts to patch up the road surfaces that are pummelled by heavy goods vehicles represents constant work in progress as potholes announce themselves in new locations – which is intimately related to a frightening rate of accidents and deaths on the road. In many ways, this could stand as a metaphor for corridor management as a whole, which necessarily tends to be much more reactive than toolkits and official pronouncements might lead one to believe. We need, therefore, to understand what the various institutional actors believe they are doing, but also to have a feel for the realities that are unfolding on the ground – realities that may be following a number of different social and temporal logics. This was, in fact, the starting point for the AFRIGOS project, which provides the backbone to this volume.

The concept of the *transport corridor* can be understood by approaching each of the signifiers separately. To begin with transport, corridors can only be held to exist in so far as the underlying infrastructure is in a condition, and if there is adequate security, to enable people and goods to move. At the very least, there needs to be a road surface that is motorable. But clearly most corridors consist of other elements as well. There are seaports, inland dry ports, multi-lane highways, navigable waterways and railways – either in existence, currently under construction or being planned. In a functioning multi-modal system, goods are expected to shift from one means of transport to another, according to the balance of affordability and convenience. Multi-modality remains an aspiration in Africa, given that most freight and passenger traffic is still conducted by road and little investment has been channelled into waterways. For example, the Walvis Bay Corridors are entirely dependent on road haulage.[14] In the wake of the privatisation of mines in Zambia, the shift in the geographical centre of mining operations and the penetration of the South African trucking business, there has indeed been a pronounced shift from rail to road in the sub-region.[15] In East and West Africa, there is more in the way of rail, much of it very old, but road transport remains dominant. As Lombard outlines (this volume), the uptake in road transport had reduced the share of the Dakar–Bamako railway to around 10 per cent. Within the East Africa Community (EAC), road accounts for 90 per cent of market share, while along the Northern and Central Corridors specifically rail carried only 6 per cent of the total volume of goods transported around 2016.[16] The completion of the Mombasa–Nairobi Standard Gauge Railway (SGR) has altered the picture somewhat. But at the time of writing, financing constraints mean that there are doubts as to whether the line will reach the border and about whether Uganda will be able to continue the line to Kampala and beyond. Tanzania is constructing another SGR along the Central Corridor, which is expected to link up to transport on Lake Victoria; but whether this line would be extended to neighbouring countries equally remains in doubt. Across the Horn, the picture is similar. Although the completion of the Addis Ababa–Djibouti Railway now provides an alternative, many users continue to prefer road transportation because of a number of logistical challenges (Chen, this volume).

---

14   Plans for a rail link between Grootfontein and Katima Mulilo in Namibia are currently on hold.

15   The Zambian Copperbelt was dependent upon the railways until the 1980s. There has since been a shift to road transport, which has to some extent shifted the financial burden onto the state. Gaël Raballand and Alan Whitworth, *Should the Zambian Government Invest in Railways?*, ZIPAR Working Paper No. 3, 2012 (Lusaka, Zambia Institute for Policy Analysis and Research).

16   Charles Kunaka, Gael Raballand and Mike Fitzmaurice, *How Trucking Services Have Improved and May Contribute to Development: The Case of East Africa*, WIDER Working Paper 152/2016, p. 3.

In theory, railways are more cost-efficient and environmentally friendly than roads. But there are two fundamental reasons why they do not carry the day. The first is that the fixed costs of establishing a railway are very high, and because they place a very visible burden of debt on government, these have ultimately to be transferred to the users. By contrast, the cost of repairing the damage done to roads by trucking is not borne by users to any meaningful extent, while the financial obligations are less visible and more incremental.[17] Secondly, the debate on road versus rail has been a highly political one since colonial times.[18] As Muñoz demonstrates in this volume, it was a significant factor in the lengthy delays to the resolution of Cameroon's transport dilemmas. In many countries today, like Ethiopia and Kenya, there remain powerful interests that insist on the primacy of trucking, which politicians ignore at their peril. As things stand, therefore, road continues to trump rail.

The corridor signifier is relatively easy to grasp. Within global trade, there is never really a clearly defined start and end point. Proponents of the corridor construct impose a boundedness for reasons of convenience. In other parts of the world, corridors are often taken to include the shipping lanes along which the container traffic moves. But in Africa, the corridor is typically considered to start at the coastal port and to end with a conurbation or a mining cluster. Part of the reason is that there little in the way of short-sea shipping. Possibly because governments and RECs are the ones pushing the agenda, the boundaries tend to be drawn at the jurisdictional limits of the state. Across Africa, there are different types of corridor. The Northern and Central Corridors in East Africa, which begin in Mombasa and Dar es Salaam respectively and extend into the Congolese interior, are classic coast-to-hinterland configurations. This is also true of the Walvis Bay–Lubumbashi–Ndola Corridor, with the difference that it is very much shaped by the demands of the mining industry. The usage of 'corridor' to refer to urban-to-urban connections is much less common in Africa, with the one important exception of the Abidjan–Lagos Corridor. Whereas the others run from the coast to the interior, this particular one links multiple cities (and ports) along the littoral (see Nugent, this volume).

Theo Notteboom reminds us that corridors should not be conceived of purely in terms of point-to-point connections and invokes the network metaphor:

[17] The ability of roads to adapt to usage was a structural difference with railways that confirmed the 'superiority of roads over railways', in the classic account of: Albert O. Hirschman, *Development Projects Observed*, Washington, D.C., 1967, p. 83.

[18] See, for example, the origins of the infamous 'road gaps' policy in the Gold Coast, G.B. Kay (ed.), *The Political Economy of Colonialism in Ghana: A Collection of Documents and Statistics 1900–1960*, Cambridge, 1972, pp. 20–25.

A transport corridor is very often viewed as a point-to-point connection. In reality, individual transport corridors are mostly part of extensive transport and logistics networks consisting of a range of corridors, each with specific characteristics in terms of scale, transport modes used, price and service quality. The future development of transport corridors will therefore have to be assessed ever more from a network perspective.[19]

However, a network configuration is only really apparent in Southern Africa where a number of corridors intersect and are expected to feed the three seaports of Walvis Bay, Lobito and Durban. A corridor network might emerge in West Africa if the mooted railway loop is ever completed, but this now seems unlikely. Across the continent, the prevailing pattern is one of a single port serving a transport corridor. This, in turn, leads to a situation of corridor competition rather than complementarity – as is explored in greater detail by Lamarque in this volume. The stakes are high when it comes to making infrastructural investments, and this serves to create something that looks rather more like a zero-sum game than a state of healthy competition. A corridor network could, of course, involve not just connectivity between railways and highways, but also the ports. In 2005, Notteboom and Rodrigue identified the limitations of older models of port development that were premised on single ports operating in close proximity to large cities. They pointed to a process of regionalisation that has led to the emergence of transshipment hubs in remote locations and dry ports and inland terminals in the hinterlands.[20] In Africa, nodes have been mapped by researchers on the basis of global maritime flows linking to dominant hubs in Europe (Rotterdam) and Asia (Singapore): namely, Alexandria, Durban, Cape Town, Pointe Noire, Casablanca, Lagos, Abidjan (albeit interrupted by years of political crisis).[21] One might also add Dakar, Lomé and Tema to the list (Lombard, Sylvanus, Byiers and Woolfrey, this volume). Tanger-Med in Morocco is a major transhipment hub. However, although it has been suggested that

19   Theo Notteboom, 'Strategies and Future Development of Transport Corridors', in Yann, Alix (ed.), *Les Corridors de Transport*, Caens, 2012), pp. 289–312 <https://www.faq-logistique.com/EMS-Livre-Corridors-Transport-18-Strategies-Future-Develoment.htm> [Accessed 27 April 2021].

20   Theo E. Notteboom and Jean-Paul Rodrigue, 'Port Regionalisation: Towards a New Phase in Port Development', *Maritime Policy & Management*, 32:3, 2005, pp. 297–313.

21   César Ducruet, Sylvain Cuyala and Ali El Hosni, 'Maritime Networks as Systems of Cities: The Long-Term Interdependencies between Global Shipping Flows and Urban Development, (1890–2010)', *Journal of Transport Geography*, 66, 2018, pp. 340–55.

Durban and a new port at Ngqura/Port Elizabeth have the capacity to perform that role in the future, transhipment operations are for the time being quite limited.[22] We can also see the beginnings of a spatial reconfiguration of the ports in the shape of inland terminals that are generally under the management of international logistics companies, and the steady growth in the number of dry ports (often under private ownership) where customs clearance for imported goods takes place.[23] But this is at a very incipient stage.

Finally, the concept of the 'development corridor' has gained some traction in Africa, not least after its endorsement by the AU and several RECs in 2008.[24] The latter shares many of the same elements as a transport corridor, but has a more explicit spatial referent that is captured in the terminology of the spatial development initiative (SDI). Whereas some transport corridors manifestly serve the extractive industries, RECs have embraced the notion that corridors ought to promote intra-regional trade and build on complementarities between African economies. In that sense, investments in corridors are intended to promote new sites of economic dynamism through a multiplier effect.[25] Investments are often located away from the main cities, and are expected to contribute to a more balanced form of national and cross-border development.[26] Special economic zones (SEZs) and industrial parks, which are springing up in a number of countries like Ethiopia, are similarly part of an effort by governments to

[22] Hwa-Joong Kim, Jasmine Siu Lee Lam and Paul Tae-Woo Lee, 'Analysis of Liner Shipping Networks and Transhipment Flows of Potential Hub Ports in sub-Saharan Africa', *Transport Policy*, 69, 2018, pp. 193–206.

[23] In 2009, South Africa had six inland terminals but only one dry port at City Deep. Erené Cronje, Marianne Matthee and Waldo Krugel, 'The Role of Dry Ports in South Africa', *Transport and Communications Bulletin for Asia and the Pacific*, 78, 2009, pp. 112–20, at p. 116. The French logistics giant, Bolloré, operates no fewer than 25 inland terminals: <www.bollore-ports.com/en/our-port-expertises/inland-container-depots.html> [Accessed 27 April 2021]; Benjamin Steck, 'L'Afrique des Ports et des Corridors: Comment Formuler l'Interaction entre Logistique et Développement', *Cahiers de Géographie de Québec*, 59:168, 2015, pp. 447–67. Transhipment has had an outsized share in the performance of ill-judged new port investments such as Kribi (Cameroon).

[24] Fourth Annual Meeting of the Infrastructure Consortium for Africa (ICA), held in Tokyo in March 2008.

[25] David Simon and Muriel Samé Ekobo, 'Walvis Bay-Swakopmund: Desert Micro-Region and Aspiring Regional Gateway', in Söderbaum and Taylor (eds), *Afro-Regions*, pp. 53–73, at p. 62.

[26] Fredrik Söderbaum and Ian Taylor, 'Considering Micro-Regionalism in Africa in the Twenty-First Century', in Söderbaum and Taylor (eds), *Afro-Regions*, p. 1.

give private investors an incentive to turn the corridor into an instrument of development. An excellent illustration of how these visions come together is provided by the Nacala Development Corridor, which is expected to run from coal mining concessions in the Tete Province of north-west Mozambique, to connect with a revamped railway line running to the north of Malawi, and then link to a modernised port at Nacala – in the vicinity of which a SEZ was established in 2009. The vision for the corridor turns not merely on mining, but also on the development of modernised agriculture in Mozambique, Zambia and Malawi.[27] A large number of other development corridors are currently mooted or are under construction, despite concerns about their environmental and economic sustainability.[28] Some are road corridors nesting within the greater Trans-African Highway project (see Oliete Josa and Magrinyà, this volume),[29] others are rebranded REC transport corridors (such as the Central Development Corridor in East Africa), while still others seem to be national initiatives linking hinterlands to ports that are intended to join up with neighbouring countries at some unspecified point in the future.[30] As things stand, the developmental outcomes remain in the future tense, with corridors tending to reinforce enclave effects. Moreover, SEZs and industrial parks have as yet failed to deliver their promised benefits. As Farole and Moberg indicate, this is partly because the choice of locations has been driven by a political calculus and partly it comes down to misplaced assumptions about where comparative advantages reside.[31] In so far as these initiatives are intended to boost intra-regional exchange (as

27 Republic of Mozambique, *The Project for Nacala Corridor: Economic Development Strategies in the Republic of Mozambique – Final Study Report*, Maputo, 2015, pp. 16–17; Euclides Gonçalves, 'Agricultural Corridors as "Demonstration Fields": Infrastructure, Fairs and Associations along the Beira and Nacala Corridors', *Journal of Eastern African Studies*, 14:2, 2020, pp. 354–74.

28 Bill Laurence, Sean Sloan, Lingfei Weng and Jeffrey A. Sayer, 'Estimating the Environmental Costs of Africa's Massive "Development Corridors"', *Current Biology*, 25, 2015, pp. 3202–08. The authors list 33 planned or existing corridors.

29 An example is the Mombasa–Nairobi–Addis Ababa Road Corridor.

30 The Mozambican government launched the Beira Agricultural Growth Corridor with donors and private investors in 2009, and the Mtwara Development Corridor with the AfDB in 2012. See <www.agdevco.com/uploads/reports/BAGC_Investment_Blueprint_rpt19.pdf> and <https://projectsportal.afdb.org/dataportal/VProject/show/P-Z1-D00–021> [both accessed 27 April 2021].

31 John Farole and Lotta Moberg, 'Special Economic Zones in Africa: Political Economy Challenges and Solutions', in John Page and Finn Tarp (eds), *The Practice of Industrial Policy: Government-Business Coordination in Africa and East Asia*, Oxford, 2017, pp. 234–51.

opposed to merely maximising overseas exports), their likely success depends on the ease of doing business across borders.

In the light of the above, the task of studying transport corridors throws up a particular set of methodological challenges for researchers. The first is that of bridging the divide between policy and everyday practice. We need to understand the perspectives of those who plan, finance and construct corridors, given that they operate according to specific temporal horizons and understandings about risks and rates of return. But we equally need to focus on those who carry out official functions – such as customs, immigration and security – as well as those who perform outsourced responsibilities such as maintenance and repair. And, of course, we need to pay close attention to the many actors who make use of the corridor – more on this below. Secondly, research has to be flexible enough to observe corridor dynamics from fixed points, such as ports or one-stop border posts (OSBPs), but also to capture the reality of people and goods as they move through space. The perspective of a trucker, a customs officer and an engineer are likely to be very different, not simply because of the work they perform, but because of their quite different fields of vision. Thirdly, there is the challenge of comparing the patterns that play out across corridors. That is, we need to be able to distinguish what is specific to a corridor from that which is more generic. A final set of challenges relates to matters of scale, to which we also return in greater detail below.

When is a Transport Corridor? Recurring Temporalities

Having dealt with what a transport corridor *is*, the next question that arises is the point from which one can meaningfully trace its emergence. It is clear that it had already begun to take shape in Europe and North America by the 1970s. As far as the World Bank is concerned, the concept arose in discussions about developing countries somewhat later, and later still with respect to Africa (Cissokho, this volume). What this already underlines is that certain conceptions about the relationship between transport and development have drifted in and out of fashion, often being repackaged in the process. Ironically, the allure of the corridor concept has resided in the notion that what is being unveiled is something fundamentally new. Today, this is reflected in the contention that global connectivity potentially unleashes all manner of synergies that did not previously exist. This is linked in particular to transformations in global shipping and port development that has enabled a prodigious number of containers to be shipped around the world at a much lower cost per unit. But shipping is precisely one of those areas where it pays to take the longer view. For historians, much of the language surrounding investments in transport infrastructure is redolent of the language of post-war developmentalism which was sold as a qualitative leap forward in much the same terms. The difference in Africa was that the infrastructure was supposed to better connect the colonies with the European 'metropole', whereas now the focus is much more upon the benefits of increasing trade with East and South-East Asia. It is clearly also the case that many of the projects that are being promoted now build upon infrastructure (notably road and rail) that was established in the colonial period or in the early years of independence.[32] Hence the Addis–Djibouti Corridor is a direct replacement for a former French colonial railway (Chen, this volume). Again, the Zambezi Valley SDI in Mozambique is effectively a dusted-down colonial project devised by Portugal and South Africa.[33] The Nacala Corridor is similarly based on a much older system of road and rail in Mozambique and Malawi, which was effectively disabled by the RENAMO insurgency four decades ago.

But there is also a case to be made for taking an even longer view. It is interesting to note that a recent report from the Asian Development Bank has pointed to precursors to contemporary transport corridors in South Asia which it dates to Mughal and East India Company initiatives.[34] Isabella Soi (this volume) similarly points to the historicity of certain trade routes that were important for established kingdoms within the Great Lakes region. Trade brought commodities in and out, but it also conferred revenues on the states that sought to regulate and tax what moved along the routes. During the heyday of the trans-Atlantic and Indian Ocean slave trades, a number of coastal ports became significant foci of maritime trade in West and East Africa. Some of these, like Mombasa and Luanda, remain important to this day. In the nineteenth century, the links

---

[32]   Charis Enns and Brock Bersaglio, 'On the Coloniality of "New" Mega-Infrastructure Projects in East Africa', *Antipode*, 52:1, 2019, 101–23. See also Johannes Theodore Aalders, 'Building on the Ruins of Empire: the Uganda Railway and the LAPPSET Corridor in Kenya', *Third World Quarterly*, published online 12 March 2020.

[33]   Milissão Nuvunga, 'Region-Building in Central Mozambique: the Case of the Zambezi Valley Spatial Development Initiative', in Söderbaum and Taylor (eds), *Afro-Regions,* pp. 74–89, at pp. 79–80.

[34]   World Bank, *The Web of Transport Corridors in South Asia*, Washington, D.C., 2018, pp. 27–48. A historic road link between Nepal and Tibet, which was effectively closed in the 1960s, has received a renewed lease of life as a consequence of Chinese investments in a strategic corridor designed to connect East and South Asia. Galen Murton, 'Trans-Himalayan Transformations: Building Roads, Making Markets, and Cultivating Consumption between Nepal and China's Tibet', in Yongming Zhou, Qu Tenglong, and Li Guiying (eds), *Roadology: Roads, Space, Culture*, Chongqing, 2016, pp. 328–40, at p. 335.

between the interior and the coastal ports were more fully elaborated, both in East and West Africa. In the case of Asante, Ivor Wilks identifies a conscious attempt to develop a system of 'great roads' converging on the capital of Kumasi from the coast and the Sahel.[35] Guaranteeing a modicum of physical security along the routes was a precondition for trade – as it certainly is today – but they had also to be actively maintained if they were to be serviceable. Challengers to the established order sought to cut the routes and/or to impose their own conditions on traders. For this reason, Peer Schouten observes that there is a prehistory to the modern roadblock in Central Africa – roughly Chad and Central African Republic – in the shape of taxes that were imposed upon people and goods at strategic chokepoints.[36] A similar logic applied to the 'protection money' demanded from the caravans that passed through Harar to Berbera by Somali clans along the route.[37]

Colonial propagandists, who were inclined to posit a sharp break with the past, were dazzled by feats of engineering, such as the Chemin de fer Congo-Océan, by which Europeans imposed their stamp on the continent, as well as on the African subjects whose labour was required to realise them. But we know that in the early twentieth century, many existing transport routes gained a second life as colonial infrastructure. Hence the ancient livestock trade route to Berbera was first valorised by the British, who channelled meat supplies towards Aden, and was then embedded when the Italian army constructed a motorable road in 1941.[38] The continuities were obvious in the case of lake transport, but they are also apparent when it comes to roads. Some road projects undoubtedly represented something novel because they were tied to new developments in mining and cash crop production.[39] But many were superimposed upon something that embodied a greater historicity. Existing routes were widened, straightened and flattened to facilitate the circulation of wheeled transport, but they connected

---

[35] Ivor Wilks, *Asante in the Nineteenth Century: The Structure and Evolution of a Political Order*, Cambridge, 1975, ch. 1.

[36] Schouten, 'Roadblock Politics', p. 2.

[37] Finn Stepputat and Tobias Hagmann, 'Politics of Circulation: the Making of the Berbera Corridor in Somali East Africa', *Environment and Planning D: Society and Space D*, 37:5, 2019, 794–813, at p. 799.

[38] Luca Ciabarri, 'Biographies of Roads, Biographies of Nations: History, Territory and the Road Effect in Post-Conflict Somaliland', in Klaeger and Michael Stasik (eds), *The Making*, pp. 116–40, at p. 120.

[39] Libbie Freed, 'Conduits of Culture and Control: Roads, States and Users in French Central Africa, 1890–1960', unpublished PhD thesis, University of Wisconsin Madison, 2006.

the same places – most notably urban settlements and port towns. Contemporary transport corridors today connect up segments of existing roads and stretches of rail that were established in the colonial period. In this we can discern longer cycles of decay as well as moments of retrofitting.[40] Much as stripping back the layers of an actual road reveal many different moments of construction, and multiple patch-ups, corridors may be seen as the accretion of so many older iterations of construction, maintenance and repair. If we start to conceive of transport corridors as explicitly modernist constructs that cover over the traces of their own pasts, we can also arrive at a more nuanced appreciation of how infrastructure actually works and is related to by local actors. Part of the reason why so many corridor interventions fail is that they are put into effect with a wilful ignorance of this history.

Scales (1): Institutional Actors

Although scale has become a contested concept within critical geography, it seems indispensable when grappling with the complexities of transport corridors – not least because it is a framing that key actors are themselves guided by. Moreover, it is the slippage between interventions at different scales that frequently explains why there is such a mismatch between grandiose visions and mundane realities.

The transport corridors that are unfolding across Africa are, at the most fundamental level, intended to facilitate access to global markets. But they are also embedded in other visions that extend well beyond the remit of corridor authorities. In the case of the Chinese Belt and Road Initiative (BRI) investments in infrastructure are solicited by African governments and delivered by Chinese companies, as part of an ambitious agenda whose origins clearly lie outside the continent (Gambino, this volume). Although corridors could be folded into the BRI agenda, they were almost incidental to the underpinning rationale. And while Africa was not originally envisioned as part of BRI, projects have been added to it in a manner that suits all the main parties (Chen, this volume). At the same time, there are the continental initiatives that are intended to link different regions through infrastructure. As Oliete Josa and Magrinyà explain (this volume), the United Nations Economic Commission for Africa (UNECA) formulated the Trans-African Highways (TAH) initiative as far back

---

40   Cymene Howe, Jessica Lockrem, Hannah Appel, Edward Hackett, Dominic Boyer, Randal Hall, Matthew Schneider-Mayerson, Albert Pope, Akhil Gupta, Elizabeth Rodwell, Andrea Ballestero, Trevor Durbin, Farès el-Dahdah, Elizabeth Long and Cyrus Mody, 'Paradoxical Infrastructures: Ruins, Retrofit and Risk', *Science, Technology and Human Values*, 41:3, 2016, pp. 547–65.

as the 1970s. In recent times, it has underpinned the African Regional Transport Infrastructure Network (ARTIN) and the African Union's Programme for Infrastructure Development in Africa (PIDA).[41] These plans for pursuing continental integration through connective infrastructure bring together the AU, the various RECs, the AfDB, the EU, donor countries and African states. The various transport corridors map onto this larger infrastructural agenda, but African countries also advance their own preferences while often paying lip-service to continental and regional plans.

National governments organise their bureaucratic functions according to a very particular sense of scale. The presidency and core ministries in the capital city decide on what the national priorities are, which opens up a field of potential contestation. Ministries of transport are often weak relative to ministries of finance and of planning, and each of these may be bypassed by presidential secretariats that are intent on bringing infrastructural projects to fruition with minimal delay (Muñoz, this volume). Who negotiates the deal with the Chinese delegation is typically revealing about where the balance of power resides within the structures of government at any given moment. Then there are those agencies that enjoy a degree of operational autonomy from the core ministries – this typically includes the port and the revenue authorities (including customs), which often fight their own turf wars.[42] Their role in collecting revenue, or making revenue collection possible, lends them a voice and often an enhanced capacity to block and deflect unwelcome changes. By contrast, while decentralisation theoretically permits sub-national bodies a degree of latitude to set priorities, this generally does not extend to national infrastructure projects. The question of adequate compensation for land that may be requisitioned to build a port or a railway is typically one of the points of friction, especially as resident populations often bear the additional inconvenience associated with long periods of construction.[43]

---

[41] The remit of PIDA is far wider than transport infrastructure and includes ICTs, energy and trans-boundary water resource management. <www.au-pida.org/pida-history/> [Accessed 27 April 2021].

[42] Lamarque, 'Profitable Inefficiency', pp. 98–99.

[43] This is true of LAPPSET. Charis Enns, 'Infrastructure Projects and Rural Projects in Northern Kenya: The Use of Divergent Expertise to Negotiate the Terms of Land Deals for Transport Infrastructure', *Journal of Eastern African Studies*, 46:2, 2017, pp. 358–76; and Ngala Chome, 'Land, Livelihoods and Belonging: Negotiating Change and Anticipating LAPSSET in Kenya's Lamu County', *Journal of Eastern African Studies*, 14:2, 2020, pp. 310–31. Hassan K. Kochore, 'The Road to Kenya? Visions, Expectations and Anxieties Around New Infrastructure Development in

As members of one or more of the overlapping RECs, African countries have signed up to regional protocols that formally commit them to the freedom of movement of people and goods along the corridors. In theory, the agendas of national governments and the RECs are perfectly aligned, but in practice governments sign up to far more than they are willing or able to implement. The REC secretariats are chronically underfunded and have limited capacity to pressure governments to honour their commitments. Like the AU, the RECs formally respect national sovereignty, but seek to persuade and cajole national governments to take their obligations seriously. Goods that are produced within the RECs that have established customs unions are permitted to cross borders free of duty, subject to local content provisions, while those that come from outside are covered by a common external tariff (CET). The harmonisation of tariffs is supposed to place member states on a level footing, but also to enhance commerce between member states. Some countries have negotiated 'temporary' exemptions for strategic commodities, and these have proved difficult to remove. The African Continental Free Trade Area (AfCFTA), which is in the process of being rolled out, is supposed to align with the existing free trade provisions of the RECs and to scale them upwards. But, given the difficulties experienced by RECs, it remains to be seen whether a continental authority would be better placed to secure compliance.

Some of the greatest challenges have arisen from a proliferation of non-tariff barriers. This includes a range of fees that are levied at the border, notably for rights of transit, but also innumerable hurdles encountered on the road (Byiers and Woolfrey, this volume). One of the most persistent challenges has been the proliferation of roadblocks thrown up by a range of agencies, typically in the name of road safety or national security. These are extreme in the DRC,[44] but they are also ubiquitous in Kenya and Ghana, whose governments are formally committed to regional integration. Along the Abidjan–Lagos Corridor, sub-units of Nigerian customs and immigration compete in the establishment of their own roadblocks (Nugent, this volume). Corridor management authorities are typically skeleton bodies with staff seconded from national ministries that have a greater or lesser input from the private sector. Their ability to shape the behaviour of governments is therefore even more limited than that of the RECs. In West Africa an additional difficulty is that the Francophone countries are

---

Northern Kenya', *Journal of Eastern African Studies*, 10:3, 2016, pp. 494–510. The speculation and outright scams surrounding compensation claims is also a factor in the equation.

44   Schouten, 'Roadblock Politics', pp. 10–14.

members of the Economic Community of West African States (ECOWAS) and of l'Union Économique et Monétaire Ouest-Africaine (UEMOA). Despite the efforts to harmonise the rules, divergences between them – for example over axel load limits – have culminated in misunderstandings and frequent stoppages. Some of the same complications occur in the Great Lakes where a number of countries are members of the East African Community (EAC) as well as COMESA.

Along the corridors themselves, officials often enjoy a degree of operational autonomy that enables them to exploit the complexities of scale and the lack of alignment between institutional actors. Officials ignore and blunt official dictats that are not to their liking and find ways of carrying out their functions in accordance with their own understandings of 'business as usual'. Although the latest directive often cascades down to the local police station or customs post, its efficacy is often limited and short-lived, as there is a keen appreciation that follow-ups are unlikely and after some time it will probably be forgotten[45]. The officials who formally do the work of government at the local level have adopted their own conventions, which are often worked out in tandem with the freight forwarders, truckers, traders and road builders who are present along the corridor. These conventions persist because they are relatively predictable – although they do not necessarily work for everyone or to the same degree – and those who are newly arrived are quickly inducted into the rules of the game. As Thomas Bierschenk indicates, such innovations should not necessarily be treated as corruption, disobedience or collusion because the reality is that policies that issue from the centre are often impractical as they stand.[46] Nevertheless, the workarounds that local actors fashion lead to a situation where the mismatch between the theory surrounding the corridor and the everyday realities is never actually bridged – and in some cases becomes even starker as time passes. This underlines a crucial finding, which is that the cumulative effects of actions taken by officials at the lowest scales often outweigh the impact of regional and national decision-makers who notionally call the shots.

---

[45] José-María Muñoz, *Doing Business in Cameroon: An Anatomy of Economic Governance*, Cambridge, 2018, pp. 158–62.

[46] Thomas Bierschenk, 'Sedimentation, Fragmentation and Normative Double-Binds in (West) African Public Services', in Thomas Bierschenk and Jean-Pierre Olivier de Sardan (eds), *States at Work: Dynamics of African Bureaucracies*, Leiden & Boston, 2014, pp. 221–45, at p. 241.

Scales (2): The States, Corporations and Small Fish

Factoring in scale is especially important for understanding the role, influence and physical presence of private sector actors along the corridors. It is a commonplace observation that the relationship between the African state and capital has been reconfigured during the 1980s and 1990s under the regime of structural adjustment. The reality that political elites could actually benefit from the logic of 'privatisation' is well-established.[47] But the withdrawal of the state has also been much exaggerated. Although African governments do not implement many infrastructural projects directly, they do finance many of them and, as importantly, they underwrite the external loans. In many countries such as Kenya, it is the politicians that have been keen to accelerate infrastructural projects, in the belief that this will play well with voters. As Lombard and Sylvanus both indicate (this volume) ports also occupy an important place in national imaginaries. In Ghana, the decision to roll out three new transport corridors from Tema to the North may be seen as a revival of the vision of achieving economic transformation through infrastructural development that Kwame Nkrumah had once championed – even if the Akuffo-Addo government belongs to the competing political tradition. In Ghana, like Kenya, promising roads and railways is part of the currency of national politics – and because it depreciates rapidly, new projects constantly have to be conceived. At the same time, nothing has been done to develop transport along the Volta Lake, which would be key to a functioning multi-modal transport network. Paradoxically, it would require much less capital investment to accomplish, but the crux is that it would yield a correspondingly lower political dividend.

The gatekeeping role that particular branches of the bureaucracy perform also has an important bearing on what gets built where, but also defines who gets to build it and under what terms and conditions. Corporate actors therefore have a vested interest in cultivating long-term relationships with the most important branches of the bureaucracy, while remaining on good terms with powerful interest groups on an everyday basis. Playing the long game, large corporate players are often prepared to take on loss leaders, such as creaking parts of rail links, in order to remain in the larger contest. Needless to say, the mutual embeddedness of corporate actors and gatekeepers frequently means that the transport configurations are not necessarily the economically optimal ones.

Two dominant perceptions about what has unfolded over the past 20 years each contain an element of truth, but need to be nuanced. The first is that states

---

[47]   Fredrik Söderbaum and Ian Taylor, 'Competing Region-Building in the Maputo Development Corridor', in Söderbaum and Taylor (eds), *Afro-Regions*, pp. 35–52.

have essentially rolled over and allowed corporate capital to assume control over transport infrastructure where the juiciest pickings are to be found. While it is true that there has been a concentration of capital in global shipping over recent decades, there has also been fierce competition between companies over access to port facilities. The intrusion of Dubai Port World (DPW), the Mediterranean Shipping Company (MSC) and China Merchant Holding International (CMHI) has reduced some of the earlier dominance of Bolloré and Maersk.[48] This has enabled governments to play a range of actors off against each other (Lombard, this volume).[49] While governments have been willing to lease container terminals to shipping and logistics companies, port authorities (PAs) have retained overall oversight. Governments have generally preferred joint ventures to outright privatisation. For example, Tema remains a public port under the control of the Ghana Ports and Harbour Authority (GPHA). In 2004, GPHA granted Meridian Port Services (MPS) the contract to build and operate a container terminal, which was opened three years later. As Brenda Chalfin underlined a decade ago, the GPHA was careful to retain a grip over the port, and this picture has not changed significantly since then.[50] In 2019, the first phase of the container port expansion was completed, with the second phase to follow in 2020. Crucially, MPS was to be jointly owned by GPHA itself (30 per cent), APM Terminals (a subsidiary of A.P. Moller/Maersk on 35 per cent) and Bolloré (35 per cent) – although the GPHA stake was effectively halved in 2016 when additional shares were issued without its knowledge.[51] Governments have also shown their willingness to flex their muscles in relation to both ports and

48 Debrié, 'West African port', p. 4.
49 When DPW won the contract to run the Berbera port, the state-owned Ethiopian Shipping and Logistics Services Enterprise (ESLSE) was cut in on the deal. Warsame M. Ahmed and Finn Stepputat, *Berbera Port: Geopolitics and State-Making in Somaliland*, Rift Valley Institute Briefing Paper, Nairobi, 2019, p. 4.
50 Brenda Chalfin, 'Recasting Maritime Governance in Ghana: The Neo-Developmental State and Port Governance in Tema', *Journal of Modern African Studies*, 48:4, 2010, pp. 573–98.
51 The scandal was unravelled in Andrew Weir, 'How Vincent Bolloré Won Control Over Ghana's Biggest Port', *Africa Confidential*, 62:7, 2021 <www.africa-confidential.com/article/id/13322/SPECIAL_REPORT_How_Vincent_Bollor%C3%A9_won_control_of_Ghana%E2%80%99s_biggest_port> [Accessed 28 July 2021]. Consortia such as this one involving the partnering of competitors are not unusual. A similar shareholding arrangement among Bolloré, APM and Cameroonian interests prevailed in the company that operated Douala's container terminal from 2003 to 2019.

railways. An illustration is that of the Doraleh Container Terminal in Djibouti which was constructed and operated by DPW, only for the government to expel the company, alleging that it had acquired the concession through bribery.

The second perception is that China has cornered the market in infrastructure by tying concessionary financing to the award of contracts. While it is true that Chinese companies have often been awarded important construction contracts, they have not, in most cases, secured the concessions to run the container terminals. When it comes to new railway projects, the Chinese role is much more visible. But Brautigam notes that China has actually only financed four 'greenfield' railway projects.[52] Of these, the Kenyan SGR is the one that has received the most attention. The Djibouti–Addis Ababa railway was a Chinese project, but Chen (this volume) points to the fact that the second main line to the north was contracted to a Turkish company. In the case of the Central Corridor railway, the first sections were awarded to a Turkish/Portuguese consortium. And finally, the Dakar–Bamako railway is an instance of retrofitting an existing railway rather than constructing something from scratch. In reality, the Chinese presence would appear to be far more important lower down the food-chain, notably in the construction of roads and highways that connect urban centres or address urban transportation – and are often not the product of Chinese financing.[53] When it comes to the infrastructure that is strung out along the corridors, it is also important to recognise the presence of other actors. In the case of the Kazangula bridge across the Zambezi River, for example, the bulk of the funding came from the Japanese development agency, JICA, while the contract was awarded to Daiwoo, a South Korean company. The Nacala Corridor is effectively a joint venture between Vale (a Brazilian mining company), Mitsui (the Japanese multinational) and the Mozambican state. In general, African companies lack the capacity to compete for major contracts to construct or to manage large infrastructure projects – with the exception of South African players like Transnet. They tend to feature more in the construction and maintenance of roads, where the award of contracts is no less murky.

Moving to transport itself, there is less concentration of capital in road haulage than in ports and railways. Across Southern Africa, there are a number of international logistics companies that operate across the region. These handle the export of minerals, notably from the Copperbelt. In South Africa

52 Deborah Brautigam, 'Chinese Loans and African Structural Transformation', in Arkebe Oqubay and Justin Yifu Lin (eds), *China-Africa and an Economic Transformation*, Oxford, 2019, pp. 129–47, at p. 140.
53 Thierry Pariault, 'China in Africa: Goods Supplier, Service Provider rather than Investor', *Bridges Africa*, 7:5, 2018, no page.

itself, Vilikazi identifies seven large logistics companies that operate vertically integrated businesses across Southern Africa, but also a significant number of smaller companies. This is significant in a context where South Africa exports a range of commodities to its neighbours.[54] In East Africa, the consolidation of a small number of large companies in Kenya, operating modern fleets of trucks, contrasts with the picture in other countries, most notably Tanzania.[55] In West Africa, the trucking industry is more highly fragmented. While transport unions are relatively influential, especially in the Francophone countries, they are made up of a large number of small operators. The bilateral agreements over division of the transit traffic is an instrument that is intended to protect their interests (Byiers and Woolfrey, this volume).

Across the continent, the cost of trucking is relatively high because of the lack of a back-load and regulations that prevent cabotage (that is, the carrying of goods in another country). Moreover, the powerful interests that coalesce around road haulage at the national level make it unlikely that this will change any time soon. Another major cost lies in delays at border crossings and the bribes demanded at roadblocks. Here, it is the limitations to the exercise of power by transport unions and logistics companies that is displayed. In West Africa, the Borderless Alliance has worked together with RECs to underline the downstream consequences of these practices, but with uneven results. TradeMark East Africa (TMEA) is a different beast because it is funded by donors and co-ordinates the delivery of corridor infrastructure like OSBPs. But it also makes the case for open borders, exploiting its excellent access to government. The functioning OSBPs in East Africa, many of which have been implemented through TMEA, have managed to significantly reduce border crossing times[56] – unlike in West Africa – but roadblocks and police corruption have proved less easy to resolve. Among the users of the various corridors, some of the most hard-worked are the drivers themselves, who bear much of the risk and inconvenience for meagre remuneration.

The corridors are, of course, intended to serve as a conduit for trade, and again there are quite different scales where this plays out. China has become the most important trading partner for African countries. But apart from the large-scale

54 Thando S. Vilikazi, 'The Causes of High Inter-Regional Road Freight Rates for Food and Commodities in Southern Africa', *Development Southern Africa*, 35:3, 2018, pp. 388–403, at p. 392. Interestingly, he points to the growing domination of a small group of larger businesses in Mozambique as well.
55 Kunaka, Raballand and Fitzmaurice, *How Trucking Services Have Improved*.
56 Paul Nugent and Isabella Soi, 'One-Stop Border Posts in East Africa: State Encounters of the Fourth Kind', *Journal of Eastern African Studies*, 14:3, 2020, p. 9.

importers and exporters, corridors have also helped to spawn a range of other actors. Many African traders make it their business to source their goods directly from China or Dubai. In a fascinating account, Haugen reveals how traders either share containers or fill their own containers using logistics agents based in southern China who, in turn, source goods directly from the factories. The agents channel the goods through the Chinese port which, at any given time, are less likely to entail physical' inspections.[57] The traders typically employ their own clearing agents in African ports who cultivate close relations with customs authorities. These containers may travel to inland cities or they may be opened close to the port where individual traders can collect their own share of the consignment. Many own their own stores, but also operate as wholesalers to smaller traders who will purchase the goods and transport them by road to their final destination. The financial margins reside in the intricacies of packing and unpacking containers, the subtleties of customs valuations and in the size of the truck loads plying the transport corridors. All these actors work the system as best they can – which entails minimising risks and being able to adapt to sudden shifts in prices and demand – while exploiting the infrastructure and logistics that is controlled by corporate business. What this also means is that many of the most important users of corridor infrastructure are small-scale enterprises, with petty traders at one end of the spectrum and larger merchants at the other end. Their interests do not necessarily align with those of corporate capital, but they are just as likely to diverge with those of domestic manufacturing interests. The latter often have an interest in reducing competition from neighbouring countries, whereas the livelihoods of traders depend on the flow of goods in infinitely variable quantities. The port and the road therefore reveal, in very sharp relief, the very different configurations of economic power along each of the corridors.

It is also important to recognise that because corridors run through African borderlands, they also have a significant impact on the populations that reside there. In East Africa, part of the rationale for the OSBPs is that they should also benefit small-scale cross-border traders. On the Uganda/Kenya border, the authorities have sought to simplify the processes of making customs declarations in an effort to encourage traders to use the facilities rather than plying the many unapproved routes – in a context where cross-border trade underpins the livelihoods of many people.[58] In West Africa, there has been much less progress on

57   Heidi Østbø Haugen, 'The Social Production of Container Space', *Society and Space*, 37:5, 2019, pp. 868–85.
58   Nugent and Soi, 'One-Stop'.

OSBPs, but the corridors often run through thickly populated border regions – especially along the Abidjan–Lagos Corridor. As Nugent (this volume) indicates, small-scale traders exploit the corridor in discrete segments because of the many disincentives to crossing multiple borders. Lomé continues to serve as a focus for Ivorian and Ghanaians traders who buy cloth, much of which is imported from China, that is transported back along the corridor by companies that specialise in this business.[59] In addition, revolving markets link traders across borders and over considerable distances. Because there is money to be made from such trade, border towns have tended to grow faster than the national average, especially in West Africa.[60] This means that corridors have also served as a conduit for migrants in search of greener pastures. Even where the border towns themselves are not the primary focus, as in Southern Africa, migrants use the very same border crossings as the trucks. Although the RECs are formally committed to freedom of movement of people, this has been controversial in South Africa in recent years. It is highly telling that when the COVID-19 pandemic struck in early 2021, South Africa closed all the borders that were associated with migration, and only allowed vehicles transporting essential goods to pass along trucking routes. In general, the potential for transport corridors to advance cross-border regionalism, in a manner which includes borderlanders, remains largely untapped.

Financial Sustainability

The final theme that needs to be raised is that of sustainability because it underpins many of the fundamental debates about transport infrastructure: such as the merits of road versus rail and the desirability of port/corridor competition. There are in fact two inter-related issues at stake here. The first is whether the infrastructural commitments that have been made are likely to deliver a rate of return that will enable them to pay for themselves, whether in the immediate future or over the long term. The second is whether African governments are in a position to commit further to ambitious plans for corridor development without incurring crippling levels of debt.

As far as the first is concerned, funding institutions have generally taken a sanguine view about investments on the basis that it is necessary to address the infrastructural deficit that acts as a dead-weight on Africa's development.

---

[59] On the changing patterns of the cloth trade, see Nina Sylvanus, *Patterns in Circulation: Cloth, Gender and Materiality in West Africa*, Chicago & London, 2016.

[60] OECD/SWAC, "Population and Morphology of Border Cities," *West African Papers*, No. 21, Paris, 2019, pp. 21–33.

On the back of years of economic growth, the argument is that Africa needs to anticipate rising demand well in advance. Hence, there has generally been financial and moral backing for the development of African ports that are often relatively close neighbours. Competition between ports tends to be regarded by economists in a positive light because it notionally drives efficiency.[61] As things stand, there is little evidence that this is actually happening. Some African ports are undoubtedly more efficient than others, but a recent World Bank report indicates that none of them fare well from international comparisons.[62] The accent has therefore tended to shift to what needs to be done to address structural inefficiencies rather than considering the possibility that coastal countries risk over-extending themselves. The COVID-19 pandemic delivered a sharp shock, which was reflected in an immediate decline in global shipping. Although this may be a temporary effect, a global recession is likely to have a significant impact on international trade in the longer term. Many countries in Africa face the prospect of a serious, and possibly prolonged economic downturn, which is likely to deliver a further blow to the continent's trade with the rest of the world. This has palpable consequences for port developments. It has been suggested that this moment might provide an occasion to build intra-regional trade rather than trying to prise a way into global value chains – something that could even help to nurture cross-border regions.[63] It is doubtful that it would make much of a difference to the viability of the ports, however, and it would depend on making additional investments in order to redress the lack of connectivity between transport corridors. Following some years in which governments have been banking on port investments to deliver economic transformation, it seems more likely that countries will be stuck with investments that will fail to pay their way. In the case of railways, the early evidence from the SGRs in Kenya and Ethiopia/Djibouti is that they are already struggling to break even. Of

61   Theo Notteboom, César Ducruet and Peter de Langen (eds), *Ports in Proximity: Competition and Coordination among Adjacent Seaports*, Abingdon & New York, 2009.

62   Martin Humphreys, Aiga Stokenberga, Matias Herrera Dappe, Atsushi Limi and Olivier Hartmann (eds), *Port Development and Competition in East and Southern Africa: Prospects and Challenges*, Washington, D.C., 2019.

63   Andrew Mold and Anthony Mveyange, "Trade in Uncertain Times: Prioritising Regional over Global Value Chains to Accelerate Economic Development in East Africa", *Brookings*, 15 April 2020 <www.brookings.edu/blog/africa-in-focus/2020/04/15/trade-in-uncertain-times-prioritising-regional-over-global-value-chains-to-accelerate-economic-development-in-east-africa/> [Accessed 27 April 2021].

course, where they entirely cannot deflect the costs, governments may choose to subsidise rail,[64] but this would come at the cost of other important public goods such as education and health. What all of this underlines is the tension inherent within a form of regionalism that hangs on the vagaries of national politics.

As far as the second issue is concerned, the overall levels of public debt began to rise in a worrying fashion well before the outbreak of the COVID-19 pandemic. According to the World Bank, the average public debt increased from 40 to 59 per cent of GDP, while the number of countries entering debt distress had increased to 18, between 2000 and 2018.[65] Whereas Africa had previously been indebted to multilateral institutions, notably the IMF and World Bank, new forms of indebtedness have arisen in the shape of non-concessionary private sector loans (typically repayable at much higher rates of interest), Eurobonds (incurred in foreign currency) and domestic bond issues.[66] As far as bilateral debts are concerned, Africans have borrowed heavily from China in order to finance infrastructural development, but opacity on the part of the main Chinese lenders means that the details are obscure.[67] Indeed, the Jubilee Debt Campaign estimated that China accounted for around 20 per cent of all African government debt in 2018.[68] At a time when the continent was experiencing years of impressive growth, the inclination of governments was to go for broke. This meant that when commodity prices tumbled in 2014, African countries – and especially oil producers – found themselves severely exposed. The pandemic

---

[64] Kenya has imposed a railway development levy on imported manufactured goods, which passes some of the costs onto consumers.

[65] Francisco G. Carneiro and Wilfried A. Kouame, 'How Much Should African Countries Adjust to Curb the Increase in Public Debt?', *World Bank Blogs*, 3 February 2020 <https://blogs.worldbank.org/africacan/how-much-should-sub-saharan-african-countries-adjust-curb-increase-public-debt> [Accessed 27 April 2021].

[66] Chukwuka Onyekwena and Mma Amara Ekeruche, 'Is a Debt Crisis Looming in Africa?', *Brookings*, 10 April 2019 <www.brookings.edu/blog/africa-in-focus/2019/04/10/is-a-debt-crisis-looming-in-africa/>. [Accessed 27 April 2021]; James C. Mizes, 'Who Owns Africa's Infrastructure', *Limn* <https://limn.it/articles/who-owns-africas-infrastructure-2/> [Accessed 27 April 2021].

[67] Ian Taylor and Tim Zajontz, 'In a Fix: Africa's Place in the Belt and Road Initiative and the Reproduction of Dependency', *South African Journal of International Affairs*, 27: 3, 2020, p. 287.

[68] Yun Sun, 'China and Africa's Debt: Yes to Relief, No to Blanket Forgiveness', *Brookings*, 20 April 2020 <www.brookings.edu/blog/africa-in-focus/2020/04/20/china-and-africas-debt-yes-to-relief-no-to-blanket-forgiveness/> [Accessed 27 April 2021].

merely brought matters to a head. According to the latest IMF data, five African countries have accumulated debts at over 100 per cent of GDP, and 13 have debts of more than 70 per cent. Of the major RECs, SADC has the greatest problem, with an average indebtedness of 70.1 per cent of GDP, whereas the EAC average is 54 per cent and that of ECOWAS is 42 per cent.[69] With the exception of Nigeria, the oil-producing countries have incurred the greatest debt burden. But it is equally clear that a number of the countries that have been investing most heavily in infrastructure – notably Djibouti (104 per cent), Mozambique (125 per cent), Zambia (110 per cent),[70] Ghana (68 per cent), Namibia (67 per cent) and Kenya (65 per cent) – are recording some of the highest levels of indebtedness. Tanzania (40 per cent) and Ethiopia (57 per cent) have fared somewhat better. It is true that there is a great deal of infrastructural expenditure, including power generation, that is not directly related to transport, but this varies by country.[71]

Before the pandemic broke, there had already been some debate about what action might be needed to mitigate the impact of indebtedness. Chen observes that China itself had already written off significant amounts of debt before 2018. In the case of the Addis–Djibouti railway, she recalls that China cancelled some of the Ethiopian loans and extended the repayment period for others.[72] In 2020, there were various responses to the reality that African countries faced the prospect of having to default. The IMF cancelled six months of debts owed by 19 African countries, the G20 countries agreed a debt freeze until the end of 2020, while China cancelled interest-free loans that would mature at the end of the year (a small percentage of the total). China's response has been distinctly

---

69   IMF Data Mapper <www.imf.org/external/datamapper/GGXWDG_GDP@ AFRREO/ZMB/NGA> [Accessed 27 April 2021].

70   For the Zambian case, see Tim Zajontz, 'The Chinese Infrastructural Fix in Africa: Lessons from the Sino-Zambian Road Bonanza', *Oxford Development Studies*, published online 21 December 2020, DOI: 10.1080/13600818.2020.1861230 [Accessed 19 March 2021].

71   According to World Bank estimates of infrastructural financing needs, less than a quarter would be required for transport, whereas 40 per cent would be required for power generation. But clearly some of what is covered under ICTs relates directly to transport corridors. Foster and Briceño-Garmendia (eds), *Africa's Infrastructure*, Overview at p. 7.

72   Yunnan Chen, 'Countries Facing COVID-19 Debt Need Flexible Financing: Lessons from China', ODI Blog 14 April 2020 <www.odi.org/blogs/16842-countries-facing-covid-19-debt-need-flexible-financing-lessons-china> [Accessed 27 April 2021].

cautious, and this may well signal a more guarded approach to infrastructure financing in the years to come.

It seems very likely that the more ambitious plans for linking corridors will have to be put on ice and that some infrastructural projects will be suspended or abandoned altogether. This would, of course, fit perfectly with a historical oscillation between caution and enchantment about the transformative potential of infrastructural investments. Indeed, today's stalled projects will provide the material for tomorrow's retro-fit. But it would appear that we may well have witnessed the end of a cycle – both of thinking and of financing. In future, one imagines that funding to cover the 'infrastructure deficit' will become much less readily accessible. It may well be that the enchantment with big infrastructure is itself beginning to fade as funders and governments alike are forced to weigh up priorities. While electrification, urban sanitation and water supply cannot be avoided, it may well be that transport corridors slip down the list of priorities or are repackaged to serve these agendas. At the time of writing, however, it is too early to tell whether we are witnessing something more profound than a temporary blip.

Transport corridors are elusive because they represent models for the way the world works, but are simultaneously embodied in material objects and immaterial flows. Capturing these complexities has been one of the principal challenges for AFRIGOS, but also for the composition of the current volume.

As indicated in the preface, this book brings together chapters that have arisen directly from the AFRIGOS project and others that were specifically commissioned with a view to achieving a more rounded coverage of continental trends while capturing the dynamics of particular regions and specific corridors. The contributors cover a spectrum that runs from conventional academia to those with a closer relationship to policy. The contributors hail from very different disciplinary backgrounds, and partly for that reasons they draw on distinct types of data that capture realities in very different registers and at very different scales – including material from World Bank, EU and national archives in Africa and Europe; statistics and reports issued by international agencies, development banks and national governments; interviews and informal interactions with actors engaged in construction, corridor management and border control; and, finally, engagements with the everyday users of corridors like small-scale traders and the general public. Some of the corridor actors are unlikely to ever meet, whereas others encounter each other on a regular basis and work collectively to reproduce and actualise a discourse surrounding what corridors are and ought to be.

Most of the contributions to the volume speak to at least one other chapter directly – and often several at once – and this has helped to inform our decisions about the structure of the book as a whole. First of all, there are chapters that are explicitly historical in focus. Sidy Cissokho explores the genealogy of the corridor concept within the World Bank. He tracks the emergence of the contemporary instantiation of the transport corridor as a conceptual synthesis that combines a traditional focus on transport with one that is directed to the facilitation of trade. The manner in which corridors are laid across older spatial logics is taken up by Isabella Soi in her account of the historicity of topography of trade and transport routes, and the rivalry between them, across East Africa and the Great Lakes region. This encourages us to think more deeply about how some colonial infrastructure built on some of what was already in existence. In his contribution, José-María Muñoz brings a different historical lens to bear in his detailed account of the wrangling between the World Bank, bilateral donors and segments of the Cameroun government bureaucracy over the realignment of the former colonial Douala–Yaounde line during the 1970s. The evolution of continental transport planning after independence also features prominently in the comparative discussion of European and African transport policy and financing by Sergio Oliete Josa and Francesc Magrinyà. Whereas Cissokho focuses on the role of the World Bank, they highlight a range of other international actors and fora where corridor policy has been forged. Whereas their focus is largely on the European Union, Elisa Gambino provides a detailed account of how African transport corridors have also been folded into the Chinese Belt and Road Initiative – further underlining the multivalence of the corridor concept.

A number of contributions address aspects of competition: notably between ports/corridors and between modes of transport. Port competition is a topic that is squarely addressed by Bruce Byiers and Sean Woolfrey, who point out that despite the large number of ports in West Africa, competition has not reduced the costs to end-users – in part because of the monopolistic hold of a handful of large logistics corporations. The substantial investments in upgrades to ports inevitably are based on future projections and a large amount of guesswork. As Jérôme Lombard indicates, the Senegalese corridor strategy has been premised on increasing the flows through the port of Dakar which, with respect to the transit trade to Mali, involves competition with the ports of Abidjan, Lomé and Tema. Distances, operating costs and security are among the main factors determining the choices that economic operators make. In the case of the transit trade with Ougadougou, the chapters by Nina Sylvanus and by Byiers and Woolfrey both indicate the success with which the port of Lomé has competed with Tema and Abidjan – which is also the source of a certain amount of civic pride. As Paul Nugent indicates, the port of Lomé continued to attract small traders from as far afield as Abidjan until the border closures that came with the COVID-19 pandemic. While many of the contributions focus on West Africa, Hugh Lamarque provides a comparable account of the high-stakes rivalry between the ports of Mombasa and Dar es Salaam – and the Northern and Central Corridors that they serve. Like Byiers and Woolfrey, he points to the array of interests that cluster around the operation of the ports and corridor management – underlining the point that the quest for greater efficiency is far from being the only factor in the equation.

When it comes to road and rail competition, Lombard indicates that road has trumped rail in the Senegambia – although, like Muñoz and Byiers and Woolfrey, he points to ongoing plans to rehabilitate the railways. Although rail is once more promoted as a viable alternative to road, notably in East Africa and the Horn, Yunnan Chen and Lamarque signal that questions remain about their financial viability. Among road transporters, there is often resistance to anything that smacks of favouritism – as has been amply demonstrated by resistance to government efforts to favour the SGR in Kenya. Byiers and Woolfrey also point to the ways in which port competition is closely bound up with struggles for control over trucking between transporters in Burkina Faso, Togo and Ghana. This has been a recurring feature along the East and Southern African transport corridors as well.

A number of contributions address corridor financing and construction – notably the chapters by Cissokho, Muñoz and Oliete and Margrinyà. As Gambino and Chen both demonstrate, the Chinese state has become important as a financier of African corridor infrastructure, but Chinese companies also play a key role in construction – often enabling African governments to bring their own pet projects to fruition. As Gambino indicates, this is true in different ways of the SGR between Mombasa and Nairobi and the Lamu port project. In a complementary chapter, Chen focuses on the role of Chinese and Turkish actors in the construction of the Djibouti–Addis Ababa railway that has been central to Ethiopian plans for redressing its landlocked status. While there is abundant evidence that African governments have been able to advance their priorities, Lamarque points to some of the problems that arise when neighbours more or less consciously undermine each other's position. Nugent reveals how the lack of consensus has played out differently along the Abidjan–Lagos Corridor where Nigerian protectionism reduced trucking to a trickle and then to nothing as the border with Benin was unilaterally closed since 2019. The manner in which vested interests cluster at the national level often means that policy interventions are thwarted at the corridor level. Where corridor management authorities exist, they tend to be toothless.

Finally, the volume pays some attention to the everyday users of the corridor. Unfortunately, the original plan for a chapter specifically on trucking in Southern Africa did not come to fruition – although a number of chapters do allude to the hardships associated with being on the road and the frustrations of being stuck at border crossings. Lombard observes that while populations living along a corridor are supposed to reap many of the rewards, they also have also been left to deal with the downsides. Along the busiest corridor routes, such as along the Northern Corridor, accidents and deaths caused by heavy trucks are a daily hazard. The neglect of secondary roads is another corridor effect that rural populations are forced to put up with. Border populations who use segments of the corridors are often subjected to everyday harassment and are forced to pay a range of bribes at the crossing points. Whereas in East Africa, there has been a conscious effort to encourage small-scale traders to make use of OSBP facilities, this has scarcely been seen as a priority along the Abidjan–Lagos Corridor. This particular corridor perhaps demonstrates the greatest mismatch between the grand designs at the continental level and what plays out on the ground. While it sometimes seems that official discourse has the miraculous capacity to conjure corridors into existence, the stark reality of border blockages can about a much-needed reality check.

Bibliography

Aalders, Johannes Theodore, 'Building on the Ruins of Empire: the Uganda Railway and the LAPPSET Corridor in Kenya', *Third World Quarterly*, published online 12 March 2020

Ahmed, Warsame M. and Stepputat, Finn, 'Berbera Port: Geopolitics and State-Making in Somaliland', *Rift Valley Institute Briefing Paper*, Nairobi, 2019.

Beck, Kurt, Klaeger, Gabriel and Stasik, Michael, 'An Introduction to the African Road', and other contributions to Gabriel Klaeger and Michael Stasik (eds), *The Making of the African Road*, Leiden, 2017.

Berg, Elliot J., 'Structural Transformation versus Gradualism: Recent Economic Development in Ghana', in Philip Foster and Aristide Zolberg (eds), *Ghana and the Ivory Coast: Perspectives on Modernisation*, Chicago & London, 1971, pp. 187–230.

Bierschenk, Thomas, 'Sedimentation, Fragmentation and Normative Double-Binds in (West) African Public Services', in Thomas Bierschenk and Jean-Pierre Olivier de Sardan (eds), *States at Work: Dynamics of African Bureaucracies*, Leiden & Boston, 2014, pp. 221–45.

Brautigam, Deborah, 'Chinese Loans and African Structural Transformation', in Arkebe Oqubay and Justin Yifu Lin (eds), *China–Africa and an Economic Transformation*, Oxford, 2019, pp. 129–47.

Caldéron, César and Servén, Luis, 'Infrastructure and Economic Development in Sub-Saharan Africa', *Journal of African Economies*, 19, AERC Supplement 11, 2010, pp. i13–i87.

Carneiro, Francisco G. and Kouame, Wilfried A. 'How Much Should African Countries Adjust to Curb the Increase in Public Debt?', 3 February 2020 <https://blogs.

worldbank.org/africacan/how-much-should-sub-saharan-african-countries-adjust-curb-increase-public-debt> [Accessed 19 March 2021].

Chalfin, Brenda, 'Recasting Maritime Governance in Ghana: The Neo-Developmental State and the Port of Tema', *Journal of Modern African Studies*, 48:4, 2010, pp. 573–98.

Chen, Yunnan, 'Countries Facing COVID-19 Debt Need Flexible Financing: Lessons from China', ODI Blog, 14 April 2020 <www.odi.org/blogs/16842-countries-facing-covid-19-debt-need-flexible-financing-lessons-china> [Accessed 19 March 2021].

Chome, Ngala, 'Land, Livelihoods and Belonging: Negotiating Change and Anticipating LAPSSET in Kenya's Lamu County', *Journal of Eastern African Studies*, 14:2, 2020, pp. 310–31.

Ciabarri, Luca, 'Biographies of Roads, Biographies of Nations: History, Territory and the Road Effect in Post-Conflict Somaliland', in Gabriel Klaeger and Michael Stasik (eds), *The Making of the African Road*, Leiden, 2017, pp. 116–40.

Cooper, Frederick, 'Modernising Bureaucrats, Backward Africans, and the Development Concept', in Frederick Cooper and Randall Packard (eds), *International Development and the Social Sciences: Essays in the History and Politics of Knowledge*, Berkeley & London, 1998, pp. 64–92.

Cronje, Erené, Matthee, Marianne and Krugel, Waldo, 'The Role of Dry Ports in South Africa', *Transport and Communications Bulletin for Asia and the Pacific*, 78, 2009, pp. 112–20.

Dalakoglou, Dimitris, *The Road: An Ethnography of (Im)mobility, Space and Cross-Border Infrastructure in the Balkans*, Manchester, 2017.

Debrie, Jean, 'The West African Port System: Global Insertion and Regional Particularities', *EchoGéo* [online], 20, 2012, no page: http://journals.openedition.org/echogeo/13070.

Debrie, Jean and Comtois, Claude, 'Une Relecture du Concept de Corridors de Transport: Illustration Comparée Europe/Amerique du Nord', *Cahiers Scientifiques du Transport*, 58, 2010, pp. 127–44.

Ducruet, César, Cuyala, Sylvain and Hosni, Ali El, 'Maritime Networks as Systems of Cities: The Long-Term Interdependencies between Global Shipping Flows and Urban Development (1890–2010)', *Journal of Transport Geography*, 66, 2018, pp. 340–55.

Enns, Charis, 'Infrastructure Projects and Rural Projects in Northern Kenya: The Use of Divergent Expertise to Negotiate the Terms of Land Deals for Transport Infrastructure', *Journal of Eastern African Studies*, 46:2, 2017, pp. 358–76.

Enns, Charis and Bersaglio, Brock, 'On the Coloniality of "New" Mega-Infrastructure Projects in East Africa', *Antipode*, 52:1, 2019, pp. 101–23.

Farole, John and Moberg, Lotta, 'Special Economic Zones in Africa: Political Economy Challenges and Solutions', in John Page and Finn Tarp (eds), *The Practice of Industrial Policy: Government-Business Coordination in Africa and East Asia*, Oxford, 2017, pp. 234–51.

Fau, Nathalie, Khonthapane, Sirivanh and Taillard, Christian (eds), *Transnational Dynamics in Southeast Asia: The Greater Mekong Subregion and Malacca Straits Economic Corridor*, Singapore, 2014.

Foster, Vivien and Briceno-Garmendia, Cecilia, *Infrastructures Africaines: Une Transformation Impérative*, Paris, 2010, p. 202.

Freed, Libbie, *Conduits of Culture and Control: Roads, States and Users in French Central Africa, 1890–1960*, unpublished PhD thesis, University of Wisconsin Madison, 2006.

Gonçalves, Euclides, 'Agricultural Corridors as "Demonstration Fields": Infrastructure, Fairs and Associations along the Beira and Nacala Corridors', *Journal of Eastern African Studies*, 14:2, 2020, pp. 354–74.

Harvey, Penny and Knox, Hannah, 'The Enchantments of Infrastructure', *Mobilities*, 7:4, 2012, pp. 521–36.

Haugen, Heidi Østbø, 'The Social Production of Container Space', *Society and Space*, 37:5, 2019, pp. 868–85.

Hirschman, Albert O., *Development Projects Observed*, Washington D.C., 1967.

Hönke, Jana and Cuesta-Fernández, Iván, 'Mobilising Security and Logistics through an African Port: A Controversies Approach to Infrastructure', *Mobilities*, 13:2, 2018, pp. 246–60.

Howe, Cymene, *et al.*, 'Paradoxical Infrastructures: Ruins, Retrofit and Risk', *Science, Technology and Human Values*, 41:3, 2016, pp. 547–65.

Hoyle, B.S. and Hilling, D., (eds), *Seaports and Development in Tropical Africa*, London, 1970.

Humphreys, Martin, *et al.* (eds), *Port Development and Competition in East and Southern Africa: Prospects and Challenges*, Washington DC, 2019.

Josa, Sergio Oliete and Magrinyà, Francesc, 'Patchwork in an Interconnected World: The Challenges of Transport Networks in Sub-Saharan Africa', *Transport Reviews*, 38:6, 2018, pp. 710–36.

Kay, G.B. (ed.), *The Political Economy of Colonialism in Ghana: A Collection of Documents and Statistics 1900–1960*, Cambridge, 1972.

Kim, Hwa-Joong, Lam, Jasmine Siu Lee and Lee, Paul Tae-Woo, 'Analysis of Liner Shipping Networks and Transhipment Flows of Potential Hub Ports in Sub-Saharan Africa', *Transport Policy*, 69, 2018, pp. 193–206.

Kochore, Hassan H., 'The Road to Kenya? Visions, Expectations and Anxieties Around New Infrastructure', *Journal of Eastern African Studies*, 10:3, 2016, pp. 494–510.

Kunaka, Charles, Raballand, Gael and Fitzmaurice, Mike, *How Trucking Services Have Improved and May Contribute to Development: The Case of East Africa*, WIDER Working Paper 152/2016.

Larkin, Brian, 'The Politics and Poetics of Infrastructure', *Annual Review of Anthropology*, 42, 2013, pp. 327–43.

Lamarque, Hugh, 'Profitable Inefficiency: The Politics of Port Infrastructure in Mombasa, Kenya', *Journal of Modern African Studies*, 57:1, 2019, pp. 85–109.

Laurence, Bill, Sloan, Sean, Weng, Lingfei and Sayer, Jeffrey A., 'Estimating the

Environmental Costs of Africa's Massive "Development Corridors"', *Current Biology*, 25, 2015, pp. 3202–08.

Masquelier, Adeline, 'Road Mythographies: Space, Mobility and the Historical Imagination in Postcolonial Niger', *American Ethnologist*, 29:4, 2002, pp. 829–56.

Mizes, James C., 'Who Owns Africa's Infrastructure', *Limn* <https://limn.it/articles/who-owns-africas-infrastructure-2/> [Accessed 27 April 2021].

Mold, Andrew and Mveyange, Anthony, 'Trade in Uncertain Times: Prioritising Regional over Global Value Chains to Accelerate Economic Development in East Africa', 15 April 2020 <www.brookings.edu/blog/africa-in-focus/2020/04/15/trade-in-uncertain-times-prioritising-regional-over-global-value-chains-to-accelerate-economic-development-in-east-africa/> [Accessed 19 March 2021].

Monson, Jamie, *Africa's Freedom Railway: How a Chinese Development Project Changed Lives and Livelihoods in Tanzania*, Bloomington, 2011.

Muñoz, José-María, *Doing Business in Cameroon: An Anatomy of Economic Governance*, Cambridge, 2018.

Murton, Galen, 'Trans-Himalayan Transformations: Building Roads, Making Markets, and Cultivating Consumption between Nepal and China's Tibet', in Yongming Zhou, Qu Tenglong and Li Guiying (eds), *Roadology: Roads, Space, Culture*, Chongqing, 2016, pp. 328–40.

Ndulu, Benno J., 'Infrastructure, Regional Integration and Growth in Sub-Saharan Africa: Dealing with the Disadvantages of Geography and Sovereign Fragmentation', *Journal of African Economies*, 15, AERC Supplement 2, 2006, pp. 212–44.

Notteboom, Theo, 'Strategies and Future Development of Transport Corridors', in Yann Alix (ed.), *Les corridors de Transport*, Caens, 2012, pp. 289–312.

Notteboom, Theo, Ducruet, César and de Langen, Peter (eds), *Ports in Proximity: Competition and Coordination among Adjacent Seaports*, Abingdon & New York, 2009.

Notteboom, Theo and Rodrigue, Jean-Paul, 'Port Regionalisation: Towards a New Phase in Port Development', *Maritime Policy & Management*, 32:3, 2005, 297–313.

Nugent, Paul, 'Africa's Re-enchantment with Big Infrastructure: White Elephants Dancing in Virtuous Circles?', in Jon Schubert, Ulf Engel, and Elisio Macamo (eds), *Extractive Industries and Changing State Dynamics in Africa: Beyond the Resource Curse*, Abingdon, 2018, pp. 22–40.

Nugent, Paul and Soi, Isabella, 'One-Stop Border Posts in East Africa: State Encounters of the Fourth Kind', *Journal of Eastern African Studies*, 14:3, 2020, pp. 433–54.

Nuvunga, Milissão, 'Region-Building in Central Mozambique: the Case of the Zambezi Valley Spatial Development Initiative', in Frederik Söderbaum and Ian Taylor (eds), *Afro-Regions: The Dynamics of Cross-Border Micro-Regionalism in Africa*, Uppsala, 2008, pp. 74–89.

OECD/SWAC, 'Population and Morphology of Border Cities', *West African Papers*, No. 21, Paris, 2019.

Onyekwena, Chukwuka and Ekeruche, Mma Amara, 'Is a Debt Crisis Looming in Africa?', *Brookings*, 10 April 2019 <www.brookings.edu/blog/africa-in-focus/2019/04/10/is-a-debt-crisis-looming-in-africa/>. [Accessed 27 April 2021].

Pariault, Thierry, 'China in Africa: Goods Supplier, Service Provider Rather than Investor', *Bridges Africa*, 7:5, 2018, no page.

Raballand, Gaël and Whitworth, Alan, *Should the Zambian Government Invest in Railways?*, ZIPAR Working Paper No. 3, 2012, Lusaka, Zambia Institute for Policy Analysis and Research.

Republic of Mozambique, *The Project for Nacala Corridor: Economic Development Strategies in the Republic of Mozambique – Final Study Report*, Maputo, 2015.

Schouten, Peer, 'Roadblock Politics in Central Africa', *Environmental Planning D: Society and Space*, 37:5, 2019, pp. 924–41.

Simon, David, and Ekobo, Muriel Samé, 'Walvis Bay–Swakopmund: Desert Micro-Region and Aspiring Regional Gateway', in Frederik Söderbaum and Ian Taylor (eds), *Afro-Regions: The Dynamics of Cross-Border Micro-Regionalism in Africa*, Uppsala, 2008, pp. 53–73.

Söderbaum, Fredrik and Taylor, Ian (eds), *Afro-Regions: The Dynamics of Cross-Border Micro-Regionalism in Africa*, Uppsala, 2008.

Steck, Benjamin, 'L'Afrique des Ports et des Corridors: Comment Formuler l'Interaction entre Logistique et Développement', *Cahiers de Géographie de Québec*, 59:168, 2015, pp. 447–67.

Stepputat, Finn and Hagmann, Tobias, 'Politics of Circulation: The Making of the Berbera Corridor in Somali East Africa', *Environment and Planning D: Society and Space D*, 37:5, 2019, pp. 794–813.

Sun, Yun, 'China and Africa's debt: 'China and Africa's Debt: Yes to Relief, No to Blanket Forgiveness' <www.brookings.edu/blog/africa-in-focus/2020/04/20/china-and-africas-debt-yes-to-relief-no-to-blanket-forgiveness/> [Accessed 19 March 2021].

Sylvanus, Nina, *Patterns in Circulation: Cloth, Gender and Materiality in West Africa*, Chicago & London, 2016.

Taylor, Ian and Zajontz, Tim, 'In a Fix: Africa's Place in the Belt and Road Initiative and the Reproduction of Dependency', *South African Journal of International Affairs*, 27: 3, 2020, pp. 277–95.

Vilikazi, Thando S., 'The Causes of High Inter-Regional Road Freight Rates for Food and Commodities in Southern Africa', *Development Southern Africa*, 35:3, 2018, pp. 388–403.

Weir, Andrew, 'How Vincent Bolloré Won Control Over Ghana's Biggest Port', *Africa Confidential*, 62:7, 2021 <www.africa-confidential.com/article/id/13322/SPECIAL_REPORT_How_Vincent_Bollor%C3%A9_won_control_of_Ghana%E2%80%99s_biggest_port> [Accessed 28 July 2021].

Wilks, Ivor, *Asante in the Nineteenth Century: The Structure and Evolution of a Political Order*, Cambridge, 1975.

World Bank, *The Web of Transport Corridors in South Asia*, Washington DC, 2018.

Zajontz, Tim 'The Chinese Infrastructural Fix in Africa: Lessons from the Sino-Zambian Road Bonanza', *Oxford Development Studies*, published online 21 December 2020, DOI: 10.1080/13600818.2020.1861230 [Accessed 19 March 2021].

CHAPTER 2

Infrastructure, Development and Neoliberalism in Africa: The Concept of Transport Corridors

SIDY CISSOKHO

Introduction

Infrastructure in general, and transport infrastructure in particular, are the focus of an increasing number of social science studies. While most have concentrated on how populations have adopted them, few have looked at how they were perceived before they were established. However, the ways these physical creations are viewed and justified do not merely stimulate a simple narrative with no connection to the uses that can be made of them. Instead, they define much of what they actually are, as well as the limits within which they are created and used. Starting out from this premise, this chapter will trace the trajectory of one of the main intellectual constructs through which roads, ports and railways are conceived by development actors in Africa: the 'corridor'.

This archaeological work is all the more important because the term 'corridor' is used both by those who think and implement these infrastructures in the expert domain, and by those who are responsible for producing a critical discourse about them in the academic domain. This situation certainly concerns other notions of the development world. However, it is not without its problems, for how can a critical discourse be produced on the physical and institutional achievements designated by the expression 'corridors' without distancing itself, at least for a time, from the forms of knowledge and presuppositions that contribute to making this category legitimate? The concept of corridors does not refer to a mere association of infrastructures: it gives it a particular meaning. It entails a certain representation of a territory based on regional, not national, divisions. In addition, the rhetoric around the formation of these transnational spaces, which are intended to be free of any constraints that might hinder the circulation of goods, makes free trade the main vector of development, thereby making transport infrastructure the material support for what is an eminently liberal project.

Rather than on infrastructure itself or the science and technology that enable its construction, this chapter focuses on how the narrative that justifies their existence has developed. This will require us to combine archival material with informal conversations and observations made during an ethnographic immersion among expert networks that advocate for this type of policies.[1] It will take us on a journey through scientific and expert publications, summary reports, audit reports, internal correspondences of international organisations (when they are available), and will even follow the work of the individuals and groups who deliver this discourse on the international stage, from one organisation or forum to another. The purpose of this chapter is not to uncover the origin of the notion of 'corridors', but rather to identify the starting point(s) of its investment by development practitioners, the variations, hesitations, as well as the contradictions inherent in the elaboration of the discourses with which this category is associated.

When everything is taken together, it reveals the intellectual history of an expression and its uses. It also exposes some of the mechanisms that have enabled the neoliberal agenda to prevail and prosper in the small world of development. Indeed, the rise of the use of the concept of 'corridors' has been in fact a response to the exhaustion of the justifications that had surrounded the construction of transport infrastructure in the development field since the post-war period. This made it possible to match the motivations surrounding this type of investment with the neoliberal thought that dominated the intellectual world in the 1970s and made the construction of transport infrastructure a necessary prelude to the creation of transnational free trade zones.[2] Since the time it was founded, this branch of public policy and the beliefs it conveys have continued their process of institutionalisation at the heart of an ensemble of international actors who still contribute to its existence today. Our review of the various stages of development and dissemination of the notion of corridors further demonstrates that

[1]   This chapter parallels the overview of various territories conducted between 2016 and 2019. It is first of all the product of a compilation of informal interviews, observations and archival work at the World Bank in Washington, D.C. and with European Union personnel in Brussels. It is also the result of observational work at meetings attended by development practitioners devoted to transport infrastructures and trade liberalisation in various West African capitals. To all of this we added the documentary research (reports, publications, documents and projects) we carried out over the course of these three years.

[2]   On the victory of neoliberal ideas during the 1970s, see Philip Mirowski and Dieter Plehwe (eds), *The Road from Mount Pelerin. The Making of the Neoliberal Thought Collective*, London, 2009.

the structures of the market economy, of which transport infrastructures have become the backbone, are the product of an ongoing political effort rather than a spontaneous natural reality.[3]

The Keynesian Moment: Transport Infrastructures and the Developmentalist Imagination

At the root of the developmentalist discourse in the immediate aftermath of the Second World War, the link between development and the construction of transport infrastructure was obvious;[4] however, this link was not made explicit until much later, at the end of the 1960s. It emerged partly from the increasing importance attributed by think tanks to the rationalisation of developmentalist thinking in the US. In the wake of the New Deal and the Keynesian thinking that still dominated certain spheres of thought at the time, heavy public investment in transport infrastructure was seen as a way of compensating for underdevelopment by contributing to the 'Big Push'.[5]

As the developmentalist paradigm gradually spread in the immediate aftermath of the Second World War financing transport infrastructure became a key activity of the international institutions.[6] The construction of railways, roads and ports is considered to be one of the essential factors – if not *the* factor – for driving development. In the early 1960s, therefore, the construction of transport infrastructure became one of the World Bank's main areas of activity. Although Africa remained neglected, the Bank was carrying out important work in this field in Latin America and India. The same was true of the European Economic

---

3   Karl Polanyi, *The Great Transformation*, Boston, 1957.
4   Gilbert Rist, *Le Développement: Histoire d'une Croyance Occidentale*, Paris, 1996.
5   On this subject, see Thomas Medvetz, *Think Tanks in America?*, Chicago, 2012. The expression is borrowed from developmental economist Paul Rosenstein-Rodan, who theorised the idea in the 1940s. It was subsequently used by Walter Whitman Rostow. For its use in connection with the development in the transport sector, see Sergio Oliete Josa and Francesc Magrinyà, 'Patchwork in an Interconnected World: The Challenges of Transport Networks in Sub-Saharan Africa', *Transport Reviews*, 38:6, 2018, pp. 710–36, p. 717.
6   Some recent works have suggested that the idea of 'development' was born in the inter-war period, thereby challenging the timeline suggested by Rist. As we are primarily interested in the institutionalisation of this school of thought, however, we adopt the timeline suggested by Rist. Véronique Plata-Stenger, 'Mission Civilisatrice, Réforme Sociale et Modernisation: L'Oit et le Développement Colonial dans l'Entre-Deux-Guerres', *Relations Internationales*, 177:1, 2019, pp. 15–29.

Community (EEC), which was also already one of six main providers of funds in this sector at the time.[7]

Transport infrastructure construction was not supported by any official discourse during this period, however. For the bureaucrats, the significance of transport infrastructures in public development policies was a natural consequence. The construction of transport infrastructure has been important element of the actions taken by the Bretton Woods organisations since their creation in the post-war context, where this type of infrastructure was particularly targeted. Also, many of the employees of organisations that were promoting the developmentalist paradigm – whether they belong to the World Bank or the EEC – had come from colonial administrations.[8] Still, transport was at the heart of the public policy being led by these administrations.[9] There was also a second pool of international civil servants responsible for designing public development policies who had come from national administrations in which transport infrastructure was also seen as an important element of growth.[10]

It was not until the early 1960s that what had seemed to be obvious actually took the form of a structured discourse in the development sector. Although the EEC was already one of the largest providers of infrastructure construction, it was not in its immediate environment that this discourse was being developed, but rather in Washington, D.C.[11] One particular research programme was emblematic of the formation of this discourse: the Transport Research Program, which was financed through a co-operation between the US and the World Bank. It was created in the early 1960s, and distributed its final publication at the end of the

7   Wilfred Owen, *Strategy for Mobility*, Washington, D.C., 1964, p. 171.
8   Véronique Dimier, 'Politiques Indigènes en France et en Grande-Bretagne dans les Années 1930: Aux Origines Coloniales des Politiques de Développement', *Politique et Sociétés*, 24:1, 2005, pp. 73–99.
9   Hélène d'Almeida-Topor, Chantal Chanson-Jabeur and Monique Lakroum (eds), *Les Transports en Afrique XIXe–XXe Siècle*, Paris, 1992.
10   See, for example, Hugh S. Norton, *National Transportation Policy: Formation and Implementation,* Berkeley, 1967, but also, more broadly, works such as John K. Galbraith, *Le Nouvel État Industriel: Essai sur le Système Économique Américain*, Paris, 1968.
11   Until the 1990s, and even later, the European Union did not make its presence felt as a meaningful producer among the players in international aid. See: Véronique Dimier, *The Invention of a European Development Aid Bureaucracy: Recycling Empire*, Basingstoke, 2014, in particular p. 152.

1980s.[12] One of America's oldest and largest think tanks, the Brookings Institution, was commissioned to carry out the work. In order to do so, it brought together not only its permanent think tank employees but also outside consultants from academia, who were exclusively economists. All together, they exported their conception of transport infrastructure role in economic development forged in the US national context, in the development field.

The arguments that were developed in the various publications associated with this programme are symptomatic of the justifications elaborated during the 1960s and 1970s around the construction of transport infrastructure in Sub-Saharan Africa. In order to understand the emergence of this discourse at that particular moment, we need to look at the history of the institution from which it originated. The birth of the Transport Research Program corresponded to the shift by many Washington think tanks from national policies to development policies. The Brookings Institution belongs to the first wave of American think tanks created in the US in the early twentieth century by forward-thinking philanthropic businessmen.[13]

After playing an important role in defining the central elements of US domestic policy, these institutions espoused the immediate post-war movement designed by the US, which was increasingly invested in international affairs.[14] The type of discourse think tanks delivered also benefited from the significant status acquired by the expertise gained from legitimising public policy during the war effort. These institutions won numerous foreign policy contracts from the American government and other Washington-based organisations, not just nationally, but also internationally.

[12] A series was published as part of this project. All the published works were reviewed in the various specialist journals of the time. *Strategy for Mobility*, by Owen Wilson; *Transport Investment and Economic Development*, edited by Gary Fromm; *Government Controls on Transport: An African Case*, by Edwin T. Haefele and Eleanor B. Steinberg; *The Impact of Highway Investment on Development*, by George W. Wilson, Barbara R. Bergmann, Leon V. Hirsch and Martin S. Klein; *Transport and the Economic Integration of South America*, by Robert T. Brown; *Soviet Transport Experience: Its Lessons for Other Countries*, by Holland Hunter; and *Distance and Development: Transport and Communications in India*, by Wilfred Owen.

[13] Donald E. Abelson, 'From Policy Research to Political Advocacy: The Changing Role of Think Tanks in American Politics', *Canadian Review of American Studies*, 25:1, 1995, pp. 93–126; Gerald Freund, *Narcissism and Philanthropy: Ideas and Talent Denied*, New York, 1996.

[14] See in particular the chronology produced in Donald E. Abelson, *Do Think Tanks Matter? Assessing the Impact of Public Policy Institutes*, Montreal, 2002, pp. 17–49.

The career path of Wilfred Owen, the director of the programme, makes this interweaving of national administrations, international administrations and networks of experts that was specific to the US capital easier to understand.[15] Wilfred Owen was educated as an economist at Harvard in the early 1930s.[16] Immediately after graduating, he joined the Highway Research Board in Washington, a division of the US National Research Council. Created in the early 1920s, the Highway Research Board advised the US administration at a federal level. Throughout the 1940s, he was one of the experts on the National Resources Planning Board, which Roosevelt had created to support his New Deal policy by providing studies on a number of important topics. He then moved into the private sector and joined the Brookings Institution, where he started out producing analyses of US domestic transport policy.[17] When the organisation became increasingly involved in drafting reports on US foreign policy and foreign countries, Wilfred Owen's career became international. His expertise in transport grew, and he worked on the preparation of reports for the World Bank, the US Agency for International Development (USAID), the Asian Development Bank and the Ford Foundation in Asia, Africa and Latin America.

The discourse that developed in the various studies from the Transport Research Program was clear. The challenge was to bring the relationship between transport and economic growth up to date, and so transport, and through it the mobility of goods and people, was placed at the heart of the development issue. The construction of transport infrastructure was not the only condition for economic development, but it was a central one. Other intellectual output from organisations on a similar path to the Brookings Institution reinforced this argument, as was the case, for example, with the 'mobility index' developed from the statistical work carried out by the International Road Federation. This organisation had played an important role in disseminating road-building standards in the immediate post-war era, and its experts now collaborated with the United Nations, and even the World Bank, in the 1960s.

The index below reproduces the major distinction between 'developed' and 'undeveloped' countries popularised by the American discourse in the immediate post-war period. It introduces another division between 'mobile' and 'immobile'

15   See also the career path of Albert O. Hirschman, which is retraced in Jeremy Adelman, *Worldly Philosopher: The Odyssey of Albert O. Hirschman*, Princeton, 2014.

16   A piece by Graeme Zielinski published in the *Washington Post* on 6 December 2001 on the death of Wilfred Owen.

17   Charles L. Dearing and Wilfred Owen, *National Transportation Policy*, Washington, D.C., 1949.

societies. As a result of this rhetorical work, the discourse on infrastructure is directly superimposed on that on development.

Table 2.1. Index of per capita GNP and the mobility of nations, 1961.

Country	GNP	Freight mobility	Passenger mobility
Immobile nations			
Ethiopia	3.2	1.7	1.7
Pakistan	5.5	6.7	8.3
India	5.9	10.0	11.5
Ghana	14.6	10.1	9.5
Columbia	20.8	11.3	9.2
Peru	13.3	12.7	10.8
Algeria	20.6	17.3	16.0
Greece	31.7	17.8	18.7
Mexico	23.0	27.8	22.8
Mobile nations			
Japan	37.2	30.5	46.3
Spain	27.5	33.2	34.8
Chile	33.3	38.2	36.2
UK	104.0	86.0	94.5
Sweden	130.8	93.0	104.5
France	100.0	100.0	100.0
West Germany	105.4	99.3	91.0
US	207.3	189.0	147.2
Canada	147.9	223.1	148.9

Source: Adapted from Owen, *Strategy for Mobility*, p. 14.

Beyond the simple correlation between development and mobility revealed by the use of numbers, the challenge at the time was to manage the causal link between the two elements in a way that reflected the canons of scientific discourse as closely as possible. Was transport infrastructures a condition or a consequence of development? In the literature produced by expert circles in Washington, proof of this causal link necessitated repeated calls for examples from American history in which roads and, even more, railways, occupied a

SSIDY CISSOKHO

significant place.[18] In the context of the Cold War, however, the example of communist countries served as a foil. Behind the opposition to it lay criticism of the Soviet Union's planning policies, and to a lesser extent those of China.[19] The leverage effect on development induced by investment in transport infrastructure was also seen as being closely linked to the forms taken by existing political and social structures. The combination offered by the examples of developed countries – the Soviet Union aside – therefore served to define a path to development through transport.

Wilfred Owen's adaptation of the famous stages of development of industrial societies, which had been theorised by the economist Walt Whitman Rostow a few years earlier, shows that undeveloped countries corresponded to stages 1 and 2 and communist countries to stage 3, notably due to their emphasis on rail.[20] The US corresponded to stages 4 and 5.

First was the period of immobility and traditional society. In this period, it was difficult and costly to develop trade and cultural relations on any large scale except where channels of communications were provided by the rivers and oceans. The pattern of living emerging from these conditions was predominately one of localised agriculture and handicraft industries with a minimum of economic integration and social intercourse. Most people of the world still live in this initial stage of primitive transport, and their efforts to break out of a subsistence environment and to achieve a better life are being thwarted by the same barriers to movement that plagued all generations before them.

A second stage of transport development was the period of internal improvements and the growth of trade. Human and animal power was made much more effective by the development of turn pikes and canals, which reduced the cost of transport by traditional methods of moving on land and water. This period of declining transport cost saw both an expansion of capacity and a lengthening of the radius of trade and travel.

A third stage in the evolutionary process toward greater mobility and higher standard of living was the period of transport mechanisation and industrialisation. This was the period of steam power, which introduced both the steamship and the first railways. It was a period marked by heavy

18 Robert W. Fogel, *Railroads and American Economic Growth: Essays in Econometric History*, Baltimore, 1964.

19 Ernest W. Williams, *Freight Transportation in the Soviet Union, including Comparisons with the United States*, Princeton, 1962.

20 Walt Whitman Rostow, *The Stages of Economic Growth: A Non-Communist Manifesto*, Cambridge, 1960, in particular pp. 4–16.

investments in transportation, as well as the establishment of a wide assortment of manufacturing industries.

A fourth period in the evolution of transport has been the development of motorisation and the new mobility. This has been an era marked by growing dependence on trucks, buses and automobiles, and by extensive effort to provide all-weather roads. This is the period when people and economic activity were freed from the limited mileage of fixed routes provided by railways ad water ways.

A fifth stage still in the process of development is the air age and the conquest of distance, a period in which the world is being united by transport speeds that are obliterating political boundaries and adding a third dimension to the solution of transport problems. This stage, however, has not yet affected local and short-haul transport that comprises a major part of the transport problem.[21]

We should not over-emphasise the producers' reasoning in this discussion, however, as the extract suggests, for those who believed in the link between mobility and development, the issue of the specificity of the social, political and economic structures of so-called undeveloped countries raised the question of the relevance of this model outside the West. What was being questioned was not the model to be achieved – which was that of the US – but rather the inescapable nature of the steps required to achieve it. According to the prevailing economic theories of the time, the heavy public investment in transport infrastructure had to enable developing countries to catch up, without repeating the mistakes made by their North American 'big brother'.

The role of the US, and especially Washington, in creating schools of thought on the place of transport infrastructure in the development process, may seem surprising in view of the other development topics from the same period. It is linked above all to the available sources, which originated in the American capital and its microcosm of experts, think tanks and national and international officials, the main producers of the discourse associating transport infrastructure with development. Representatives of other organisations located in Europe or elsewhere that were involved in financing infrastructure construction did also have their own vision of the role of transport infrastructure in development. During this period, for example, the media division of the Directorate-General for International Cooperation and Development of the European Union (Le Courrier Afrique – Caraïbes – Pacifique – Union Européenne) kept track of

---

[21]   Owen, *Strategy for Mobility*, pp. 35–37.

this thinking in opinion pieces produced by European Union officials.[22] But it was only in the US that we saw a systematic shaping of this belief in the form of research projects, scientific articles, books, indicators and a field of research in its own right.[23] Over the next few decades, the central importance of Washington only increased, as the World Bank's dominance in the production of development knowledge became more significant.

The Neoliberal Moment:
Transport and Free-Trade Infrastructures

The belief in a link between development and the construction of transport infrastructure continued to form the basis for justifying transport infrastructure projects, even though it may have been the subject of heated discussions. The ways in which this belief was expressed modified though to accommodate changes in the developmental paradigm, especially with the advent of the Washington Consensus.[24] At the end of the 1980s, the myth that associated the construction of transport infrastructure with development was perpetuated through the notions of 'transport corridors', 'economic corridors' and later 'development corridors'. The formation of transnational spaces in which goods would be able to circulate unhindered became one of the preferred paths to development. More than mobility, it was now free trade that infrastructure had explicitly come to support. This reformulation was essentially the product of World Bank personnel, whose transport discourse dominated the 1990s.[25]

Apparently, the World Bank's use of the term did not just signal the proximity of the sphere of development to the economy, as it had in the immediate

---

22   Behind these seemingly rational narratives, it would seem that political interests were at the forefront. Infrastructure was used as a way of buying African elites, who were easily able to capitalise on their construction. See Véronique Dimier, *Recycling Empire*, in particular p. 152.

23   See, for example, the birth of the *Journal of Transport Economics and Policy* in 1967.

24   Yves Dezalay and Bryant Garth, 'Le "Washington consensus": Contribution à une Sociologie de l'Hégémonie du Néolibéralisme', *Actes de la Recherche en Sciences Sociales*, 121–22, 1998, pp. 3–22.

25   For more on this subject, see Josa and Magrinyà's review paper, 'Patchwork in an Interconnected World', at p. 7. The role of this organisation in the formulation of the logic that underlies a large number of development policies has been highlighted in numerous studies. See, for example, Michael Goldman, 'The Birth of a Discipline: Producing Authoritative Green Knowledge, World Bank-Style', *Ethnography*, 2:2, 2001, pp. 191–217.

post-war period, but also to geography, given that the concept actually appeared in that field in the 1960s. Little is known about the shift of this notion from the scientific to the decision-making sphere. In the best-documented North American context, it seems to have been driven by the increased proximity of certain experts in the field to the federal administration after the Second World War.[26] Jean Debrie and Claude Comtois are the only geographers who have attempted to trace the genealogy of the concept of corridors and, to a lesser extent, the conditions under which it made the shift from the scientific world to government administration. In their view, the notion first appeared in so-called developed countries during the 1970s.[27] The concept of corridors was thus used in the development field as early as the 1970s, and therefore at the same time as in national bureaucracies.[28] It was used in a loose sense, however, and the word 'corridor' was primarily employed as a synonym for terms like 'transport system'.[29] In fact, the word was applied mainly to refer to a simple chain of different types of transport infrastructure.

As a sign of the progressive empowerment of the development industry, the shift from the notion of US and European national administrations to the development world could no longer be explained by the career path taken by individuals such as Wilfred Owen two decades earlier. The porosity between national and international bureaucracies remained, however, in the form of areas that grouped their representatives together on specific topics. In the case of World Bank personnel, which is the best documented situation, this was manifested by the fact that employees of the organisation participated in numerous international conferences, where they sat alongside officials and experts involved in making policies for Western countries. Similar spaces were also developed within the World Bank itself, where weekly training for the organisation's staff included

26 Thomas J. Wilbanks, 'Geography and Public Policy at the National Scale', *Annals of the Association of American Geographers*, 75:1, 1985, pp. 4–10. For a more recent review of these relationships between government and geography, see National Research Council, *Rediscovering Geography: New Relevance for Science and Society*, Washington, D.C., 2000, pp. 109–37.

27 Jean Debrie and Claude Comtois, 'Une relecture du concept de corridors de transport: illustration comparée Europe/Amérique du Nord', *Les Cahiers Scientifiques du Transport*, 58, 2010, pp. 127–44.

28 See, for example, in the case of Latin America: Debrie and Comtois, 'Une relecture', pp. 127–44.

29 Yann Alix (ed.), *Les corridors de transport*, Cormelles-le-Royal, 2012.

North American or European experts, who were expected to provide potential models for public development policies intended for developing countries.[30]

It was only from the end of the 1980s that the concept of 'corridor' became the subject of a true definition and delimitation of studies. This moment in time combined with two important turning points in the development industry. First, this theoretical elaboration was mainly produced by personnel from one organisation, the World Bank. The construction of a discourse that legitimised infrastructure projects no longer took place outside international organisations, as had been the case in the immediate post-war era with think tanks in the US capital, but directly within the bank. This shift in the location of expertise marked the beginning of the international financial institution's affirmation as a knowledge producer.[31] Second, while reflections on the link between transport and development had mainly focused on Asia, and to a lesser extent Latin America, the concept of corridors was being developed based on considerations that were germane to the African continent. This change reflected a move in the World Bank's interests, and with it those of the entire development industry, towards Africa.[32]

When viewed through the World Bank's archives, the process that led to the reformulation of the link between transport infrastructures and development emerges as being linked to the affirmation of the organisation's so-called 'technical' staff at the end of the 1980s more than to any sort of ideological upheaval.[33] A study of the correspondence by the infrastructure division personnel, who were mainly engineers, suggests that the commitment to the concept of corridors coincided with a dwindling of the prior justifications for the construction of transport infrastructures in developing countries among this group, and the simultaneous rise of a sense of weariness. The personnel questioned the nature of the projects that

---

30 In particular, the weekly Wednesday seminars at the organisation's headquarters during a part of the 1980s come to mind.

31 This upheaval is represented by the expression 'knowledge bank', which has given rise to a significant body of literature. Teresa Kramarz and Bessma Momani, 'The World Bank as Knowledge Bank: Analyzing the Limits of a Legitimate Global Knowledge Actor', *Review of Policy Research*, 30:4, 2013, pp. 409–31; Goldman, *The Birth of a Discipline*; Olivier Nay, 'International Organisations and the Production of Hegemonic Knowledge: How the World Bank and the OECD Helped Invent the Fragile State Concept', *Third World Quarterly*, 35:2, 2014, pp. 210–31.

32 John P. Lewis, Richard C. Webb, and Devesh Kapur (eds), *The World Bank: Its First Half Century: History, Vol. 1*, Washington, D.C., 1997, in particular pp. 16–21.

33 S. Cissokho, 'Reflections on the Washington Consensus: When the World Bank turned to free trade for its transport infrastructure projects', *Politix*, 128:4, 2019, 179–205.

had been undertaken up to that point, and the recurring failings of infrastructure construction despite the enormous investments that had been made.

At the same time, an internal reform of unprecedented significance modified the functions of these same individuals, giving them greater reach in the development of projects. The new 'task team leaders' were responsible for the composition of their teams, the development of the logic behind their projects, the sourcing of funding within the institution to complete their projects and, of course, the task of convincing the bank's clients and their superiors of the merits of the project they were taking on.[34] In other words, they became real promoters of projects within the new reticular organisation of the World Bank, which was unique to the emerging management ideology.[35] The bank's engineers – who had once been confined to technical expertise – seized this reform and the new roles it created to change the meaning of transport infrastructure projects. This was reflected in the creation of a multi-donor research programme – the Sub-Saharan Africa Transport Policy Program (SSATP) – which was closely controlled by the bank, and brought economists and engineers together to produce an in-depth reflection on public transport policies in Sub-Saharan Africa.[36] It was notably in this area that work on defining the World Bank's transport infrastructure policies, as well as that of all donors in Africa throughout the 1990s, was carried out.[37]

---

[34] For a more detailed explanation of the role currently being played by the TTL, see Lavagnon Ika, 'Opening the Black Box of Project Management: Does World Bank Project Supervision Influence Project Impact?', *International Journal of Project Management*, 33:5, 2015, pp. 1111–23.

[35] Luc Boltanski and Ève Chiapello, *Le Nouvel Esprit du Capitalisme*, Paris, 1999, pp. 99–167.

[36] This situation would lead to a profound crisis at the end of the 1990s and the partial overhaul of the programme. John Bruce Thompson, 'Africa's Transport: A Promising Future. A Review of Africa's Achievements', SSATP Advocacy Paper, Washington, D.C., 2011, pp. 12–13.

[37] In his foreword to the history of the SSATP, John Bruce Thompson, a former European Commission official, writes: 'The European Commission, as a leading transport donor in Sub-Saharan Africa with activities covering 30 countries, needed a sectoral approach to sustain its major investments. SSATP policy principles and good practices guided my development of the EC transport sector guidelines. Similarly, SSATP experience was shared with the European Union member states resulting in an EC Communication on promoting sustainable transport in development co-operation. Lately, SSATP transport corridor expertise contributed to the EC Communication on the EU-Africa Infrastructure Partnership, which through a Trust Fund fosters interconnection along the Trans-African transport corridors': Thompson, *Africa's Transport*, p. vii.

There was also a similar expansion in another, more ideological context, however. The end of the 1980s saw the institutionalisation of structural adjustment policies. It emerges from the archives of the bank's infrastructure division that highlighting these policies and aligning them with those of the World Bank and the objectives it set out jeopardised infrastructure projects as they had previously existed. 'Corridor' projects allowed them to be placed in a broader context than before: the promotion of free trade. This enabled the infrastructure division to maintain the size of its budget, which had been endangered during the 1980s, after an unprecedented growth during McNamara's presidency. In a series of letters to its operating teams, the infrastructure division's management encouraged corridor projects in the hope that thanks to this type of project it would be able to show that it fully supported the organisation's joint effort to restore the recipient countries' trade balances by facilitating interregional trade, thereby benefiting from the lines of credit associated with structural adjustments.

It would be wrong, however, to believe that use of the word 'corridor' inside the bank became a fixture as soon as it first appeared. According to the organisation's official documents, the notion of corridors was first seen as a response to the natural problem of landlocked countries. In the late 1980s, therefore, it was first of all a question of enabling countries with no direct access to the sea to limit their import and export costs by creating road or rail infrastructures with links to one or more ports. At the beginning of the 1990s, the problem of regional integration, which is considered here from the economic point of view alone, became part of the mix. The combination of infrastructures was supposed to enable the creation of new roads, and thus facilitate the formation of regional markets governed by common legislation. Later in the 1990s, what became known as 'first-generation regional transport and trade projects' systematically accompanied the regional-scale infrastructure construction of institutional reforms.[38] In this version of corridor projects, infrastructure remained the basis for the projects, but served as a lever to trigger institutional reforms such as the reorganisation of customs services, the harmonisation of laws, or even the creation of public–private partnerships. In addition to the shift in meaning of infrastructure investments, new 'instruments of government' emerged.[39]

One sign of how the meaning and instruments associated with this solution were solidifying, a 'toolkit' of all the reforms tied to this category was published

---

[38] Abel Bove, et al., 'West and Central Africa Trucking Competitiveness', SSATP Working Paper 108, Washington, D.C., 2018, p. 52.

[39] Christopher C. Hood, *The Tools of Government*, London, 1983.

by the bank in 2014.[40] This type of document is common in the organisation. It encapsulates solutions that are considered to be part of the bank's classic repertoire, and includes condensed government instruments that otherwise exist independently, but that together form this category of public policy. Corridors are seen as a set of measures, laws, institutions, customs reforms and infrastructures that combine to facilitate free trade at a regional level. This type of policies within the bank was also crystallised in way the bank was organised, as starting in the 2000s, a working group specifically dedicated to sharing experiences on corridor projects took shape. Rather than by regular meetings alone, this group's existence was first given substance in mailing lists across which so-called corridor projects circulated so that they could be submitted for a joint review before being examined by the bank's management. Though intangible, these internal networks helped spread these policies through the organisation beyond Africa and infrastructure departments, and established peer reviews of these applications.

The concept of corridors thus allowed the faith in the links between transport infrastructure and development to continue to thrive in a renewed form at the end of the 1980s. In a context in which neoliberal thinking now dominated the developmentalist discourse, it allowed the World Bank employees responsible for infrastructure projects to create a connection between the achievements of their project, free trade and development. Once again, the centre of gravity of this discursive production seemed to be Washington – or more precisely the World Bank – thereby following a path that resembled the way development knowledge was produced. This discourse has, however, now been taken up on several occasions by a number of international organisations, whose policies it echoes.

Well-established Belief

The actions of the bank's staff alone are not enough to explain why this category and the tools of government it embodies still endure. In fact, they are also supported by a network of actors stretching beyond the World Bank's circle of employees. Representatives of the European Union, national co-operation agencies, the African Development Bank, regional economic communities (RECS), all kinds of consultancy firm, national administrations, and even the business community all form an ensemble of actors who exist because of this solution just as much as they contribute to its existence. The challenge of this last section, which takes the form of an epilogue, is not to create an exhaustive

---

[40]   Charles Kunaka and Robin C. Carruthers, *Trade and Transport Corridor Management Toolkit*, Washington, D.C., 2014.

mapping of this set of actors and the places where they come together.[41] It is more modest than that: it is a question of using our interviews and observations in an attempt to sketch out a few hypotheses to explain what may have governed the spread of this approach beyond World Bank programmes alone since the 2000s.

Hegemonic Discourse

The cultural hegemony of the bank's discourse is first and foremost the product of the balance of power in the development world. In terms of corridors, this hegemony is reinforced by the opaque nature of speeches on transport infrastructure policy by donors such as the European Union. Although the European Union's aid policies focused on this type of achievement at the outset, officials at DG DEVCO adopted the instruments and discourse developed by the Bank during the 1990s.[42] Subsequent staff cuts at the Directorate General for International Cooperation and Development from the end of the 1990s only increased the dependency of this area of the European Union's administration on the World Bank. The dominance of the bank's infrastructure discourse has been further enhanced by the growing value of co-financed project that have associated the bank with national co-operation agencies such as those of Germany (GIZ), the US (USAID) and Japan (JICA), for which the challenge is to use these collaborations as a way of magnifying the impact of their own projects.

The success of this category may, however, be due to how it has been shaped. In a context in which development aid is increasingly subject to measured targets, the turnkey quantification instruments provided with this type of public action facilitate its spread to other national co-operation organisations concerned about being able to quantify their actions and impacts.[43] The malleability of the concept, and even the blurring that surrounds this category, is a

---

41 See for example on this subject, studies using social network analysis: SWAC/ OECD, *Cross-Border Co-operation and Policy Networks in West Africa*, Paris, 2017, pp. 67–75 and 162–91.

42 Dimier, *Recycling Empire*, in particular p. 152.

43 Kevin P. Donovan, 'The Rise of the Randomistas: On the Experimental Turn in International Aid', *Economy and Society*, 47:1, 2018, pp. 27–58; just like international public policies: Patrick Le Galès, 'Performance Measurement as a Policy Instrument', *Policy Studies*, 37:6, 2016, 508–20. See, for example, the standardisation proposed in Kunaka and Carruthers, *Trade and Transport Corridor Management Toolkit*, pp. 29–69.

'catch-all', making corridors 'boundary objects'.[44] It unites professionals from different development circles specialising in infrastructure, transport, borders, regional integration and the free movement of goods, all of which can be found in one or more of the components of this type of standard public policy.

The scale of regional actions this category embraces has a certain resonance among a number of international organisations that lack recognition. Representatives of the RECs and the African Union see promotion of the regional level as a means of asserting their authority by strengthening the regional integration process and providing their respective administrations with the resources they lack. They enable representatives of the continent's regional organisations to rely on the influence of donors to make their respective organisations' regulatory production effective at a national level. In addition, we see the production and dissemination of idealised representations of the continent in the formulation of projects such as the Trans-African Highway, NEPAD, PIDA and more recently the AfCFTA.

The notion has also been established in advocacy speeches by interest groups representing the economic world, with the support of national co-operation agencies in both West and East Africa. Over the years since 2010, organisations like the Borderless Alliance in West Africa and the East African Business Council in East Africa have seized on the notion in order to pressure national governments and RECs and advocate for lower export taxes. The sensitivity of national administrations to the discourse of business-oriented interest groups has also been reinforced by the increasing importance of indicators such as the 'Doing Business Index', which is directly based on business perceptions, as well as by the new conditionalities associated with International Monetary Fund funding and the 'improvement of the business climate'.[45]

---

[44] See also the seminal article by Susan Leigh Star and James R. Griesemer, 'Institutional Ecology, 'Translations' and Boundary Objects: Amateurs and Professionals in Berkeley's Museum of Vertebrate Zoology, 1907–39', *Social Studies of Science*, 19:3, 1989, pp. 387–420. In the development field, see the Camille Al Dabaghy's work on the Malagasy decentralisation programme: Camille Al Dabaghy, 'Pour ou Contre les Centres d'Appui aux Communes: Controverse sur les Instruments dans le Tout Petit Monde Transnationalisé de la Décentralisation Malgache', a presentation at the AFSP congress in Bordeaux in 2019.

[45] Timothy Besley, 'Law, Regulation, and the Business Climate: The Nature and Influence of the World Bank Doing Business Project', *Journal of Economic Perspectives*, 29:3, 2015, pp. 99–120.

The Formation of a Small Community

Beyond these various reappropriations, the institutionalisation of this category and the instruments of government it conveys depend on the forums in which they are debated. Again, World Bank staff play a leading role in facilitating and organising these networks. At a continental level, one of the major forums is the SSATP, which is still hosted by the bank as we are writing these lines. Based on the annual meetings of the programme, it was decided in 2004 to create an annual conference that would bringing the various actors from the public and private sectors that are supposed to be involved in the development of corridors together at a continental level. This forum is known as the REC-TCC (Regional Economic Communities Transport Coordination Committee). It is reinforced by numerous other forums organised by business representatives in West and South Africa.[46] While these may be less prestigious, they also see representatives from the private and public sectors come together on the subject of corridors with the same frequency.

According to our observations,[47] these social spaces are undoubtedly areas of confrontation between different visions of what corridors are or, more broadly, the general level of interest in them. This includes opposition between representatives of the private and public sectors, between the different areas of the national administration, between regional and national administrations, and even between competing regional bureaucracies such as between representatives of WAEMU and ECOWAS in West Africa. However, they are also – and perhaps above all – places where there it is possible to disseminate ideas and good practices associated with this category policy. Against the backdrop of PowerPoint presentations or less formal discussions in reception rooms or hotel buffets, the same arguments are repeated, the same examples circulate, and the same people meet. The spread of this type of policy also flows from a certain type of elite sociability that is re-created in these forums, akin to that of clubs, and common to representatives of the private sector and the internationalised public sector.[48] This community is further reinforced by the existence of other similar spaces at national and regional levels, where presentations are held and debates are organised on related themes in the meeting rooms of the same hotels,

---

[46] Borderless Alliance, East African Business Council.

[47] Cissokho, S., 'Fabriquer son "accès" à l'État: Ethnographie d'un espace de rencontre international entre représentants du secteur privé et public (Afrique de l'Ouest)', *Anthropologie et Développement*, 51/2021 (to be released).

[48] Dominique Connan, 'Une Réinvention de la Différence Élitaire: Un Rotary Club dans le Kenya de Mwai Kibaki', *Critique Internationale*, 73:4, 2016, pp. 133–55.

and bring together representatives of the same national administrations, the same international organisations and the same interest groups. These sociabilities are further perpetuated in the management organisations that embody most corridors today.[49]

These spaces embrace certain skills and resources that enable the movement of individuals from one organisation to another. National administrations thus serve as a reservoir not only for international organisations, but also for expert firms with which national co-operation organisations contract in order to set up their programmes. This is the case with the most senior customs officers, who are particularly envied for the networks of officers they have at various border crossings and for their knowledge of the complex rules governing the movement of goods. They can thus be found in large numbers in both RECs and organisations representing the interests of business communities at a national and regional level, such as the Borderless Alliance in West Africa, or in funds that bring together donors of all kinds, such as TradeMark East Africa.[50] These forums are therefore also, and sometimes first and foremost, places where national administrative staff seeking to internationalise are recruited, as well as places for discussion. As in other areas of public development policy, this situation cannot exist without generating professionalisation, once again making a contribution if not to the spread, then at least to the maintenance of this category, which is now associated with the interests of a specific social group.[51]

Conclusion

The story of the journey of the corridor concept in the development industry provides more than just a reflection on infrastructure or even the construction of a category of policy: it offers a perspective on how the neoliberal agenda has prevailed in the development field. This process includes the already well-known role of the World Bank, which, as in many other areas of development, is the

---

[49] These organisations exist for the Abidjan-Lagos, North, Central, Walvis Bay, Maputo and Dar es Salaam corridors. For more information, see: Yao Adzigbey, Charles Kunaka and Tesfamichael Nahusenay Mitiku, 'Mécanismes Institutionnels de Gestion des Corridors en Afrique Subsaharienne', SSATP Working Paper 86, Washington, D.C., 2007; or John Arnold, Gerald Ollivier and Jean-Francois Arvis, *Best Practices in Corridor Management*, Washington, D.C., 2005.

[50] See, for example, the recent ECOWAS Task Force project.

[51] See, for example, the work on transitional justice by Sandrine Lefranc and Frédéric Vairel, 'The Emergence of transitional justice as a professional international practice', ECPR International Congress, Reykjavik, Iceland, August 2011.

main producer of the conceptual framework that is bringing this reversal about. More unexpected, however, are the phenomena behind the dissemination of this agenda. Across the transport infrastructure sector, they are not so much the product of an ideological battle as of the affirmation of certain categories of employees within the World Bank. In addition, the dissemination and maintenance of this new framework is not a matter of conviction, but rather a set of beliefs and institutions based on a certain type of sociability and expertise.

Bibliography

Abelson, Donald E., *Do Think Tanks Matter? Assessing the Impact of Public Policy Institutes*, Montreal, 2002.
— 'From Policy Research to Political Advocacy: The Changing Role of Think Tanks in American Politics', *Canadian Review of American Studies*, 25:1, 1995, pp. 93–126.
Adelman, Jeremy, *Worldly Philosopher: The Odyssey of Albert O. Hirschman*, Princeton, 2014.
Adzigbey, Yao, Kunaka, Charles and Mitiku, Tesfamichael Nahusenay, Mécanismes Institutionnels de Gestion des Corridors en Afrique Subsaharienne, SSATP Working Paper 86, Washington D.C., 2007.
Alix, Yann (ed.), *Les Corridors de Transport*, Cormelles-le-Royal, 2012.
d'Almeida-Topor, Hélène, Chanson-Jabeur, Chantal and Lakroum, Monique (eds), *Les Transports en Afrique XIXe–XXe Siècle*, Paris, 1992.
Arnold, John, Ollivier, Gerald and Arvis, Jean-Francois, *Best Practices in Corridor Management*, Washington DC, 2005.
Besley, Timothy, 'Law, Regulation, and the Business Climate: The Nature and Influence of the World Bank Doing Business Project', *Journal of Economic Perspectives*, 29:3, 2015, pp. 99–120.
Boltanski, Luc and Chiapello, Ève, *Le Nouvel Esprit du Capitalisme*, Paris, 1999.
Bove, Abel, *et al.*, 'West and Central Africa Trucking Competitiveness', SSATP Working Paper No. 108, Washington DC, 2018.
Cissokho, S. 'Reflections on the Washington Consensus: When the World Bank turned to free trade for its transport infrastructure projects', *Politix*, 128:4, 2019, 179–205
Cissokho, S., 'Fabriquer son "accès" à l'État: Ethnographie d'un Espace de Rencontre International entre Représentants du Secteur Privé et Public (Afrique de l'Ouest)', *Anthropologie et Développement*, 51/2021 [to be released].
Connan, Dominique, 'Une Réinvention de la Différence Élitaire: un Rotary Club dans le Kenya de Mwai Kibaki', *Critique Internationale*, 73:4, 2016, pp. 133–55.
Dearing, Charles L. and Owen, Wilfred, *National Transportation Policy*, Washington D.C., 1949.
Debrie, Jean and Comtois, Claude, 'Une relecture du concept de corridors de transport: illustration comparée Europe/Amérique du Nord', *Les Cahiers Scientifiques du Transport*, 58, 2010, pp. 127–44.

Dezalay, Yves and Garth, Bryant,'"Le 'Washington Consensus": Contribution à une Sociologie de l'Hégémonie du Néolibéralisme', *Actes de la Recherche en Sciences Sociales*, 121–22, 1998, pp. 3–22.

Dimier, Véronique, *The Invention of a European Development Aid Bureaucracy: Recycling Empire*, Basingstoke, 2014.

— Politiques Indigènes en France et en Grande-Bretagne dans les Années 1930: Aux Origines Coloniales des Politiques de Développement', *Politique et Sociétés*, 24:1, 2005, pp. 73–99.

Donovan, Kevin P., 'The Rise of the Randomistas: On the Experimental Turn in International Aid', *Economy and Society*, 47:1, 2018, pp. 27–58.

Fogel, Robert W., *Railroads and American Economic Growth: Essays in Econometric History*, Baltimore, 1964.

Freund, Gerald, *Narcissism and Philanthropy: Ideas and Talent Denied*, New York, 1996.

Galbraith, John K., *Le Nouvel État Industriel: Essai sur le Système Économique Américain*, Paris, 1968.

Goldman, Michael, 'The Birth of a Discipline: Producing Authoritative Green Knowledge, World Bank-Style', *Ethnography*, 2:2, 2001, pp. 191–217.

Hood, Christopher C., *The Tools of Government*, London, 1983.

Ika, Lavagnon, 'Opening the Black Box of Project Management: Does World Bank Project Supervision Influence Project Impact?', *International Journal of Project Management*, 33:5, 2015, pp. 1111–23.

Josa, Sergio Oliete and Magrinyà, Francesc, 'Patchwork in an Interconnected World: The Challenges of Transport Networks in Sub-Saharan Africa', *Transport Reviews*, 38:6, 2018, pp. 710–36.

Kramarz, Teresa and Momani, Bessma, 'The World Bank as Knowledge Bank: Analyzing the Limits of a Legitimate Global Knowledge Actor', *Review of Policy Research*, 30:4, 2013, pp. 409–31.

Kunaka, Charles and Carruthers, Robin C., *Trade and Transport Corridor Management Toolkit*, Washington, D.C., 2014.

Le Galès, Patrick, 'Performance Measurement as a Policy Instrument', *Policy Studies*, 37:6, 2016, pp. 508–20.

Lewis, John P., Webb, Richard C., and Kapur, Devesh (eds), *The World Bank: Its First Half Century: History, Vol. 1*, Washington, D.C., 1997.

Medvetz, Thomas, *Think Tanks in America?*, Chicago, 2012.

Mirowski, Philip and Dieter Plehwe (eds), *The Road from Mount Pelerin. The Making of the Neoliberal Thought Collective*, London, 2009

National Research Council, *Rediscovering Geography: New Relevance for Science and Society*, Washington DC, 2000.

Nay, Olivier, 'International Organisations and the Production of Hegemonic Knowledge: How the World Bank and the OECD Helped Invent the Fragile State Concept', *Third World Quarterly*, 35:2, 2014, pp. 210–31.

Norton, Hugh S., *National Transportation Policy: Formation and Implementation*, Berkeley, 1967.

Owen, Wilfred, *Strategy for Mobility*, Washington D.C., 1964.

Plata-Stenger, Véronique, 'Mission Civilisatrice, Réforme Sociale et Modernisation: L'Oit et le Développement Colonial dans l'Entre-Deux-Guerres', *Relations Internationales*, 177:1, 2019, pp. 15–29

Polanyi, Karl, *The Great Transformation*, Boston, 1957.

Rist, Gilbert, *Le Développement: Histoire d'une Croyance Occidentale*, Paris, 1996.

Rostow, Walt Whitman, *The Stages of Economic Growth: A Non-Communist Manifesto*, Cambridge, 1960.

Star, Susan Leigh and Griesemer, James R., 'Institutional Ecology, "Translations" and Boundary Objects: Amateurs and Professionals in Berkeley's Museum of Vertebrate Zoology, 1907–39', *Social Studies of Science*, 19:3, 1989, pp. 387–420.

SWAC/OECD, *Cross-Border Co-operation and Policy Networks in West Africa*, Paris, 2017.

Thompson, John Bruce, 'Africa's Transport: a Promising Future – A Review of Africa's Achievements', SSATP Advocacy Paper, Washington D.C., 2011.

Wilbanks, Thomas J., 'Geography and Public Policy at the National Scale', *Annals of the Association of American Geographers*, 75:1, 1985, pp. 4–10.

Williams, Ernest W., *Freight Transportation in the Soviet Union, including Comparisons with the United States*, Princeton, 1962.

CHAPTER 3

Hidden in Plain Sight: The Temporal Layers of Transport Corridors in Uganda

ISABELLA SOI

Introduction

It is often claimed that modern trade corridors are based on the colonial infra-structures that were created to carry goods from the African interior to the coast. When the Europeans arrived in Buganda in the mid-1800s, however, the region was already part of a long-distance trading system made up of roads and trade centres (market towns) that linked the Great Lakes Region and the Eastern coast. When the British arrived and settled there, they recorded what they found and used this remarkable transport system for their own colonial interests. The British colonial road system was therefore built on top of the pre-existing regional network. As has been the case in Europe, where the modern trans-European networks are partially a consequence of the road system of the Roman Empire, modern-day transport corridors in Africa are the result of a system that was first used centuries ago as a way to improve trade, move troops and assert political control over the region.[1] This chapter strips away the layers of history and seeks to demonstrate that today's trading space has a far longer history than is often thought. Its goal is twofold, therefore: firstly, to make a contribution towards showing that long-distance trade in the interlacustrine region was not an outside initiative, but was based on a combination of local enterprises, the experience and global connections of coastal traders, thereby demonstrating the complexity of the trade system in East Africa; and, secondly, to show that as in Europe and Asia, transport corridors in Africa have a long

---

[1]   Debra Johnson and Colin Turner, *Trans-European Networks: The Political Economy of Integrating Europe's Infrastructure*, London, 1997; Cèsar Carreras and Pau De Soto, 'The Roman Transport Network: A Precedent for the Integration of the European Mobility', *Historical Methods: A Journal of Quantitative and Interdisciplinary History*, 46:3, 2013, 117–33.

historical trajectory that links different times and experiences in the form of overlapping maps of transport networks.

Transport Corridors and Long-Distance Trade

Transport corridors are seen as a modern means of boosting economic development and stimulating regional integration through trade. This concept and argument has been widely applied to European integration and the use of the road networks built by the Roman Empire after 300 BCE as 'the first inland transport network in Europe and the basis of most national road systems in the European nations over the centuries up to the present'.[2] In East Asia, too, modern transport corridors have a long history of shared space with ancient trade routes, whose shape and location depended on both the administrative structures that controlled them and the commercial and economic needs of those who used them.[3] Describing what he saw when he arrived on the shores of Lake Victoria in 1863, John Hanning Speke described the Buganda system thus: 'The roads, as indeed they were everywhere, were as broad as our coach-roads, cut through the long grasses, straight over the hills and down through the woods in the dells – a strange contrast to the wretched tracks in all the adjacent countries.'[4] Obviously, another major change was the technological advances in transport techniques, such as the introduction of motor vehicles.

In some ways, all this is also true of East Africa. The main modern Northern transport corridor in East Africa links the port of Mombasa to Rwanda and DRC, passing through Uganda and connecting the states of the East African Community. In fact, however, this corridor is actually mainly based on the colonial – and in some cases pre-colonial – transport system that has been used for trade and political purposes for centuries. The correspondence of the location of the corridor in the Kenyan section from Mombasa to Lake Victoria (which can be seen by simply superimposing a contemporary map on to a colonial map) is less obvious in the Ugandan section. This is in part as a result of the very limited number of available maps of the early transport system in Uganda (if any exist at all). It is this area that this chapter will analyse, focusing on south-west Uganda as the portion of the current corridor where local trading activities linking different

2   Carreras and De Soto, 'The Roman Transport Network', p. 1.
3   Asian Development Bank (ADB); UKAID; JICA; World Bank Group, *The WEB of Transport Corridors in South Asia*, Washington, D.C., 2018.
4   J. H. Speke, *Journal of the Discovery of the Source of the Nile*, Edinburgh and London, 1863. Among the first accounts of Buganda, see also John Roscoe, *The Baganda*, London, 1911.

regions (cross-border trade) were not only influenced by external events such as the arrival of Europeans, but were also closely related to, and determined by, local dynamics. Despite the very local characteristics of the trade routes we analyse here, we can see that they answered – albeit indirectly – to external demands and stimuli, as was the case in other parts of the world, such as South Asia.[5]

Dubbed 'untouched' Africa by some authors due to its lesser level of involvement in the slave trade, the Great Lakes Region has long been seen as an isolated region that was not part of the trade system that connected the Swahili region globally (albeit indirectly).[6] However, a few more recent studies have established that the Great Lakes Region was linked to the coast by an extensive and quite well-maintained mobility system.[7] The main aim of this chapter is therefore to offer a contribution to a better understanding of the socio-economic context of this region prior to the arrival of the Europeans. Among the key conclusions of this chapter is that colonial structures and systems responded to colonial needs, but were also built on to pre-existing networks.

Comparison and Organisation of the Chapter

In Africa, as in Europe, the modern transport systems that connect the various regions of the continent were built on to the existing structures that linked different regions, the Roman Empire's road system being their most sophisticated and widespread ancient antecedent. Studies on European commercial routes have proved that the Roman Empire's decision to build a road network was influenced by both economic and political reasons, as was the case in other regions such as in Rome's contemporary, Persia.[8] The case of the Roman Empire's transport network provides us with an example of how transport infrastructures are sometimes built in accordance with both economic and political logics, but it also offers evidence of the relationship between roads and urban centres (spaces of trade and political power), and how these strategies and locations can persist over time, connecting both different places and different eras.

---

[5]   ADB, *et al.*, 44.

[6]   Among others see Richard Gray and David Birmingham (eds), *Pre-Colonial African Trade: Essays on Trade in Central and Eastern Africa before 1900*, London 1970.

[7]   For example Karin Pallaver, 'Nyamwezi Participation in Nineteenth-Century East African Long-Distance Trade: Some Evidence from Missionary Sources', *Africa: Rivista Trimestrale di Studi e Documentazione dell'Istituto Italiano per l'Africa e l'Oriente*, 61:3/4, 2006, pp. 513–31.

[8]   Carreras and De Soto, 'The Roman Transport Network'.

In many cases, modern-day transport corridors are not a new invention, just as they were not a colonial creation. In our case, we see the evolution of an earlier trade and transport system that consisted mainly of paths, but also included routes by water across Lake Victoria and Lake Tanganyika, connecting the interlacustrine kingdoms with the Swahili region.[9] This chapter is based on both archival and published materials, and focuses on the nineteenth century and the great transformations, both economic and political, that that took place during this period. The 1800s marked the beginning of the colonial era but, as we will see, it was also a time of major changes in internal equilibria among different kingdoms and peoples, when new ideas and technologies arriving from outside Africa merged with internal changes and practices that persisted, sometimes underground, despite colonial efforts to modify them.[10] Owing to the breadth of the topic and the lengthy timeframe, this chapter focuses exclusively on those routes (across Uganda) and markets that later became part of the modern Northern trade corridor. Waterways, particularly those across the lakes, will not be analysed for the same reasons. Using established historical works such as those by Jan Vansina and David Newbury, it will show that this region of Africa did not diverge very much from Europe and Asia (despite the obvious differences) as regards colonial and modern political and economic attitudes towards building on existing systems to enhance or create modern infrastructures and practices.

Another essential element of this story is markets, which were a crucial component of the infrastructures that linked different kingdoms and opened up the allegedly 'untouched' region to the rest of the continent. The importance of markets also lay in the extra-economic role they played: as places where people gathered, and which were often located close to courts, they had a political, legal and cultural function. They were places where people found out the latest news or gained access to the ruling powers. We have included markets in our analysis, both as places and as a principal component in economic terms because of their

---

9   In this work, the author uses the term 'interlacustrine kingdoms' to refer to the kingdoms that developed in the territory that is now Uganda, which were broadly speaking situated between Lake Victoria, Lake Albert and Lake Edward. From east to west, they are Busoga, Buganda, Bunyoro, Toro and Ankole.

10   There are many examples of local practices that persisted despite colonial projects. One interesting example that has received only limited academic attention so far is the change in the currency used in the continent. Among others, see Karin Pallaver, '"The African Native Has No Pocket": Monetary Practices and Currency Transitions in Early Colonial Uganda', *International Journal of African Historical Studies*, 48:3, 2015, pp. 471–500.

importance for proving that a commercial structure and trade infrastructures existed before the arrival of either the coastal traders or the Europeans.[11] In this sense, roads and markets are essential parts of a trading system in which local people were already actively involved in their trade with neighbouring populations and polities (whether or not they were centralised kingdoms) before outside traders and authorities arrived. This does not mean that we are denying or underestimating the external influences in any way, but simply that as they expanded, upgraded infrastructures, and reorganised trading structures, the Europeans built on existing structures that had been created by local authorities – although they naturally responded to different needs and interests, and so the structure was changed whenever it suited them.[12]

While we have an abundance of sources describing markets and trade routes in West Africa because of its long-standing links with the Mediterranean world, which have led to a far lengthier and deeper knowledge of commerce in the area, the existence of markets and trade links in the interlacustrine region was only first described by the Europeans who arrived in the area in the nineteenth century.[13] Most works on modern Uganda therefore focus on the two most powerful (and antagonistic) kingdoms in the area: Buganda and Bunyoro. The pre-eminence of the former during the nineteenth century is undeniable, and it was also there that the first Europeans to reach the region were accommodated, but despite its efficient centralised system and regional role, it is not the only protagonist of this chapter.[14] Among the most important regional

---

[11] On the debate on the concept of 'market' and the origins of marketplaces in Africa see, among others: B. Turyahikayo-Rugyema, 'Markets in Precolonial East Africa: The Case of the Bakiga', in *Current Anthropology*, 17:2, 1976, pp. 286–90; G. N. Uzoigwe, 'Precolonial Markets in Bunyoro-Kitara', *Comparative Studies in Society and History*, 14:4, 1972, pp. 422–55; B. W. Hodder, 'Some Comments on the Origins of Traditional Markets in Africa South of the Sahara', *Transactions of the Institute of British Geographers*, 36, 1965, pp. 97–105; Charles M. Good, 'Markets in Africa: a review of research themes and the question of market origins', *Cahiers d'Études Africaines*, 13:52, 1973, pp. 769–80.

[12] Olivier Pétré-Grenouilleau, 'Long-Distance Trade and Economic Development in Europe and Black Africa (Mid-Fifteenth Century to Nineteenth Century): Some Pointers for Further Comparative Studies', *African Economic History*, 29, 2001, pp. 163–96, at pp. 192–93; Alberta O. Akrong, 'Trade, Routes Trade, and Commerce in Pre-Colonial Africa', in N. N. Wane (ed.), *Gender, Democracy and Institutional Development in Africa*, Cham, 2019, pp. 67–98.

[13] Good, *Markets in Africa*, pp. 769–80.

[14] John A. Rowe, 'The Western Impact and the African Reaction: Buganda 1880–1900', *The Journal of Developing Areas*, 1:1, 1966, pp. 55–66; Buganda is usually described

kingdoms, Bunyoro has a twofold significance, as the place where many markets were organised,[15] and as a centralised power that controlled a broad swathe of territory, including essential areas that produced two vital items for inter-kingdom trade – salt and iron. The kingdom of Bunyoro was what remained of the earlier empire of Bunyoro-Kitara, which fell in the 1800s.[16] According to Uzoigwe, Bunyoro-Kitara's economy was reasonably diversified and specialised, which led to a proliferation of markets that were later seriously affected when the kingdom of Tooro proclaimed its independence from Bunyoro in the 1830s. This meant exclusion from direct access to the trade routes to the coast and losing the salt mines of Katwe and Kibiro.[17]

Two Elements of the Equation: Routes and Markets

The region's trade system was made up of various levels and types of trade, depending on the goods being traded (and their strategic importance) and the distances covered. The model described by Jan Vansina in the case of trade in Central Africa can also be applied to East Africa to some degree. Three types of trade can be distinguished: local (from village to village, exchanging local products in local markets), interregional (involving neighbouring people trading in border markets or large trade centres and exchanging both local and long-distance products), and long-distance (involving mainly non-African products in exchange for slaves, ivory and copper).[18] According to Charles Good, on the other hand, the type of trade that connected different polities can also be referred

---

as a centralised kingdom, with the Kabaka as a clear central authority, but this description overshadows the presence of different cultures and peoples within Bugandan territory, particularly regarding its 1800s acquisitions and at its periphery. The nature of the kingdom is not the focus of this chapter, but it is important to remember that these kingdoms were far more varied than they have often been described to be: Aidan Stonehouse, 'The Bakooki in Buganda: Identity and Assimilation on the Peripheries of a Ugandan Kingdom', *Journal of Eastern African Studies*, 6:3, 2012, pp. 527–43.

15   Charles M. Good, 'Markets in Africa', p. 773.
16   On the history of Bunyoro-Kitara and its fall, see, among others: G. N. Uzoigwe, 'Bunyoro-Kitara Revisited: A Reevaluation of the Decline and Diminishment of an African Kingdom', *Journal of Asian and African Studies*, 48:1, 2012, pp. 16–34; A. R. Dunbar, *A History of Bunyoro-Kitara*, Oxford, 1965.
17   Uzoigwe, 'Precolonial Markets', p. 433; Uzoigwe, 'Bunyoo-Kitara Revisited', p. 24.
18   Jan Vansina, 'Long-Distance Trade Routes in East Africa', *Journal of African History*, 3, 1962, pp. 375–90.

to as the 'king's trade': long-distance/interstate trade with other kingdoms, where traders needed personal favours and permission from a king, for example the Omugabe of Ankole.[19] Alongside a classification of the various types of trade, we also find a category of the different types of market, even though it may not have been created with evidence from Africa, such as the one proposed by William Skinner for China, which was re-elaborated by Uzoigwe in 1972.[20] In Uzoigwe's study, we find three types of market: (1) local, serving a village or group of villages; (2) royal, situated near a palace in order to trade close to the source of power; and (3) specialised, established close to where a certain product is produced or manufactured.[21] Frontier markets, which are located between two different authorities or two different regions, make up a special category.[22] In this case, markets appear near lines of cultural differentiation, in transitional and peripheral areas, to some extent in accordance with Igor Kopytoff's later study on frontiers, and those proposing a wider pattern of buffer zones that become borders, and markets that become the focal point of border towns.[23] Following Newbury's idea, markets were likely to crop up in peripheral areas, where goods and people meet.[24]

In modern Uganda, both the eastern and western regions were frontier zones where there were no strong kingdoms to govern what are now borderlands. There were 'buffer' kingdoms that traded very actively, however, and small towns with good links to neighbouring areas and active markets. Conversely, peripheral markets and towns in regions with strong or large kingdoms such as Buganda seem to have been less important, as the central power had more control over them, leaving them with fewer opportunities for growth.[25]

Trade in the interlacustrine region expanded considerably in the mid-1800s, due mainly to increased international demand for ivory and slaves to work in the plantations of Zanzibar.[26] This meant that coastal traders played a newly active role in regional commerce, not by creating a new trade network, however,

[19] Charles M. Good, *Rural Markets and Trade in East Africa. A Study of the Functions and Development of Exchange Institutions in Ankole, Uganda*, Chicago, 1970, p. 151.

[20] G. William Skinner, 'Marketing and Social Structure in Rural China', *The Journal of Asian Studies*, in three parts), 24:1, 1964, 2, 1965.

[21] Uzoigwe, 'Precolonial Markets', p. 438.

[22] Ibid.

[23] David Newbury, 'Lake Kivu Regional Trade in the Nineteenth Century', *Journal des Africanistes*, 50:2, 1980, pp. 7–30.

[24] Newbury, 'Lake Kivu', p. 28.

[25] Good, *Rural Markets*.

[26] Pallaver, 'Nyamwezi Participation'.

but by using the one that was already there.[27] At the time, there were three main trade routes in the region: one in the south linking Kilwa to the interior, one in the north towards the coast of Kenya, and one in the centre linking Bagamoyo with Lake Tanganyika.[28] This last one, the central caravan route, on which coastal traders and the Nyamwezi were particularly active, is the most important for our story. This new era of regional trade was not only the consequence of new external demands for African goods, however: it was also the outcome of new balances of power within the kingdoms and people of the region, such as Buganda's prominence and the development of a new class of Nyamwezi traders, the *wandewa*.[29]

The key area in all of this is south-west Uganda (Ankole and especially Kigezi), which was the 'frontier' zone between or adjacent to some of the region's most important kingdoms in the nineteenth century – Bunyoro and Buganda and Rwanda – and various economic zones, where trade offered a comparative economic advantage.[30] The presence of a number of different kinds of terrain, production (agricultural, mineral and handcraft) and polities made the region particularly rich in terms of trade and exchanges, creating a special economic and cultural environment in which the local and regional combined and were in some way inter-dependent.[31] Different people and polities met in these frontier markets, creating the lively locations that remain a dynamic borderland to this day. At the time, most of the goods that were exchanged between the interlacustrine region and the coast passed through Ankole and Kigezi, not from eastern Uganda. Goods arrived from the Swahili regions thanks to merchants who used

[27] John Tosh, 'The Northern Interlacustrine Region', in R. Gray and D. Birmingham (eds), *Pre-Colonial African Trade: Essays on Trade in Central and Eastern Africa before 1900*, London, 1970, pp. 103–118, at p. 111; Pallaver, 'Nyamwezi Participation', p. 514.

[28] Pallaver, 'Nyamwezi Participation', p. 513.

[29] Pallaver, 'Nyamwezi Participation', p. 515.

[30] The Baganda were not particularly active in regional trade outside their kingdom (despite some later attempts at sending expedition directly to Zanzibar, as in the case of Mutesa in 1870). Before the mid-1800s, they tended to wait for merchants to reach Buganda to trade, focusing their activities beyond their borders on demands for tributes, conquests and plundering. Despite this, Buganda undeniably played a central role in regional trade in view of their requirements of salt and iron and their production of bark cloth.

[31] On trade by Ankole see, among others, the always interesting Good, *Rural Markets*.

caravan routes that mostly began in Zanzibar.[32] According to Edward Alpers, merchants from Zanzibar had been attracted by the possibility of exploiting the region as a source of ivory since the early 1800s, when the Sultan of Oman moved its capital to Zanzibar.[33] The ivory trade was especially lucrative during this period, not only due to high demand from non-African markets, but also, and in particular, because of the large numbers of elephants in the area and the quality of their ivory, the so-called 'soft type', which was ideal for carving.[34]

Coastal traders set up their main stations in Karagwe (now north-west Tanzania),[35] most of them close to the capital but some in the north near the Buganda's border, which was proof of their preference for the southern (land) and Victoria (water) routes rather than the eastern (Kenyan) one as a way of reaching the Indian Ocean – favouring what is now the Ugandan border with Rwanda and Tanzania rather than the border with Kenya.[36] Their choice was dictated by their need to be close to Buganda, which they entered in 1840s, and which became their main trading partner, thanks in part to the Kabaka's openness to outside opportunities. However, he was always careful not to give them too much space or power, which is probably one of the reasons why they were kept close to the court, and were not free to settle wherever they wanted.[37] In an attempt to cut rival kingdoms out of the coastal trade, this special relationship with Buganda in the second half of the 1800s essentially became an exclusive one, especially in the case of Zanzibar. This isolated Bunyoro, which

[32]   When referring to traders from Africa's east coast, many sources refer to Muslim traders, and others to Arab traders, in addition to Swahilis. These terms are not synonymous, and they often refer to different peoples, but considering the objectives of this chapter and to make it simpler, the author uses the generic term 'coastal traders', when referring to merchants from the coastal region who were active in long-distance trade.

[33]   Sayyid Said ibn Sultan, the ruler of Oman, moved its capital from Muscat to Zanzibar in 1840; Edward A. Alpers, 'The East African Slave Trade', in Z. A. Konczacki and J. M. Konczacki (eds), *An Economic History of Tropical Africa. Volume One – The Pre-Colonial Period*, London, 1977, pp. 206–15.

[34]   R. W. Beachey, 'The East African Ivory Trade in the Nineteenth Century', *The Journal of African History*, 8:2, 1967, pp. 269–90.

[35]   According to Henri Médard, during the late 1800s the region south of Lake Victoria was the main route linking Unyamwezi and Zanzibar: Henri Médard, *Le Royaume du Buganda au XIXe Siècle*, Paris, 2007, p. 182.

[36]   Tosh, 'The Northern Interlacustrine Region', pp. 111–12; Rowe, 'The Western Impact', p. 55.

[37]   Good, *Rural Markets*, p. 151.

was Buganda's principal antagonist at the time.[38] Despite this attempt, some coastal traders visited Bunyoro in 1877, bypassing Buganda and opening up a new route, but they were not granted access to Rwanda until the 1880s, when the need for weapons overshadowed Rwandan suspicions.[39]

Coastal traders reached Buganda from their base in Karagwe in the 1840s, and Ankole as late as the 1870s.[40] In fact, they did not cross into Ankole or Rwanda for many years. Ivory was brought to them by others, probably from Unyamwezi.[41] Unyamwezi was another key location in long-distance trade. It lay at the junction of a number of different commercial routes, and was the main place where porters were hired to take ivory to the coast.[42] It has been estimated that half a million porters passed through Tabora every year and they were preferred to slaves for transporting such a difficult, heavy and valuable cargo.[43] While Ankole had irregular and indirect trade contacts with Karagwe, the Baganda, in a break with their usual customs, travelled to Karagwe to trade before the coastal people arrived, and also maintained contacts with polities along the southern shore of Lake Victoria.[44] Buganda's traders and envoys were no strangers to using the lake to reach places such as the Speke Gulf on the southern shore of Lake Victoria.[45] Another factor that helped Buganda's trade was its relations with the Kooki kingdom. Kooki was situated at the south-west periphery of Buganda, and had always been an important ally, but it only became a part of Buganda in the late 1800s. Buganda was its main trading partner, and it was a key to commerce because of its privileged geographical position at the junction of various different markets: Bakooki merchants traded actively with

---

38 Tosh, 'The Northern Interlacustrine Region', p. 112.
39 R. M. A. Van Zwanenberg and Anne King, *An Economic History of Kenya and Uganda, 1800–1970*, London, 1975, p. 170; Tosh, 'The Northern Interlacustrine Region', p. 113.
40 Good, *Rural Markets*, pp. 165–6.
41 Direct trade between Unyamwezi and Zanzibar dated back to the early 1800s, if not earlier. Sayyid Said ibn Sultan sent at least one large caravan to Unyamwezi, mainly to trade in ivory: Alpers, 'Slave Trade', p. 213.
42 Pallaver, 'Nyamwezi Participation', p. 515.
43 Beachey, 'Ivory Trade', p. 276.
44 Good, *Rural Markets*, 164; Gerald W. Hartwig, 'The Victoria Nyanza as a Trade Route in the Nineteenth Century', *The Journal of African History*, 11:4, 1970, pp. 535–52.
45 Hartwig, 'Victoria Nyanza', p. 541.

Ankole (for salt) and Tooro (for ivory), and these coastal traders played a major role in regional trade in the 1800s.[46]

To complicate the picture even further, the rivalry between Buganda and Bunyoro played a relatively important role in the coastal traders' inability to expand their activities beyond Buganda.[47] This proved not to be an impediment to regional trade, however, because, while coastal merchants were involved, they did not control it. Their activity consisted in trading with locals, changing their business partners if needed, and taking their goods to the coast. Despite the fact that there is little evidence so far that there were any full-time professional local traders (most were also involved in agriculture or in producing the goods they were exchanging), locals did not give up their roles, and managed the organisation of regional trade, apart from the transport of goods for long distances.[48]

As we have seen, the network of regional trade formed the basis for, or a small segment of, long-distance trade routes.[49] In the case of interlacustrine trade (in modern Uganda) one of the main links to the outside world, heading south through modern Rwanda, was the Nyamwezi and their trade network. The Nyamwezi had long traded goods such as iron, salt, slaves, cattle and goats, but they became particularly well-known on the east coast of Africa (particularly Zanzibar) in the 1800s as a link between non-African economies (Europe, India and America) and the source of ivory in central Uganda.[50] The Nyamwezi mainly used two trade routes to reach the coastal region, one through Sangu to Lake Tanganyika, and one through Unyanyembe (Tabora) to Lake Tanganyika, or heading north through Rusubi and Busambiro.[51]

What Goods? Salt, Iron and Ivory

As we have seen, the ivory trade was central to the development and expansion of trade networks in the 1800s. It had had a small local market before that time, as it was mainly for non-African outside markets and was therefore less significant because of its limited value for the local population (it was mainly restricted to being a symbol of chieftainship).[52] Furthermore, the ivory trade

---

46 Stonehouse, 'Bakooki', p. 533.
47 Good, *Rural Markets*, p. 165.
48 Tosh, 'The Northern Interlacustrine Region'.
49 Andrew Roberts, 'Nyamwezi Trade', in *Pre-Colonial African Trade*, pp. 39–74.
50 Roberts, 'Nyamwezi Trade', pp. 47–9.
51 Roberts, 'Nyamwezi Trade', p. 50; Beachey, 'ivory trade', 218; The former is more or less where the modern central railway line from Dar es Salaam to Tabora now runs.
52 Roberts, 'Nyamwezi Trade', pp. 47, 51.

also had the side-effect (besides the increased development of long-distance routes) of helping trade in other local goods that were exchanged along the route, particularly salt (such as that produced in Vinza, east of Lake Tanganyika) and iron (produced north-west of Unyamwezi), which were used by long-distance caravans as currency to pay tributes or buy food along the route, and in some cases ivory itself.[53] Another local good with a key role in the ivory trade was slaves. Most were initially taken to Zanzibar, but with the abolition of the slave trade in the sultan's dominions in the 1870s, they became a commodity to be traded locally, and were often employed in the hunting of elephants as a source of ivory.[54]

While ivory became the principal commodity in long-distance trade (its extraction was mainly a royal monopoly), particularly from the time of Kabaka Semakokiro's kingdom (1787–1814), because of external demand, the two key goods in regional trans-kingdoms trade were historically salt and iron. Salt was an essential and strategic commodity because of its scarcity (not many areas produced a high-quality version) and the location of the main production area, Kigezi (in south-west Uganda), which was a frontier zone between two kingdoms that fought constantly for control of the salt fields. The salt trade was therefore of particular importance for the region, above all as regards the salt produced in Katwe, which linked the Lake Edward town to Congo, Rwanda, Ankole and Buganda.[55] Other sources were Kasenyi, on the shores of Lake George, and Kibiro, on the eastern shore of Lake Albert, which was closer to Bunyoro's centre of power than Katwe, and more oriented towards the north and east.[56] The main salt producers areas were therefore in territories controlled by Bunyoro-Kitara, which had a monopoly of both salt production and trade routes until the early to mid-1800s.[57]

---

53 Roberts, 'Nyamwezi Trade', p. 53.
54 Roberts, 'Nyamwezi Trade', p. 61.
55 Despite the significance of salt production for Katwe, it is important to point out that it was not its exclusive activity. Because of fluctuating production levels, people in Katwe engaged in other activities such as agriculture to ensure they could make a living: Kathryn Barrett-Gaines, 'The Katwe Salt Industry: A Niche in the Great Lakes Regional Economy', *African Economic History*, 32, 2004, pp. 15–49.
56 Graham Connah, 'The Salt of Bunyoro: Seeking the Origins of an African Kingdom', *Antiquity*, 65:248, 1991, pp. 479–94; Charles M. Good, 'Salt, Trade, and Disease: Aspects of Development in Africa's Northern Great Lakes Region', *The International Journal of African Historical Studies*, 5:4, 1972, pp. 543–86, at p. 565.
57 Uzoigwe, 'Precolonial Markets', pp. 442–45.

A thriving salt trade was common to the entire western region, but the role of Katwe is particularly important for the purposes of this chapter because it was mainly the salt from there that went south, especially to modern-day Rwanda, through Kigezi. According to Charles Good,[58] the main land route from Katwe crossed Ankole, 'ultimately linking up with Kigezi, Ruanda and Karagwe'. The feature of the route through Kigezi was that the trade in salt was supported by exchanges with other goods through the intervention of part-time traders (who were also involved in agricultural and pastoralist activities), making the route particularly important (and sustainable) for the economy of the region. On the other hand, Kasenyi's salt became key in the late 1800s, when the long-distance trade route from the coast crossing Tabora reached Kitagwenda, east of Lake George, where some of Kasenyi's salt was traded.[59] The situation changed in the mid to late 1800s, when a trade shift took place in the region for geopolitical reasons: Tanganyika became more important, and the salt route shifted south.[60] In some ways, there was already competition between the North and Central trade corridors, as there is today.

Kigezi therefore played a special role. It formed a kind of buffer zone between the centralised kingdoms, with a long history of migration from the south (Rwanda) and to central and southern Uganda.[61] Because theirs was a segmentary society, Bakiga markets were not politically controlled, unlike in neighbouring Bunyoro and Buganda, where the king controlled the main markets, usually keeping them close to the court and demanding a fee.[62] Despite the lack of a central authority, 'prominent people in society such as the elders, medicine men and rain-makers were particularly important as the rulers of the Basigi, especially before their migration from Rwanda in the 1800s. The role of the rain-makers and medicine men and Nyabingi priests becomes meaningful in the context of their function as economic managers of their society'.[63] The physical location of markets also depended on the availability of goods (mainly the food and commodities needed for everyday life), which made them particu-larly active during droughts or other times of shortages and important for their role as a space where people could meet, come together and find out the latest

---

58 Good, 'Salt, Trade, and Disease', pp. 558–59.
59 Good, 'Salt, Trade, and Disease', pp. 561–62.
60 Newbury, 'Lake Kivu', p. 20.
61 Grace Carswell, 'Soil Conservation Policies in Colonial Kigezi, Uganda: Successful Implementation and an Absence of Resistance', in W. Beinart and J. McGregor (eds), *Social History and African Environments*, Oxford, 2003, pp. 131–54.
62 B. Turyahikayo-Rugyema, 'Markets in Precolonial East Africa', p. 288.
63 Turyahikayo-Rugyema, 'Markets in Precolonial East Africa', pp. 288–89.

news.[64] The economy of the area was mainly based on agriculture and trade: the Bakiga produced a surplus of food crops (primarily peas and beans) that was traded in neighbouring areas, proving that the dichotomy between food and cash crops does not always apply.[65] Its location was particularly favourable for this purpose, due to the diverse agro-ecological neighbouring zones, the flexibility of its agricultural system, and the important trading route (mainly for Katwe salt) that passed through its territory.[66]

Kigezi was formally acquired by the British in 1912 as a consequence of the Anglo-German-Belgian Boundary Commission of 1911, which settled the claim by the three parties that wished to gain control of Kigezi.[67] When the British found that there was no recognisable or usable system of government, they established their own administration using Baganda agents, as they had in other regions such as the Eastern Province, which altered the social balance.[68] Despite their poor understanding of the size, shape and characteristics of the region, the British recognised that Katwe's salt and position was key to their situation, and so, on his arrival in 1891, Lord Lugard built a fort (Fort George) in Katwe, which had always been disputed by various powers.[69] Katwe's importance was later confirmed by the British decision to guard it as a means of combating Kabarega (the defiant King of Bunyoro) in order to prevent his invasion of Tooro (which controlled Katwe at that time), and at the same time seeking to obtain revenues for the government through trade.[70] The British also maintained a defence force in Tooro in the early 1900s to 'keep a watch on the salt lakes and the Belgian frontier'.[71] The British underestimated the local production of food and cash crops, however, and unsuccessfully attempted to introduce new cash crops for export, particularly coffee, flax and tobacco.[72] This colonial policy was also impacted by a marketing strategy, because the newly-introduced cash crops had to be sold through the colonial authorities, while other (pre-colonial) cash crops were sold directly in markets. This stimulated the smuggling of coffee to the Belgian Congo, where sellers could obtain higher prices and avoid colonial

64   Turyahikayo-Rugyema, 'Markets in Precolonial East Africa', p. 288.
65   Grace Carswell, 'Food Crops as Cash Crops: The Case of Colonial Kigezi, Uganda', *Journal of Agrarian Change*, 3:4, 2003: pp. 521–51, at p. 523.
66   Carswell, 'Food Crops', p. 525.
67   Good, 'Salt, Trade, and Disease', p. 568.
68   Carswell, 'Food Crops', p. 526; Carswell, 'Soil Conservation Policies', p. 133.
69   Good, 'Salt, Trade, and Disease', p. 568.
70   Barrett-Gaines, 'The Katwe Salt Industry', p. 22.
71   Reported in Good, 'Salt, Trade, and Disease', p. 569.
72   On the reasons behind this failure, see Carswell, 'Food Crops', p. 533.

taxation.[73] Famers preferred to produce goods they could maintain control over for marketing and consumption purposes, not least because the new cash crops could not be eaten in the event of a poor harvest. In a nutshell, one might say that the strength of local market and cash crop production made a powerful contribution to the failure of colonial policies, a failure inspired by a lack of knowledge of the local systems of production and trade.

Post–1800s: Colonial Infrastructures and Regional Trade

With the proclamation of the East African Protectorate (now Kenya) and the Uganda Protectorate in the late 1800s, Great Britain established a colonial project founded on its capacity to build and control a feasible, working and efficient transport system to connect the port of Mombasa, the main exit point for African products, to the interior of the region. Of particular importance was the need to link the interior close to Lake Victoria with the coast, thereby seeking to make the most of possible waterways for the movement of goods. There was also the symbolic value of the lake and the sources of the River Nile for the British colonial plan. One key element in the control of the traffic of both goods and people (mainly the troops required for the colonial enterprise) was the construction of the so-called Uganda Railway. In colonial projects, railways were not just a means of transport; they represented modernity and efficiency, and were a symbol of the process of civilisation that theoretically inspired the colonial venture. While the railway is not among the topics of this chapter, it represents another example of continuity in routes and infrastructures. It was seen as a competitor to road-building at the time, but the two (roads and railway) were actually complementary.[74] The Uganda Railway is, in fact, one of the colonial railroads that is still in use today (naturally after modernisation and in some cases rebuilding), not only because of a dependence on colonial transport models but also – according to recent studies from the Centre for Economic Policy Research – because it was constructed in the perfect location, based on cost analysis reports.[75] In colonial times, the railway line across Kenya was considered to be the main competitor of road transport and trade, which

---

[73]   Carswell, 'Food Crops', p. 536.
[74]   Patrick Y. Whang, 'Regional Derailment: the Saga of the East African Railways', *Journal of Eastern African Studies*, 12:4, 2018, pp. 716–34.
[75]   Rémi Jedwab, Edward Kerby, Alexander Moradi, 'How Colonial Railroads Defined Africa's Economic Geography', <https://voxeu.org/article/how-colonial-railroads-defined-africa-s-economic-geography>, published online on 2 March 2017 [Accessed 5 August 2019].

was a system based on motor vehicles, and on porters before that, and diverted part of the trade from the central caravan route (through Tanganyika) to the northern one (through Kenya).[76]

As we have seen, long-distance trade was not an invention of the colonial rulers, and they did not organise it. The Great Lakes Region was already linked to the Swahili region through a well-organised trade system that included the active participation of local traders. There was also a reasonably good network of paths connecting the various areas of the Great Lakes Region and facilitating the movement of people and traders all over the area. The local economies and local trade in the area were also flexible and reactive to external stimuli, proving African initiative and 'continuity from earlier processes of economic change'.[77] Finally – and this was probably the main change – there was the marginalisation of African traders from the system. The other change was, at least in part, the subsequent diversion of the trade route from Tanganyika to Kenya, which inspired the more recent competition between the Northern and Central corridors. All this happened outside Uganda, however, and within Uganda itself colonial rule did not totally alter the pattern of trade and route networks. In 1953, in its *Report of Enquiry into Road Transport Conditions in the Protectorate of Uganda*, which analysed the condition of the 'Kampala–Masaka–Mbarara–Kabale–Kisoro–Ruhengeri (Ruanda)' route, the East Africa Royal Commission stressed that 'the route between Kampala and Kabale must in the future become one of the most important in the Protectorate', even though it was 'clear that this route will not be served by railway in the foreseeable future and therefore every encouragement is present for the setting up of a reliable and adequate service for passengers, mail and freight'.[78]

Notwithstanding the initially good impression the British had of Ugandan roads and its trade network, they soon realised that they were not suited to their requirements and that they should encourage improvements, introducing reforms to adjust the trade system to their needs. After a few years, however, it became clear that the colonial investment had been inadequate and, in the 1950s, on the eve of independence, the British administration deemed the trade system to be unsatisfactory for the development of the protectorate. Upgrading the routes to roads suitable for motor vehicles was particularly problematic, and Indian enterprises were favoured over African companies because they had more

---

76   Pallaver, 'Nyamwezi Participation', p. 531.
77   Roberts, 'Nyamwezi Trade', p. 74.
78   London, The National Archives, Commercial and Industrial Development, CO 892/15/10.

assets and greater access to cash and lorries. As reported in the *Kigezi District Annual Report for 1930* 'there is no doubt that Indians are capturing much of the trade which was formerly in the hands of natives, e.g. Katwe salt and locally-caught fish'.[79] For the British administrators, the scarce participation by African traders was particularly worrying:

> African traders are severely handicapped by the lack of organized transport systems in the Protectorate resulting in unreliability of service and high costs. It is considered that it would be of some assistance in the problem if private enterprise could be encouraged to establish a Clearing House system extending into up-country centres and providing the facilities for the development of regular trunk and small traffic services. This idea has been discussed with the responsible Officer of the Traffic Control Board and will be further pursued. It is considered important that as far as possible the development of such a system should be based on private enterprise in which Africans should play a prominent part.[80]

Conclusion

As was the case with the Roman Empire, the road and waterway systems (such as the canoes used in the Buganda Kingdom) the British found were used not only to facilitate trade, but also as a way of asserting political control over the region by the various kingdoms. One of the hegemonic polities in the area in the nineteenth century was Buganda, which lay in what is now the southern-central region of Uganda. Buganda was part of the trade network that linked Lake Victoria to the east coast of Africa, which was mediated by local and coastal traders.[81] The kingdom and its wealth (mainly its 'access' to ivory and slaves)

79 Good, 'Salt, Trade, and Disease', p. 580.
80 London, The National Archives, Report on African Participation in Trade, 1953, Commercial and Industrial Development: CO 892/15/10.
81 Abdul Sheriff, *Slaves, Spices and Ivory in Zanzibar. Integration of an East African Commercial Empire into the World Economy, 1700–1873*, London, 1987; Bashir Ahmed Datoo, *Port Development in East Africa: Spatial Patterns from the Ninth to the Sixteenth Centuries*, Kampala, Nairobi and Dar es Salaam, 1975; Erik Gilbert, *Dhows and the Colonial Economy of Zanzibar, 1860–1970*, Oxford, 2004; Richard Gray and David Birmingham (eds), *Pre-Colonial African Trade: Essays on Trade in Central and Eastern Africa before 1900*, London, 1970; B. S. Hoyle, 'Early Port Development in East Africa: An Illustration of the Concept of Changing Port Hierarchies', *Tijdschrift voor Economische en Sociale Geografie*, 58, 1967, pp. 94–102; Karin Pallaver, 'The African Native Has No Pocket'.

were not unknown to the external world; they belonged to it as a result of the kingdom's widespread road system and a wider trade network that went beyond the African continent, as was the case with the East/South Asian corridors of the eighteenth and nineteenth centuries.[82]

The communication routes of Buganda, Bunyoro and other kingdoms formed the basis for controlling the commercial network, which was kings' main goal for gaining wealth and prestige. They even promoted the development of a fleet of large canoes that was capable of crossing the lake, which was a target of expansionist ambitions that were not limited just to the mainland.[83] The backbone of the trade and transport system in the area remained its land routes, however. The pre-colonial routes, and the markets alongside them, were proof of how dynamic the population of the area was in terms of exchanging goods and their interest in an active trade environment in the 1800s. South-west Uganda is of special interest here because of its dynamic trade network, its frontier characteristics, and the major changes it underwent over the course of a few decades. It was an established trade hub controlled by local populations during the 1800s, and it was during the colonial period that Africans lost control of the system, especially to Indian enterprises. This created an economic and social disruption rather than a real change in the location of trade paths, however.

In conclusion, what is generally seen as a modern solution to boost African economies and regional integration is not a recent invention at all. The colonial powers did not bring integrated transport systems to East Africa: a fairly detailed and widespread transport system (using water and land routes) already connected the eastern coast of the continent to its interior. Indeed, the well-known Swahili trade network linked up with a well-maintained network of paths in the west to Congo, using the lake trade network, which was controlled by local traders and connected by coastal traders. Another element that should not be forgotten is the relationship between economic and political influences in maintaining an efficient communications network, which was confirmed by the positions adopted by Buganda and Bunyoro in the 1800s. Political opportunities and geopolitical views are important factors for deciding the fate of modern transport corridors today, but this also applied to their historical precursors. Despite the differences in time and space between the experience of the Roman Empire in Europe and the road networks in East Africa in the 1800s, we have

---

[82] John M. Gray, 'Ahmed bin Ibrahim—The First Arab to Reach Buganda', *Uganda Journal*, 11:2, 1947, pp. 80–97; ADB, *et al.*

[83] Richard Reid, *Political Power in Pre-Colonial Buganda. Economy, Society & Warfare in the Nineteenth Century*, Woodbridge, 2002.

seen that they both responded to economic/trade and political/military needs (as Bunyoro's attempts to control the salt trade demonstrate), reminding us that if we only take the economic requirements of a given region into account when we study and analyse transport corridors, and ignore history, we can only ever have an incomplete picture.

Bibliography

CO 892/15/10, *Commercial and Industrial Development*, The National Archives, London.

MPK 1/161, Map of Africa, from the Equator to the Southern Tropic 1853, The National Archives, London, UK).

MR 1/1013, Sketch of country near Fort Ternan, Eastern Province Uganda Protectorate 1901, The National Archives, London, UK).

Akrong, Alberta O., 'Trade, Routes Trade, and Commerce in Pre-colonial Africa', in N. N. Wane (ed.), *Gender, Democracy and Institutional Development in Africa*, Cham, 2019, pp. 67–98.

Alpers, Edward A., 'The East African Slave Trade', in Z. A. Konczacki and J. M. Konczacki (eds), *An Economic History of Tropical Africa. Volume One – The Pre-Colonial Period*, London, 1977, pp. 206–15.

Asian Development Bank (ADB); UKAID; JICA; World Bank Group, *The WEB of Transport Corridors in South Asia*, Washington, D.C., 2018.

Barrett-Gaines, Kathryn, 'The Katwe Salt Industry: A Niche in the Great Lakes Regional Economy', *African Economic History*, 32, 2004, pp. 15–49.

Beachey, R. W., 'The East African Ivory Trade in the Nineteenth Century', *The Journal of African History*, 8:2, 1967, pp. 269–90.

Carreras Cèsar and De Soto, Pau, 'The Roman Transport Network: A Precedent for the Integration of the European Mobility', *Historical Methods: A Journal of Quantitative and Interdisciplinary History*, 46:3, 2013, pp. 117–33.

Carswell, Grace, 'Food Crops as Cash Crops: The Case of Colonial Kigezi, Uganda', *Journal of Agrarian Change*, 3:4, 2003, pp. 521–51.

— 'Soil Conservation Policies in Colonial Kigezi, Uganda: Successful Implementation and an Absence of Resistance', in W. Beinart and J. McGregor (eds), *Social History and African Environments*, Oxford, 2003, pp. 131–54.

Connah, Graham, 'The Salt of Bunyoro: Seeking the Origins of an African Kingdom', *Antiquity*, 65:248, 1991, pp. 479–94.

Datoo, Bashir Ahmed, *Port Development in East Africa: Spatial Patterns from the Ninth to the Sixteenth Centuries,* Kampala, Nairobi and Dar es Salaam, 1975.

Dunbar, A. R., *A History of Bunyoro-Kitara*, Oxford, 1965.

Gilbert, Erik, *Dhows and the Colonial Economy of Zanzibar, 1860–1970*, Oxford, 2004.

Good, Charles M., 'Markets in Africa: a Review of Research Themes and the Question of Market Origins', *Cahiers d'Études Africaines*, 13:52, 1973, pp. 769–80.

— Rural Markets and Trade in East Africa. A Study of the Functions and Development of Exchange Institutions in Ankole, Uganda, Chicago, 1970.

— 'Salt, Trade, and Disease: Aspects of Development in Africa's Northern Great Lakes Region', *The International Journal of African Historical Studies*, 5:4, 1972, pp. 543–86.

Gray, John M., 'Ahmed bin Ibrahim—The First Arab to Reach Buganda', *Uganda Journal*, 11:2, 1947, pp. 80–97.

Gray, Richard and Birmingham David (eds), *Pre-colonial African Trade: Essays on Trade in Central and Eastern Africa before 1900*, London, 1970.

Hartwig, Gerald W, 'The Victoria Nyanza as a Trade Route in the Nineteenth Century', *The Journal of African History*, 11:4, 1970, pp. 535–52.

Hodder, B. W. 'Some Comments on the Origins of Traditional Markets in Africa South of the Sahara', *Transactions of the Institute of British Geographers*, 36, 1965, pp. 97–105.

Hoyle, B. S., 'Early Port Development in East Africa: An Illustration of the Concept of Changing Port Hierarchies', *Tijdschrift voor Economische en Sociale Geografie*, 58, 1967, pp. 94–102.

Jedwab, Rémi, Kerby, Edward, and Moradi, Alexander, 'How Colonial Railroads Defined Africa's Economic Geography' <https://voxeu.org/article/how-colonial-railroads-defined-africa-s-economic-geography>, published online on 2 March 2017.

Johnson, Debra and Turner, Colin, *Trans-European Networks: The Political Economy of Integrating Europe's Infrastructure*, London, 1997.

Médard, Henri, *Le Royaume du Buganda au XIXe Siècle*, Paris, 2007,

Newbury, David, 'Lake Kivu Regional Trade in the Nineteenth Century', *Journal des Africanistes*, 50:2, 1980, pp. 7–30.

Pallaver, Karin, '"The African Native Has No Pocket": Monetary Practices and Currency Transitions in Early Colonial Uganda', in *International Journal of African Historical Studies*, 48:3, 2015, pp. 471–206.

—'Nyamwezi Participation in Nineteenth-Century East African Long-Distance Trade: Some Evidence from Missionary Sources', *Africa: Rivista Trimestrale di Studi e Documentazione dell'Istituto Italiano per l'Africa e l'Oriente*, 61:3/4, 2006, pp. 513–31.

Pétré-Grenouilleau, Olivier, 'Long-Distance Trade and Economic Development in Europe and Black Africa (Mid-Fifteenth Century to Nineteenth Century): Some Pointers for Further Comparative Studies', *African Economic History*, 29, 2001, pp. 163–96.

Reid, Richard, *Political Power in Pre-Colonial Buganda. Economy, Society & Warfare in the Nineteenth Century*, Woodbridge, 2002.

Roberts, Andrew, 'Nyamwezi trade', in R. Gray and D. Birmingham (eds), *Pre-colonial African Trade: Essays on Trade in Central and Eastern Africa before 1900*, London, 1970, pp. 39–74.

Roscoe, John, *The Baganda*, London, 1911.

Rowe, John A., 'The Western Impact and the African Reaction: Buganda 1880–1900', *The Journal of Developing Areas*, 1:1, 1966, pp. 55–66.

Sheriff, Abdul, 'Slaves, Spices and Ivory in Zanzibar. Integration of an East African Commercial Empire into the World Economy, 1700–1873', London, 1987.

Skinner, G. William, 'Marketing and Social Structure in Rural China', *The Journal of Asian Studies* (in three parts), 24:1, 1964, 2, 1965.

Speke, J. H., *Journal of the Discovery of the Source of the Nile*, Edinburgh and London, 1863.

Stonehouse, Aidan, 'The Bakooki in Buganda: Identity and Assimilation on the Peripheries of a Ugandan Kingdom', *Journal of Eastern African Studies*, 6:3, 2012, pp. 527–43.

Tosh, John, 'The Northern Interlacustrine Region', in R. Gray and D. Birmingham (eds), *Pre-Colonial African Trade: Essays on Trade in Central and Eastern Africa before 1900*, London, 1970, pp. 103–18.

Turyahikayo-Rugyema, B., 'Markets in Precolonial East Africa: The Case of the Bakiga', in *Current Anthropology*, 17:2, 1976, pp. 286–90.

Uzoigwe, G. N., 'Bunyoro-Kitara Revisited: A Reevaluation of the Decline and Diminishment of an African Kingdom', *Journal of Asian and African Studies*, 48:1, 2012, pp. 16–34.

— 'Precolonial Markets in Bunyoro-Kitara', *Comparative Studies in Society and History*, 14:4, 1972, 422–55.

Van Zwanenberg, R. M. A. and King, Anne, *An Economic History of Kenya and Uganda, 1800–1970*, London, 1975.

Vansina, Jan, 'Long-Distance Trade Routes in East Africa', *Journal of African History*, 3, 1962, pp. 375–90.

Whang, Patrick Y., 'Regional Derailment: The Saga of the East African Railways', *Journal of Eastern African Studies*, 12:4, 2018, pp. 716–34.

CHAPTER 4

From Priority Projects to Corridor Approaches: African and European Transport Networks in Perspective

SERGIO OLIETE JOSA AND FRANCESC MAGRINYÀ

Introduction:
Are African and European Transport Networks Comparable?

In many ways, European integration has inspired African states to move towards a more ambitious African Union, and there are clear parallels between the institutional arrangements of the AU and the EU. However, a number of authors have warned of the limitations involved in making any comparisons, starting from the fact that African states have ceded very restricted sovereignty at a supranational level compared with Europe. In this chapter, we pose the question of whether the African transport network and the Trans-European Transport Network (TEN-T) are comparable. We want to see whether the criticisms of and lessons learned from the European experience are applicable to the development of the African Regional Transport Infrastructure Network (ARTIN), as supported by the Programme for the Infrastructure Development of Africa (PIDA). By reviewing the literature that highlights the methodological shortcomings in the planning process of the TEN-T, we analyse the similarities and differences between the two continental ambitions from different standpoints: official narratives, stakeholder analysis and planning and funding instruments. We conclude that support for the transport sector is an appropriate way of strengthening African integration, but any ambitions to do so need to be balanced in accordance with the existing resources. In particular, the completion of 'missing links' can have significant structuring effects, but it should not be done at any cost, because planning errors can have very negative consequences. National political interference, low cost-effectiveness and a high environmental impact are common criticisms in the case of the TEN-T. Africa suffers considerably from the same drawbacks, with the additional problems of higher investment needs, insufficient funding, a larger surface area to cover, lower densities and lack of maintenance. By looking at the European experience, Africa may be able to improve and accelerate its own process.

Transport is one of the necessary conditions for achieving Africa's aspirations as they have been set for 2063, but it is not adequate in itself.[1] It is one of the sectors that has the most investment needs and the highest cost of maintenance.[2] It is also one of the key sectors of an economy in which the provision of infrastructure is lower than it is on other continents. In Sub-Saharan Africa, the population lives far from economic markets: on average, it is located 13 per cent further away than populations in other parts of the world. This figure increases to almost 50 per cent when compared to Europe.[3] 16 out of the 54 countries are landlocked, and even some of those with direct access to the sea have vast inland areas located far from the coast, as is the case with DRC. The railway network has hardly expanded at all since colonial times, the lines are unevenly located (they are mostly in Southern Africa) and density is low, ranging from 30 to 50 kilometres per million people, or about 2.5 kilometres per thousand square kilometres.[4] In Europe, the density of the rail network is between 200 kilometres and 1,000 kilometres per million people, nearly 50 kilometres per thousand square kilometres. Similarly, road density in Africa – 3.4 kilometres per thousand people – is less than half the global average, and this is reduced to one-fifth when comparing its paved roads with those on other continents.[5] In Europe, according to Eurostat, road density is about 8.1 kilometres per thousand people.

---

1   In 2063, Africa will commemorate 100 years since the Organisation of African Unity (OAU) was established: Africa Union <https://au.int/en/agenda2063/aspirations>.

2   V. Foster and C. M. Briceño-Garmendia (eds), *Africa's Infrastructure: A Time for Transformation*, The World Bank, 2010, pp. 6–7.

3   P. Manners and A. Behar, *Trade in Sub-Saharan Africa and Opportunities for Low Income Countries*, Background Paper for the World Development Report 2009: Reshaping Economic Geography, Washington, D.C., 2009, p. 5 <http://hdl.handle.net/10986/9242>.

4   African Development Bank, *An Integrated Approach to Infrastructure Provision in Africa*, Tunis, 2013, pp. 13–14 <https://www.afdb.org/fileadmin/uploads/afdb/Documents/Publications/Economic_Brief_-_An_Integrated_Approach_to_Infrastructure_Provision_in_Africa.pdf>.

5   K. Gwilliam, 'Africa's Transport Infrastructure: Mainstreaming Maintenance and Management', Washington, D.C., 2011, pp. 22–26 <http://hdl.handle.net/10986/2275>.

In Sub-Saharan Africa, there is a vicious circle of a lack of competitiveness, poor domestic revenue mobilisation, low investment in transport infrastructure and high transport costs. Transport prices are not the result of a lack of good infrastructure alone, however; they are also related to a chain of defects caused by non-physical barriers along the transport corridors, starting at the ports. Ports are essential elements of the inter-modal connectivity of these corridors, as they are giving access to inland areas and landlocked countries. Africa is highly dependent on ports in order to have access to international trade. While it only contributes to 2.7 per cent of global trade by value, its ports represent 7 per cent of global loaded tonnage and 5 per cent of unloaded tonnage.[6] In general, however, they do not fulfil their function satisfactorily. Their performance levels are poor, and their infrastructures and services are not up to international standards. The containerisation of African ports remains low, and globally they only receive and dispatch 4 per cent of containers, mainly to import manufactured goods. Only four of the top 100 global container ports are in Africa. The low level of efficiency is also reflected by crane productivity and dwell times: while crane productivity is 25–40 moves per crane per hour on average, in West Africa it is only 20 moves. Cargo dwell time is also high in Sub-Saharan ports: on average, cargo spends more than two weeks at the ports, while on other continents the average period is less than a week.

An increasingly challenging situation for African ports is their interface with inland transport modes (road and rail). Many urban areas around ports are becoming increasingly congested, and goods cannot be easily warehoused or moved of cities. Dry ports on the outskirts of densely-populated urban areas would be vital to increase the efficiency of the logistics chains. Overall, poor infrastructure in urban nodes (by-passes, public transport, underground railway systems, etc.) is becoming a major obstacle that must be added to the already flawed land transport.

A number of authors have looked at the challenges faced by African transport networks and emphasised the influence history and geography have on them.[7] These two factors lie at the origin of the major differences between African and

6   UNCTAD (United Nations Conference on Trade and Development), *Review of Maritime Transport*, Geneva, 2017 <https://unctad.org/es/node/29022>.

7   W. Naudé, 'Geography, Transport and Africa's Proximity Gap', *Journal of Transport Geography*, 17:1, 2009, 1–9; J. Debrie, 'From Colonization to National Territories in continental West Africa: the Historical Geography of a Transport Infrastructure Network', *Journal of Transport Geography*, 18:2, 2010, 292–300; S. Oliete Josa and F. Magrinyà, 'Patchwork in an Interconnected World: the Challenges of Transport Networks in Sub-Saharan Africa', *Transport Reviews*, 38:6, 2018, 710–36.

European transport systems. The Sahara desert, the difficult living conditions in the Equatorial forests and a lack of navigable rivers are some of the geographical determinants that are considered to have had a historical impact on the development of transport networks. Low density and sparse urbanisation have also heavily influenced their development. These problems do not exist in Europe. Furthermore, the way the borders of colonial empires were established created terminuses for many roads and railways. The political legacy and poor economic performance of the newly-independent states have also unquestionably made a contribution towards holding back transport in Africa.

With all these substantial differences, does it make any sense to compare transport networks in Africa and Europe? As we will see in the paragraphs that follow, the discourses in Africa are more about connectedness (*connexité*), where the connections between nodes have not been completed yet (missing links). As Dupuy has defined it,[8] the term *connexité* means the links between subsystems. In Europe, the network is completed in most cases: it is more an issue of connectivity (bottlenecks), understood in the sense of the existence of a multiplicity of links within a connected network.

If one takes the historical context and technological progress into consideration, it would be a mistake to assume that African networks will follow the same path towards attaining full connectedness as Europe's did. However, as many authors have noted,[9] there are common specificities and logics of transport networks that correlate with territorial organisation. In this chapter, we argue that despite there being major differences, there are also similarities between African and European transport networks, in particular with regard to recent planning and decision-making processes. Good practices, as well as the errors made, in the European context may help improve policy-making and project implementation in Africa. We will first analyse the differences between transport policies on the two continents and then assess the current infrastructure development programmes in Europe and Africa.

---

8   G. Dupuy, 'Propriétés des Réseaux', *Systèmes, Réseaux et Territoires. Principes de Réseautique Territoriale*, Paris, 1985, pp. 65–100.

9   E. J. Taaffe, R. L. Morrill and P. R. Gould, 'Transport Expansion in Underdeveloped Countries: A Comparative Analysis', *Transport and Development*, London, 1973, pp. 32–49; Dupuy, 'Propriétés des Réseaux'; B. Hoyle and J. Smith, 'Transport and Development: Conceptual Frameworks', in B. Hoyle and R. Knowles (eds), *Modern Transport Geography* (2nd edn), Chichester, 1998, pp. 13–40.

Transport Policies in Africa and Europe: An Apparently Far-fetched but Useful Comparison

Before analysing the African and European programmes for developing their respective transport corridors, it is important to examine more thoroughly the process of regional integration in both continents and its consequences for transport policies. Fioramonti and Mattheis[10] have suggested a framework for comparing the construction of the two continental unions that shows that despite certain symbolic institutional similarities where the AU has been inspired by the EU, the integration logics applied on the two continents differ. For instance, in contrast with the African experience, Europe's has been characterised by a gradual process of integration starting out from six countries, restrictive membership requirements and the transfer of significant sovereignty roles to a supranational level. However, the main distinction between the two processes that influences how the transport sector is addressed resides in 'the drivers of regionalism'. While European integration has been driven by trade integration, market liberalisation and to some extent social cohesion, integration in Africa has focused on peace and security issues. The low volumes of intra-African trade (estimated to be 12.8 per cent of total African international trade) are fundamental when it comes to explaining the low level of competitiveness of many countries.[11] Except for certain limited experiences at a regional level, it was only in 2019 that the African Continental Free Trade Area (AfCFTA) came into effect, and it is still difficult to precisely anticipate the pace of implementation, the increases in trade flows and the advantages of the AfCFTA for African economies. Conversely, the project to connect Europe with transport corridors is a 'by-product of the European single market project'.[12]

In view of this major difference in terms of drivers of continental integration, it is important to study how it affects transport continental policies in Europe and Africa and if it has practical consequences for the implementation of their respective infrastructure programmes. Three different aspects are considered and compared in the following sections: the key players, the official narratives and the planning tools.

---

[10]   L. Fioramonti and F. Mattheis, 'Is Africa Really Following Europe? An Integrated Framework for Comparative Regionalism', *JCMS: Journal of Common Market Studies*, 54(3), 2016, pp. 674–90.

[11]   M. Bosker and H. Garretsen, 'Economic Geography and Economic Development in Sub-Saharan Africa', *The World Bank Economic Review*, 26(3), 2012, pp. 443–485 <doi: 10.1093/wber/lhs001>.

[12]   A. Aparicio, 'The Changing Decision-Making Narratives in 25 Years of TEN-T Policies', *Transportation Research Procedia*, 25, 2017, pp. 3715–24.

An Analysis of the Key Players

Overall, institutional arrangements seem to be similar on both continents: planning is at a central level, while implementation is at a national level. In Africa, PIDA officially covers development of the transport network. In Europe, the programme guiding transport infrastructure is the TEN-T. In theory, where priority projects are to be adopted, the decision-making process is in both cases the result of a bottom-up consulting process in which proposals put forward by member states are validated at a high political level after being reviewed by experts. In Africa, the AU Assembly of Heads of State and Government takes these decisions, while in Europe they are adopted by the EU Transport Ministers at the Council of the European Union. African regional economic communities (RECs) often play a more important role in the choice of priority projects than do countries, as is often the case in other areas (for example, monetary and security). RECs usually have their own regional infrastructure master plans, which have been the basis for the elaboration of the PIDA at a continental level.

In practice, the African and European institutional architectures are quite different. Europe's relatively longer experience has helped it reduce complexity and provide more flexible arrangements. These days, the TEN-T is seen more as a policy than an infrastructure programme. The development of the Trans-European corridors is guided by work plans that outline the objectives for action up to 2030. They include investments, preparatory activities, studies and policy-oriented actions. They are updated regularly on the basis of stake-holder consultations[13] and new technical studies. For each of the nine corridors and two horizontal priorities, the European Commission appoints 'European Coordinators', high-level figures in charge of overseeing, facilitating and reporting on the work plans. One important aspect of their mandate is consul-tation with corridor forums, which are consultative bodies made up of member states and significant stakeholders. In addition, for more than a decade, TEN-T Days have brought together ministers, members of the European Parliament, the European Coordinators and representatives of the European Investment Bank, the European Commission and TEN-T stakeholders to discuss progress on the implementation of the trans-European transport network.

In support of these work plans, the European Commission has put in place a number of funding instruments that combine grants, loans, guarantees and other innovative financial instruments. In particular, the Connecting Europe Facility

---

[13] Generally, stakeholders include member states, infrastructure managers/authorities, regional and territorial representatives, municipalities, metropolitan authorities and transport operators.

(CEF), which is managed by the Climate, Infrastructure and Environment Executive Agency (CINEA), co-finances actions submitted by the various stakeholders and selected through competitive calls for proposals. Nevertheless, although several other funding sources exist, such as the European Structural and Investment Funds and the European Fund for Strategic Investment, the largest portion of funding comes from the member states' national budgets.

In Africa, the current Institutional Architecture for Infrastructure Development in Africa (IAIDA) governing PIDA is the result of a series of attempts to accommodate numerous initiatives that have emerged with the aim of effecting a rapid reduction of the infrastructure deficit. Many of the initiatives in recent decades have been proposed by charismatic African presidents like Mbeki and Zuma in South Africa, Wade in Senegal and Kagame in Rwanda. Once a political action of this kind has been launched, it has been extremely difficult to reach a compromise to avoid adding institutional complexity. When these new structures are created at a national level, new management units are generated that absorb agents and officials. These programmes are difficult to dismantle once they have attained their objective or, as is usually the case, they are not considered to be efficient enough and are superseded by new, and supposedly improved, initiatives. A good example of this phenomenon is the frequent reforms that the New Partnership for Africa's Development (NEPAD) has undergone since its creation in 2001. It is still hard for an outsider to understand the division of labour between the NEPAD mandate and the AU Commission. The most recent redesign and attempt at rationalisation was the transformation in 2018 of NEPAD's structures into the African Union Development Agency, which is known by the acronym AUDA-NEPAD. This agency, together with the African Union Commission (AUC), the African Development Bank (AfDB), the United Nations Economic Commission for Africa (UNECA) and the RECs, is now seen as the lead organisation supporting the member states in their implementation of the PIDA.

At a planning level, the AU has also made efforts to rationalise the myriad consultative entities intended to assist the decision-making process. The most recent unifying strategy was the Agenda 2063, which was launched in 2013, and sets out the AU's long-term development vision. The PIDA is the continental framework for Africa 2063's infrastructure development as decided at the Malabo Conference of Ministers for Transport in 2014.

Like TEN-T Days, the PIDA Week has been organised annually since 2015 to co-ordinate and create synergies among the different stakeholders. Although it is not a statutory AU event, it brings the PIDA's leading implementing organisations together with representatives from, for example, the PIDA Steering Committee, the Council for Infrastructure Development, the Infrastructure

Consortium for Africa, the Continental Business Network. Member states also usually attend PIDA Weeks, often in the form of representatives from ministries, the private sector, civil society, bilateral and multilateral development finance institutions, among others.

From Official Narratives to Special Interests

Modern inter-state initiatives for the development of continental transport infrastructure are actually older in Africa than in Europe. The UN Economic Commission for Europe (UNECE) began to define the E-Road network in Europe in the 1950s, but it was not until the 1990s that Europe established a common planning and funding scheme. In Africa in the early 1970s, UNECA defined a network of roads linking all the capitals of the continent to be known as the Trans-African Highway (TAH), which consisted of nine main roads with a total length of 59,100 kilometres (see Map 4.1). The alignment of some of them, like the Trans-Saharan Highway, had already been designed by the colonial powers. Starting with the Lagos–Mombasa highway, implementation of the TAH network was monitored by intergovernmental co-ordinating committees, with UNECA leading the process as the executing agency. Since then, the TAH network concept has been the prevalent accepted point of reference for African states, RECs and donors. For instance, since the establishment of the TAH, the project appraisal documents produced by many development agencies have justified the choice of a specific road by the fact that it constitutes a section of a trans-African highway. In 2012, the TAH network was used as the basis for the definition of the Africa Regional Transport Infrastructure Network (ARTIN), which is the reference point for the PIDA. The ARTIN consists of the TAH network, which now has 10 axes, plus 40 key corridors.

As mentioned above, European integration was driven by the goal of the single market, and the notion of a trans-continental transport infrastructure was closely connected to it. Likewise, in the case of Africa, the motivation behind the initial TAH network was economic integration and increasing African trade, with one noteworthy difference from Europe: 'opening up new areas with promising agricultural and mineral potential'.[14] In both cases, however, besides the trade angle, other interests and arguments have emerged to drive development of the transport agenda. In the first place, there is the pursuit of political legitimation

---

[14]   Economic Commission for Africa, *Resolution Adopted by the Conference of Ministers, 226(l): Trans-African Highway*, Tenth Session, Conference of Ministers, Tunis, 8–13 February 1971.

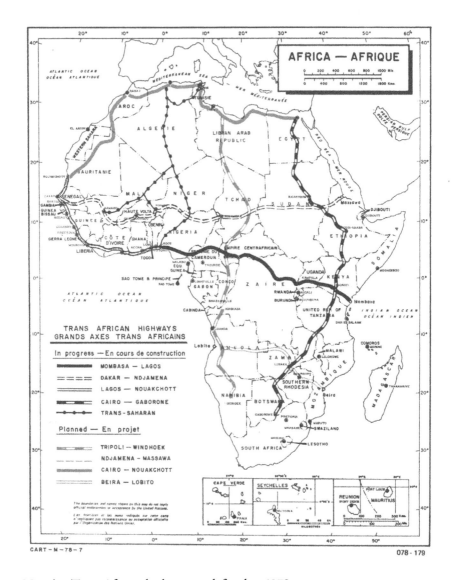

Map 4.1. Trans-African highways as defined in 1978.
(Source: Ousmane Gueye, Bangui Conference on Transport and Communications,
UN Economic Commission for Africa, 1978.)

by regional organisations. In Africa, in the early decades following independence, there was a strong rivalry between the Organisation of African Unity (OAU), the UN Development Programme (UNDP) and UNECA.[15] For the latter, the TAH network, and later the UN Transport and Communications Decade in Africa (1978–1988), were initiatives that made it possible for the organisation to bring advisory and co-ordination functions together on issues of major importance for the African states. Later on, as we explained in the previous section, this role was gradually transferred from UNECA to NEPAD and the AUC.

In Europe, like agriculture and the free movement of people, services and capital, the common transport policy was introduced by the Treaty of Rome, which created the European Economic Community in 1957. However, it was not until the Maastricht Treaty was signed in 1993 that the Trans-European Networks were adopted as an integral part of Community policy. This was because for the member states, the TEN-T policy *de facto* represented a transfer of critical decisions on important aspects of their territorial sovereignty,[16] and they only agreed to move forward when the European Court of Justice intervened.[17] As a result, by adding long-term planning responsibilities to the TEN-T, the European Commission gained significant power and visibility *vis-à-vis* European citizens.

Another narrative besides economic integration is the contribution made by transport networks towards strengthening a shared continental identity. In Europe, this coalesces around the cohesion policy, of which the TEN-T is a central tool for reducing regional disparities. Behind the official rhetoric of 'harmonious development'[18] promoting balanced and sustainable growth, Europe has faced the need to rally citizens from poorer countries that are suffering from the consequences of liberal policies inherent in the single market.[19] In this sense, cohesion has been presented as an expression of solidarity, as a policy to make Europe's values a reality. In practical terms, it results in the choice

15   S. Misteli, 'Gardiner, Robert Kweku', *IO BIO, Biographical Dictionary of Secretaries-General of International Organisations*, Bob Reinalda, Kent J. Kille and Jaci Eisenberg (eds) <www.ru.nl/fm/iobio> [Accessed 15 August 2019].

16   F. Piodi, 'The Financing of Trans-European Transport Networks', *Directorate General for Research, Working Document Transport Series E-4*, Brussels 1997, pp. 24–25.

17   A. Faludi, 'Territorial Cohesion Policy and the European Model of Society', *European Planning Studies*, 15:4, 2007, pp. 567–583 <DOI: 10.1080/09654310701232079>.

18   Article 174 of the Treaty on the Functioning of the European Union.

19   D. Peters, 'Cohesion, Polycentricity, Missing Links and Bottlenecks: Conflicting Spatial Storylines for Pan-European Transport Investments', *European Planning Studies*, 11:3, 2003, pp. 317–39.

of priority projects based on political commitments and not on cost-effective considerations. In Africa, where insufficient internal trade and low levels of inter-state traffic make it hard to justify the economic feasibility of some of the trans-African highways, recourse to pan-African ideals can easily be discovered behind the official storylines. From an economic point of view, linking all the African capitals by road makes little sense in some cases, in particular where long distances have to be travelled across the Sahara Desert or tropical forests. At the same time, it is a reasonable political aspiration for Africa to think that all its capitals can be joined by road from the neighbouring country. In fact, some prominent African decision-makers, like Adebayo Adedeji, who was UNECA's Executive Secretary during the UN Decade for Transport and Communications, have openly expressed their scepticism about focusing on trade to boost African integration and have advocated backing it with infrastructure development.[20] As is the case with the European cohesion policy, the goal of opening up landlocked countries and isolated regions is customarily included in official African documents on transport. As a 2011 preparatory study for the PIDA noted, continent-wide ambitions have proved to be hard to achieve: 'Lack of alignment with national and regional priorities is a primary failure factor, as good ideas become orphan projects. For example, segments of the Trans-African Highways that correspond to the priorities of the country involved have been built, but segments that do not fit country priorities have stagnated.'[21]

This brings us back to the economic justification for trans-continental corridors. In the case of Europe, Peters[22] mentions other storylines, such as polycentricity and bottlenecks. Polycentricity is a narrative that proposes competition and complementarity between cities and regions in the context of the common market. This is a controversial line of reasoning because it might be argued that it goes against cohesion policy. While the 'EU's cohesion policy aims to strengthen economic and social cohesion by reducing disparities in the level of development between regions,'[23] the principle of polycentricity is that cities should be interconnected by high-speed transport, while many rural areas and peripheral regions may be bypassed. In the case of Africa, even though the concept of growth poles is often utilised at the national level, the logic of polycentricity is not on the agenda at a continental level, probably because of

[20]   S. K. B. Asante, *African Development: Adebayo Adedeji's Alternative Strategies*, London, 1991, pp. 8–13 and pp. 105–06.

[21]   SOFRECO, Study on Programme for Infrastructure Development in Africa (PIDA), Phase I Study Summary. Clichy, 2011.

[22]   Peters, 'Cohesion, Polycentricity, Missing Links and Bottlenecks', pp. 317–39.

[23]   https://ec.europa.eu/regional_policy/en/policy/what/glossary/c/cohesion-policy.

the small size of the market. The bottleneck storyline is evoked in the African context, but almost exclusively to describe congestion in ports due to a lack of appropriate infrastructure, and more especially to their management failings. In Europe, by contrast, the concept is far more widespread. It is associated with the insufficient capacity of already existing connections, in particular between or through urban nodes. Again according to Peters, the bottleneck is a concept that is not exempt from controversy. Policy-makers have not defined it accurately, and it raises environmental concerns as to the limits to which infrastructure capacity can be expanded. In addition, it is a notion that is associated with places where infrastructure already exists, and these are normally the wealthier ones.

A very common current argument is built around the notion of 'missing links'. It was introduced in official documents in both unions dating back to the 1980s, albeit with different implications. In Africa, as we mentioned earlier, it refers mainly to matters of *connexité*: that is, sections of the trans-African highways that really do not exist, or are surfaced with earth and gravel and need to be upgraded to paved standards. In 2017, according to the AUC's estimates, TAH missing links covered 4,300 kilometres out of a total of 61,870 kilometres. In Europe, most links already exist in one mode or another, and the objective is to reduce time or increase capacity, in particular on cross-border sections: it is simply a matter of improving connectivity. In both cases, however, behind the rhetoric of 'missing links' lies the need to justify significant investments, the economic returns from which are not evident. The choice of these priority projects is often political, as we have seen in the previous paragraphs but, as Peters[24] points out for the case of Europe, the construction industry also lobbies extensively in favour of them. In Africa, while the interests of construction firms carry less weight, the 'missing links' attract great interest from the ruling class, not only due to political benefits but also because of the personal gains they can obtain in a corrupt procurement system. For their part, donors and development banks play a central role in promoting the completion of inter-state infrastructure. Firstly, the increase in intra-African trade is a top priority in aid agendas today, even though, in many cases, the transport demand that will be generated will be low in the short and medium term. Secondly, massive public spending on infrastructure is still viewed as a stimulus for the economy. Last, but not least, 'missing links' can help maintain lending operations at satisfactory levels because they are usually funded with regional allocations, which are easier to mobilise (they come at the top of countries' strategies and are not in competition with other national priorities).

[24]   Peters, 'Cohesion, Polycentricity, Missing Links and Bottlenecks', pp. 317–39.

Planning Methods and Financing Tools

As we have seen in both Europe and Africa, planning of trans-continental corridors is to some extent transferred to a union level, while the implementation of projects remains the responsibility of member states. Although the decision-making concept may be used in official documents, notably by the AU, the word 'planning' seems to be more appropriate in both cases because the inclusion of a project in the PIDA or the TEN-T does not mean that it has actually been 'decided'. In practical terms, there is a major difference between the two processes: the AU does not provide funds for investment in infrastructure from its own budget; at most, it mobilises grants from international donors and channels them to certain projects or uses them for institutional support.[25] The absence of AU funding instruments to support the PIDA is an institutional weakness that limits its capacity to influence how member states prioritise trans-continental projects. In Europe, the situation is rather different, and the existence of various sources of funding facilitates the elaboration of work plans as an inclusive decision-making process with a high likelihood of being implemented. However, some authors[26] have criticised the European planning process for not taking efficiency and environmental aspects into adequate consideration and exaggerating the added value of some projects. Instead of promoting sustainable, balanced and genuinely pan-European projects, the TEN-T decision-making process is, according to these studies, not transparent enough, and is heavily biased by corporate demands and national politics.

In any case, one common occurrence that has a major impact on the materialisation of both the PIDA and the TEN-T is the lack of sufficient public funding to reach the envisaged infrastructure levels. In addition, debt sustainability is a crucial issue, whichever continent is being considered. In the case of European national governments, their contributions to the EU budget, which in turn are invested back through the TEN-T funding instruments, is one way of achieving improved compliance with public debt and deficit requirements,[27] but it is still not enough. This is why there has been a global emergence in recent years of new financial instruments with the purpose of creating leverage of public budgets and acting as a catalyst to attract additional funding from the private sector. For instance, many public–private partnerships (PPP) have been conceived in order

25 For instance, see the activities of the Joint Africa-EU Strategy (JAES) Reference Group on Infrastructure (RGI) <https://au.int/fr/node/34309>.
26 Peters, 'Cohesion, Polycentricity, Missing Links and Bottlenecks', pp. 317–39; Aparicio, 'The Changing Decision-Making Narratives', pp. 3715–24.
27 M. Turro, *Going Trans-European: Planning and Financing Transport Networks for Europe*, Oxford, 1999, Pergamon, pp. 102–03.

to contain public debt: the private operator contracts for a loan, while the public stakeholder pays those costs that cannot be recovered from the users directly. In practice, PPPs create fiscal risk and, in the case of Africa, low technical capacity is a major constraint to developing PPPs in fragility contexts. According to the World Bank, the global transport sector received US$636 billion in public-private investment between 1990 and 2018, and 1,861 projects reached financial closure.[28] During the same period, Sub-Saharan Africa received only US$23.7 billion across 113 projects. Private financing in Sub-Saharan Africa has mostly been channelled into the ports sector, which has seen over 50 per cent of the investment volume.

We cannot end this section without mentioning two important actors involved in the implementation of the PIDA and the TEN-T: the African Development Bank (AfDB) and the European Investment Bank (EIB). These two banks are respectively viewed as the 'African' and 'European' banks. AfDB is the lead financial institution for the PIDA and its logo appears next to those of the AU, UNECA and NEPAD in all official PIDA documents. What is more, AfDB defines itself as the 'Executing Agency' of the PIDA.[29] In the case of TEN-T's official documents, EIB is also explicitly, and almost exclusively, identified as the bank providing the loans and guarantees that complement the European budget grants. However, AfDB and EIB are neither AU nor EU institutions. EIB's shareholders are the 27 member states, and their share of the bank's capital is based on their economic weight within the EU at the time of their accession. With regard to the AfDB, 41 per cent of the shareholders and five of the top ten countries involved are non-African. In both banks, the governing statutory bodies are accountable to the shareholders, and not directly to the respective unions. This 'independence' is an aspect that is worthy of attention. Banks' strategies are driven by the credit risk of their operations and the need to keep their turnover at certain levels. The choice of projects to be financed is not always aligned with official strategies, does not appropriately respond to economic needs or does not fully integrate country debt sustainability considerations.[30] In addition, in contrast to other multilateral development banks, both the EIB and AfDB have the challenge of being dominated by their borrowers in terms of voting share.[31]

---

[28]   <https://ppi.worldbank.org/en/snapshots/rankings>.

[29]   <https://www.afdb.org/en/topics-and-sectors/initiatives-partnerships/programme-for-infrastructure-development-in-africa-pida> [Accessed May 2022].

[30]   See, for instance, the European Court of Auditors, 'Report on the European Fund for Strategic Investments', published in 2019 <https://www.eca.europa.eu/en/Pages/DocItem.aspx?did=49051>.

[31]   N. Birdsall, *The Dilemma of the African Development Bank: Does Governance Matter for the Long-Run Financing of the MDBs?*, Working Paper 498, Washington D.C.,

The Current TEN-T Policy and the PIDA Priority Action Plan (PAP) for Transport: A Practical Comparison

As we mentioned in the introduction to this chapter, despite major differences between the transport systems of the two continents, there are some parallels that merit analysis. In the first place, the process for defining priority projects has evolved in similar ways. In Europe, from its initial 30 priority projects, the TEN-T has adopted a multimodal corridor approach since 2013 with a significant emphasis on regulation and non-infrastructural aspects (Map 4.3). Similarly, the definition of the transport component of the PIDA in 2012 expanded the trans-African highways concept and applied a corridor approach to transport (Map 4.2). On both continents, there is now a backbone network, the ten trans-African highways in Africa and the nine European Transport Corridors in Europe. Alongside this, there is a broader 'second layer' of transport infrastructure that in Africa is made up of the remaining 40 corridors of the ARTIN and in Europe is known as the Comprehensive Network. Next to the physical corridors, Europe also has two Horizontal Priorities – the European Rail Traffic Management System and Motorways of the Sea – themes that are also reflected in the most recent policy documents in Africa as a result of including a transport strategy in the Agenda 2063.

However, despite the official rhetoric on corridors, the first PIDA PAP still follows a patchwork approach, mode of transport by mode of transport, and lacks coherence in many cases. For instance, the creation of a tenth TAH is still not reflected in some official documents and, in the PIDA database, many projects are placed under programmes labelled as 'multimodal transport corridor', but this denomination does not correspond to a specific TAH, as in the case of the Abidjan–Ouagadougou–Bamako Multimodal Transport Corridor. In fact, considerable doubt arises where in several AU documents there is a differentiation between the TAH and the (new) African Integrated High Speed Railway Network (AIHSRN). In short, while African institutions do not clearly differentiate between the transport corridor and the transport mode, the EU has reached a consensus about the notion of corridor. We should also recall here that in the case of Europe this approach was to a large extent adopted thanks to the reinforced competences that have been transferred to the European Commission, in particular to CINEA.

As a consequence of this diverse interpretation of the notion of the transport corridor in Africa, it is difficult to compare the current TEN-T and PIDA in

2018, pp. 1–5 <https://www.cgdev.org/sites/default/files/dilemma-afdb-does-governance-matter-long-run-financing-mdbs.pdf>.

terms of investment. However, we can compare the 30 priority projects planned for 2020 in Europe with the first PIDA PAP, which was effective until 2020. As we have said, the 30 priority projects have been replaced by a corridor approach since 2013, but they are still a valid point of reference for gaining a greater appreciation of the order of magnitude of the investment in both continents. The 231 PIDA transport projects can be grouped into 24 programmes whose

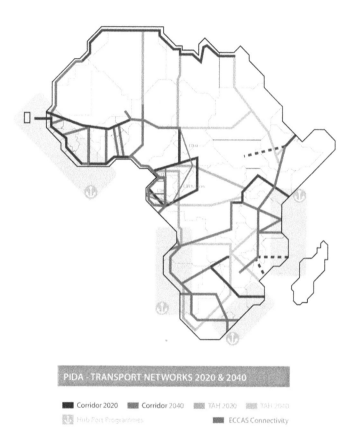

PIDA - TRANSPORT NETWORKS 2020 & 2040

■ Corridor 2020   ■ Corridor 2040   ▒ TAH 2020   ▒ TAH 2040
▒ Hub Port Programmes   ■ ECCAS Connectivity

Map 4.2. The transport networks to be supported by the first PIDA PAP by 2020 and 2040.
(Source: African Union 2011. Programme for Infrastructure Development in Africa. (2012). Interconnecting, integrating and transforming a continent, Addis Ababa, African Union, www.afdb.org/fileadmin/uploads/afdb/Documents/Project-and-Operations/PIDA%20note%20English%20for%20web%200208.pdf.)

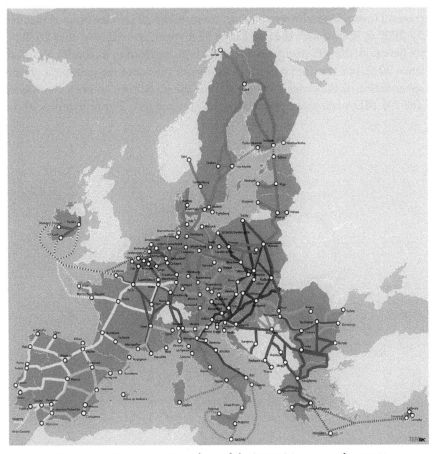

Map 4.3. European Transport Corridors of the TEN-T as revised in 2021. (Source: European Commission (2021), Creating a green and efficient Trans-European Transport Network, Factsheet, https://ec.europa.eu/commission/presscorner/detail/en/ip_21_6776.)

scale is comparable to that of the 30 European priority projects.[32] Taking into consideration the fact that the TEN-T priority projects were conceived to be implemented over 25 years and the PIDA-PAP is an eight-year plan, we can

---

[32]   <https://www.au-pida.org/pida-projects/>. There are discrepancies in some official documents. For instance, the PIDA Week 2018 concept note mentions 235 projects grouped under 25 programmes.

estimate that in Europe, yearly investments have reached about €16 billion, while in Africa the investment is supposed to have been around €10 billion per year (see Table 4.1). The average size of a project/programme is close to €530 million in Europe and €416 million in Africa.

Table 4.1 TEN-T and PIDA PAP 1 transport priority projects.

	TEN-T 30 priority projects	PIDA-PAP 1 transport
Budget period	1995–2020	2012–2020
Overall investment	€398,340,000,000	€79,927,863,636
Investment per year	€15,933,600,000	€9,990,982,955
Number of priority projects	30	24
Investment per project	€531,120,000	€416,290,956
Total length – Priority projects (km)	47,882	62,000
Rail	*33,698*	*29,500*
Road	*10,691*	*32,500*
International waterways	*3,493*	*Not mentioned*

Sources: Programme for Infrastructure Development in Africa, <www.au-pida.org/pida-projects/> [Accessed 23 February 2022]; €1 = US$1.1.

More recently, it has been estimated in Europe that by 2030 the financial investment required for the completion of the TEN-T Core Network Corridor alone is €21 billion a year, or a total of approximately €750 billion of investment over 35 years. In Africa, the AfDB[33] estimates that transport infrastructure development requires between €31 billion and €42 billion annually. These amounts include both the PIDA and national needs. If we take into account the fact that yearly disbursements oscillate between €22 billion and €31 billion, the financing gap may be more than €10 billion, depending on the year. However, two important points arise when placing African investment needs and Europe's requirements for the TEN-T side by side. The former is related to the baseline for the calculation of infrastructure deficit in Africa. While the order of magnitude of financing needs declared in official documents may be comparable, Africa basically has two objectives: interconnecting capitals, ports, border crossings and secondary cities with a good quality road network; and

---

[33]   African Development Bank, *African Economic Outlook 2018*, 2018, p. 70 <www.afdb.org/fileadmin/uploads/afdb/Documents/Publications/African_ Economic_Outlook_2018_-_EN.pdf>.

providing all-seasons road access in rural areas. As we have said, the priority is to provide full connectedness or *connexité*. At the same time, improved connectivity through multimodal systems (for example, high speed railways) is acquiring space on political agendas, which means that the threshold for estimating the infrastructure gap will be raised, and funding needs will increase. Secondly, in Africa, the operation, maintenance and rehabilitation costs of preserving the investments are estimated to be 80 per cent of total investment needs, and only 20 per cent is allocated to upgrading and new construction.[34] The problem in Africa is that the notion of *connexité* is very frequently breached because of a lack of maintenance and road protection. This means that, in addition to missing links, there are links that 'disappear' and need to be rebuilt several times. In short, it is very difficult for Africa to begin investing in improved connectivity when basic *connexité* is not guaranteed.

Conclusions

Among all the policies and programmes undertaken by the AU, transport is one of the sectors in which it can first engage in order to strengthen continental integration. This may seem paradoxical, since the internal market is not large enough to justify many of the international links. At the same time, it is claimed that interconnecting the continent will boost commercial exchanges, another assumption that should be made cautiously. On this point, it is not advisable to establish parallels between transport policies in Europe and Africa. Transport infrastructure is tangible and politically attractive, and can act as a catalyst for pan-African integration, but this process should in all cases be begun between densely-populated nearby territories that have the capacity to constitute a market.

The TEN-T's planning and implementation modalities have evolved significantly over time, but the various institutional arrangements have not been exempt from criticism. In particular, national and special interests seem to have prevailed in the selection of a number of projects, a circumstance that has been favoured by deficiencies in the evaluation methods. As we have seen, inadequate cost–benefit analyses or poor environmental impact assessments have contributed to the choice of projects whose added value has been exaggerated. Nevertheless, the corridor approach adopted for the TEN-T in recent years allows for a more coherent and participative framework in which governance

---

[34]   African Development Bank, *African Economic Outlook 2018*, p. 70.

involving an important number of stakeholders is clearer, and the territorial impact better delimited.

In Africa, it is difficult to implement a similar corridor approach because of the problems associated with connectedness or *connexité*. In this case, the narrative of 'missing links' is still a valid one, provided that these links connect points with minimum density levels. The impact of a two-lane asphalt road connecting urban centres, which might seem marginal in advanced economies, may have significant structuring effects in developing countries.[35] At the same time, we have raised the question of whether full *connexité* must be achieved at all costs, and whether it is more urgent than improving connectivity between nodes where considerable levels of exchange already exist. In this respect, appropriate planning tools, as well as a broadly participatory approach, are needed to guide the decision-making process. Since reinforcement of the networks needs to focus on places where there is a sufficient population and the systems of the cities are structured, the PIDA should prioritise interventions in those territories with the highest density levels, such as the north of Africa, West African countries and the region along the Indian Ocean (see Map 4.4).

Expanding the notion of corridors and moving away from the patchwork method, as has been the case in Europe, would be fundamental for increasing transparency, better defining the scope of decisions and specifying the appropriate level where they should be adopted. A sustainable and harmonious development of African transport networks is exposed to threats similar to those identified in Europe. However, because Africa suffers from meagre public budgets and a maintenance backlog, every effort should be made to avoid the proliferation of 'white elephants'. In this regard, it is essential that corridor approaches should first target the consolidation of territories with a sufficient network density.

Since the AU does not have funding of its own to develop the network, it lacks the capacity to incentivise better planning instruments. In addition, readily available funds without significant social and environmental safeguards make it particularly difficult for African countries to abstain from accepting offers of aid from certain partners, notably China. These external interests, which are often driven by mining industries, find support among political and financial elites and prevent a thorough analysis to determine whether the overall conditions of a particular deal are favourable for the country.

One asset the AU possesses, which does not exist in Europe, is the existence of RECs, and current PIDA implementation relies heavily on them. The

---

[35]   B. Steck, 'Transport et Développement', in M. Brocard (ed.), *Transports et Territoires. Enjeux et Débats*, Paris, 2009, pp. 125–55.

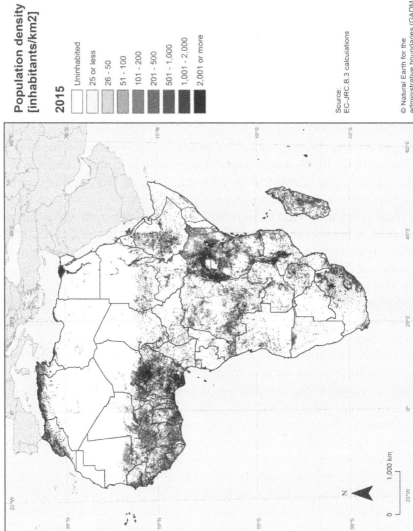

Population density [inhabitants/km2]

2015

- Uninhabited
- 25 or less
- 26 - 50
- 51 - 100
- 101 - 200
- 201 - 500
- 501 - 1,000
- 1,001 - 2,000
- 2,001 or more

Source:
EC-JRC.B.3 calculations

© Natural Earth for the
administrative boundaries (GADM DB)

0   1,000 km

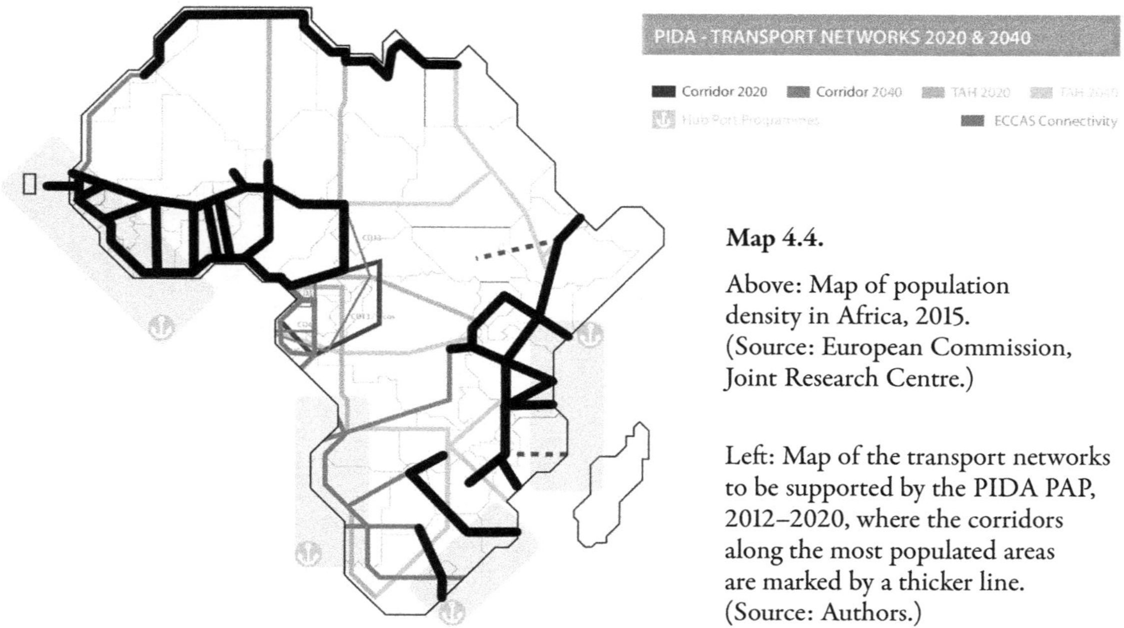

Corridor 2020 Corridor 2040 TAH 2020 TAH 2040
Main Port Programmed ECCAS Connectivity

Map 4.4.

Above: Map of population density in Africa, 2015. (Source: European Commission, Joint Research Centre.)

Left: Map of the transport networks to be supported by the PIDA PAP, 2012–2020, where the corridors along the most populated areas are marked by a thicker line. (Source: Authors.)

establishment of African transport networks should continue to be supported by this intermediate level. At the same time, the AU should rationalise its project preparation facilities and keep the focus on building the capacity of its member states to plan and implement infrastructure projects. The second PIDA PAP will present a good opportunity for addressing these issues.

Bibliography

African Development Bank, *African Economic Outlook*, 2018 <www.afdb.org/fileadmin/uploads/afdb/Documents/Publications/African_Economic_Outlook_2018_-_EN.pdf> [Accessed 27 April 2021].

— *An Integrated Approach to Infrastructure Provision in Africa*, Tunis, 2013.

— Project for Infrastructure Development in Africa, <www.afdb.org/en/topics-and-sectors/initiatives-partnerships/programme-for-infrastructure-development-in-africa-pida> [Accessed August 2019].

Aparicio, Ángel, 'The Changing Decision-Making Narratives in 25 years of TEN-T Policies', *Transportation Research Procedia*, 25, 2017, pp. 3715–24.

Asante, S. K. B., *African Development: Adebayo Adedeji's Alternative Strategies*, London, 1991.

Birdsall, Nancy, *The Dilemma of the African Development Bank: Does Governance Matter for the Long-Run Financing of the MDBs?*, Working Paper 498, Washington D.C., 2018, <https://www.cgdev.org/sites/default/files/dilemma-afdb-does-governance-matter-long-run-financing-mdbs.pdf> [Accessed 27 April 2021].

Bosker, Maarten and Garretsen, Harry, 'Economic Geography and Economic Development in Sub-Saharan Africa', *The World Bank Economic Review*, 26:3, 2012, pp. 443–85.

Debrie, J., 'From Colonization to National Territories in continental West Africa: the Historical Geography of a Transport Infrastructure Network', *Journal of Transport Geography*, 18:2, 2010, 292–300.

Dupuy, G., 'Propriétés des Réseaux', *Systèmes, Réseaux et Territoires. Principes de Réseautique Territoriale*, Paris, 1985, pp. 65–100.

Economic Commission for Africa, '*Resolution 226(l)a Trans-African Highway*', Tenth Session, Conference of Ministers, Tunis, 8–13 February 1971.

European Commission, 'Cohesion Policy' <https://ec.europa.eu/regional_policy/en/policy/what/glossary/c/cohesion-policy> [Accessed 27 April 2021].

Faludi, Andreas, 'Territorial Cohesion Policy and the European Model of Society', *European Planning Studies*, 15:4, 2007, pp. 567–83.

Fioramonti, Lorenzo and Mattheis, Frank, 'Is Africa Really Following Europe? An Integrated Framework for Comparative Regionalism', *JCMS: Journal of Common Market Studies*, 54:3, 2016, pp. 674–90.

Foster, Vivien and Briceño-Garmendia, Cecilia (eds), *Africa's Infrastructure: A Time for Transformation*, Washington D.C., 2010.

Gwilliam, Ken, *Africa's Transport Infrastructure: Mainstreaming Maintenance and Management*, Washington D.C., 2011.

Haggett, Peter, Frey, Allan, and Cliff, A. D., *Locational Analysis in Human Geography*, London, 1977.

Hoyle, Brian and Smith, Jose, 'Transport and Development: Conceptual Frameworks', in B. Hoyle and R. Knowles (eds), *Modern Transport Geography*, Chichester, 1998, pp. 13–40.

Manners P. and Behar, A., *Trade in Sub-Saharan Africa and Opportunities for Low Income Countries*, Washington D.C., 2009.

Misteli, Samuel, 'Gardiner, Robert Kweku', *IO BIO, Biographical Dictionary of Secretaries-General of International Organisations*, Bob Reinalda, Kent J. Kille and Jaci Eisenberg (eds) <www.ru.nl/fm/iobio> [Accessed 15 August 2019].

Naudé, W., 'Geography, Transport and Africa's Proximity Gap', *Journal of Transport Geography*, 17:1, 2009, 1–9.

Oliete Josa, S. and Magrinyà, F., 'Patchwork in an Interconnected World: the Challenges of Transport Networks in Sub-Saharan Africa', *Transport Reviews*, 38:6, 2018, 710–36.

Peters, Deike, 'Cohesion, Polycentricity, Missing Links and Bottlenecks: Conflicting Spatial Storylines for Pan-European Transport Investments', *European Planning Studies*, 11:3, 2003, pp. 317–39.

Piodi, Franco, *The Financing of Trans-European Transport Networks*, Brussels, 1997.

Program for Infrastructure Development in Africa, 'PIDA Projects Dashboard' <www.au-pida.org/pida-projects/> [Accessed 27 April 2021].

SOFRECO, *Study on Programme for Infrastructure Development in Africa (PIDA)*, Phase I Study Summary, Clichy, 2011.

Steck, Benjamin, 'Transport et Développement', in M. Brocard (ed.), *Transports et Territoires*, Paris, 2009, pp. 125–55.

Taaffe, E. J., Morrill, R. L. and Gould, P. R., 'Transport Expansion in Underdeveloped Countries: A Comparative Analysis', *Transport and Development*, London, 1973, pp. 32–49.

Turro, Mateu, *Going Trans-European: Planning and Financing Transport Networks for Europe*, Oxford, 1999.

United Nations Conference on Trade and Development (UNCTAD), *Review of Maritime Transport*, Geneva, 2017.

World Bank, 'Featured Rankings, 1990 to 2019' <https://ppi.worldbank.org/en/snapshots/rankings> [Accessed 27 April 2021].

CHAPTER 5

The Political Economy of West African Integration: The Transport Sector on Two Port Corridors

BRUCE BYIERS AND SEAN WOOLFREY

Introduction

Studies have shown that transport and transit costs in Mali, Burkina Faso and Niger are up to 50 per cent higher than for countries with direct access to the sea.[1] High transport costs raise the cost of doing business and trading across borders, hampering private investment, and undermining opportunities for job creation and poverty reduction, particularly in the hinterland countries and regions of West Africa.

Given an over-supply of small independent truckers who operate on relatively thin margins, 'the poverty and social impact of trucking reform will be considerable'.[2] While this may be the case on paper, given the political sensitivities of such reforms, it is important to understand where the main barriers and opportunities for transport reform lie, domestically and in regional terms.

Recent analysis and anecdotal evidence also suggest that user charges in West African ports are above average, and may be inflated. This is despite the rise in 'landlord ports' whose container terminal operations have been concessioned to private sector operators, ostensibly to boost efficiency and bring down costs for users. These high costs are surprising given the proximity of at least six ports along the coast between Benin and Côte d'Ivoire.

While there is arguably 'a good case for more co-operation between West African countries on port reform, competition and regulation', the challenge is

[1]   Frank Hollinger and John Staatz, *Agricultural Work in West Africa. Market and Policy Drivers,* Rome, 2015.

[2]   World Bank, *Program Information Document, Concept Stage. Regional Trade Facilitation and Competitiveness DPO,* IV Poverty and Social Impacts and Environment Aspects, Washington, D.C., 2014.

to see where the interests for this might lie in reality – who currently collects what rents in the current system; what is the distribution of gains within and between countries; and who would incur losses from modernising the sector?[3]

This chapter aims to respond to these questions for the ports and road transport markets in West Africa. It focuses on the corridors connecting Ouagadougou in Burkina Faso to Lomé in Togo, and to Tema in Ghana.

The analysis suggests that the interests of the hinterland population and private sector in accessing cheaper goods and inputs through lower transport costs are placed below the goal of ensuring Burkina trucks carry Burkina-bound goods, with costs to overall efficiency and to the detriment of efficiency-seeking reforms.

Intra–regional Competition or Collusion?

Foundational Factors Shaping Regional Transport Dynamics

Physical Factors

A map of the region with its ports and road and rail connections is sufficient to see that, in principle, Côte d'Ivoire, Ghana and Togo compete (along with Senegal and Benin) to serve as gateways to Burkina Faso and the other Sahelian countries, especially Niger and Mali. In principle, importers and exporters in the hinterland have a choice of which corridor and port to use (Map 5.1). The resulting competition would be expected to help lower transport prices for hinterland consumers.

While corridors vary in length, road quality, and the choice between road and rail, ports also vary in depth – this determines the size of ships that can dock, with larger ships offering the potential to offload more goods in one visit. Lomé is regularly cited as the deepest natural port in the region at 15 metres, with Tema and others in the region requiring regular dredging. At the same time, an in-depth study by JICA finds that though the route with the longest section in a poor state to Ouagadougou, the Lomé Corridor has the least roadblocks and is the least expensive in the region – this has also made it the most frequented in terms of traffic volume.[4]

---

3   World Bank, *Western Africa. Making the Most of Ports in West Africa*, Report No: ACS17308, Washington, D.C., 2016.

4   Japan International Cooperation Agency (JICA), *Projet du Plan Directeur de l'Aménagement des Réseaux Logistiques pour l'Anneau de Croissance en Afrique de l'Ouest, Rapport d'Avancement*, Tokyo, 2016.

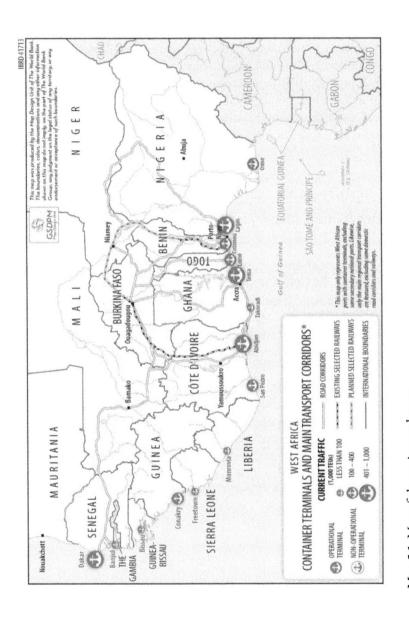

Map 5.1. Map of the region and ports.
(Source: World Bank, Western Africa. Making the Most of Ports in West Africa, Report No: ACS17308, Washington D.C., 2016.)

These all potentially affect the cost equation for transporters and therefore for shippers from hinterland countries like Burkina Faso. In principle, the country that manages to best align public and private sector actors around its port and facilitating trade should be able to reap benefits along with hinterland transporters and shippers.

But these physical aspects are only some of the factors that determine which goods travel along which corridor. Tufour cites the following: direct transit cost, transit time and the reliability of the corridor, safety and security, as well as language difficulties or incompatibility between stakeholders in given countries as equally important factors that determine corridor choices.[5] For instance, at different times, the Côte d'Ivoire civil wars in the first decade of the 2000s, strict Ghanaian axle load limit enforcement, Togo road damage and Benin customs procedures all affected traffic volumes on the different corridors, thus affecting the corridor choice of shippers.[6]

Port and terminal strategies also shape trade flows and shipper decisions. Security is particularly important with there being a pressing need to find alternative routes when tensions in coastal countries affect transit, as in Côte d'Ivoire from 2002 to 2011 or Togo from the mid-1990s until 2006. Thus, the choice of corridors for Burkina Faso and other hinterland countries ostensibly promotes competition but also provides alternative routes when instability erupts.

Regional Port Strategies

While the continual drive for economies of scale in global shipping leads to large 'hub' ports that serve as gateways and trans-shipment hubs, the interest in maintaining corridor and port options in West Africa also aligns with interests in each of the port countries. Together these lower the level of port consolidation that might otherwise take place.[7]

Beyond interests in maintaining national ports, only a small number of private companies dominate the sub-region's ports. Bolloré Africa Logistics is a major player with significant presence in all major ports. They operate terminals in joint ventures with APM Terminals in Abidjan and Tema, while the Mediterranean

---

5   Augustine Kwabena Tufour, 'Critical Factors that Influence the Attractiveness of Ghana's Corridor to Stake-Holders Engaged in the Transit Business of Landlocked Burkina Faso', *Africa Development and Resources Research Institute Journal*, 25:3, 2015, pp. 69–82.

6   World Bank, *Western Africa*.

7   Jean Debrie, 'The West African Port System: Global Insertion and Regional Particularities', *EchoGéo* [online], 20, 2012, no page<http://journals.openedition.org/echogeo/13070>.

Shipping Company (MSC) operates terminals in Lomé. Debrie points to the network strategy used by companies around key ports and corridors with port concessions.[8] According to one view, Bolloré expects to lose money on serving the remote ends of its 'vital corridors', but believes maintaining the network will put it in a better position to bid for supplying lucrative mining projects.[9] World Bank describes a 'region-wide quasi duopoly of two dominant TOCs (terminal operating companies, namely Bolloré and APM Terminals), which compete or co-operate in different ports and together control around 80 per cent of container throughput'.[10]

While diversification across ports can be seen as a legitimate strategy for private operators in view of past instability, the market structure for port terminals limits competition. As such, even with concessioning and growing trade volumes, 'prices for end users have not gone down and have increased significantly in some cases, generating substantial profits for ToCs'.[11] The same report also highlights that 'shippers have far less service options and far less bargaining power, and therefore face greater risks [than shipping lines, the other port user]'. Combined with the understandable lack of willingness of countries to rely on a port in a single neighbouring country, there is a 'continuation of multiple, sub-optimal size facilities which are naturally monopolistic and suggest the need for economic regulation'. Recent scrutiny of terminal concession processes both in the countries analysed here and elsewhere suggest that Bolloré is particularly seen as wielding political power both through its importance as a French overseas interest, and its role in supporting political campaigns (further discussed below). This suggests that shippers' interests have limited influence on vested interests, with political considerations trumping efficiency concerns.

Economic Structures, Political Consequences

Underlying economic factors are also important in shaping transport patterns and costs: 'The structural imbalance of West African economies ... results in an equation which is difficult for the shipping lines to solve'.[12] The major market imbalance between transit imports and exports clearly affects costs due to empty return journeys, whether from the port for exports or from Ouagadougou for

8　　Debrie, 'West African Port System', no page.
9　　Economist, *Network Effects: Connectivity and Commitment Pay Dividends in African Transport*, 16 October 2008 <www.economist.com/node/12432456> [Accessed 27 April 2021].
10　World Bank, *Western Africa*.
11　World Bank, *Western Africa*.
12　Debrie, 'West African Port System', no page.

imports. The types of goods flowing south along corridors (e.g. livestock, cotton, minerals) are different from those flowing north (consumer goods and capital goods), creating trade imbalances but also often requiring different types of trucks. This affects the profitability of trucks, particularly newly imported trucks, also leading to practices of overloading to raise the value of each trip. This model, with low revenues of truckers, appears to undermine the argument made by Teravaninthorn and Raballand, for example, that while transport prices are high to shippers, the costs to transport firms are low.[13]

But more than the economic challenge this poses, these imbalances have political repercussions. Burkina Faso's reliance on access to inputs and consumer goods in particular, and the threat of instability in neighbouring countries, creates political pressure to minimise reliance on the trucking industries of other countries. This amplifies the political importance of the Burkinabè trucking industry, its transport unions, organisations such as the Conseil Burkinabè des Chargeurs (Burkina Shippers Council, CBC), and their relations to the coastal country transport actors.[14] The importance attributed to transport is also reflected in government strategies that refer to the importance of regional infrastructures and transport to support planned growth poles and the priority sectors of agriculture, mines, crafts and SMEs and 'promotion of economic integration and Foreign Trade'. It is also seen through the priority given by the government to renewing the truck transport fleet, with a recently adopted decree to allow duty-free and VAT-free importation of 900 vehicles over a period of two years from May 2016, the fourth such exercise since 1985.[15]

This is similar for Togo, where the economic weight of the port is large in a small economy. That differs from Ghana (or Côte d'Ivoire), where domestic markets are much larger, reducing the relative importance of transit traffic.[16]

---

13 Supee Teravaninthorn and Gaël Raballand, *Transport Prices and Costs in Africa: A Review of the International Corridors*, Directions in Development; Infrastructure, Washington, D.C., 2009.

14 The Burkina Transport Minister is also responsible for Infrastructure and 'Disenclavement'.

15 R. F. Dandjinou, 'Burkina Faso: Conseil des Ministres – Importation de 900 Véhicules de Transport Exonérés de Droits de Douanes et de Tva', *AllAfrica* [online], 26 May 2016. <https://fr.allafrica.com/stories/201605261191.html> [Accessed 27 April 2021].

16 G. Raballand, *et al.*, *Why Does Cargo Spend Weeks in Sub-Saharan African Ports? Lessons from Six Countries. Directions in Development—Trade*, Washington, D.C., 2012; they then associate this with Lomé offering exceptionally long free time for traffic in transit.

In 2013 transport services as a share of commercial service exports represented 53.1 per cent for Togo, compared to 29.6 for Ghana and 17.6 for Côte d'Ivoire.[17]

The seasonality in trade also adds to the economic and political challenges. While there can be transport shortages at certain times of year such as harvest time for export crops, and Ramadan when imports of basic goods such as rice and sugar to hinterland countries go up, imbalances reportedly also lead to an oversupply of trucks at quiet times of year. This puts pressure on the unions operating at the ports and on transport contractors in terms of distributing the little freight there is.[18]

'Rules of the Game'

Formal Institutional Factors

A range of both formal and informal institutions also govern the transport sector in West Africa, where 'institutions' are interpreted as 'rules of the game'.[19] These include unwritten rules about ways of working and expected practices that nonetheless govern behaviour.

At a formal level, Togo and Burkina Faso are members of eight-member West African Economic and Monetary Union (UEMOA), while all three plus Ghana are part of the 15-member Economic Community of West African States (ECOWAS), which includes all UEMOA members. The two francophone states are also part of a loose network of 'like-minded' nations under the Conseil d'Entente, again not including Ghana.[20] While ostensibly this creates some hurdles for transit through Ghana given its distinct currency, administrative language and regulatory processes, Ghana is nonetheless an observer of UEMOA and indeed was one of the first to implement the UEMOA axle load limit, a

---

[17] World Development Indicators, last updated 5 February 2016

[18] When doing interviews for this study with the Togo transport union, only five containers were available for transporting, compared to a list of more than 100 trucks waiting for freight.

[19] For example, see: Douglass C. North, *Institutions, Institutional Change, and Economic Performance*, Cambridge, 1990.

[20] The Conseil de l'Entente (Council of Accord or Council of Understanding) is a West African regional co-operation forum. It was established in May 1959 by Côte d'Ivoire, Niger, Upper Volta (now Burkina Faso) and Dahomey (now Benin), and joined in 1966 by Togo, having grown out of the short-lived Sahel–Benin Union, a successor to the dissolved French regional colonial federation of French West Africa. Since 1966 the Council has possessed a permanent administrative secretariat based in Abidjan. A mutual aid and loan guarantee fund exists to assist poorer members from a common pool <https://en.wikipedia.org/wiki/Conseil_de_l%27Entente>.

key issue affecting costs between corridors today.[21] Paying bribes in Cedi is also reportedly cheaper than the CFA Franc bribes expected along the other corridors.

Bilateral Freight Quotas

In addition to regional regulations, the transport sector has long been shaped by bilateral arrangements to share transit freight between the arrival and destination country: two-thirds of each consignment of containers should go to Burkinabé transporters, and one-third to the coastal country transporters. The issue of freight quotas between Burkinabe and coastal truckers is a major component of the system that limits competition in the transport sector, thus affecting prices in the region.

Given that 'the CBC has the responsibility of ensuring that this rule is enforced' through agents in each port, this puts considerable power in the hands of the CBC to determine freight allocation across transporters, even if rules are not always applied.[22] Importantly, the quota applies to shipments on a case-by-case basis, not to the average overall volume of goods or number of containers over a day or week. This means that for each consignment of three containers, two must be carried by Burkinabè transporters, or negotiated over with the CBC. Where formal agreements do exist, cabotage is not allowed, meaning that no foreign truckers can be involved in the transport of domestic cargo.

The origins and validity of these agreements across the corridor countries are not clear. Terevaninthorn and Raballand state that the 'bilateral treaties are in place because after a crisis that followed the 1992 transport deregulation, the government of Burkina Faso signed an agreement with all its corridor partners (Ghana, Côte d'Ivoire, Togo and Benin) to establish quotas'.[23] But while other studies refer to a 1984 bilateral agreement between Haute Volta (now Burkina Faso) and Togo to limit haulage of transit freight imported to Burkina Faso through Lomé to Togolese and Burkinabè trucks in the ratio one-third, two-thirds respectively, more recent information suggests that Ghana has in fact no such formal agreement.[24]

---

21 While UEMOA countries adopted regulation (règlement) 14 on axle load and harmonisation of standards and procedures across countries, this has not been fully enforced, with no systematic sanctions for noncompliance.

22 Teravaninthorn and Raballand, *Transport Prices and Costs*.

23 Teravaninthorn and Raballand, *Transport Prices and Costs*.

24 Protocole d'Accord de Transports Routiers entre la République Togolaise et la République de Haute-Volta, Lomé, 14 April 1984; West Africa Trade Hub (WATH), *Transport and Logistics Costs on the Lomé-Ouagadougou Corridor*, Report #47,

Though the Burkinabé would like such an arrangement with Ghana, Ghanaian truckers are reluctant to acquiesce. According to Luguje, Ghana's ports handled no (from the late 1980s to early 1990s), or only negligible amounts of transit freight (until the second half of the 1990s).[25] Perhaps for this reason, freight sharing along that corridor was never fully formalised. Nonetheless, in July 2015 Burkinabè concerns about loss of access to their own transit freight led to the border being closed and renewed pressure on Ghana to accept an agreement stipulating that Burkinabé truckers carry two-thirds of shipments and coastal country truckers one-third.[26]

Whether formal or informal, the system in place gives the CBC monopoly power in the way freight is distributed. According to interviews this is to secure Burkinabè access to necessary imports, but also to address concerns about employment and the 'social dimension of the sector' leading them to protect their transport sector. This then promotes close linkages between CBC and OTRAF (Organisation des Transporteurs du Faso), representing a key aspect of the way the sector is governed. In effective terms, the sector is organised so as to protect Burkinabè truckers at the expense of the wider population. This is a fundamental reality that must be taken account of in any attempts to encourage trade facilitation and transport sector reform.

---

no place of publication, 2012, also cites Burkina Faso ministerial decree number 82–0358/CMRPN/PRES/MTP.T.URB.

25   Luguje, 2004.

26   For example, see *Les Echos du Faso*, 'Altercation entre Chauffeurs Burkinabè et Ghanéens des Problèmes de Chargements Évoqués' 30 July 2015 on recent tensions between Ghanaian and Burkinabe drivers over freight sharing <http://lesechos-dufaso.net/altercation-entre-chauffeurs-burkinabe-et-ghaneens-des-problemes-de-chargements-evoques/> [Accessed 27 April 2021]. Interviews in the field suggest that little has changed since Teravaninthorn and Raballand's report of 2009: 'The unofficial rules in a port in West Africa are as follows: A shipper informs the CBC it has a shipment to be transported to Burkina Faso. The CBC then informs the OTRAF, the Burkinabè truckers union, about this shipment and all its details. It may or may not negotiate the tariff with the shipper. OTRAF turns to its constituents and assigns the load on a first come–first served basis. This tour de rôle is updated in real time: when a truck arrives in the port, the driver goes to the OTRAF representative to be added to the waiting list. Once the contract is established, the trucker pays its due to the association (FCFA 10,000) for the service it provided and to the CBC (FCFA10,200) for the loading authorisation.' The only difference, discussed by corridor, relates to the first-come-first-served basis, which is also reportedly subject to flexible, informal arrangements.

Additional 'informal' or unwritten rules also shape the transport sector and the political weight given to strengthening regional connections. These relate to the way that 'formal' rules and agreements are applied – axle load limits have been a 'rule' since the 1980s but not fully applied, leaving application open to abuse and by those monitoring transport along the corridors. The freight-sharing quota agreements are also reportedly only applied at certain times, when tensions mount or when volumes are highest, and open to negotiation between shipper and OTRAF.

Overall, a range of different foundational and institutional factors underlie regional relations, all affecting the way in which the transport sector is organised within each of the affected countries. While there is the potential for competition between corridors, this is dampened by the structure of the ports market and relations between transport operators between countries. The broad structural and institutional factors felt at the regional level then affect the political weight of the transport sector across countries, with implications for the political power of different actors within the countries.

Corridor Actors and Interests

The Lomé–Ouagadougou Corridor

Given the importance of the port in Togo for the broader Togolese economy, what takes place around it is also politically important. While donors like GIZ see Togo as being on the path of democracy, the IMF highlights that 'political risks hinge on the government's capacity to deliver its promises of economic growth, social spending and job creation'.[27] As this section discusses, this has led to policies to encourage investment and reforms in the port and beyond that ostensibly aim to improve the efficiency of the economy. These reforms have met with some resistance and strikes that have so far been overcome.

Port Dynamics

Togo's port at Lomé has long played an important role in the country's economy, reportedly responsible for 80 per cent of overall customs revenues and indirect taxes. Its importance to the economy is also highlighted in various formal

---

[27] 'Le Pays se Trouve Aujourd'hui dans une Phase de Démocratisation', *Deutsche Gezellschaft für Internationale Zusammenarbeit* (GIZ), 'Togo Website' <www.giz.de/en/worldwide/26441.html> [Accessed March 2016]; International Monetary Fund (IMF), Country Reports 15/309, *Togo: 2015 Article IV Consultation-Press Release; Staff report; and Statement by the Executive Director for Togo*, p. 6, Washington, D.C., 2015.

documents including the government's national development strategy. Further underpinning the corridor approach, Togo Invest Corporation was established as a state-owned enterprise in 2014 to implement Togo's corridor vision for economic development. This company is meant to become a major actor around the corridor and in shaping interests relating along the corridor.

The vast majority of Lomé's transit traffic is destined for Ouagadougou.[28] This raises the importance of Togo–Burkina relations at a political level, but also between actors in the freight chain. Further, the government growth strategy highlights the role of the port authority given that '90 per cent of Togo's foreign trade passes through the PAL [Port Autonome de Lomé]'.[29]

There is also considerable unrecorded trade to countries in the region. It is among the largest 'under-invoicers of export proceeds', with illicit outflows from Togo reportedly averaging 66 per cent of GDP between 2002 and 2011 – peaking at 140 per cent of GDP in 2008, more than four times the annual budget.[30]

The Lomé port falls under the authority of the PAL, which handles clinker, wheat and hydrocarbons, while container traffic comes through two terminal concessions. One of these was awarded to Bolloré Africa Logistics under a 35-year concession that was awarded in 2010; and another to a joint venture between MSC and China Merchant Holding International (CMHI) also under a 35-year concession since October 2014, with options for ten more years to operate the brand-new Lome Container Terminal (LCT), reportedly representing the largest private sector investment in Togo. Though the 'concessions have provided Governments with millions of dollars in revenue through entry tickets, annual fees and royalty payments on traffic handled by concessionaires' the exact level of financial contributions of the port to government coffers is hard to gauge.[31]

The concession process has not been without controversy. There is anecdotal evidence suggesting that the awarding of concession contracts has been used as an instrument to help the incumbent regime, also supported by business

28 JICA, *Projet du Plan*.
29 IMF, Country Reports 14/224, *Togo: Poverty Reduction Strategy Paper*, p. 76, Washington, D.C., 2013.
30 Dirk Kohnert, 'Togo Country Report', in D. Kar and J. Spanjers (eds), *Illicit Financial Flows from Developing Countries: 2003–2012,* New York, 2014. Informal trade with Nigeria in cars, fuel, rice and fabrics is substantial. Though on a smaller scale compared to Benin, this shapes political dynamics around the port.
31 Christopher Clott and Bruce C. Hartman, 'Supply chain integration, landside operations and port accessibility in metropolitan Chicago', *Journal of Transport Geography* 51 (2016), 130–39.

networks operating in France and Togo. At the same time, Bolloré's interest in the port of Lomé is seen by some as a defence of its interests elsewhere in the region, with articles citing internal communication at Bolloré concerned about how investment in Lomé might undermine their investments elsewhere, most notably in Abidjan.[32] News reports cite opposition party members complaining about the insignificant 'crumbs' that the port contributes to the budget.[33]

MSC's entry into Lomé is seen as 'an entry point into a closed market' that may alter port dynamics and indeed the role of Togo in the region.[34] LCT, aiming for a capacity of 1.5 million TEU (twenty-foot equivalent units) in the long run, is intended as a hub port for MSC.[35] Its move into Lomé in 2014 followed a previous investment in San Pedro, Côte d'Ivoire in 2008, but which was disrupted by Côte d'Ivoire's subsequent instability, again highlighting the role of peace and security in determining port investment choices. Lomé is intended principally as a hub port for transhipment services linking to nine ports in the region, serving its Africa Express service arriving from key Asian ports via Durban and Cape Town, and potentially helping to lower prices. The intention is thereby to offer a hub and spoke service to deep-sea West Africa liner services.[36]

The MSC-run terminal being deeper (16.6 metres) than Bolloré's (12–15 metres), larger ships can dock.[37] Moreover, future price cuts may favour greater containerisation, for example for mining and forestry products.[38] Anecdotally, high-level political discussion and external pressure also led MSC to promise to focus on transhipment, not gateway traffic, which was to be left to their

32 R. Lecadre, 'Bolloré et Dupuydauby, Deux Requins dans les Ports Africains', *Libération*, 3 June 2009.

33 K. Mensah, 'Togo, un Pays en Faillite qui Enfante des Milliardaires, *TOGO-online*, 16 February 2016 <https://togo-online.net/togo/togo-un-pays-en-faillite-qui-enfante-des-milliardaires/> [Accessed 27 April 2021].

34 Hartman 2016; Olivier Caslin and Andrew Lynch, 'À Lomé, MSC inaugure un nouveau concept', *Jeuneafrique*, 23 December 2015 <https://www.jeuneafrique.com/mag/287892/economie/andrew-lynch-a-lome-msc-inaugure-nouveau-concept/> [Accessed 27 April 2021].

35 Kohnert, 'Togo Country Report'.

36 The ports are: Abidjan, Cotonou, Douala, Freetown, Lagos (Tin Can), Libreville, Monrovia, Takoradi and Tema; PortStrategy, *From Famine to Feast*, 10 February 2015 <www.portstrategy.com/news101/world/africa/w-africa-article#sthash.P2mWxFBV.dpuf> [Accessed 27 April 2021].

37 JICA, *Projet du Plan*.

38 JICA, *Projet du Plan*.

competitors. While this may be the case, the MSC decision to invest was also shaped by interest in Lomé as a gateway port connecting to the regional rail ring foreseen for the region.[39] Since 2014, the volume of its container traffic has tripled.[40]

Beyond private sector interests, President Faure Gnassingbe has reportedly also put forward his country as the 'West African staging point for China's Silk Road initiative, as countries on the continent begin to warm up to the Asian giant's plan to be a major geopolitical player'.[41] Transformation of the transport and logistics sector into a modern industry has become a first strategic priority in its National Development Plan 2018–2022.[42] The entry of MSC into Lomé port and their direct line from East Asia appear to at least partially confirm this.

Again reflecting the broader reliance on transport in Togo, the PAL has a strategy targeting transit traffic with Lomé as a gateway port: while domestic goods can remain for free in port for only four days, Raballand *et al.* say that this rises to 21 days for transit goods – 'the Port Authority of Lomé seems reluctant to use pricing to lower dwell time for fear of losing competitive advantage over other ports'.[43]

However, transporters and the port authority complain of a wide range of costs and charges that they say lowers the competitivity of the Lomé Corridor. In particular, UEMOA regulation 14 is seen as a key challenge for the sector. Reportedly (according to interviews) due to its recent heavy investments in road infrastructure, the Togolese government began to strictly impose the UEMOA axle load limit as of January 2016, seen by some interviewees as having undermined Lomé and its transporters' competitiveness. As the West African Trade Hub (WATH) state: 'Trucking prices are basically a function of load—the more tonnes carried the lower the cost per tonne—and whether the cargo is containerised or not.'[44] While 1 June 2016 was agreed on as the date to implement regulation 14 across the region, it is not yet clear what has happened in this regard.

Another frequently raised concern of transporters and the PAL is the so-called Bordereau Electronique de Suivi de Cargaison (BESC) or electronic shipment

39   Caslin and Lynch, 'À Lomé, MSC Inaugure un Nouveau Concept'.
40   Abel Bove, *et al.*, 'West and Central Africa Trucking Competitiveness', SSATP Working Paper No. 108, Washington, D.C., 2018.
41   President Faure Gnassingbe in interview with Chinese state news agency Xinhua <http://news.xinhuanet.com/english/2016–05/28/c_135394923.htm>.
42   Bove, *et al.*, *Trucking Competitiveness*.
43   Raballand, *et al.*, *Why Does Cargo?*
44   WATH, *Transport and Logistics Costs on the Lomé-Ouagadougou Corridor*.

form. Formally speaking, the BESC is meant to provide statistics, identification of merchandise, transport cost control and traceability of goods.[45]

Various elements have led to controversy around this shipping requirement that is reportedly not required along the other corridors. While initially managed by the Togo Shippers Council (the Conseil National de Chargeurs Togolais, CNCT), under President Gnassingbé's brother, 'opacity' around how it was being managed led the government to put its management out to tender, won by a Belgian company and leading to a four-fold cost increase to CFA70,000 per container.[46] In addition, Burkinabe importers reportedly already pay the BESC for tracking by the CBC, leading to double-payment of this charge for which there is little understanding of the benefits.[47]

Other issues raising costs along the Lomé Corridor relate to: deposits for containers that remain high, encouraging destuffing and axle overloading; customs scanning, where goods periodically appear as 'unreadable' due to specific packaging materials, opening the way for perfectly 'readable' goods being classified as unreadable and container stripping, opening up opportunities for corruption; a *droit de passage* (DDP) imposed by the Chambre du Commerce du Burkina Faso (CCBF) to finance the bonded warehouse it operates; charges to use rest areas by truckers (around US$20 for a night); GPS tracking to avoid transit goods going missing *en route* to Ouagadougou where fines are imposed due to batteries running down either due to not being charged, or because of unexpected delays caused by technical faults etc.[48] Drivers also report theft of these transmitters, which is suspected as being done in collaboration with Cotecna staff.[49]

To add to this, trucks reportedly do too few trips to allow profitability – the OTRAF president is quoted as saying that 'while in developed countries the truck does 30,000–50,000 kilometres per month, Burkinabe trucks do a maximum of 20,000 kilometres per year'.[50] Transporters therefore complain of the underlying low profitability of trucking despite the high prices they charge.

45   See more at <www.lexportateur.com/faq.asp?id_page=205#sthash.ILf8pNDy. dpuf>/.

46   Conseil National des Chargeurs du Togo, 'Trafic General', 2016 <https://cnct.tg/ wp-content/uploads/2017/09/Trafic-General-2016.pdf>.

47   Interviewees, various.

48   WATH, *Transport and Logistics Costs on the Lomé-Ouagadougou Corridor*.

49   Interview, Lomé, May 2016.

50   'Crise à l'OTRAF: Les Chauffeurs Transporteurs Interpellant le Premier Ministre Yacouba Isaac Zida' *aOuaga.com*, 31 July 2015 <http://news.aouaga.com/h/73076. html> [Accessed 27 April 2021]. While these average figures for developed countries

Freight Distribution

As the discussion thus far suggests, the costs involved in transporting goods from Lomé to Ouagadougou result from a range of different practices, by different public and private agents. This encourages a range of practices to recuperate costs, not least through overloading trucks. However, a key issue in the cost calculation is also access to freight, where the system described above lowers competition among truckers, protecting inefficient, single-truck operators at the expense of the wider population.

A recent JICA report estimates that between 60 and 80 per cent of freight is transported as break-bulk, rather than in containers.[51] The WATH also cites similar figures, estimating that 60–70 per cent of transit containers are stripped (unloaded) and the goods trucked to landlocked countries as break bulk, while 30–40 per cent of transit containers continue to Ouagadougou, 20 per cent of them under a 'through bill of lading'.[52] The through bill of lading implies that the shipper pays for door-to-door delivery with a transport company, encouraging the use of containers and thus reducing axle overloading. However, the through bill of lading does not guarantee that the contracted company will carry the goods, as described below, with all goods essentially subject to rules on access to freight, managed by the CBC and the transport union OTRAF.

In essence, while CBC is informed of all information regarding transit traffic, this is then passed on to OTRAF for distribution among carriers. OTRAF themselves see their role as protecting the two-thirds vs one-third quota, as reflected in interviews and their report from the first quarter of 2015, for example.[53] That means that OTRAF is essentially the gatekeeper to transit traffic, imposing the two-thirds one-third rule on freight that arrives without a predetermined carrier (the through bill of lading), leaving UNATROT (L'Union Nationale des Transporteurs Routiers du Togo, the Togo union) to allocate freight to its truckers on a first-come-first-served basis: the infamous *tour de rôle*.

Perhaps more interestingly, even when freight arrives with a through bill of lading, implying that the shipper has already taken out a contract with a transporter to ensure door-to-door delivery of goods, this shipment is nonetheless

---

may be exaggerated, the main point made by Yssouf Maïga, President of OTRAF, remains valid.

51   JICA, *Projet du Plan*.

52   WATH, *Transport and Logistics Costs on the Lomé-Ouagadougou Corridor*.

53   'Transport Routier: L'OTRAF Appelle Ses Membres au Respect Scrupuleux de la Charge à l'Essieu', *LeFaso*, 12 August 2015 <http://lefaso.net/spip.php?article66328> [Accessed 27 April 2021].

subject to the quota. Take for example a shipment of nine containers bound for Ouagadougou with a through bill of lading. Six of the nine containers are the responsibility of a logistics company, with a contract with one transport company, and are subject OTRAF demands. For the remaining three containers, the same companies may be able to carry one or two, depending on negotiations with UNATROT.[54]

Further, the driver chosen for a load pays a fee to the transporters' associations from both countries for the allocation service and assistance when travelling along the corridor, and also to drivers' unions from both countries, the OTRAF and the UNATROT. This is defended as being for assistance during the trip.[55]

This system then implies that a contracted transporter must fully carry the risk of using the transporter allocated by OTRAF or UNATROT. In cases where unionised individual truckers have not enough insurance to cover the merchandise being carried, it is known for contract transport companies to take out additional insurance, charge this to OTRAF or UNATROT, in order for the transport to take place. Companies have been known to refuse trucks deemed not to be in good enough condition, but this then also risks hold-up from OTRAF or UNATROT who essentially wield power in the ports by blocking entry or exit of specific goods or trucks. At the same time, contracted companies can be held responsible for poorly maintained trucks imposed by the unions that then break down on their way to Ouagadougou, implying substantial additional costs and losses than then must be negotiated with the union in question.

This means that, in practice, the quota, freight distribution system and goods with through bill of lading are subject to negotiation between transporters, OTRAF and UNATROT. Freight distribution also depends on the availability of trucks, and the levels of freight passing through the port. It can happen that a contracted transport company manages to carry its full consignment (e.g. of nine containers), but this would mean that in a future consignment it might be obliged by OTRAF and/or UNATROT to forego freight to 'pay back' for what it was allowed to take.[56]

While little of this is formally stated or established, in spite of the formal bilateral agreement around the quota, what emerges is that regardless of the contracts established, UNATROT and OTRAF manage to hold transporters to ransom in order to gain access to freight. While in interviews the unions defend their practices as defending the access to freight of single-truck, driver-owner

54 Interview, Lomé, May 2016.
55 WATH, *Transport and Logistics Costs on the Lomé-Ouagadougou Corridor*.
56 Interviewee.

transporters, and thus what one might call inclusivity, critics from within the transport sector also point to preferential treatment within the unions – more powerful or influential members of UNATROT can pay to be put at the front of the queue. Similarly, interviewees suggest that import agents are known to take the fee for importing goods but then selling the access to these goods to the highest bidder (who may then also sell this on to another person) introducing additional transaction costs and lowering the price ultimately received by the transporter.

While Burkina Faso has been going through important political changes, with President Compaoré driven from office by popular protests in December 2014, demands for political change also carried over to OTRAF. Protesting truckers forced the previous OTRAF head to resign in December 2014 after being in position for 19 years, amid accusations of nepotism, tariffs charged and preferential distribution of freight to the OTRAF president's family and close acquaintances.[57] News articles from July 2015 continued to refer to the issue of OTRAF distributing freight in Lomé and Tema according to payments made by their truckers to the detriment of Burkinabe truckers, reflecting the internal incentives at OTRAF to maximise payments rather than necessarily ensuring freight distribution to their members, leading Burkinabe truckers to close the frontier in 2015.

According to Gueh-Akué, the environment for unions, or *syndicats*, in Togo is characterised by fragmentation, 'permanent social tension', use of strikes as the only collective negotiation tool and a deficit of other alternatives.[58] Drivers and transporters therefore use blockages at truck parks and around ports and towns to arbitrarily demand contributions.[59] While there is an implicit understanding that the unions wield political power to create instability, it may be that recent reforms have reduced previous hostility – one report suggests that

---

[57] 'Les manifestants ont pris d'assaut les bureaux de l'organisation qu'ils ont presque mis à sac. Ils reprochent au président Sankara d'occuper son poste depuis 19 ans et d'avoir placé des membres de sa famille et connaissances aux postes influents. Les chauffeurs se plaignent aussi des tarifs appliqués sur les voyages. Boukaré Sankara et ses proches, selon toujours les manifestants, se partageraient les bons de transport, occasionnant un manque de travail et de revenus réguliers pour le reste des transporteurs'; Stella Nana, 'Ouaga: Les chauffeurs et transporteurs exigent et obtiennent le départ du président de l'OTRAF', *Burkina24*, 1 December 2014 <www.burkina24. com/2014/12/01/ouaga-les-chauffeurs-et-transporteurs-exigent-et-obtiennent-le-depart-du-president-de-lotraf-2/> [Accessed 27 April 2021].

[58] N. Goeh-Akue, 'Etude sur Le Paysage Syndical au Togo', 2015 <https://library.fes. de/pdf-files/bueros/benin/12374.pdf>.

[59] Ibid.

though strong in 2012 with unions managing to bring mass protests, unions are far more divided today with certain key figures joining the government 'regime' and government quickly managing to point to a minority 'privileged handful'.[60]

The impact of the current system is to limit the amount of freight available among transporters, therefore raising the pressure to carry as much freight as possible in one trip, bringing the discussion back full circle to axle regulation imposition and transport costs. The combination of factors is reportedly shrinking and closing several formal transport companies in Togo.

Current strategies underway to promote formalisation include the formation of co-operatives. However, rather than numerous co-operatives emerging, UNATROT created one co-operative for all of its members, CNATROT (La Coopérative Nationale des Transporteurs Routiers du Togo), formed in February 2016 with the Ministry of Infrastructures and Transport 'inviting' transporters to join.[61]

As the above discussion suggests, there are many internal bargaining processes and power games within UNATROT that therefore also seem likely to affect the impact of this initiative.

Tema Corridor Storylines

Although the port sector in Ghana is also considered a vehicle for economic growth, Tema Port lags behind its main regional competitors, Abidjan and Lomé, in terms of competing for transit traffic to landlocked West African countries. While investments such as the US$1.5 billion expansion project at Tema announced in 2015 reflect an interest in attracting more transit traffic and positioning Tema Port as a regional hub, growing domestic trade volumes provide another rationale for such investments. Certainly, the vast majority of traffic passing through Tema Port (Table 5.1) is accounted for by Ghanaian imports and exports. In 2014, for example, only 5 per cent of the 11 million tonnes of freight that passed through Tema was transit freight. That stands in contrast to Lomé, discussed above.

60   Olivier Rogez, 'Togo: le Systéme Faure', RFI, 4 May 2015 <http://www.rfi.fr/fr/afrique/20150504-togo-systeme-faure-gnassingbe-eyadema-unir-jean-pierre-fabre-anc-cap-2015-election-> [Accessed 27 April 2021].
61   Hélène Dubidji, 'Les Transporteurs Routiers en Coopérative pour Faire Face aux Défis du Secteur', iciLome.com, 18 February 2016 <https://news.icilome.com/?idnews=819221> [Accessed 27 April 2021].

Table 5.1. Freight traffic through Tema Port, 2013–2015 (tonnes).

Year	Vessel calls (units)	Total freight traffic	Export	Import	Transit	Transhipment	Container traffic (TEUs)
2013	1,553	12,180,615	1,493,956	10,014,243	620,668	51,748	841,989
2014	1,504	11,126,355	1,463,273	8,922,550	577,227	163,305	732,382
2015	1,514	12,145,496	1,303,090	10,043,146	722,508	76,752	782,502

Source: GPHA; <www.ghanaports.gov.gh/Files/TEMAPORTPERFORMANCE2003-2015.pdf>.

The Tema–Ouagadougou Corridor is key to growing transit freight volumes, as 80 per cent of transit traffic through Ghana is accounted for by Burkina Faso (see Table 5.2). Transit trade with Niger and Mali has declined in recent years and given the geography of the region, there is little obvious potential for growing the currently marginal volumes of transit trade with these countries.[62] It does seem, however, that the focus in Ghana is much more on satisfying the domestic market than on growing transit trade volumes. For example, stakeholders at Tema Port claim that the port – and Ghana in general – does a bad job 'marketing' the Tema–Ouagadougou Corridor to shipping lines, and does not make enough effort to attract transit traffic.[63] This is despite the fact that the port offers some advantages over other ports in the region.

Port Dynamics

The Ghana Ports and Harbours Authority (GPHA) is a public company established under the Ministry of Transport to build, plan, develop, manage, maintain, operate and control Ghana's ports. GPHA acts as a landlord at Tema Port, but also provides a number of services at the port, including marine services (pilotage, towage and mooring), stevedoring (and allocating private stevedores), cargo handling and security. In addition, GPHA sets maximum port tariffs. The fact that GPHA acts as both an operator and a supervisory authority at Tema Port means that it plays a complex role. While such a situation could in theory lead to inefficiencies and conflicts of interest, interviewees in Ghana did not suggest that the position of GPHA was a major contributor to the challenges highlighted at the port.

---

[62] JICA, *Projet du Plan.*
[63] Discussion at Tema Port (CBC, BAL).

In August 2004, the concession for the development and operation of a container terminal was awarded for 20 years to Meridian Port Services (MPS), a partnership between the companies APMT and BAL (35 per cent each) and the GPHA (30 per cent).[64] The terminal became partly operational in April 2007, with an annual capacity of 0.5 million TEUs, which was expanded in June 2013 to 1 million TEUs. Around 20 per cent of container traffic is handled in multipurpose berths run by GPHA and other local operators.

A recent study noted a number of advantages of Tema Port *vis-à-vis* its competitors in the region. These include: relatively competitive (official) port tariffs; daily departure of loaded trucks; safety of freight cargo in the port; electronic tracking along Ghanaian corridors; and dedicated infrastructure for handling transit freight.[65] Security at Tema Port is generally thought to be better than in other ports in the region.[66] Interviewees also noted the relative stability and reliability of the port (including the fact that it is 'never closed'), the port's responsiveness to users (a transit shipper committee meets every quarter to address challenges), and the effectiveness of the 'berthing window' at the port.[67]

Conversely, relatively long clearance times at Tema Port represent a major bottleneck on the Tema–Ouagadougou Corridor.[68] One of the main reasons for the long clearance times is the complexity of administrative procedures and the number of agencies involved. There used to be 29 regulatory agencies involved in the clearance chain, but through engagement with stakeholders and the government, GPHA was able to successfully push for the number to be cut down to 14 by December 2015 (with the hope that the full implementation of the single window will improve the situation even further). According to GPHA, the impact of this reduction has been noticeable for port users.[69] Other factors contributing to long clearance times at Tema include the inefficiency of customs clearance procedures (which, according to some, is used as a tactic to solicit unofficial payments); the fact that agents clearing cargo at the port are often servicing multiple clients; the fact that the 'single window' is not yet fully operational; persistent congestion problems resulting from a lack of storage (something that should be addressed by

---

[64] World Bank, *Western Africa*.
[65] JICA, *Projet du Plan*; It should be noted, however, that while official tariffs at Tema are competitive relative to neighbouring ports, unofficial payments, including to service providers, consolidators, clearing agents and customs officials, add to the cost of moving goods through Tema Port.
[66] Discussion – CBC, BAL.
[67] Interview, Danish Embassy.
[68] JICA, *Projet du Plan*.
[69] Interview, GPHA.

ongoing and planned investment in the expansion of the port); and the 'lack of professionalism' of many shippers, who are often unfamiliar with relevant requirements, leading to delays in clearing freight.[70]

Transport Sector Dynamics and Other Factors Affecting Corridor Competitiveness

In discussions with stakeholders in the Tema–Ouagadougou Corridor, two factors stand out as significantly inhibiting the competitiveness of the corridor. The first is that the regulatory environment for the market for cross-border freight transportation between Ghana and Burkina Faso results in shippers not being able to benefit from competitive transportation services. Shippers in Tema agree that the Ghanaian trucking industry is relatively more competitive than that of Burkina Faso, as although it is made up largely of private individual operators, with small fleets and limited capacity for upgrading, it also comprises a number of well-established freight companies with a greater capacity for offering a professional service. However, due to practices around cargo allocation and restrictions on Ghanaian truckers carrying goods from Burkina Faso, shippers utilising the Tema–Ouagadougou Corridor are forced to make use of the relatively less competitive services of the Burkinabe trucking industry. The trucking sector in Ghana itself is also constrained by the fact that the country strictly regulates axle-load limits, unlike other countries in the region, putting its trucks at something of a competitive disadvantage.

The second factor inhibiting the competitiveness of the corridor is the large number of official and unofficial costs involved in moving goods from Tema Port to Burkina Faso. These include a US$200 transit charge levied by the Ghanaian Central Bank on goods transiting Ghana from Burkina Faso, numerous illicit or informal payments demanded by officials at the numerous checkpoints along the corridor and at the border crossing between the two countries and a CFA 10,000 payment demanded by informal 'agents' at the Paga border to act as intermediaries between the truckers and customs officers (apparently truckers are not allowed to give their documents directly to customs officers). Previously, efforts by advocacy groups such as Borderless Alliance to monitor the checkpoints along the corridor and the demand for informal payments demanded by officials had led to a reduction in the extent of such demands, but more recently this monitoring has been scaled back, and there is anecdotal evidence that demand for such payments has again increased.

---

70   Interview, Danish Embassy.

Transit Freight Allocation

Unlike the Abidjan–Ouagadougou and Lome–Ouagadougou Corridors, there is no formal agreement in place between Burkina Faso and Ghana setting out bilateral quotas for the allocation of transit freight destined for Burkina Faso. However, the CBC and OTRAF have been able, through their monopoly right to issue a *bon de chargement* (loading note) at Tema Port for transit freight destined for Burkina Faso – this *de facto* enforces a quota system in practice.[71] CBC describes the *bon de chargement* as a tool that gives them back control over cargo allocation to ensure that two-thirds of transit freight is allocated to Burkinabe transporters, in line with norms and practices along othe r corridors in West Africa.[72] Indeed, apart from possibly allowing for improved data collection, the *bon de chargement* does not appear to have any other purpose. CBC is also clear that ensuring cargo allocation to Burkinabe truckers is an important part of its mission.[73]

According to CBC, the *bon de chargement* system has been in place at Tema Port since the 2000s, and it is true that tensions over transit freight allocation practices on the Tema–Ouagadougou Corridor – as well as CBC and OTRAF's role in these practices – have arisen periodically since at least the early 2000s. Nevertheless it appears that transit freight allocation and the use of the *bon de chargement* became particularly contentious issues during 2015 and 2016, while the system continues in 2020.[74] This is possibly due to the fact that prior to that, CBC and Burkinabe customs/border authorities were less concerned with enforcing freight-sharing quotas.[75]

---

71 According to data collected by the Joint Association of Port Transport Unions (JAPTU), the umbrella body at Tema Port representing Ghanaian transporters, in recent months about 80% of transit freight has been allocated to Burkinabe trucks; Interview, JAPTU, Ghana Haulage Transport Owners Association (GHATOA), and Ghana Haulage Transport Drivers Association (GHTDA).

72 Interview, CBC and OTRAF, May 2016.

73 Interview, CBC and OTRAF, May 2016.

74 Romuald Ngueyap, 'Burkina Faso: Le Gouvernement Met de l'Ordre dans la Gestion du Fret en Provenance et à Destination du Pays', *Agence Ecofin* [online], 27 February 2020 <www.agenceecofin.com/transports/2702–74283-burkina-faso-le-gouvernement-met-de-l-ordre-dans-la-gestion-du-fret-en-provenance-et-a-destination-du-pays> [Accessed 27 April 2021].

75 It was also suggested by officials of the Ghana Shippers Authority that enforcement was tightened up following the signing of a decree to that effect by a minister in the previous Burkinabe government.

This concern for enforcing freight sharing comes from CBC claims of increasingly unhappy Burkinabe truckers due to Ghanaian truckers carrying 'everything' to Burkina Faso, while they were having to wait up to a couple of months at Tema Port to be allocated freight.[76] This situation reportedly led to Burkinabe truckers 'attacking' the OTRAF head office in Ouagadougou.[77] CBC also claims that its role in 'organising' transit freight allocation is partly to address the fact that the system at Tema Port lacked transparency and had become 'corrupted' by 'coxeurs', well-connected middlemen who are able to use their connections to ensure freight landing at Tema Port is allocated to their preferred transporters, much as in the other ports.[78] CBC claims that, in the case of transit freight, such a situation was not, and would never be, acceptable to Burkina Faso.

In practice, the use of *bons de chargement* to enforce bilateral quotas raises the cost of transporting freight through the Tema–Ouagadougou Corridor, as the prices demanded by the Burkinabe transporters assigned by OTRAF are generally higher than the market rate (i.e. what Ghanaian transporters would charge).[79] In addition, forwarders at Tema complain that Burkinabe drivers are less professional than those provided by the Ghanaian (or Burkinabe) transport companies that the forwarders would prefer to work with, and cause delays due to their dealing with 'their own people' at the Ghana–Burkina Faso border.

Some have noted that these issues never arose under the previous government in Burkina Faso (under Blaise Campaoré), which may point towards changes in political economy dynamics in Burkina Faso. Interestingly, Burkina Faso periodically seeks to renew road haulage fleet and, to this end, in May 2016, the Burkinabe government temporarily suspended VAT and import duties on haulage and road transportation vehicles.[80] According to CBC, however, the enforcement of the *bon de chargement* requirements has nothing to do with attempts to promote the trucking industry in Burkina Faso, and is simply about fairness.[81]

---

[76]   A situation CBC describes as 'unacceptable' and as prompting a need to take action to ensure fairness for Burkinabe truckers. Interview, CBC and OTRAF, May 2016.

[77]   Interview, CBC and OTRAF, May 2016.

[78]   Interview, CBC and OTRAF, May 2016.

[79]   The reference price that for Burkinabe transporters to transport freight from Tema to Ouagadougou is CFA 40,000 per tonne.

[80]   'Le Pays', GIZ.

[81]   Interview, CBC and OTRAF, May 2016.

Conclusion

Although in principle governments, transporters, shippers and port operators all seek to improve the efficiency of the transport sector, in practice this cannot always be assumed to be the top priority. Many different parties benefit from current inefficient practices in different ways and at different scales – including low-income individuals.

Burkinabe interests and concerns about maintaining a strong Burkinabe transport sector shape much of the transport sector dynamics that we see, with concern for transport jobs and maintaining a 'national transport sector' apparently overriding considerations for the price to importers and exporters. The Burkina transporters union, OTRAF and the CBC between them shape the use (or not) of the bilateral freight cargo quotas between countries, while the transporter union in Togo governs freight distribution among transporters. The unions in Ghana are seen to be less influential or effective in asserting the interests of Ghanaian truckers with regards transit traffic, also reflecting a more market-based system.

In the ports, Bolloré Africa Logistics and the Maersk Group – through its port subsidiary APM Terminals – apparently carry considerable political influence in the countries in which they operate, despite some competition from MSC as the one other major terminal operator in the region. Beyond these, a lot of influence is held by customs authorities, whether as a distinct revenue-raising body, or as part of an autonomous revenue authority (the OTR in Togo). Nonetheless, the influence and importance of the transport and transit sectors vary in weight across countries. In Ghana, efforts to professionalise the private-operator segment of the trucking industry are hampered by stricter enforcement of axle-load limits, which puts Ghanaian truckers at a competitive disadvantage

The interests of shippers – consumers, producers and traders – are conspicuous by their absence in discussions of regional transport, with only a few cases emerging of coalitions of reform among citizens or firms, though ports appear more aware of the need to respond to shippers' needs to promote port interests.

One major game changer may be the envisaged rehabilitation of the Abidjan–Ouagadougou Railway Corridor, and the planned investments in the railway belt linking Cote d'Ivoire, Burkina Faso, Niger, Benin and finally Togo. Yet, such major multi-country investment programmes suffer from a range of institutional dysfunctions and political uncertainties in different belt countries.

While the focus here is on the port and the transport corridors, the study also points to the strong linkages between narrower corridor development reforms and the broader transport sector reforms, part of which are aimed at professionalising the trucking industry and modernising the trucking market over time. Context-specific foundational factors such as being landlocked, and contextual variables such as economic imbalances between countries, insecurity or the influence of dominant private stakeholders shape the institutional and incentive background against which coalitions prioritise sector reforms or problem solving.

Bibliography

aOuaga.com, 'Crise à l'OTRAF: *Les Chauffeurs Transporteurs Interpellant le Premier Ministre Yacouba Isaac Zida, a Ouaga.com*',31 July 2015 <http://news.aouaga. com/h/73076.html> [Accessed 27 April 2021].

Bove, Abel, *et al.*, 'West and Central Africa Trucking Competitiveness', SSATP Working Paper No. 108, Washington D.C., 2018.

Caslin, Olivier and Andrew Lynch, 'À Lomé, MSC Inaugure un Nouveau Concept', *Jeuneafrique*, 23 December 2015 <www.jeuneafrique.com/mag/287892/economie/ andrew-lynch-a-lome-msc-inaugure-nouveau-concept/> [Accessed 27 April 2021].

Clott, Christopher, and Bruce C. Hartman, 'Supply chain integration, landside operations and port accessibility in metropolitan Chicago', *Journal of Transport Geography* 51 (2016): 130–39.

Conseil National des Chargeurs du Togo, 'Trafic General', 2016 <https://cnct.tg/ wp-content/uploads/2017/09/Trafic-General-2016.pdf>.

Dandjinou, R. F., 'Burkina Faso: Conseil des Ministres – Importation de 900 Véhicules de Transport Exonérés de Droits de Douanes et de TVA, *AllAfrica* [online]. 26 May 2016. <https://fr.allafrica.com/stories/201605261191.html> [Accessed 27 April 2021].

Debrie, Jean, 'The West African Port System: Global Insertion and Regional Particularities', *EchoGéo* [online], 20, 2012, no page: http://journals.openedition. org/echogeo/13070.

Deutsche Gezellschaft für Internationale Zusammenarbeit (GIZ), 'Togo Website' <www.giz.de/en/worldwide/26441.html> [Accessed March 2016].

Dubidji, Hélène, 'Les Transporteurs Routiers en Coopérative pour Faire Face aux Défis du Secteur', *iciLome.com*, 18 February 2016 <https://news.icilome. com/?idnews=819221> [Accessed 27 April 2021].

Economist, *Network Effects: Connectivity and Commitment Pay Dividends in African Transport*, 16 October 2008 <www.economist.com/node/12432456> [Accessed 27 April 2021].

Goeh-Akue, N. 'Etude sur Le Paysage Syndical au Togo', 2015 <https://library.fes.de/ pdf-files/bueros/benin/12374.pdf>.

Hollinger, Frank and Staatz, John, *Agricultural Work in West Africa. Market and Policy Drivers*, Rome, 2015.

International Monetary Fund, Country Reports 14/224, *Togo: Poverty Reduction Strategy Paper*, p. 76, Washington D.C., 2013.

— International Monetary Fund, Country Reports 15/309, *Togo: 2015 Article IV Consultation-Press Release; Staff Report; and Statement by the Executive Director for Togo*, p. 6, Washington D.C., 2015.

Japan International Cooperation Agency (JICA), *Projet du Plan Directeur de l'Aménagement des Réseaux Logistiques pour l'Anneau de Croissance en Afrique de l'Ouest, Rapport d'Avancement*, Tokyo, 2016.

Kohnert, Dirk, 'Togo Country Report' in D. Kar and J. Spanjers (eds), *Illicit Financial Flows from Developing Countries: 2003–2012*, New York, 2014.

Lecadre, R., 'Bolloré et Dupuydauby, Deux Requins dans les Ports Africains', *Libération*, 3 June 2009.

LeFaso, 'Transport Routier: L'OTRAF Appelle Ses Membres au Respect Scrupuleux de la Charge à l'Essieu', *LeFaso*, 12 August 2015 <http://lefaso.net/spip.php?article66328> [Accessed 27 April 2021].

Luguje, M.A., 'A comparative study of import transit corridors of landlocked countries in West Africa', Unpublished Ph.D. (World Maritime University).

Mensah, K., 'Togo, un Pays en Faillite qui Enfante des Milliardaires, *TOGO-online*, 16 February 2016 <https://togo-online.net/togo/togo-un-pays-en-faillite-qui-enfante-des-milliardaires/> [Accessed 27 April 2021].

Nana, Stella, 'Ouaga: Les Chauffeurs et Transporteurs Exigent et Obtiennent le Départ du Président de l'Otraf', *Burkina24*, 1 December 2014 <www.burkina24.com/2014/12/01/ouaga-les-chauffeurs-et-transporteurs-exigent-et-obtiennent-le-depart-du-president-de-lotraf-2/> [Accessed 27 April 2021].

Ngueyap, Romuald, 'Burkina Faso: Le Gouvernement Met de l'Ordre dans la Gestion du Fret en Provenance et à Destination du Pays', *Agence Ecofin* [online], 27 February 2020 <www.agenceecofin.com/transports/2702–74283-burkina-faso-le-gouvernement-met-de-l-ordre-dans-la-gestion-du-fret-en-provenance-et-a-destination-du-pays> [Accessed 27 April 2021].

North, Douglass C., *Institutions, Institutional Change, and Economic Performance*, Cambridge, 1990.

PortStrategy, *From Famine to Feast*, 10 February 2015 <www.portstrategy.com/news101/world/africa/w-africa-article#sthash.P2mWxFBV.dpuf> [Accessed 27 April 2021].

Raballand, Gael, *et al.*, *Why Does Cargo Spend Weeks in Sub-Saharan African Ports? Lessons from Six Countries. Directions in Development*, Washington D.C., 2012.

Rogez, Olivier, 'Togo: Le Système Faure', *RFI*, 4 May 2015 <www.rfi.fr/fr/afrique/20150504-togo-systeme-faure-gnassingbe-eyadema-unir-jean-pierre-fabre-anc-cap-2015-election-> [Accessed 27 April 2021].

Teravaninthorn, Supee and Raballand, Gaël, *Transport Prices and Costs in Africa: A Review of the International Corridors. Directions in Development; Infrastructure.*, Washington D.C., 2009.

Tufour, Augustine Kwabena, 'Critical Factors That Influence the Attractiveness of Ghana's Corridor to Stake-Holders Engaged in the Transit Business of Landlocked Burkina Faso', *Africa Development and Resources Research Institute Journal*, 25:3, 2015, pp. 69–82.

West Africa Trade Hub, *Transport and Logistics Costs on the Lomé-Ouagadougou Corridor*, Report #47, no place of publication, 2012.

World Bank, *Program Information Document, Concept Stage. Regional Trade Facilitation and Competitiveness DPO,* IV Poverty and Social Impacts and Environment Aspects, Washington D.C., 2014.

— World Bank, *Western Africa. Making the Most of Ports in West Africa*, Report No: ACS17308, Washington D.C., 2016.

CHAPTER 6

The Dakar–Bamako Corridor:
Between Boom and Contradictions

JÉRÔME LOMBARD

'Among the challenges to overcome in order to ensure the successful implementation of the Plan for an Emerging Senegal (PES) it was noted that
some fall under the infrastructure and transport sector, notably roads,
through the reduction of the infrastructure deficit and the strengthening
of regional interconnection.'[1]

Introduction

Among the assumptions underlying the PES (Plan for an Emerging Senegal) is the
need – if not the obligation – to have high-quality infrastructure and transport,
which requires the construction of new roads and, above all, the development of
interconnections with neighbouring countries. With the PES, the tone has been
set. Senegal is developing its new infrastructure programme, which was launched
in 2014 by the president of the republic, Macky Sall, and has the goal of inserting
itself more effectively in international, continental (and intercontinental) trade
networks. In view of the importance of the Autonomous Port of Dakar (Port
Autonome de Dakar, PAD), efforts are focused in particular on strengthening
the Dakar–Bamako axis, especially the road network, while waiting for the
railway to regain its former glory. What matters to the government of Senegal is
the possibility that goods will be able to circulate more easily between Dakar and
Bamako, which is the basis of Senegal's attractiveness to international donors,
shipowners and logistics operators.

---

[1] Ministère des Infrastructures, des Transports Terrestres et du Désenclavement,
Plan Stratégique de Développement de l'AGEROUTE Sénégal 2017–2021, Dakar,
2016, p. 2.

By focusing on interconnection, Senegal is playing the modernity card, for which mobility has been regarded a watchword for more than a decade.[2] Like the new city of Diam-Niadio, the new airport of Ndiass and the Dakar–Thiès–Mbour–Touba motorway, the Dakar–Bamako axis, which has been renamed the 'corridor', must in the short term characterise the country's entry into a new era and highlight a process of radical change, making Dakar an 'infrastructure metropolis'.[3]

What works in favour of Senegalese policy-makers, port authorities and international donors (increased traffic and transit along the axis in question) raises a number of questions, however. Aside from the fact that no credible alternative to road transport seems to be in the making, the impact of increased road traffic on the spaces crossed and on towns and villages seems to have barely been taken into account. However, already-old work[4] has cast doubt on the structural effects of transport infrastructure on the space. More recent analyses highlight the fact that the transport facilities located between central areas and territorial peripheries have deepened inequalities.[5] Olivier Ninot insists on the need for much more empirical work in order to better understand what is being achieved by infrastructure, and what falls under public policy, stakeholder strategies and local decision-making.[6] Along the Dakar–Bamako Corridor, the question of the growth-generating effects is still being raised. Policy-makers seem to be obscuring it, however, even as traffic increases and the axis polarises economic and social activity.

In this chapter, we will begin by discussing the role of the port of Dakar in Senegal's economy. We will then look at the current claims about the place occupied by the Dakar–Bamako Corridor in Malian transit and the competition represented by other locations. Finally, we will re-explore the conflicted relationship between the fluidity of international traffic and local development of the spaces crossed by the corridor.

2   Peter Adey, *Mobility*, London, 2000.
3   C. Prélorenzo and D. Rouillard, *La Métropole des Infrastructures*, Paris, 2009 pp. 189–99.
4   J.-M. Offner, 'Les « effets structurants » du transport : mythe politique, mystification scientifique', L'Espace Géographique, 3,⊠ 1993, pp. 233–42,
5   Danny MacKinnon, Gordon Pirie and Matthias Gather, 'Transport and Economic Development', in R. Knowles, J. Shaw and I. Docherty (eds), *Transport Geographies*, Oxford, 2008, pp. 10–28.
6   Olivier Ninot, 'À propos des relations entre transports, territoire et développement', *L'Espace Géographique*, 1, 2014, pp. 61–62.

Senegal, Gateway to the Countries of the Interior

The Dakar–Bamako road axis has seen unprecedented growth since the early 2000s, which it owes to the geographical location of the port of Dakar on the network map of shipping lines as the first unloading platform on the west coast of Africa. The continuous improvement of roads in Senegal, particularly those leaving the agglomeration of Dakar to the east, also promotes the development of national and international communications.

The Privileged Situation of the Port of Dakar

Senegal's reputation was built on the presence of a 'good port', which was developed in the early decades of the twentieth century due to its geographical location on the 'fork in the lines of communication leading to South America in one direction and to the Indian Ocean in the other'.[7] In 1970, Assane Seck was the first geographer to emphasise the importance of the port of Dakar for the development of Senegal's international relations.[8] Until recently, it was still the main entry and exit port for Mauritanian, Gambian or Guinea-Bissau trade. In the 1980s, the government justified its necessary adaptations of the Senegalese economy due to 'deterioration in terms of trade'. This phrase is part of the regime's ideological framework for explaining economic problems and having the solutions for emerging from them accepted: 'According to the Senegalese government's analyses, the new economic policy implemented is essential for ensuring economic development, participatory growth and a reduction in social cost that forced adjustment does not allow.'[9]

The country then found a new slogan for development: without mobility, there is no salvation. In the name of adjustment programmes, development requires the support of all economic actors and the population to connect the country to the world and locate it on the best international trade and transport routes. In a speech delivered in January 1988, the president of the republic presented the new philosophy guiding the country:

> In this race for economic progress and social welfare, placed in this global context, Senegal, a country largely open to the Atlantic Ocean, a traffic distribution hub, the hub for the continent, has the assets required to join

7   Frederick Cooper, *L'Afrique depuis 1940*, Paris, 2008, p. 244; André Siegfried, 'Les routes maritimes mondiales', *Les Études Rhodaniennes*, 17:1–2, 1942, pp. 5–20.
8   Assane Seck, *Dakar, métropole ouest-africaine*, Dakar, 1970.
9   Momar Diop and Mamadou Diouf, *Le Sénégal sous Abdou Diouf: État et société*, Paris, 1990, p. 150.

the NPI club tomorrow .... With the prodigious development achieved
by means of communication, the question is no longer confined to inter-
African trade and extends to the whole world, and our country could
become one of *the* offshore centres of the world economy.[10]

The programme stresses the need for good tertiary services to boost the
Senegalese economy in its internationalisation phase in a pragmatic way.

> As we enter the post-industrial era in most countries, regardless of
> their level of development, the service sector will become increasingly
> important in the economic game. To this end, our country and its capital
> at the extreme tip of West Africa have a privileged role to play as a centre
> of production and trade and shining home of a rapidly expanding array
> of services.[11]

In view of Senegal's position on the world map and in Africa itself, international
transport is vital for the country.

From 2000, investment in the New Partnership for Africa's Development
(NEPAD) by the new president of the republic, Abdoulaye Wade, confirmed the
Senegalese authorities' desire to tie the country to Africa as a whole. Conceived
as a long-term programme to eradicate poverty and integrate the continent into
world trade, NEPAD emphasises the fields of telecommunications and transport,
repeatedly stressing the strengthening of infrastructure, improved accessibility,
public–private partnerships and regional connections.

It is President Abdoulaye Wade's intention to strengthen the pre-eminent
position of the port of Dakar in West African maritime transport, with the
objective of making Dakar a global hub for maritime traffic and a compulsory
point of passage for all shipping lines active along the West African coast. The
nautical conditions and the situation of the basins on the eastern part of the
Cape Verde peninsula are remarkable assets. Modernisation of the port is being
led by a director-general who is close to President Wade and has experience
working on ports, and who, following foreign leaders in shipping, is driving
unprecedented development. Until the early 2000s, the container terminal was
mainly reserved for vessels registered by the companies belonging to the Union
of Transport Auxiliaries of Senegal, which were Sdv and Saga (subsidiaries of

---

10   See the Senegalese daily newspaper *Le Soleil* of 11 January 1988, quoting the speech
     delivered the previous day by the outgoing president, Abdou Diouf, at the extraor-
     dinary congress of his party establishing him as a candidate for the presidential
     election in February 1988.

11   Ibid.

Photo 6.1. Dubai Port World container terminal at Dakar port, 2015. (Source: J. Lombard, 2015.)

Bolloré), Maersk Sealand, Simar and even Msc. The major new development of the Wade presidency is to break with this past. In 2007, Dubai Port World was awarded the new concession for the terminal for a renewable period of 25 years, with an investment commitment of CFA francs 333 billion (Photo 6.1). International competition requires new arrangements if Dakar's place in the extensive growth in containerised traffic in Africa is to be consolidated.

In 2012, Dubai Port World began the construction of a new terminal called the 'Port of the Future', which will have a capacity of 1.5 million TEU (twenty-foot equivalent units).

Increased Port Traffic

In the 2000s, an acceleration of the growth in imports led to an increase in port traffic from four million tons in 1997 to more than nine million tons in 2012, out of a total of almost 12 million tons.[12] Progress has continued steadily, and

12   Autonomous Port of Dakar, 2013.

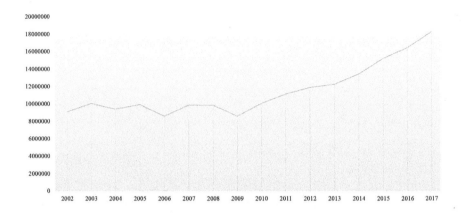

Figure 6.1. Traffic trend in the port of Dakar, 2002–2017 (Tons).
(Source: Dakar Port Authority; ANSD, 2019.)

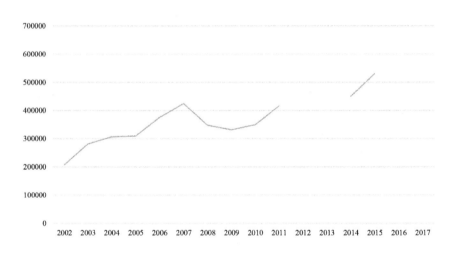

Figure 6.2. Container traffic at the port of Dakar, 2002–2017 (TEU).
(Source: Dakar Port Authority.)

in 2017 the overall volume reached 18.2 million tons (Figure 6.1). Development of the terminal has also boosted container traffic, which now exceeds 500,000 TEU. This only includes a small portion of the volume destined for Mali (at best 20 per cent, according to the SSATP study on road transport in West and Central Africa).[13] Much of it is made up of goods that arrive in containers leaving for Mali on conventional trailers (Figure 6.2).

The growth of the Senegalese population (from seven million in 1988 to 15.7 million in 2018), especially in the capital (from 1.586 million in 1990 to 3.067 million in 2015), is one of the main drivers behind the development of the port of Dakar.[14] The urban logistics within the agglomeration are an increasing element to which the port must constantly adapt.[15] The other challenge is to consolidate its role in serving Mali. The Ivorian crisis of the 2000s[16] stepped up the process of bringing West African ports into competition with each other, leading to the emergence of outgoing Malian traffic from ports in Ghana or Togo.[17] The Senegalese Corridor also strengthened its grip on Malian transit, making Dakar the leading service port for Mali (Figure 6.3). Fluctuating between 300,000 and 600,000 tons in the decade beginning in 2000, Malian transit through Dakar jumped after 2010, reaching more than 2.6 million tons today.[18]

Despite Senegal's ambitious port policy over the past two decades, the port of Dakar must still constantly seek to strengthen its attractiveness, lest traffic be lost. Notwithstanding the improved local services and remarkable nautical conditions, its location at the heart of an urban fabric limits the possibilities for expansion and hinders its ability to compete with its most serious competitors. A new port is also expected to be established further east in Rufisque Bay. The condition of the road on part of the route connecting Dakar to Bamako (not to

---

13 Abel Bove, *et al.*, *Le transport routier en Afrique de l'Ouest et Centrale*, SSATP Working Paper No. 108, Washington, D.C., 2018.

14 Africapolis <www.africapolis.org/data> [Accessed 27 April 2021].

15 N. Mareï and Olivier Ninot, 'Transformation des transports en Afrique: Vers des systèmes à plusieurs vitesses?', *Questions Internationales*, 90, 2018, pp. 27–31.

16 In 2002, Côte d'Ivoire was split in two, with its northern part occupied by belligerents considered by the Abidjan authorities to be rebels. Economic activity slowed down and rail transport was interrupted completely. International transit to and from the port of Abidjan was partially suspended until 2003, forcing shipowners to move to other West African ports.

17 ISEMAR, *Enjeux et position concurrentielle de la conteneurisation ouest-africaine*, 104, 2008, p. 4.

18 Ministère de l'Économie et des Finances, *Situation Économique et Sociale du Sénégal. Édition 2009*, Dakar, 2010; Port Autonome de Dakar, 2013, 2017.

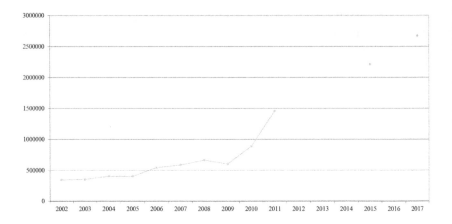

Figure 6.3. Transit traffic to Mali at the port of Dakar, 2002–2017 (Tons). (Source: Dakar Port Authority.)

mention that of the railway) is variable, increasing transport times and forcing operators to opt for diversifying their logistics solutions and not favouring the Senegalese route at the expense of others.[19] The extension of the motorway to Kaolack (190 kilometres east of Dakar) should reassure operators for a time. Finally, the transit times at the port of Dakar are still a disadvantage for the rapid clearing of containers.

The growth of port traffic in Dakar benefits both the Senegalese national market and Malian trade. The geographical advantage of the Dakar peninsula, which is the first major stopping point for ships operating on the Europe–Africa lines, is accompanied by active lobbying by the port authorities and the Senegalese powers in an extremely competitive West African landscape.

The Dakar–Bamako Corridor in Regional Competition

Service to Mali from the port of Dakar evolved throughout the twentieth century. Road transport has now overtaken river and rail, making the Dakar–Bamako

---

19   Jérôme Lombard, Benjamin Steck and Sidy Cissokho, 'Les transports sénégalais: Ancrages internationaux et dérives locales', in M.C. Diop (ed.), *Sénégal, 2000–2012: Les institutions et politiques publiques à l'épreuve d'une gouvernance libérale*, Dakar, 2013, pp. 642–71.

route the number one trade route with the outside world for Mali; however, competition from other transport routes and West African ports is a constant threat to Dakar's leadership.

From Rail to Road

The difficulties involved in transport by rail between Dakar and Bamako have made the need for a quality road axis more pressing. Since 2008, the completion of the asphalting of the different sections has allowed Senegalese and Malian operators to circulate their goods more easily.[20]

The Virtual Disappearance of the Railway Line

In the Senegal–Mali international arena, trade was first conducted by the river infrastructure, which from the nineteenth century served as an axis of penetration for the colonial conquest towards French Sudan and supported all the fortified towns, from Dagana to Kayes. This golden age was short-lived, however. From 1923, with the Thiès–Kayes rail link, the waterway saw its traffic decrease and 'enter, from that moment on, a period of sleep which endures today'.[21] During the first 60 years of the twentieth century, the railway operator, whose network covered the entire Groundnut Basin, responded to the economic development challenges of the colony and then of the independent state. The shift of economic activity from the Senegal River Valley to the centre of the country reinforced the railway's primary role in west–east relations. In 1923, the traffic between Thiès and Kayes amounted to 447,500 passengers and 133,000 tons (civil servants, military personnel, traders); in 1966, freight traffic was approximately 150,000 tons.

In the last 30 years of the twentieth century, international rail traffic grew significantly (reaching 431,000 tons in 1998). However, operational difficulties coupled with the dilapidated condition of the railway caused accidents and derailments, which resulted in a rapid deterioration in rail activity, and by 2000 traffic had dwindled to 345,700 tons.[22] With the privatisation of the operation in 2003 and its takeover by an international consortium with Canadian and French capital (Canac–Getma), international flows of goods

---

[20] 'Inauguration de la route Didiéni-Diéma: un boulevard sur Dakar et Nouakchott', *L'Essor*, 21–27 July 2008.

[21] R. Keita-Ndiaye, 'Kayes et sa région: Étude de géographie urbaine au Mali', unpublished PhD thesis, Université Louis Pasteur, 1971, p. 69.

[22] Ministère de l'Équipement et des Transports, *Mémento des Transports Terrestres du Sénégal,* Dakar, 2002.

appeared to be rising again – by approximately 9 per cent in 2004, due to an increase in traffic in the Senegal–Mali direction.[23] In 2007, Transrail was acquired by the Advens group of Franco-Senegalese businessman Abbas Jaber, and was managed on a day-to-day basis by Vecturis, which specialises in rail transport in Africa. However, the volume of traffic failed to take off, falling below 300,000 tons in 2011,[24] and continued to decrease thereafter, to 288,086 tons in 2013, 244,858 tons in 2014, 210,008 tons in 2015 and 74,989 tons in 2016.[25] In 2015, operation of the line by Advens was terminated, and in 2016, Transrail was replaced by the Dakar Bamako Railway (DBF), a transitional manager until a permanent solution could be found.[26]

The Dominance of Road Traffic

Since the end of the 1990s, roads have played an important part in the transport of goods to and from Mali as a result of the end-to-end completion of an asphalted route between Dakar and Bamako.[27] Rapid changes have been seen over the course of 20 years. Observations made at the customs post on the Senegalese–Malian border (Photo 6.2) or the Kayes bridge in Mali (Photo 6.3) confirm the upward trend. In 2001, nearly 50 lorries weighing between 10 and 30 tons, mainly loaded with hydrocarbons, building materials (lime and cement) and foodstuffs (salt, fish and various others) crossed the border from Senegal towards Mali every day. In 2006, according to the Malian press, more

23 Ministère de l'Économie et des Finances, *Situation Économique et Sociale du Sénégal. Édition 2004*, Dakar, 2004.

24 Ministère de l'Économie et des Finances, *Situation Économique et Sociale du Sénégal. Édition 2011*, Dakar, 2013.

25 ANSD, *Situation Économique et Sociale du Sénégal en 2016*, Dakar, 2019. The decrease in freight traffic is creating real financial difficulties for Transrail. See Sidy Dieng, 'Transrail. Le plan de sauvetage vaut 177 milliards', *Wal Fadjri*, 16 May 2012 <http://fr.allafrica.com/stories/201205161173.html> [Accessed 27 April 2021].

26 The fall in international passenger rail traffic has been going on for several decades: in 1998, 41,900 passengers travelled by train between Senegal and Mali, while in 2000, there were only 30,800. Over the period from 1995 to 2007, the decrease was 42%. Since 2018, passenger rail traffic has been totally interrupted on the international line and the internal link between Bamako and Kayes.

27 Road passenger traffic is also steadily increasing between the Malian capital and Dakar: 17,000 travellers in 2005 compared to 7,000 in 2002. In 2009, no fewer than ten coaches with approximately 50 seats left Bamako every day for Kayes, with some continuing on to Dakar. In the other direction, several vehicles left the Senegalese capital for Mali every night.

Photo 6.2. Queue of trucks waiting at the Malian border, 2001.
(Source: J. Lombard, 2001.)

Photo 6.3. Convoy of tankers in the city of Kayes, Mali, 2009.
(Source: J. Lombard, 2009.)

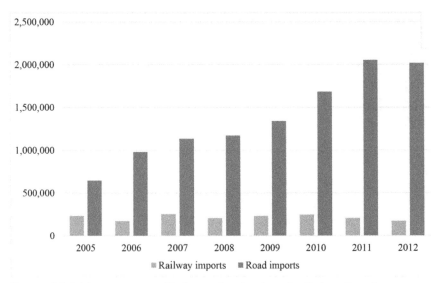

Figure 6.4. Malian import traffic by road and rail on the Dakar–Bamako
Corridor, 2005–2012.
(Source: Malian Port Authority in Senegal, 2013.)

than 100 lorries from all over Mali and its neighbouring countries (including Burkina Faso .and Niger) crossed Kayes daily towards Senegal.[28] In 2009, according to the prime minister of Mali, this number stood at more than 200. Today, according to the aforementioned SSATP study, nearly 400 vehicles use this corridor on a daily basis.[29]

Between 2005 and 2012, the total volume transported along this corridor (imports and exports), road and rail combined, increased approximately 2.6 times, from 897,691 tons in 2005 to 2,326,802 tons in 2012. Road transport accounts for almost 90 per cent of Mali's overall traffic passing through Senegal, compared to 10 per cent by rail. Table 6.1 and Figures 6.4 and 6.5 illustrate the dominance of road over rail supply.

Table 6.1. Evolution of freight traffic on the Dakar–Bamako Corridor (in tons, 2005–2012).

	2005	2006	2007	2008	2009	2010	2011	2012
Imports by rail	233,410	171,935	254,353	207,503	230,572	245,830	206,356	171,838
Imports by road	644,707	978,995	1,133,173	1,171,088	1,339,574	1,681,812	2,050,257	2,016,142
Exports by rail	9,481	11,819	15,028	52,644	39,580	29,315	43,181	70,266
Exports by road	10,093	21,166	20,090	16,585	11,190	20,628	52,322	68,556

Source: Entrepôts Maliens au Sénégal (EMASE), 2013.

The Introduction of Competition between Corridors by Mali

Although the Senegalese Corridor is the main route of choice for Malian operators, other African corridors are equally advantageous. The development of the Entrepôts Maliens ('Malian Warehouses') organisations abroad has promoted competition among states on the Atlantic Ocean, for the benefit of

---

[28] 'Kayes amorce son décollage: Le soleil se lève à l'Ouest', *L'Essor*, 20 September 2006.
[29] Bove, *et al.*, *Le transport routier en Afrique de l'Ouest et Centrale*.

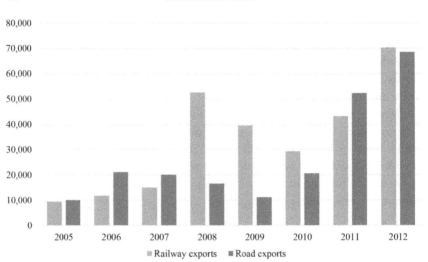

Figure 6.5. Malian export traffic by road and rail on the Dakar–Bamako Corridor, 2005–2012.
(Source: Malian Port Authority in Senegal, 2013.)

Mali, whose isolation is thereby diminished and its dependence on any one of them reduced.[30]

'Closing the Gap between the Coast and the Interior'[31]

In a context characterised by the opening up of African economies to imports and the capitalisation of their exports, the landlocked West African states (Mali, Burkina Faso, Niger) have opted for policies that diversify their supply and shipping routes. Rather than relying too heavily on the strategies of port authorities in the context of increasing competition among maritime entities that can sometimes benefit from political instability in order to gain market shares, these states have adopted a logic of pitting different platforms against each other.[32] The aim of this is to restore the balance of power, and to make port authorities more attentive to – and even dependent on – national strategies. In Mali, as in Burkina Faso or Bouaké in the north-central part of

---

30 There are also Entrepôts Maliens in Côte d'Ivoire, Senegal and Togo (EMACI, EMASE and EMATO respectively).
31 According to the expression of a Malian official interviewed in 2010 in Bamako.
32 Jean Debrie and Sandrine De Guio, 'Interfaces portuaires et compositions spatiales: Instabilités africaines', *Autrepart*, 32:4, 2004, pp. 21–36.

Côte d'Ivoire, 'dry port' projects located within the borders or closer to the barycentre of national territories demonstrate the desire to circumvent the congestion problems of coastal ports, to reduce transit times by eliminating customs operations on landing, and to develop storage facilities in the territory of the destination country, 'to ensure regular supply to the population as well as the main sectors of the economy'.[33]

The existence of transport corridors should be seen as more than a means of reducing isolation, and as the horizon of national and international transport policies. In Mali, the Shippers' Council (Conseil Malien des Chargeurs, CMC) seeks to develop winning strategies to improve the country's land-based services and support industrialists and traders, and to take on some of the logistics and transport operations by attracting them to Mali and entrusting them to national operators.[34]

The First Transits of Malian Freight through the Port of Dakar

Observations of the evolution of the links between Mali and the Atlantic Ocean highlight the existence of multiple possible routes. The link to Côte d'Ivoire has been added to the route that has passed through the west of Mali toward Dakar since 1923, which since 1934 has linked the railway between Abidjan and Ferkessédougou, and then the track and road to Bamako, via Sikasso. These routes have long dominated Mali's land transport and communications landscape, with the link to Côte d'Ivoire overtaking the route to Senegal in the 1990s because of operational problems encountered on the Bamako–Dakar railway and the Ivorian port's efforts to attract Malian operators.[35] With the 1999 coup in Côte d'Ivoire and the country's split into two separate parts, the situation changed completely in favour of Dakar. Malian operators also look

[33] Jean Tape Bidi, 'Quelques réflexions sur l'existence d'un port sec à Bouaké en Côte d'Ivoire', in K. Fodouop and J. Tape Bidi (eds), *L'armature du développement en Afrique. Industries, transports et communications*, Paris, 2010, pp. 77–86; Harouna Cisse, 'La création des ports secs au Mali', Communication to the International Workshop *Systèmes de transport de marchandises en Afrique de l'Ouest*, World Road Association, Ouagadougou, 13–15 June 2005, p. 2.

[34] The CMC brings together an assembly of more than 250 industrialists and traders each year. While the secretary-general is a Malian sate official, the president and vice-presidents are business leaders.

[35] In 1996, the Abidjan–Mali axis handled almost 940,000 tons (imports and exports combined), while the Dakar axis handled only 431,000 tons: Entrepôts Maliens au Sénégal and the Senegal Department of Transport.

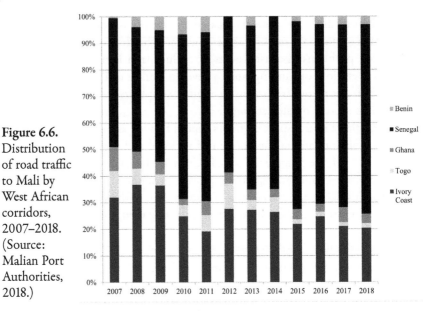

Figure 6.6. Distribution of road traffic to Mali by West African corridors, 2007–2018. (Source: Malian Port Authorities, 2018.)

to Togo (Lomé: 26 per cent of Malian transit in 2004) and Ghana (Tema and Takoradi: 17.8 per cent).[36]

Over the past 15 years or so, the Senegalese corridor has made gains over its competitors (Figure 6.6 and Map 6.1). At the end of the 2000s, the Dakar–Bamako axis took 50 per cent of Malian traffic, but this percentage grew steadily from 2013, rising to nearly 70 per cent in 2018. Malian transit traffic has continued to decline at the port of Abidjan, by almost 40 per cent in the 2000s, but by only 20 per cent in 2018. As for Ghana's ports (Takoradi and Tema), which were able to capture 10 per cent of Malian transit for a time, their share fell to less than 5 per cent because of long waiting times at the port and difficulties with access (untimely roadblocks).[37]

The advantages of the Dakar–Bamako Corridor are still undeniable. According to importers we interviewed in 2013 as part of a study on the

36   See Jacky Amprou, *Crise ivoirienne et flux régionaux de transport*, Paris, 2005.
37   Herve Deiss, 'Afrique de l'Ouest: Le portuaire joue la carte de la solidarité avec les pays enclavés', *Ports et Corridors* <https://portsetcorridors.com/2019/ports/afrique-de-louest-le-portuaire-joue-la-carte-de-la-solidarite-avec-les-pays-enclaves/> [Accessed 27 April 2021].

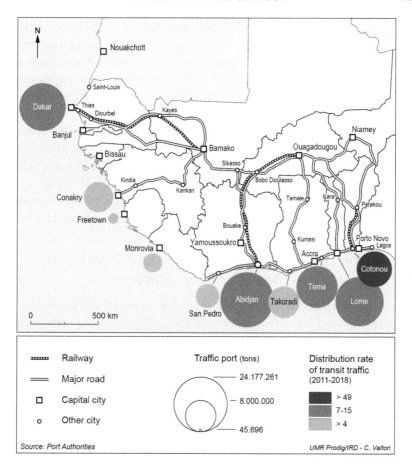

Map 6.1. Total traffic and share of transit traffic in West African ports, 2011–2018.
(Source: Port authorities.)

transportation of Senegalese goods by road, the corridor benefited from the Ivorian crisis and the resulting insecurity on the roads.[38] The distance between Bamako and the other ports (Cotonou, Lomé and Accra), which are located about 2,000 kilometres from the Malian capital, is turning into an advantage for Dakar, which is only 1,200 kilometres away. In addition to providing an alternative to the northern corridor, the implementation of the southern corridor (Tambacounda–Kédougou–Saraya–Kita–Bamako) in 2014 shortened the

---

[38] State of Senegal and the European Union, 2013.

Dakar–Bamako road link to 1,000 kilometres. According to the oil carriers we interviewed, there are also other factors that favour the Senegalese corridor, including the section of road that passes near the gold mines of the Kayes region (which are heavy consumers of diesel) and the reduction in waiting times at the Dakar refinery, which allows four monthly rotations per tanker truck, compared to two in Abidjan.

For almost two decades, the policy adopted by the port of Dakar and the construction of additional roads have consolidated Senegal's place in trade with Mali. Competition from Abidjan, which is in search of its former glory, is currently below what it might have been until the end of the 1990s. The current challenge for the Dakar–Bamako Corridor is to maintain its attractiveness for international transport operators and the populations residing along its route.

When the Dakar–Bamako Corridor Emancipates Itself from the Territory

Efforts by Senegalese actors to make the Dakar–Bamako axis the main choice for transport and logistics operators are increasing. With the opening of the second axis toward the Malian border, which crosses Senegalese mining areas, the corridor has become a national issue for the country. The aim of this policy, which is supported by international donors, is to improve traffic flows along this double axis. One question remains unresolved, however: is this objective becoming exclusive, or can it accommodate a more balanced territorial development?

Prioritising Fluidity

The development of international trade between Senegal and Mali is founded on a favourable and long-standing backdrop of improving road links between African capitals.[39] Support for corridors linking ports to capital cities in landlocked countries has become even stronger as one sees significant declines in transport costs along heavy traffic routes.[40] Donors, meeting the interests of landlocked countries and the major domestic and international operators, are pushing to strengthen corridors, with the goal of improving traffic flows on major roads and minimising

---

[39] Club du Sahel et de l'Afrique de l'Ouest, *Atlas régional des transports et des télécommunications dans la CEDEAO*, Paris, 2005.

[40] Supee Teravaninthorn and Gaël Raballand, *Transport Prices and Costs in Africa: A Review of the International Corridors*, Directions in Development; Infrastructure, Washington, D.C., 2009.

existing barriers, including so-called abnormal practices.[41] Improving traffic on the main West African roads is becoming the backbone of the development of transport systems in Africa, and is one of the strategic axes of transport policies, led by continental organisations such as NEPAD.[42]

The focus on international infrastructure and the consolidation of international corridors stems from the credit they enjoy in the dominant discourse and the extensive projects envisioned for the continent. International donors and global operators see this as an easy way of duplicating what is being done elsewhere. The corridor is viewed as the only alternative to a lack of international connections. In a sense, the prophecy of the corridor is self-fulfilling, in the words of Robert King Merton, and is also referred to by J.-F. Staszak.[43]

The notion of the corridor is presented as one of the elements of the relationship between transport, regional integration and the development process. The corridor promotes institutional integration, which enables the development of international co-operation, the creation of public–private partnerships, and changes in legislation and inter-state agreements. Logistical and economic successes, which are given value by the prevailing narratives about the future of transport in West Africa, establish it as a new paradigm.[44] As a 'programming and governance tool', it tends to be organised into a functional (and efficient) space, concentrating infrastructures, flows, operators and public

---

41 Borderless Alliance <www.borderlesswa.com>; checkpoints (customs, police, etc.) along international roadways have been identified as additional cost factors (due, for example, to illegal taxes, bribes) and significant delays. They are monitored by a collective of public and private interests called 'Borderless', which aims to improve trade and transport conditions in West Africa. See comment prepared in 2018 by a Senegalese representative of the Observatory of Abnormal Practices (OPA – Observatoire des Pratiques Anormales): <www.dakaractu.com/Corridor-Dakar-Bamako-D-excellents-resultats-ont-ete-enregistres-en-2016-Mbaye-Chimere-Ndiaye_a137029.html> [Accessed 27 April 2021].

42 West Africa Trade Hub, *Coûts du transport et de la logistique sur le corridor Lomé–Ouagadougou*, Report #47, no place of publication, 2012; Jérôme Lombard, Olivier Ninot and Benjamin Steck, 'Corridors de transport en Afrique et intégration territoriale en questions', in A. Gana and Y. Richard (eds), *Les intégrations régionales dans le monde*, Paris, 2014, pp. 245–64.

43 Robert King Merton, *Éléments de théorie et de méthode sociologique*, Paris, 1953/1997; Jean-Francois Staszak, 'Prophéties auto-réalisatrices et géographie', *L'Espace Géographique*, 29:2, 2000, pp. 105–19.

44 Vivien Foster and Cecilia Briceno-Garmendia, *Infrastructures africaines: Une transformation impérative*, Paris, 2010, p. 202; Yann Alix (ed.), *Les corridors de transport*, Cormelles-le-Royal, 2012.

and private authorities.[45] Its operation is reduced to the establishment of simple accelerators of flows: that is, roads connecting two points – in this case capitals such as Dakar, Bamako, Ouagadougou, Abidjan, Accra and Lomé. These continental hubs exert their influence over the entire area being served and ensure the redistribution of goods in their inland areas. The pursuit of the technical–economic logic of corridors leads to territories dominated by fluidity and only slightly structured by the diversity of the transport systems. The example of the Maputo Corridor is emblematic of the development of this type of heavy axis in Africa, which benefits only international trade, and only rarely local traffic.[46]

What are the Effects for the Territories Crossed?

The quest for fluidity on the Dakar–Bamako Corridor raises certain questions. The tunnel effect is often the first outcome of the concentration of efforts on a single axis. It results in low interdependence between long-distance traffic and local spatial dynamics. As transit traffic grows, small towns scattered along the axis become no more than milestones for drivers and exit and redistribution points for freight and passengers.[47]

The corridor is designed by globalised economic actors as a logistical axis, which under optimal conditions must enable flows of traffic and ensure the maximum profitability of these flows, dictated by the needs of both shipping customers and consumers of the products being transported. At the same time, it is presented by institutional leaders as a development tool that benefits the territories crossed and as a resource for improving the accessibility of inhabited areas. There is no guarantee, however, that these populations will notice any positive impact, with the discourse on the structural effects obscuring the negative aspects, which include inconveniences such as pollution and accidents, and even insecurity and land pressures.

[45] Jean Debrie and Claude Comtois, 'Une relecture du concept de corridors de transport: Illustration comparée Europe/Amérique du Nord', *Les Cahiers Scientifiques du Transport*, 58, 2010, pp. 127–44.

[46] Frederik Söderbaum and Ian Taylor (eds), 'Competing Region-Building in the Maputo Development Corridor', in F. Söderbaum and Ian Taylor (eds), *Afro-Regions: The Dynamics of Cross-Border Micro-Regionalism in Africa*, Uppsala, 2008, pp. 35–52.

[47] A former Senegalese driver interviewed in 2000 when he was the caretaker of a transport company, who had left a small town in the centre of the country to settle in Dakar, repeatedly told of seeing tanker trucks passing by on the road to Mali, no longer stopping in what had been the company's stronghold for 50 years: "Even breakdowns are repaired from Dakar", he added.

In the 1990s, one of Africa's top transport specialists, the economist Xavier Godard, underlined the importance of linking international and local flows.[48] The corridor can aid the process of bringing them together provided that it is not thought of just as a fluid axis of circulation, but is also viewed as an interface space. The existence of secondary intermediate hubs, holders of relay functions (transport, logistics, trade), and the polarisation of jobs and financing is one of the conditions. On the Dakar–Bamako Corridor, the question arises of the role and future of the towns and villages located along the road axis. The life generated by the flows results in a reduction of activities toward the axis, where sustainable human settlements and the seeds of future agglomerations emerge (Koumpentoum in the region of Tambacounda, in Senegal, or Diéma and Didiéni between Kayes and Bamako, in Mali). Corridors become tools of territorial reconfiguration, offering benefits to the territories. On the one hand, there is the possibility that people will benefit from what is circulating by offering numerous goods and services (fuels, various repairs, restoration and accommodation) and, on the other, there is also the potential capacity to meet travellers' needs at the stops with food products, construction materials, energy resources (for example charcoal) and handicrafts. The growing numbers of trips made by government officials and private companies, and even private vehicles, are creating a traffic market from which the local population can benefit. Finally, being located on a corridor means having easier access to health, education and administrative services.

Another major issue is the destruction of infrastructures. Between Tambacounda and Kedougou, the axis is in poor condition, as it also is between Kedougou and the Malian border.[49] The Kayes Bridge, which spans the Senegal River, has been weakened by uninterrupted truck crossings for almost two decades, as it was not built to take such a high level of traffic. In 2016, it was even closed for reconstruction, forcing vehicles over 40 tons in weight to travel by the southern route.[50] The main explanation for this was the systematic

48   Xavier Godard, 'Transport local, transport global, quelle articulation ?' in SITRASS, *Efficacité, Compétitivité, Concurrence: la chaîne de transport en Afrique Sub-Saharienne*, Lyon-Arcueil, 1996, pp. 339–43.

49   See Boubacar Dembo Tamba, 'Le corridor Dakar–Tambacounda–Bamako via Kédougou se dégrade dans sa partie située entre Niéméniké et Moussala', *Radio Tamba Online*, 23 December 2017 <www.tambacounda.info/2017/12/23/ corridor-dakar-tambacounda-bamako-via-kedougou-se-degrade-partie-situee-entre- niemenike-moussala/> [Accessed 27 April 2021].

50   Since 2021, a second bridge over the Senegal River relieves the old bridge of part of its traffic. See Aminata Sanou, 'Inauguration du 2ème pont de Kayes: contribuer à la

overloading of heavy goods vehicles in contravention of West African Economic
and Monetary Union (WAEMU) community regulations (to which Mali and
Senegal are subject), in particular regulation 14/2055/CM/WAEMU, on the
harmonisation of standards and procedures for the control of the gauges, weights
and axle load of haulage vehicles. Overloading is often used to compensate for
low freight prices and the almost constant empty return journeys. A 2013 study
on the state of road freight transport in Senegal indicated that at the Diam
Niadio weighing site at the exit from the Dakar agglomeration, 78 per cent
of heavy goods vehicles were overloaded. The same study concluded that the
lifespan of the infrastructure has been drastically reduced (from 15 to five years).

The rail transport alternative represents one way of addressing the problem
of vehicle overloading and destruction of infrastructure. On the link between
Dakar and Bamako, however, despite repeated promises to boost use of the
line, no large-scale plan has been envisaged to permit the complete restoration
of the track or, presumably, widening it to standard gauge.[51] Moreover, there
is nothing that says that the revival of rail transport will benefit the localities
crossed or their populations. In fact, the example of the Abidjan–Ouagadougou
line, which is operated by SITARAIL, a subsidiary of the Bolloré group, shows
the opposite: a reduction in the number of stops at passenger stations and a
concentration of investment in freight trains.[52] On the Dakar–Bamako line, the
impact for the territories has been disastrous: since the takeover of operations
by private funds in 2003, residents have complained about the disappearance of
the passenger service, which was sometimes the only way available to them to

croissance économique et assurer la continuité du trafic du corridor Dakar-Bamako
!', Maliactu.net, 2 March 2021 <https://maliactu.net/mali-inauguration-du-
2eme-pont-de-kayes-contribuer-a-la-croissance-economique-et-assurer-la-conti-
nuite-du-trafic-du-corridor-dakar-bamako/> [Accessed 8 June 2021].

51   Khadim Mbaye, 'Macky Sall réitère son plaidoyer pour le développement du ferroviaire en Afrique', *La Tribune Afrique*, 25 September 2017 <https://afrique.latribune.
fr/finances/investissement/2017–09–25/macky-sall-reitere-son-plaidoyer-pour-le-
developpement-du-ferroviaire-en-afrique-751648.html> [Accessed 27 April 2021];
Michel Lachkar, 'Moderniser la ligne de train Dakar-Bamako, un projet stratégique
pour le Sénégal', *franceinfo*, 11 August 2018 <www.francetvinfo.fr/monde/afrique/
senegal/moderniser-la-ligne-de-train-dakar-bamako-un-projet-strategique-pour-le-
senegal_3054631.html> [Accessed 27 April 2021].

52   Foussata Dagnogo, 'Rail-route et Dynamiques Spatiales en Côte d'Ivoire', unpublished PhD thesis, Université de Paris 1 Panthéon-Sorbonne, 2014.

travel outside their isolated region.[53] The revitalisation of the line has not been integrated with transport/space interactions in mind, and the only underlying goal has been the fluidity of traffic between the two terminals.

Conclusion: Senegal's Corridor at the Tip of Africa

By focusing its energy on infrastructure development, particularly that of the Dakar–Bamako road axis, Senegal comes across as a country committed to change. The Dakar–Bamako Corridor is apparently a project that serves a dominant vision of the economy, in which accelerating and securing intercontinental traffic are the fundamental principles.

However, Senegal's territory lies at the 'tip of the network', at the far end of the axis from Mali, and thus from central West Africa. Policies to strengthen national infrastructure in the direction of Dakar, coupled with disagreements with The Gambia, Mali and Mauritania, have highlighted Senegal's focus on itself and contributed towards distancing it from its neighbours, to the point where international land connections remain difficult: the Tambacounda/Malian border axis was only asphalted in 1999 and there is no bridge across to Banjul in The Gambia or to Mauritania, while routes to Guinea or Guinea Bissau are few and in poor condition. Nationally, therefore, Senegal is a country that is turned towards its capital, while at a continental level it is relegated to a peripheral position that is no more favourable in terms of better integration into West African trade than that of landlocked Mali and Burkina Faso, which seem to be more in control.[54]

On the African chessboard, the question is whether the Senegalese economy can turn the advantage the location of the port of Dakar represents for international sea routes into a permanent asset, and attract global and West African

---

[53] See the two-part film by Julien Merlaud, 2007, who interviewed all the rail transport actors in Mali and investigated the entire Bamako–Kayes train route: *Bamako–Kayes Parts I–II*, film, Julien Merlaud <www.dailymotion.com/video/x4phtd_bamako-kayes-part1_news> and <www.dailymotion.com/video/x4pgyq_bamako-kayes-part2_news> [both accessed 27 April 2021].

[54] See Olivier David, 'Les Réseaux Marchands Africains face à l'Approvisionnement d'Abidjan', unpublished PhD thesis, Université Paris X, 1999 on onions from the Sahel exported to the Ivorian economic capital (more than 1,500 kilometres away); Audrey Fromageot, 'Dépasser l'Enclavement: Le Maraîchage des Savanes et l'Approvisionnement d'Abidjan', *Espace-Populations-Sociétés*, 1, 2005, 83–98, on market gardening in the savannas of southern Burkina Faso, the production of which is also intended for Abidjan (more than 700 kilometres away).

transport operators in spite of competition from other ports such as Abidjan, Tema and Lomé, and soon Nouakchott and Conakry. In addition, the trade between Dakar and Bamako makes an uneven contribution to the development of national territories. While the two cities benefit, other spaces such as landlocked urban neighbourhoods and rural peripheries remain isolated from the advantages that should come with the traffic that passes through them. The rhetoric of the structural effects of infrastructure mobilised by Senegal and donors remains wishful thinking.

Bibliography

Adey, Peter, *Mobility*, London, 2000.

Alix, Yann (ed.), *Les corridors de transport*, Cormelles-le-Royal, 2012.

Amprou, Jacky, *Crise Ivoirienne et Flux Régionaux de Transport*, Paris, 2005.

ANSD, *Situation Économique et Sociale du Sénégal en 2016*, Dakar, 2019.

Bidi, Jean Tape, 'Quelques Réflexions sur l'Existence d'un Port Sec à Bouaké en Côte d'Ivoire', in K. Fodouop and J. Tape Bidi (eds), *L'Armature du Développement en Afrique. Industries, Transports et Communications*, Paris, 2010, pp. 77–86.

Bove, Abel, *et al.*, *Le Transport Routier en Afrique de l'Ouest et Centrale*, SSATP Working Paper No. 108, Washington D.C., 2018.

Cisse, Harouna, 'La Création des Ports Secs au Mali', Communication au Séminaire International *Systèmes de Transport de Marchandises en Afrique de l'Ouest*, World Road Association, Ouagadougou, 13–15 June 2005.

Club du Sahel et de l'Afrique de l'Ouest, *Atlas Régional des Transports et des Télécommunications dans la CEDEAO*, Paris, 2005.

Cooper, Frederick, *L'Afrique depuis 1940*, Paris, 2008.

Dagnogo, Foussata, *Rail-route et Dynamiques Spatiales en Côte d'Ivoire*, unpublished PhD thesis, Université de Paris 1 Panthéon-Sorbonne, 2014.

David, Olivier, 'Les réseaux marchands africains face à l'approvisionnement d'Abidjan', unpublished PhD thesis, Université Paris X, 1999.

Debrie, Jean and Comtois, Claude, 'Une Relecture du Concept de Corridors de Transport: Illustration Comparée Europe/Amérique du Nord', *Les Cahiers Scientifiques du Transport*, 58, 2010, pp. 127–44.

Debrie, Jean, and De Guio, Sandrine, 'Interfaces Portuaires et Compositions Spatiales: Instabilités Africaines', *Autrepart*, 32:4, 2004, pp. 21–36.

Deiss, Herve, 'Afrique de l'Ouest: Le Portuaire Joue la Carte de la Solidarité avec les Pays Enclavés', *Ports et Corridors* <https://portsetcorridors.com/2019/ports/afrique-de-louest-le-portuaire-joue-la-carte-de-la-solidarite-avec-les-pays-enclaves/> [Accessed 27 April 2021].

Dieng, Sidy, 'Transrail. Le Plan de Sauvetage Vaut 177 milliards', *Wal Fadjri*, 16 May 2012 <http://fr.allafrica.com/stories/201205161173.html> [Accessed 27 April 2021].

Diop, Momar and Diouf, Mamadou, *Le Sénégal sous Abdou Diouf: État et Société*, Paris, 1990.

L'Essor, 'Inauguration de la Route Didiéni-Diéma: Un Boulevard sur Dakar et Nouakchott', *L'Essor*, 21–27 July 2008.

— 'Kayes Amorce son Décollage: Le Soleil se Lève à l'Ouest', *L'Essor*, 20 September 2006.

Foster, Vivien and Briceno-Garmendia, Cecilia, *Infrastructures Africaines. Une Transformation Impérative*, Paris, 2010, p. 202.

Fromageot, Audrey, 'Dépasser l'Enclavement: Le Maraîchage des Savanes et l'Approvisionnement d'Abidjan', *Espace-Populations-Sociétés*, 1, 2005, pp. 83–98.

Godard, Xavier, 'Transport Local, Transport Global, Quelle Articulation?' in SITRASS, *Efficacité, Compétitivité, Concurrence. La Chaîne de Transport en Afrique Sub-Saharienne*, Lyon-Arcueil, 1996, pp. 339–43.

ISEMAR, *Enjeux et Position Concurrentielle de la Conteneurisation Ouest-Sfricaine*, 104, 2008.

Keita-Ndiaye, R., 'Kayes et sa Région: Étude de Géographie Urbaine au Mali', unpublished PhD thesis, Université Louis Pasteur, 1971.

Lachkar, Michel, 'Moderniser la Ligne de Train Dakar-Bamako, un Projet Stratégique pour le Sénégal', *franceinfo*, 11 August 2018 <www.francetvinfo.fr/monde/afrique/senegal/moderniser-la-ligne-de-train-dakar-bamako-un-projet-strategique-pour-le-senegal_3054631.html> [Accessed 27 April 2021].

Lombard, Jérôme, Ninot, Olivier and Steck, Benjamin, 'Corridors de Transport en Afrique et Intégration Territoriale en Questions', in A. Gana and Y. Richard (eds), *Les Intégrations Régionales dans le Monde*, Paris, 2014, pp. 245–64.

Lombard, Jérôme, Steck, Benjamin and Cissokho, Sidy, 'Les Transports Sénégalais. Ancrages Internationaux et Dérives Locales', in M. C. Diop (ed.), *Sénégal (2000–2012): Les Institutions et Politiques Publiques à l'Épreuve d'une Gouvernance Libérale*, Dakar, 2013, pp. 642–71.

MacKinnon, Danny, Pirie, Gordon and Gather, Matthias, 'Transport and Economic Development' in R. Knowles, J. Shaw and I. Docherty (eds), *Transport Geographies*, Oxford, 2008, pp. 10–28.

Mareï, N and Ninot, Olivier, 'Transformation des Transports en Afrique: Vers des Systèmes à Plusieurs Vitesses?', *Questions Internationales*, 90, 2018, pp. 27–31.

Mbaye, Khadim, 'Macky Sall Réitère son Plaidoyer pour le Développement du Ferroviaire en Afrique', *La Tribune Afrique*, 25 September 2017 <https://afrique.latribune.fr/finances/investissement/2017–09–25/macky-sall-reitere-son-plaidoyer-pour-le-developpement-du-ferroviaire-en-afrique-751648.html> [Accessed 27 April 2021].

Merton, Robert King, *Éléments de Théorie et de Méthode Sociologique*, Paris, 1953/1997.

Ministère de l'Économie et des Finances, *Situation Économique et Sociale du Sénégal. Édition 2004*, Dakar, 2004.

— Ministère de l'Économie et des Finances, *Situation Économique et Sociale du Sénégal. Édition 2009*, Dakar, 2010

— Ministère de l'Économie et des Finances, *Situation Économique et Sociale du Sénégal. Édition 2011,* Dakar, 2013.

Ministère de l'Équipement et des Transports, *Mémento des Transports Terrestres du Sénégal,* Dakar, 2002.

Ministère des Infrastructures, des Transports Terrestres et du Désenclavement, *Plan Stratégique de Développement de l'AGEROUTE Sénégal 2017–2021,* Dakar, 2016

Ninot, Olivier, 'À Propos des Relations entre Transports, Territoire et Développement', *L'Espace Géographique,* 1, 2014, pp. 61–62.

Offner, J.-M., 'Les « effets structurants » du transport : mythe politique, mystification scientifique', L'Espace Géographique, 3, 1993, pp. 233–42,

Prélorenzo, Claude and Rouillard, Dominique, *La Métropole des Infrastructures,* Paris, 2009 pp. 189–99.

Sanou, Aminata, 'Inauguration du 2ème Pont de Kayes: Contribuer à la Croissance Économique et Assurer la Continuité du Trafic du Corridor Dakar-Bamako!', *Maliactu.net,* 2 March 2021 <https://maliactu.net/mali-inauguration-du-2eme-pont-de-kayes-contribuer-a-la-croissance-economique-et-assurer-la-continuite-du-trafic-du-corridor-dakar-bamako/> [Accessed 8 June 2021].

Seck, Assane, *Dakar, Métropole Ouest-Africaine,* Dakar, 1970.

Siegfried, André, 'Les Routes Maritimes Mondiales', *Les Études Rhodaniennes,* 171–2, 1942, pp. 5–20.

Söderbaum, Frederik and Taylor, Ian (eds), 'Competing Region-building in the Maputo Development Corridor', in F. Söderbaum and Ian Taylor (eds), *Afro-Regions: The Dynamics of Cross-Border Micro-Regionalism in Africa,* Uppsala, 2008, pp. 35–52.

Staszak, Jean-Francois, 'Prophéties auto-réalisatrices et géographie', *L'Espace Géographique,* 29:2, 2000, pp. 105–19.

Tamba, Boubacar Dembo, 'Le Corridor Dakar–Tambacounda–Bamako via Kédougou se Dégrade dans sa Partie Située entre Niéméniké et Moussala', *Radio Tamba Online,* 23 December 2017 <www.tambacounda.info/2017/12/23/corridor-dakar-tambacounda-bamako-via-kedougou-se-degrade-partie-situee-entre-niemenike-moussala/> [Accessed 27 April 2021].

Teravaninthorn, Supree and Raballand, Gaël, *Transport Prices and Costs in Africa: A Review of the International Corridors,* Directions in Development; Infrastructure, Washington D.C., 2009.

West Africa Trade Hub, *Coûts du Transport et de la Logistique sur le Corridor Lomé–Ouagadougou,* Report #47, no place of publication, 2012.

CHAPTER 7

Privatising the Port: Harbouring Neoliberalism in Lomé

NINA SYLVANUS

Introduction

The micro-nation of Togo is one of the poorest countries in the world. Situated on the Gulf of Guinea, Togo's coastline is a mere 56 kilometres long. It is one of the smallest countries on the African continent, a narrow strip that stretches roughly 560 kilometres north from the coast to Burkina Faso with a population of approximately eight million. What is more, its highly protected national labour code would imply that Togo is an unattractive locale for global capital. How has this marginal place become a site of one of West Africa's leading transshipment container ports? Why is Togo so attractive to global (maritime) capital despite its lack of natural resources? And what makes Togo an 'investment destination' for new infrastructures of trade and transportation - a logistics and maritime hub at the core of a new transport corridor – notwithstanding regional competition from the ports of Tema and Cotonou, national unions and the propensity for labour to strike?

This chapter explores the political economy of Lomé harbour to illustrate why Togo, despite the aforementioned labour and economic conditions, is so attractive to global capital. Since its colonial inception, the small Togolese entrepôt nation has been an important economic frontier zone on the Gulf of Guinea, a centre for capitalist commodification and a major hub in the coastal corridor that connects Abidjan via Accra–Lomé–Cotonou to Lagos. The chapter sketches how recent shifts in port governance – the transformation of the old state-centric port system to the new privatised port - have left a vacuum for (corporate) capital to fill, while limiting the capacity of the state and labour to place restrictions upon it.

A theory of the south story, this chapter analyses the relationship between Togo's postcolonial past and the neoliberal present. It starts from the premise that if we want to understand the port's current conjuncture we must move beyond contingent explanations of the present to capture *how* the history of the *longue durée* works itself out as the history of capital and the history of the modern state. In so doing, the chapter argues for a political economic explanation that shows *why* the counterintuitive of the port's unlikely success has occurred in the way that it has.

Received Explanations

In Togolese popular discourse, the media, the milieu of national and expat port professionals, as well as scholarly work, four existing species of explanations-ecological, geographical, global financial and political economic - describe the phenomenon of the port's success.

Ecology

Perhaps the most common explanation given by World Bank technocrats, the Togolese Port Authority, the media and Togolese citizens that accounts for the success of the Lomé port concerns its *naturalness*. "Our port is the only natural deep-water seaport on the coast between Senegal and Angola", said the head of the port authority's communications department, to an audience of Burkinabe traders visiting the harbour in August 2017. "Other ports need expensive dredging if they want to berth bigger ships with more cargo", he continued with no uncertain pride, "but our port is the only port in the region that can handle the new megaships". The port authority's ecological explanation for being the first container port in West Africa is echoed by the private corporations that operate the two container terminals, the press, as well as ordinary Togolese. For example, an expatriate manager explained to me that a key reason for investing in Togo was indeed techno-ecological: "The natural draft is 14 metres, we only had to dredge minimally." Similar explanations on the implication of the deep water can be found both in the local and international press: 'Lomé, the first container port in West Africa... the only natural deep-water port in the region, and currently the only port capable of handling the third generation of cargo ships'.[1] It also features in World Bank reports and feasibility studies. For the technocrat, the media, the professional and the port bureaucrat, the techno-ecological explanation was one of the critical reasons the port is significant today.

---

[1]   Nadoun Coulibaly, 'Togo: Une Plateforme Logistique pour Désengorger le Port de Lomé', *Jeune Afrique*, 11 June 2019 <www.jeuneafrique.com/mag/786032/economie/togo-une-plateforme-logistique-pour-desengorger-le-port-de-lome/>.

Accounts by ordinary Togolese were especially poignant, not least for the way nature assumed a special quality that appeared to make Togolese subjects who they are in space and time. "It's nature's gift to us", said a taxi driver when I asked him why the port had become so big in recent years as we could see the massive crane infrastructure looming on the horizon. A trader in the market also commented on the ecological dimensions, namely the 'nature' of both port *and* nation: "Togo is a small country. It's poor. We don't have gold or oil like Ghana, but we have been blessed with our port… it's naturally deep and we have trade." As Togolese of different walks of life reflected upon their national port, the resort to the ecological and the natural was potent. For the trader, nature indeed had two sides: the nature of the country (i.e. ecological) and the nature of the nation (i.e. sociological). The port thus appeared to link the two sides of nature, both its ecological dimension and the sociological reality of a small nation bereft of natural resources. What makes the Togo port intrinsically Togolese in this account is 'our nature' in the dual sense of the term.

Geography

If the small size of a country has the capacity to naturalise the intrinsic nature of Togo, its geographical position places it strategically in the West African region. 'Togo, the Gateway to West Africa', is a slogan the government frequently uses to advertise Togo's strategic location to, and in, the world. One such *mise en scène* of the port's geographic advantage was the African Union's maritime summit, recently held in Togo; here the harbour was presented as 'the only port on the West African coast from which you can get to several capitals in one day'.[2]

The geographical explanation is also common to the discourse and the logic of the shipping lines as they seek to secure regional hubs for the transshipment of their cargo. Indeed, the Mediterranean Shipping Company (MSC), the world's second largest shipping line, has made Lomé the centre for their transshipment to the subregion. The strategic advantage of the Gulf of Guinea location, as the company's director in Togo explained, is that it "allows controlling regional cargo flow, reduce transit time, and regulate port congestion". For MSC, the Lomé Container Terminal (LCT), a joint venture between MSC's subsidiary TIL and China Merchants Port (CMP), serves as a high-capacity hub for its fleet of feeders that go from Lomé to Lagos and Port Harcourt, Cotonou, Tema and Takoradi, Abidjan and San Pedro, Monrovia and Freetown as well as Libreville, Luanda and Durban. Explaining this system of transshipment, whereby so-called

---

[2]   'Protect Our Oceans' Summit, Lomé, Togo, 15 October 2016 <www.african-union-togo2015.com/en/togo/opportunites>.

motherships from Europe and Asia arrive in Lomé, he recalls the techno-ecological advantage of the container port terminal, namely its "depth of nearly 16.6 metres" that accommodates "large ships of more than 360 metres length". Indeed, for the shipping professional, the significance of the geographical fuses with the technical and the ecological.

Then too, there are everyday explanations Togolese give about the way they relate to their country's geography, and thus to the world. Echoing the trader's comment about the smallness of Togo and its capacity for trade, many spoke about the necessity to engage with neighbouring countries.[3] "We have no choice but to be open to the world, to Europe, to China, but also to be connected to the sub-region", said an accountant. For him, Togo's economy was tied to geography: "without Burkina Faso and other landlocked countries in the Sahel, and Benin, Nigeria and Ghana, we couldn't exist economically", he concluded. Others, still, spoke of the country's historical triangulations, namely the Black Atlantic and subsequent colonial economies of extraction. While the geographical explanation of the Togo port phenomenon appears straightforward, if not deterministic, the global financial account takes us to a different scale.

Global Finance

A French financial director with a decade-long experience in the African maritime sector explained the Lomé port phenomenon to me by way of its financialisation. Because port infrastructures are especially capital intensive, there is a great deal at stake, not least in relation to how multinational corporations assemble financial capital for maritime investments. "Corporations hate government backed loan arrangements in developing countries", he began to explain. For him, the financial capital that foreign corporations had effectively mobilised and drawn into the privatised concessions of the Togo port was the quintessential example of how to create the possibility of a magnet effect. Each of the three corporations that had obtained the operating rights to the concessions for 30 plus years – namely, the Swiss terminal operator TIL, the French group Bolloré Africa Logistics, and the Spanish maritime group Boluda - used

---

3   This trade economy explanation is not unique to Togo. It is an effective argument micro-nations have successfully mobilised around the world. The most potent example is Singapore, where the government popularised the term 'small red dot' as in Singapore is just a small red dot on the (geopolitical) map, without natural resources, hence they had to be resourceful. But of course this is said from a position of economic domination in the region.

a distinct financial model. TIL utilised multilateral financial institutions and development banks for the construction and commercial exploitation of Lomé Container Terminal (LCT); later, it also drew on Chinese corporate state capital. Bolloré, by contrast, used its own corporate holding to finance the infrastructural and logistical upgrading of Togo Terminal (TT). Finally, the tugboat operator Boluda used a mix of corporate and commercial capital to acquire the operating rights for its lucrative concession. For the maritime finance expert it was the confluence of these three models of port finance that made Lomé a success.[4]

The financial model of the port concession was a necessary condition to revitalise and increase the port's influence in the region; this, in the absence of the state's capacity to leverage capital, and, importantly, to financialise capital amidst fiscal deficit and debt loan repayments. Indeed, the financialising of the Togo port was advantageous to a Togolese government that was, on the one hand, relieved of the commercial risk and financial liability of operating the port, while, on the other, extracting revenue from the concessions through tariffs, royalties and taxation. The financialisation of the port placed Togo firmly on the map of global trade and shipping. A recent IMF report, for instance, praised the role of the port in relation to growing GDP while emphasising the potential for future growth of Togo as a regional logistical hub and a dynamic financial centre. Thus, according to this explanation, it was global finance that created the conditions for the Togo port phenomenon.

The global financial explanation also resonates with scholarly work. For example, African ports have been described as 'sites of financial innovation'.[5] In the case of Tema's multilateral funding context, Brenda Chalfin suggests that two types of capital, namely development capital and commercial capital, underwrite each other, not least by combining the logics of 'extraversion and statism'.[6] In Togo, by contrast, the state does not participate in the commercial governance of the concessions, nor in the financing of the port. A port manager in Lomé made this clear: "The last thing you want is a joint-venture with a national port authority slowing down each and every decision you need to make, it's a nightmare." This was said on the basis of first-hand experience, acquired at several container ports in Africa and the Middle East where the national port authority was part of the joint venture that managed the container terminals. In Togo, government bureaucracy did not interfere with the decision-making

---

4   Whether these three models were developed in this specific context, which would suggest that Lomé was precisely their experiential ground, is an open question.
5   Brenda Chalfin, 'Recasting Maritime Governance in Ghana: The Neo-Developmental State and the Port of Tema', *Journal of Modern African Studies*, 48:4, 2010, p. 585.
6   Ibid.

processes of the port concessions. Instead, the Togolese state has retreated from the port as a passive landlord that administers the land while extracting rents from its privatisation.

Political–Economy

From an analytical perspective, the most significant explanation of the port's success is the political economic story. While other accounts merely offer functional explanations, the political economic account exceeds in importance, not least because it has different dimensions. Firstly, it concerns the retraction of the state and the political vacuum; secondly, it has to do with the privatisation of the port; and, thirdly, it relates to the discourse of informal transactions.

State Retraction

From the perspective of those Togolese who have long worked in the port system, the transformation of the harbour has to do with the neoliberal moment: "Before they liberalised the port, there was solidarity and hierarchy: it was Togolese and we worked together", summarised the driver of a medium-sized logistics company. The freight-forwarding company he worked for was one of the few that had maintained national ownership in the aftermath of the crisis of the state – that critical moment of the 1990s when non-state actors stepped into the political void of state retraction.[7] In fact, his company was created in the early 1990s, at a time when a strike had paralysed the port for almost a year amidst political crisis and state violence. As ships abandoned the harbour and the port city was emptied of its residents (fleeing the army's attack on an interim government that had temporarily stripped the president-dictator of its power), Eyadéma incentivised citizens to recapture port activity. Today, his company struggled to maintain its position in a market increasingly dominated by international corporations. "In the past", he further explained "it was buzzing, there was work, lots of it, but now? the multinationals have taken over." The view of this driver, who, like many, had seen his livelihood diminished and threatened in contradistinction to the promise of democracy and liberalisation, was reflected by many in the maritime industry (private sector and public employees, low-wage earners and top managers alike).

The retraction of the state is significant as a political economic explanation as to why the Togo port is a successful exception. At its most fundamental, state retraction is the complement to financialisation. Indeed, financialisation would not be possible without the withdrawal of the state from the management of the

---

7   Charles Piot, *Nostalgia for the Future: West Africa after the Cold War*, Chicago, 2010.

harbour. From the perspective of corporate capital, the withdrawal of the state allows for the emergence of private indirect governance, a form of 'privatised sovereignty'[8] in which state actors concede their authority to non-state actors, namely corporations. Accordingly, the capacity to run a large and effective port is made possible by virtue of financialising the port in the political vacuum. The political vacuum gets the state out of the way, and therefore capital can lay its claim.

This neoconservative argument is not new. Nor is it specific to the African continent. However, it is an argument that economists have long used to celebrate the withdrawal of the state as the necessary condition that allows free range to capital, which, in turn, creates the possibility for capital to operate a successful entrepreneurial operation. This corporate argument is hardly echoed in Togolese ordinary discourse. However, it genuinely resonates with the views of corporate port managers. Many of them believe that for a corporation to work in a country like Togo where skilled labour is scarcer, it best to not have the state intervene. Togo offered just the right kind of environment where the state gets sufficiently out of the way for corporations to open a space for, and to protect, various projects of corporate expansion; after all, corporations are there to make money.

This political economic explanation of the political void is echoed in the scholarly literature on the so-called shrinking of the state.[9] Charlie Piot[10] has described the evisceration of the Togolese state in the context of the political crisis of the 1990s. For Piot, the unravelling of the Eyadéma authority complex must be understood in relation to the end of the Cold War – i.e. the moment when Western aid was terminated and the regime was pressured to liberalise the political sphere. As national structures unravelled amidst market liberalisation, this 'post-Cold War moment'[11] became the critical turning point in the organisation of political power. For Piot, reminiscent of Foucault,[12] power shifted from a vertical patrimonial state to a horizontal neoliberal state, turning into a regime that was rooted in the 'logic of the market' and the 'rationality of the

---

8   Achille Mbembe, 'On Private Indirect Government', in *On the Postcolony*, Berkeley, 2001, pp. 66–101.

9   Jean-François Bayart, *L'État en Afrique: La Politique du Ventre*, Paris, 1989; Jean-François Bayart, Stephen Ellis and Béatrice Hibou, *The Criminalisation of the State in Africa*, Bloomington, 1999.

10 Piot, *Nostalgia for the Future*; Charles Piot, *The Fixer*, Durham, 2019.

11 Piot, *Nostalgia for the Future*, p. 19.

12 Michel Foucault, *The Birth of Biopolitics: Lectures at the College de France, 1978–1979*, Michel Senellart (ed.), translated by Graham Burchell, New York, 2008, p. 49.

commodity form'. This new political moment under neoliberalism paved the way for 'private indirect government'.[13] And it is in this space, where capital gets financialised, that corporations can do exactly what they want.

Privatisation

Another explanation is given from a scholarly perspective, the view of organic intellectuals and global technocrats. For Beatrice Hibou,[14] privatisation is the dialectical complement of the retraction of the state and the political vacuum. This, of course, is a cherished argument that World Bank technocrats have long advanced as they pushed African governments into modernising their outdated (or 'failing') port infrastructures. The need for privatisation was confirmed by many Togolese in the port system. Consider a supervisor at Lomé Container Terminal who acknowledged the benefit of privatisation: "The port had to be modernised, it was all falling apart... we badly needed the investment to privatise... the state is incapable of running the port, it was completely dysfunctional." The managing director of a tug boat company echoed the supervisor's view by confirming the port's operating deficit: "When we obtained the concession for managing the port's towage and mooring services in 2017, it was operating at a loss." One of the tug boat captains, a Togolese who had previously worked for the state-run towage service added critical nuance as he spoke about the lack of maintenance and theft that had made what should be a highly lucrative business into a deficient operation: "The tugboats weren't properly serviced ... engines would break down and spare parts were often unavailable and required a lengthy bureaucratic process to order." A high-ranking employee at the port authority agreed with the captain's assessment: "One day, we caught a guy with his *zemidjan* (taxi-moto) filling his empty tank from the tug boat's gasoline container! We fired him. But there are many other instances, and that's why things weren't working before the harbour was privatised." Still, another praised the competition and alleged efficiency that privatisation brings to the Togo port sector: "African governance is not conducive to port efficiency", said this Togolese private sector employee. For him, 'African governance' ought to be replaced by corporate governance, namely its alleged structure of accountability (i.e. structures that he considered incompatible with the former).

Many Togolese considered the privatisation of the port as a good thing, if not the primary reason behind the success of a harbour that ought not to be especially

---

13   Mbembe, 'On Private Indirect Government'.
14   Beatrice Hibou, 'From Privatising the Economy to Privatising the State', in B. Hibou (ed.), *Privatising the State*, New York, 2004, pp. 1–46

successful or important. This view resonates with the technocratic-developmentalist explanation for port privatisation. By World Bank measures, African port governance has essentially been deemed deficient for reasons that range from port congestion, outdated infrastructures to managerial failure. In Togo, as elsewhere, World Bank technicians prescribed the bank's favoured 'landlord model' to structurally adjust, i.e. liberalise, the port for greater efficiency. While the Togolese state began to privatise the port according to the Bank's model during the early 2000s, large-scale private investments in the container port's infrastructure did not materialise until the early 2010s. As foreign companies took over port operations, the port authority's role was scaled back to basic administration as per the landlord model. The result was the privatisation of state function for the said benefit of national development.

Informal transactions

Some see informal transactions as an important variable that can facilitate the success of a port. There are two dimensions to the discourse of informal transactions: firstly, informal transactions understood as informal economy (ordinary licit informal transactions), and, secondly, informal transactions understood as bribery and corruption (illicit informal transaction).[15] Both occur, and both are said to spark and energise economies. Discursively these two are fused but analytically they are of course separate. An accountant at a logistics company claimed that most companies in Togo, foreign and national, have special accounts for what he called "extra expenses". Such expenses, or informal transactions, can range from the transfer of monies to the ruling party during elections, sending beverages for the annual Evela wrestling contest in the northern city of Kara (the birthplace of the Gnassingbé 'clan'), paying off union leaders for settling labour resistances, to paying bribes to win bids for port concessions. In the port, he suggested, such informal transactions are widely enacted if they do not constitute the norm: "Everyone knows about Bolloré mingling in our 2010 election ... we know for a fact that the president has a 20 per cent share in Togo Terminal [i.e. Bolloré]", he exclaimed without the slightest hint of hesitation. What this accountant described is often thought of as corruption (indeed, in 2018, French industrial magnate Vincent Bolloré was arrested in Paris over corruption charges in the acquisition of container terminals in the ports of Lomé and Conakry). But, from the perspective of capital it is thought of as the ordinary cost of

---

[15] On the renaming of the illicit in the context of law laundering, see John L. and Jean Comaroff, 'Law and Disorder in the Postcolony: An Introduction', in J. L and J. Comaroff (eds), *Law and Disorder in the Postcolony*, Chicago, 2006, pp. 1–56.

business. According to this corporate argument, the ordinary cost of business (i.e. corruption taken as illegitimate distribution) actually facilitates the port as a highly successful operation. If there were no such costs, it would be much harder for corporations like Bolloré to get labour to do what it wants, or, for that matter, to get government licences when needed.

The explanation of shadow transactions facilitating capital flow in the Togo port economy was shared by a local legal counsel: "There are always ways around the law. You can see this all over the world, in some places it's called corruption, in others it's called a fee of consolidation", he stated sharply. Though highly critical of Bolloré's dealings in the Lomé port, he nonetheless acknowledged that informal transactions can get around labour and capital blockages, such that payouts guarantee maximum profitability. Indeed, from the perspective of those who see the port as an efficiency problem, the payment of secondary order costs constitute a form of capital management that makes the harbour functional to the logic of capital accumulation. Of course, this is not unique to Togo. Though compliancy regulations have changed the conduct of business in a shipping industry with long-standing monopoly systems,[16] customary pay-off transactions, and various practices of financial compensation, the odd corruption case breaks the news ever so often.[17] Indeed, the recent example of German shipowners taking multi-million euro bribes from a Danish marine paint manufacturer is a case in point.[18] Thus, the question of how tightly secret commissions are governed by the law, as people rarely get arrested for insider trading or malfeasance, remains a murky one. In short, what these examples illustrate is that secondary payments facilitate the wheels of capital and therefore make possible things that otherwise trigger blockages in legal and regulatory systems.

[16] The March 2017 Big Box Club meeting, an exclusive club of shipping magnates, was intercepted by the FBI on the suspicion of antitrust violations. On the issuing of subpoenas by the US Department of Justice to the CEOs of the world's largest shipping lines, see: JOC, 'US antitrust regulators raid Box Club meeting', JOC, 20 March 2017 <www.joc.com/maritime-news/us-antitrust-regulators-raid-box-club-meeting-serve-subpoenas_20170320.html> [Accessed 27 April 2021].

[17] On corruption, the HR director of a major European container terminal recounted to me how in the age of pre-compliancy it was standard practice for suppliers of personal protection equipment (hard hats, steel-toe boots, overalls) to throw lavish parties for the port's purchasing department. The latter's managers were said to wear the most elegant suits in the port.

[18] Martin Kopp, 'So Lauft das Korrupte Geschaeft mit den Schiffsfarben', *Hamburger Abendblatt*, 8 August 2016 <www.abendblatt.de/hamburg/article208374737/So-laeuft-das-korrupte-Geschaeft-mit-den-Schiffsfarben.html>.

Taken together, the different versions of political economic explanation of the port's success – the first emphasising the retreat of the state and the political vacuum, the second emphasising privatisation, and the third emphasising informal transactions – constitute three pieces of a broader category of neoliberal political economy that we shall return to in the fourth part of this chapter. The next section seeks to assess in what measure the four existing species of explanations (ecological, geographical, global financial and political economic) are in fact necessary, incomplete and/or partial.

Received Explanations, Revisited

Ecology Revisited

The harbour's natural deep seawater characteristic *is* a necessary condition for the port to have achieved its current glory. Lomé is the only natural deep-water harbour with a draft of 16.6 metres, which places it ahead of its immediate competitors, specifically the neighbouring ports of Cotonou (Benin) and Tema (Ghana). Indeed, some of the large container ships that use the Lomé port simply cannot enter its Benin counterpart; still, others are constrained to stay at anchorage off the coast until the port's access channel becomes navigable with tidal changes.

When travelling on a fully loaded medium-sized container ship from Lomé to Cotonou, I witnessed the significance of the port's draft first hand.[19] Our ship had left the Lomé docks several hours late due to last-minute changes in cargo-loading procedures. The captain, hence, was anxious to reach Cotonou in time for the ship's allotted berthing window; he was especially concerned about the effects the tidal change would have on the draft of the navigation channel that leads into the port.[20] A captain's biggest fear, I learnt, was not bad weather but a ship hitting the seabed running aground. Throughout the six-hour long journey, he was busy calculating the commensurability of the ship's draft with the depth of the port access channel. And incommensurable it was. By the time we reached Cotonou, the harbour master instructed a visibly irritated captain to spend the

---

[19] I wish to thank MSC, and particularly MSC's managing Togo director Grégory Krief, for allowing me to embark as a passenger on MSC *Angela*. I am deeply grateful to the ship's crew, in particular its captain, Predrag Petzi.

[20] To wit, there are three types of drafts: first, the ship's draft (a measure of the minimum depth of water a ship can safely navigate); second, the draft of the port's access channel (i.e. the channel depth); and, third, the depth of the port basin at dock (i.e. basin depth).

night at anchorage. Not only was the captain unhappy to not keep to the ship's schedule (anticipating further delays in the next port of Lagos, a harbour notoriously known for congestion and long dwell-times), but he was also wary of the risk of piracy with the recent surge in this area of the Gulf of Guinea.[21] By contrast, in Togo – a low-risk piracy zone - large container ships do not encounter delays related to draft.

From this perspective, the ecological explanation of the deep-water characteristic of the Togo port holds true. However, it is not a sufficient condition. Nor is it the only reason accounting for its success. Certainly, a deep-water port with a restrictive state would not produce the effect that has been produced in Togo. What is more, the new Tema terminal with its dredged 16-metre draft is likely to displace Lomé's position as the first container port in West Africa.[22] In sum, the functionalist explanation of natural deep-water is insufficient in accounting for the port's success.

Geography Revisited

Government and corporate discourse ascribe the Togo port phenomenon to its strategic geographical position. Indeed, the geographic explanation also constitutes a necessary condition but it is not a sufficient one. For sure, Lomé is geographically well positioned at the core of critical coastal and hinterland transport corridors: namely, the Abidjan–Lagos Corridor, the Lomé–Ouagadougou Corridor, and the Lomé–Niamey Corridor. But there is much competition between ECOWAS (Economic Community of West African States) member states over the control of trade with Sahelian countries.[23] For example, the Niger mining industry depends especially on the Cotonou transport corridor, whereas Burkina Faso relies on both the corridors of Lomé and Tema. But Lomé, unlike Abidjan, does not have a railway connection to Ouagadougou despite recent governmental efforts to attract investors for the 760-kilometre

---

21   According to a 2019 Commercial Crime Services (ICC) report, the Gulf of Guinea was the leading zone of piracy attacks in 2018. For a detailed account, see <www.icc-ccs.org/piracy-reporting-centre/request-piracy-report> and <https://iccwbo.org/media-wall/news-speeches/pirate-attacks-worsen-waters-off-gulf-guinea/>.

22   A joint venture between Ghana Port Authority (GPHA) and the corporate giants APMT and Bolloré. The new container port is managed by Meridian Port Services (MPS), in which all three shareholders have stakes.

23   Paul Nugeent, 'Africa's Re-Enchantment with Big Infrastructure: White Elephants Dancing in Virtuous Circles?', in J. Schubert, U. Engel and E. Macamo (eds), *Extractive Industries and Changing State Dynamics in Africa: Beyond the Resource Curse*, London & New York, 2018, pp. 22–40.

railway project (Lomé–Cinkassé).[24] Similarly, Ghana is expected to begin the Eastern Railway line project that will link coastal ports to inland dry ports.[25]

The geographic explanation, therefore, is both partial and reductionist. Indeed, if another port could be put in the next country and had the same conditions it would, in all likelihood, displace Lomé. Thus, again, the explanation of Togo's geography is a supporting one but not a sufficient one. It certainly adds value to the port but it does not explain why it has become the first container port in West Africa. By contrast, the geography of a port like Walvis Bay in Namibia is critical because Botswana is landlocked.[26] Similarly, the geographical explanation of Durban port is a critical one because there is no other access for KwaZulu-Natal and Lesotho.

Global Finance Revisited

The resort to global finance and foreign direct investment in port infrastructure and technology was both critical and necessary to the harbour's success. Global finance is irrefutably a necessary condition, but its capacity to act as a magnet effect would be much less effective in a political context where the state looms large in the economy of the port. For foreign direct investment to be as effective as it has been in Togo requires an eviscerated state that provides free range to capital, namely attractive tax, property and investment codes. But the Togolese state is not entirely withdrawn, much to the dismay of corporations. Indeed, the foreign companies that operate the port have complained about the restrictiveness of labour laws and residence regulations.

Political Economy Revisited

The political economic explanation is the most viable of the four species of explanations because it gestures towards a new political moment under neoliberalism. What is more, the three elements of political economy capture the structural aspects of the postcolonial past in the neoliberal present.

---

[24] On the Togo railway project, see Togo Invest <https://togoinvest.tg/en/the-projects/rail-project/>.

[25] For details on Ghana's Eastern Railway, see <https://dailyguidenetwork.com/2-2bn-eastern-railway-project-ready-to-take-off/>.

[26] The new $400 million China-backed container terminal at Walvis Bay port was opened in August 2019. Built by China Harbor Engineering Company (CHEC), the port's total capacity today is 750,000 TEU. Lomé Container Terminal alone has a capacity of 2.2 million TEU. On the new Walvis Bay port see 'New China-Backed Africa Terminal Unveiled', in *Port Technology*, 5 August 2019.

State Retraction Revisited

There is evidence that before the state withdrew from the management of the port, its structure was less rhizomatic: "There was a system in place, a system with clear hierarchies, but now?" lamented a high-ranking customs officer with 20 years of experience in the old state-centric port. Indeed, the work of customs has increasingly been outsourced to non-state entities from cargo scanning to GPS tracking technologies. As container movement is securitised through satellite vehicle tracking systems, technologies of logistics slip into an instrument of privatised governance à la Mbembe.[27] Thus, with the deinstitutionalisation of the state and state sovereignty, corporate capital has inserted itself into the political void of the state, effectively paving the way for capital to experiment. Its effects were acutely felt by those working in the private port sector. Freight forwarders and transport union members were worried about the future of their businesses, which had long generated reliable returns. Now, they feared being sidelined by the foreign logistics companies that private terminal operators privileged, had stakes in, if they did not own them altogether.

Privatisation Revisited

It is common cause for those working in the harbour system to attribute the transformation of the port to its radical privatisation: "They sold our port", said a retired employee of a shipping agency. While some agreed that the port had to be privatised, namely because its dated infrastructure required the kind of financial investments the port authority was unable to generate, others were suspicious about the way this had occurred. Still, others were angry that the authorities had not managed the port properly. In short, there is ample evidence that Togolese were ambivalent about the port's success; they questioned who was benefiting from its makeover, not least because some Togolese port businesses were receiving less, instead of more, cargo. In effect, their assessment captured the apparent contradiction of the port's success: How could Lomé be at once West Africa's first transshipment container port - as per the standard measure for containerised cargo, the twenty-foot Equivalent Unit (TEU) - with the highest regional cargo throughput, yet have less domestic cargo to transact in?

This explanation is underscored by what dockers had to say about the rationalisation of their labour amidst privatisation and global capital's latest quest to replace labour by intelligent, semi-automated machines. Crudely aware of their inherent

---

[27]   In her pioneering 2010 work on cargo inspection at Tema port, 'Recasting Maritime Governance in Ghana', Brenda Chalfin has powerfully shown how a process of public knowledge making has morphed into a process of enclosure.

disposability under current conditions of containerisation, they blamed the privatisation of the port's stevedoring operations and the port authority's diminishing power: "Why isn't the port helping us to get work at Bolloré, at LCT? and why are our wages so much lower than those paid by the terminals?" questioned a docker with 25 years' port experience. The docker's poignant observation points to the port authority's (in)ability to manage the fluctuating (i.e. diminishing) labour demands of the privatised port. This had two effects: first, it suggests changes in the management of labour regimes and their reorganisation along new metrics of optimisation; second, it points to the erosion of the port authority's power. Indeed, the influence of new ownership structures and foreign investment was ubiquitous.

Informal Transactions Revisited

If secondary order costs were seen to have enabled the control of the private in the same of the public, they are also the result of the end of the *longue durée* of privatisation. As new forms of capital management were rationalised as ways of tackling the port's inefficiency, private indirect governance was met with both suspicion and critique. The Togolese press had long reported on port mismanagement, including the embezzling of public funds: from stories of port monies going into private bank accounts of politically-connected businessmen, illicit payments to shadow companies, the over-invoicing of port services to the explosive uncovering of the Bolloré corruption scandal. But does this narrative of illegitimate, yet necessary or otherwise economically productive, distribution amount to a convincing account of its historical workings? To wit, the political-economic explanation of the port's transformation has multiple dimensions. While in Togo the state was never a Keynesian social-democratic state per se – i.e. not a metropolitan state but rather a (post/colonial) 'state *sans* nation'[28] – its tendency to reverse from a function of the state collecting private funds for the collective good to one in which it distributes public funds to the private sector, is nonetheless significant.[29] In sum, changes in state function at this new political moment under neoliberalism - whence the state is no longer the sole sovereign - enabled the privatisation of the port and, hence, its ultimate success. To fully grasp how these changes came about requires historicising the present moment of privatised/neoliberal port governance.

Taken together, the four species of explanations are compelling: some due to necessary but insufficient conditions (ecological and geographical), some, in the case of the (il)licit economy, because they capture the reality of the

28 John L. Comaroff, 'Reflections on the Colonial State, in South Africa and Elsewhere: Factions, Fragments, Facts and Fictions', *Social Identities* 4:3, 1998, p. 346.
29 Jean Comaroff and John L. Comaroff, *The Truth About Crime*, Chicago, 2016.

presence, but because of their presentism they also dehistoricise a process that is profoundly historical. Therefore, the next section seeks to place the Togo port phenomenon into historical perspective. In what follows, we thus move away from a presentist argument – i.e. a view of the port's success as contingent event rather than historical product - to a dialectical account that attends to the structural processes of the longer run.

The Future in the Past: Historicising the Problem

It is no historical accident that Lomé harbour has become a major transshipment port on the African continent. Since its colonial inception, Togo has been a particularly effective economic frontier zone extracting value from its borders. In fact, it was the lucrative contraband trade with the British Gold Coast that gave rise to the Lomé port-city, which, until the late nineteenth century, was little more than a fishing village.[30] By the early twentieth century, Lomé and its roadstead port became the centre of colonial capitalism.[31] The administration of German Togoland ran an effective logistical operation from the Lomé deep-water pier where steam cranes and railway tracks handled the bulk of

[30] From 1884 to 1914, Togo was a protectorate of the German empire. For an excellent discussion of the history of the Togo–Ghana contraband trade, see Paul Nugent, *Smugglers, Secessionists and Loyal Citizens on the Ghana–Togo Frontier*, Athens, 2002; for an analysis of the production and circulation of Dutch *genever* (gin) and German *schnaps* on the Guinea coast, particularly in precolonial Ghana, see Emmanuel Akyeampong, *Drink, Power and Cultural Change: A Social History of Alcohol in Ghana, c. 1800 to Recent Times*, Oxford, 1996.

[31] The first German wharf was destroyed by a storm soon after its inauguration in 1900. By 1904, a metallic pier had replaced its wooden predecessor. Conceived by imperial civil engineers and built by forced labour, the last vestiges of the metallic pier – that German colonial relic par excellence – are still visible today. In fact, a nearby beach bar, Le Wharf Allemand, carries its name. Popular among Loméans who enjoy spending Sunday afternoons at the beach, the bar offers views of the German foundation, as well as the adjacent, more visible, structure of the French wharf. The latter was used until 1968 when the current port was inaugurated. While Togolese hold highly critical views of the French today, the German era, surprisingly, holds nostalgic currency in the Togolese imagination; this, despite Germany having used the local population as a source of both forced labour and tax revenue. For a detailed history of the German era, including a discussion of the wharf, see Peter Sebald, *Togo 1884–1914 Eine Geschichte der Deutschen 'Musterkolonie' auf der Grundlage Amtlicher Quellen*, Berlin, 1988.

the *Musterkolonie* (model colony) trade economy.[32] Not surprisingly, the Lomé wharf was the only port structure on the Gulf of Guinea that imported twice as much as it exported.[33]

The German colonial administration built roads, bridges and rail lines linking coast to hinterland, thus effectively organising its empire through an infrastructure of transportation. If the German colonial administration was primarily geopolitical, in the sense that it invested in the territorial securing of space, it was also what geographer Deborah Cowen[34] has called 'geoeconomic' in its effort to secure economic spaces, markets and commodity flows by controlling key transportation corridors. This geoeconomic shift echoes the way global corporations and investors today have been securing long-term lease agreements (i.e. concessions) along the world's key shipping routes. The history of the Lomé port fits well into this model, first as a site for colonial capital to extract and secure territorial space, and later for corporate capital to experiment at the geographical margin.

Multi-modal *avant la lettre*, as it were, the German port infrastructure remained roughly intact until the late 1920s when it was modernised by the French colonial/mandate administration.[35] The French structure featured a longer wharf with additional steam cranes and rail tracks. However, by the

---

32 Bearing the traces of a crude history of colonial exploitation and forced labour, the old Prussian railway system eventually connected the pier to Aného, the initial capital of the German protectorate. Located roughly 45 kilometres east of Lomé, Aného was the centre of the booming palm oil trade that German traders had come to control once they had sidelined the powerful trading clans of the coast. See Nicoué Lodjou Gayibor, 'Histoire des togolais, des origines à 1884', *Presses UB, Lomé* 1 (1997), 13–68; Sebald, *Togo 1884–1914*. With the emergence of Lomé as the new commercial centre of German Togoland, steamship liners abandoned the Aného surf port. The latter was located off the shores of Aného, which meant that goods had to be transferred from the steamer on to smaller pirogues for coastal transport across the dangerous surf. This process was not only dangerous and time-consuming, but it also led to the loss of merchandise and people (further railway lines were built by Prussian engineers to transport cotton, rubber and cocoa).

33 Nicoué Lodjou Gayibor, 'Histoire des togolais, des origines à 1884', *Presses UB, Lomé* 1 (1997).

34 Deborah Cowen, *The Deadly Life of Logistics: Mapping Violence in Global Trade*, Minneapolis, 2014.

35 Togo under French mandate was no less economically viable. If Togo under German protectorate was nicknamed *Musterkolonie*, it becomes France's *vitrine colonial*. Two factors explain its special status, firstly France had sent an elite of colonial administers to redress German Togoland and, secondly, it benefited from a particularly

late 1950s – amidst the nationalist movement and calls for independence from France – the French pier lacked the capacity to handle larger ships. Indeed, the invention of the container in the late 1950s fundamentally changed the nature of seaborn trade. As containerised shipping became the standard for the new logics of multi-modal transportation systems – along with new management systems and the 'logistics revolution'[36] - port infrastructure had to accommodate the new imperative. Subsequently, an infrastructure of deep-water berths and stevedoring cranes came to increasingly replace the manual dock labour required for break-bulk shipping. Hence was born the project for the first commercial container port of independent Togo. In 1960, Togo's first president, Sylvanus Olympio, signed an accord of technical co-operation with the German government for the construction of the deep-water seaport.[37]

Legally created on 7 April 1967, the Port Autonome de Lomé (PAL), the Autonomous Port of Lomé, was inaugurated in 1968. Designed as a free port zone that served as a major transit point for international cargo, it was initially created to handle 400,000 tons of goods per year, including the shipping of phosphates, one of Togo's major products. A symbol of commercial prosperity and independence, the national port was directed from the proud anchor-shaped building of the central port administration. Its modernist architecture captured the hopeful style of a postcolonial nation steering its economic future. Soon, the Togo free port became an important maritime frontier in the region, benefiting from the protectionist trade policies of its Soviet-leaning neighbours while pushing a pro-trade agenda.

Like other micro-states, Singapore being the most prominent example, Togo's postcolonial state had to be resourceful to make up for its lack of natural resources. Presiding over a classic entrepôt economy, it continued much of the form and structure of the colonial state, notably its ongoing ties to the metropole and a focus on extracting value from its borders, including the lucrative contraband trade. Because Togo never had a national economy, it had to Singaporianise itself by way of mobilising its geography and history of colonialism. Instead

---

lax colonial commercial policy while important economic investments were drawn into the new colony.

36 Cowen, *The Deadly Life of Logistics.*

37 But Olympio, the initiator of the port project, did not survive the port's inauguration, nor its construction. Killed in a 1963 military coup by General Gnassingbé Eyadéma, it was nonetheless Olympio who had negotiated and signed the 1960 economic-technical co-operation agreement with the German government. Executed by three German engineering companies, the construction of the port began in 1964.

of building national industries, General Gnassingbé Eyadéma (in power since 1967) made the shadow economy essentially a state imperative. Indeed, by the 1980s, the Lomé port had become a regional platform for the narcotics and arms trade, and soon Togo was characterised a 'shadow' and 'smuggling state'.[38] This, of course, is part of the immanence of the colonial and the history in the present.

Until the end of the Cold War, that critical moment of political rupture as we shall see below, the port provided a stable source of employment for many, ranging from low-skilled manual laborers and clerical workers in the port administration to big man style directors and customs officers. For the latter, the port also functioned as a site of unfettered personal enrichment and extraction. But it also worked as a critical site of economic redistribution, not least through the informal chain of workers (money brokers, mechanics, etc.) to the buzzing market and makers' spaces that emerged around the port. On one hand, the regime's barons had placed their people – from high-ranking customs officers and key administrators who, allegedly, helped funnel port revenues into private accounts to providing special accommodations for wealthy businessmen and women controlling various commodity trades (rice, second-hand cars, etc.) – while, on the other hand, the freight-forwarding business was thriving, and, along with it, the informal economy. During the 1970s, when export prices for phosphate (Togo's key asset) quintupled, the dictatorial state was flush with money and foreign investment. Lomé also became a financial centre with African banks establishing their headquarters in the capital.[39] However, by the mid-1980s, as world phosphate prices fell, several state-owned enterprises (the infamous ailing white elephants) had collapsed. When the World Bank ushered the Togolese government into structural adjustment programmes and austerity measures that led to the privatisation of most state-owned companies (and the opening of an export processing zone[40]), the state was essentially reorganised through the market.

---

38 Bayart, Ellis and Hibou, *The Criminalisation of the State in Africa*.
39 Togo was nicknamed Africa's 'Little Switzerland', a status that referred as much to the concentration of banks as it did to money laundering, not least for French political parties.
40 SAZOF was directed by Eyadéma's son, Kpatcha Gnassingbé. SAZOF operated under a less restrictive labour code, and authorised to hold foreign currency-denominated accounts, stipulating that Togolese must be employed on a priority basis, foreign workers cannot account for more than 20 per cent of total workforce. Though SAZOF is located in the port zone (with free trade zone sites, employing total of 12,000 people, 65 companies), the free trade zone status in fact applies all over the country, allowing investors to benefit from the free-trade zone status outside.

Meanwhile, much of the 1990s was marked by crisis, including capital flight and the termination of Western aid. During this critical post-Cold War moment, which Piot[41] has described as a moment of radical rupture with both the colonial and the postcolonial past, the organisation of state power/sovereignty changed. Indeed, when President-dictator Eyadéma was pressured to liberalise the political sphere by an international community that had long turned a blind eye to his strongman ways, a period of political violence and strikes ensued that brought the port to a standstill. Subsequently, ships were diverted to the neighbouring ports of Cotonou and Tema. But, ultimately, Eyadéma broke the strike by fragmenting the dock labour union on one hand, and, on the other, by incentivising the creation of new maritime businesses consigning/chartering cargo ships to Lomé.

The IMF and the World Bank soon rated the Lomé port as deficient. By the year 2000, following the bank's prescription to reform and privatise the port, an increasingly eviscerated state had ordered the harbour's privatisation by governmental decree. Soon, tenders were launched for different concessions, which ultimately would be obtained by Bolloré and TIL (i.e. MSC). In this new era of privatised governance, the splintering of sovereignty between state and corporations was palpable. When Eyadéma died in 2005 and his ambitious young son, Faure Gnassingbé, was put into power by the military,[42] the relationship between port governance, capital and the state changed further. In the post-dictatorship era, the state increasingly worked like a corporate actor concerned with asset management and the attraction of foreign direct investment – a shift that was further facilitated by the return of foreign capital and international donor monies in 2008.

The new president made the redevelopment of Togo's maritime frontier one of the centres of his political ambition. He effectively courted French, Chinese and Middle Eastern capital, while his government created further tax incentives for global port investment. But the young president and his ruling party also faced opposition from civil society over his 2010 re-election campaign. These political contestations revived earlier arguments about the unconstitutionality of Faure's ascent to power, in 2005, amidst allegations of election fraud. The president's weakness at this fragile pre-election moment was cleverly tapped into by corporate giant Bolloré. In a strategic move akin to corporate state capture, the Bolloré corporation financed and executed Faure's electoral campaign through the group's media structure (Havas). To little surprise, the container

41 Piot, *Nostalgia for the Future.*
42 Though the installation of Faure was unconstitutional (the speaker of parliament should have led a transitional government and called elections within 60 days), the transition of power was carefully planned. It notably involved the resort to the law; hence the constitution was amended to reduce the eligible age of presidency to 35.

port concession was transferred to Bolloré just prior to Faure's re-election.[43] Conceivably, this was corporate capital's effort to engage with the state in order to capture the public domain; or, perhaps, it was the effort to establish a form of corporate sovereignty over Togo's political economy *tout court*. Of course, the state was also harnessing the corporation by privatising the port and then demanding royalties. Indeed, from the perspective of the state, which had outsourced the state function of running the port, the harbour is treated much like taxation, i.e. as a site of rents.

The triangulated relationship between port governance, capital and the state played out in a different key when a tender for a second container terminal was launched in 2011. The concession was for a so-called greenfield project, which refers to the commercial exploitation of underdeveloped and, in this case, partially reclaimed, land. But this time, Bolloré was not the only contender. Bidders included the powerful shipping lines; indeed, the latter had begun consolidating their activities in the aftermath of the 2008 global shipping crisis, which resulted in the merging of the world's biggest shipping lines into powerful consortiums (the 'big alliances'), running ever bigger ships, consolidating their services while also operating their own terminals.[44] Following a long and murky bid with many twists and turns – some companies were rumoured to have exercised intense pressure on the Togolese government – it was the shipping line MSC that obtained the contract for developing and operating the US$450 million greenfield project through its subsidiary TIL. By 2014, the new terminal, Lomé Container Terminal, was inaugurated, and a new era of sovereignty, one marked by competition between corporations, began.

---

[43] In April 2018, Vincent Bolloré was arrested in France for meddling in the Togo and Guinea 2010 election campaigns. According to *Le Monde*, the allegations concerned the Bolloré group's media agency Havas, which, in exchange for lucrative container port terminal contracts, ostensibly provided below market rate services to support the election campaigns of President Faure Gnassingbé in Togo and presidential candidate Alpha Condé in Guinea.

[44] The container terminal market is complex: on the one hand, there are operators like PSA International (Singapore) and ICTS (Manila) who exclusively run terminals, while, on the other hand, there are the increasingly powerful shipping lines (Maersk, MSC, CMA-CGM, Cosco) who run their own terminals. In the shipping industry, the future and further consolidation of lines and terminal operators is intensely debated. Even though PSA is probably the most powerful terminal operator in the world (present in strategic ports like Rotterdam), the competitive advantage of shipping lines having their own terminals that serve their ships first (speed is money) appears to be the mode of the future.

The promise of multi-modal transportation systems, i.e. a containerised rail network that links the sea port to a grid of dry ports across the country, also features in the government's 2018–22 National Development Plan (NDP). Indeed, the making of Togo into a major logistics hub in the region constitutes the first of three axes the plan proposes. Poignantly, the NDP was officially launched at the recent EU–Togo Summit where no less than former IMF director Dominque Strauss-Khan (aka DSK) promoted the plan's vision and potential. When discussing the summit in relation to the scope and ambition of the new development plan, a Togolese journalist commented sarcastically: "Whose development? Come on! Faure is preparing for next year's election, there won't be *any* national development!" His critique of the current political order, what one might call *neopolitics*, cynically captures the new political-economic moment under neoliberalism. Indeed, Faure ran the country much like a corporation, surrounding himself with a team of influential presidential advisors that, in addition to DSK, also includes Tony Blair. The latter's economic development consulting has worked through the Tony Blair Institute for Global Change. And so it was Blair himself who blatantly spoke about economic opportunity at the recent Togo–UK Investment Summit in London where he praised Togo's potential to become a major logistics centre in West Africa.[45]

Togo's neopolitical moment did not just come along, just as neoliberalism does not come along and do stuff. Ultimately, by historizing, one sees that the move to the neoliberal moment is not something that has arisen by contingency. Instead, it emerges as a process of the *longue durée* in which colonialism and its complicated processes paves the way for this to happen. It is precisely for these reasons that the ecological, the geographical and the global financial explanations are merely symptomatic and contextual – i.e. a series of necessary but insufficient conditions – whereas political economy, and its three elements, is the most persuasive explanation. Not simply because they are political economy but rather because they are the dissemination of a history of the *longue durée* without which they simply look like the happenstance of capital and the state.

Conclusion

Why did Lomé become this successful port despite the odds of being located in one of the poorest and smallest countries in the world? What is more, why should this have happened in the first place? The answer to these questions has to

---

45   See Tony Blair's 16 June 2019, speech at the Togo–UK Summit: 'Tony Blair urges investors to "Go To Togo!"' <www.youtube.com/watch?v=KfiTZwe9iZc>.

do with the specific history of how global capital/ism has re/made Lomé harbour from its edges. And there is an important comparative point to be made about the way the story of Togo harbour (hence privatised port governance) fits into global patterns of how capital is shaping and securing port and transportation infrastructure elsewhere.

The restructuring of African ports and their privatisation is not unique to Togo. Nor is it new. Indeed, the wave of port privatisation began in the 1980s when World Bank analysts considered those infrastructures to be failing, prescribing port reform according to the landlord model. It is during this time that French logistical giant Bolloré snatched up the lion share of African port concessions while also acquiring various (French colonial and postcolonial) transportation companies. To wit, today Bolloré has over 20 port concessions in Africa, in addition to rail concessions and numerous transport and logistics companies. However, it is only since 2008, in the aftermath of the global financial crisis and its impact on the global shipping industry, that we see drastic transformations in the African port and logistics sector. These transformations are related to the entry of global corporate capital.[46] They hinge on two important developments: first, the consolidation/alliances of shipping lines and terminal operators; and second, the need for modernised port infrastructure to handle the new generation of container ships. The state-of-the-art logistical infrastructure at Lomé Container Terminal – notably the giant steel structure of so-called Super-Post-Panamex cranes looming behind electric fences in strange humanoid-*animalis* form – matched the imperative of global shipping.

Lomé was the first port to feature the kind of rationalised global port infrastructure that facilitates global circulation in the era of the mega ship, yet we see the same pattern emerge across the region. A case in point is the new Tema container terminal, which was built on reclaimed land and inaugurated in June 2019. Another, particularly compelling, case is the port of Cotonou. Not only is it in the process of being fully restructured and privatised, but the Cotonou

---

[46]   Certainly, the forms this has taken have fundamentally changed with Chinese capital entering the African continent, i.e. what many view as China's geopolitical securing of major transportation networks and corridors. And such perspectives have a point. Though one might wonder if instead of conceptualising China's renewed and intensifying presence on the African continent – including investments in Africa's maritime infrastructure as part of China's Belt and Road Initiative (BRI) – might not be better thought of as Chinese corporate capital *tout court*. Then too, what makes Chinese corporations such as the shipping giant COSCO, or port equipment manufacturer ZPMC different from European corporations such as MSC, TIL or Koncecrane?

port authority is currently managed by the Port of Antwerp. There are few cases in the world where a port authority is managed by a foreign entity. The Greek port of Piraeus is perhaps the most prominent example, when, in the midst of the Greek sovereign debt crisis, the Chinese state-owned shipping company Cosco acquired the Piraeus concession and a 65 per cent stake in the port authority.[47]

Might this not be a textbook illustration of the Comaroffs'[48] conceptualisation of the Global South as the critical site where the future is being anticipated, where neoliberal patterns are rehearsed and practised as deregulated capital gets to experiment? The old model of the concession gains new currency in the remaking of a global transport infrastructure. It emerges as a new site of infrastructural, logistical and financial innovation designed to facilitate the mobility of goods and capital.

Bibliography

Akyeampong, Emmanuel, *Drink, Power and Cultural Change: A Social History of Alcohol in Ghana, c. 1800 to Recent Times*, Oxford, 1996.

Bayart, Jean-François, *L'État en Afrique: La Politique du Ventre*, Paris, 1989.

Bayart, Jean-François, Stephen Ellis and Béatrice Hibou, *The Criminalisation of the State in Africa*, Bloomington, 1999.

Chalfin, Brenda, 'Recasting Maritime Governance in Ghana: The Neo-Developmental State and the Port of Tema', *Journal of Modern African Studies*, 48:4, 2010, pp. 573–98.

Comaroff, Jean and John L. Comaroff, *Theory from the South: Or, How Euro-America Is Evolving Toward Africa*, Boulder, 2011.

— *The Truth About Crime*, Chicago, 2016.

Comaroff, John L., 'Reflections on the Colonial State, in South Africa and Elsewhere: Factions, Fragments, Facts and Fictions', *Social Identities* 4:3, 1998, pp. 321–61.

Coulibaly, Nadoun, 'Togo: Une Plateforme Logistique pour Désengorger le Port de Lomé', *Jeune Afrique*, 11 June 2019 <www.jeuneafrique.com/mag/786032/economie/togo-une-plateforme-logistique-pour-desengorger-le-port-de-lome/>.

Cowen, Deborah, *The Deadly Life of Logistics: Mapping Violence in Global Trade*, Minneapolis, 2014.

Foucault, Michel, *The Birth of Biopolitics: Lectures at the College de France, 1978–1979*, Michel Senellart (ed.), translated by Graham Burchell, New York, 2008.

Gayibor, Nicoué Lodjou, 'Histoire des togolais, des origines à 1884', *Presses UB, Lomé* 1 (1997), 13–68.

---

[47] For a fascinating structural Marxist critique of the Piraeus case, see <logisticalworlds.org>.

[48] Comaroff and Comaroff, *Theory from the South*.

Hibou, Beatrice, 'From Privatising the Economy to Privatising the State', in B. Hibou (ed.), *Privatising the State*, New York, 2004, pp. 1–46.

JOC, 'US antitrust regulators raid Box Club meeting', JOC, 20 March 2017 <www.joc.com/maritime-news/us-antitrust-regulators-raid-box-club-meeting-serve-subpoenas_20170320.html> [Accessed 27 April 2021]

Kopp, Martin, 'So Lauft das Korrupte Geschaeft mit den Schiffsfarben', *Hamburger Abendblatt*, 8 August 2016 <www.abendblatt.de/hamburg/article208374737/So-laeuft-das-korrupte-Geschaeft-mit-den-Schiffsfarben.html>

Mbembe, Achille, 'On Private Indirect Government', in *On the Postcolony*, Berkeley, 2001, pp. 66–101.

Nugent, Paul, *Smugglers, Secessionists and Loyal Citizens on the Ghana–Togo Frontier*, Athens, 2002.

— 'Africa's Re-Enchantment with Big Infrastructure: White Elephants Dancing in Virtuous Circles?', in J. Schubert, U. Engel and E. Macamo (eds), *Extractive Industries and Changing State Dynamics in Africa: Beyond the Resource Curse*, London & New York, 2018, pp. 22–40.

Piot, Charles, *Nostalgia for the Future: West Africa after the Cold War*, Chicago, 2010.

— *The Fixer*, Durham, 2019.

Sebald, Peter, *Togo 1884–1914 Eine Geschichte der Deutschen 'Musterkolonie' auf der Grundlage Amtlicher Quellen*, Berlin, 1988.

CHAPTER 8

A Time for Realignment? Retrofit in the Golden Era of the Cameroonian Railways

JOSÉ-MARÍA MUÑOZ

Introduction

This chapter explores the irruption of the notion of corridor in the vocabulary of those with a stake in transport infrastructure investments in the African continent.[1] I document this process in a particular context, that of the relationship that the World Bank and the Cameroon government forged around railways in the 1970s and, more specifically, around a project to realign the Douala–Yaounde railway line, whose construction dated back to colonial era. This reconstruction project was distinctive in that it confronted both national and international participants with what a group of scholars has recently called the paradox of retrofitting.[2] Coming as it did in the shadow of substantial new construction, the project forced all parties involved to reckon with an onerous, decaying infrastructural legacy. The 1970s were a time of increasing complexity in both planning processes in general and co-ordination of financial arrangements behind large-scale investments in particular. In the transport sector, this complexity partly derived from the coexistence of alternative modes. My

1   This work draws on research funded by the European Research Council within the framework of the African Governance and Space (AFRIGOS) project (ERC-ADG-2014–670851). I could not have done it without the outstanding support I received from Shiri Alon, Bertha Wilson and other staff at the World Bank Archives. I want to thank the other members of the AFRIGOS team and my colleagues at the University of Edinburgh's Centre of African Studies for their constant intellectual stimulus. I am also grateful to the Johns Hopkins University's School of Advanced International Studies (SAIS) for hosting me as visiting scholar while I worked on this text. I would like to give special thanks to Ulf Engel, Robert McDonald, Olivier Walther and the volume's editors for their close reading of earlier drafts.
2   Cymene Howe, *et al.*, 'Paradoxical Infrastructures: Ruins, Retrofit, and Risk', *Science, Technology and Human Values*, 41:3, 2016, 547–65.

argument is that the question of intermodal transport co-ordination was at the heart of the then emergent policy construct of corridor. The centrality of co-ordinated planning in rail and road investments seems to have receded in later decades, as if the concept of corridor had outgrown it. Intermodal co-ordination has as a result received limited attention in the scholarly and policy literatures on corridors, on which the challenges of landlockedness and regional integration have loomed larger (Cissokho, in this volume)

Questions around the feasibility of the realignment of the Douala–Yaounde railway and its timing called for a kind of technical work whose duration and complexity confounded initial expectations. It was a long-drawn endeavour that took almost a decade to be settled. As we will see, the initial task of justifying a railway project largely in its own terms was reframed with the passage of time to foreground its intermodal implications. The exercise to establish a justification for a railway investment thus explicitly became a study of optimal formulas to coordinate rail and road investments. At this juncture, 'corridor' starts to pop up in the archival record as a shorthand for such a broadened approach.

Railroad competition was by no means a new problem in the region. In the 1950s, for example, the paving of the road between Douala, Cameroon's main port, and Edea, an important town on the way to Yaounde, the capital city, had a noticeable impact on the railway company's finances. The 'brutal methods' the railway company Regifercam subsequently adopted to fend off road competitors led in 1956 to a rail–road consultative conference at the Chamber of Commerce. As the doyen of transport history in Cameroon Albert Dikoumé showed, Regifercam's methods included both officially sanctioned measures (such as a drastic drop of ton/km tariffs for cocoa and the enforcement of exacting weigh limits at the Edea rail–road bridge) and outright *tracasseries* (abuses, in this case in the form of deliberately long interruptions of road traffic at level crossings).[3] A year later the government had to intervene to regulate what types of freight could be transported by road between Douala and Yaounde. Similarly, new railway construction in the 1960s and 1970s was accompanied by agreements on intermodal distribution between Regifercam and the national truckers' association. For cargo in transit to and from northern Cameroon and Chad, truckers would thereby cease to operate in the sections covered by the railway network. More broadly, of course, the colonial and independent governments had incorporated intermodal considerations in their planning of transport infrastructures. As we will see, such considerations were integral to the northward expansion

---

[3]   Albert Dikoumé, 'Les Transports au Cameroun de 1884 à 1975', unpublished PhD thesis, École des Hautes Études en Sciences Sociales, 1982, p. 148.

of the railway network, which was conceived in conjunction with an ambitious programme of road construction. With its methods of economic analysis and computational tools, the novelty of exercises like the 'corridor study' advocated by the World Bank in this case was seen to reside in the rigour and systematicity that they brought to the co-ordination of investments.

In trying to tell as richly as possible what is an intricate story, I take heed of recent calls for new research 'to document the technical work of planning and to analyse its place within historical trajectories'.[4] The World Bank archives, where the core of my research materials come from, lend themselves particularly well to such a task. When approached with the tools of critical historiography, these materials provide rare insights into the dynamics that shape planning processes. The correspondence folders that I was able to consult shed precious yet partial light into some of the negotiations, conventions, compromises, misunderstandings and conflicts that policy visions and investment decisions are made of. Archival work took place during two visits to Washington D.C. in November 2017 and December 2018.

Retrofit in the Golden Era of Cameroonian Railways

For Cameroon, as for most African countries south of the Sahara, the first substantial exchanges with the World Bank came in the late 1960s. As the then director of the newly created Western Africa Department would later explain, '[The Bank] knew relatively little about Africa and we were a new donor ... [Others] had established themselves there ...We had to establish our credibility ... We had to start with some projects ... We had to do the legwork.'[5] In Cameroon, some of the first projects through which the bank found their place in an already crowded landscape of development assistance providers concerned transport infrastructure. The Highway, Railway, and Douala Port projects were appraised in quick succession over the course of 1970. It was just the first batch of more to come.

In the conversations that led to this first loan for railways, the rehabilitation of the Douala–Yaounde line was a focal point from the start (Map 8.1). Its 308 kilometres had been constructed in two stages: 1909–1914 under German

---

4   Boris Samuel, 'Planifier en Afrique', *Politique Africaine*, 145, 2017, pp. 5–26, at p. 26.
5   Roger Chaufournier, interview by Robert W. Oliver, 22 July 1986, Oral History Program, WBGA, pp. 42–43. After the reorganisation of 1972, Chaufournier was chosen to head the Western Africa vice-presidency. He acted as the most senior regular interlocutor for Cameroonian officials in the years covered in this chapter.

domination and 1922–1927 during the period of French rule.[6] Accordingly, the railroad bore the technological marks of the time of its construction, out of which resulted its twisting alignment, severe gradients and sharp curves. By the late 1960s, the stability of a vital steel bridge (the Japoma Bridge over the River Dibamba) was imperilled by the sinking and tilting of its piers. Another source of concern were the rails, 30 per cent of which dated back to 1914 and 1926. Moreover, 143 kilometres of the line had been laid in very light rail (26–27.8 kg/m). The age and lightness of rails meant that the line had around 40 derailments in 1969, with the associated disruption and losses.[7] These inadequacies had become glaring at a point in time when, as a result of the Biafran War (1967–1970) cutting access to the Port of Lagos for nearly two years, the lion share of Chad's imports of consumer goods and exports of cotton had been diverted towards Douala via the Transcamerounais.[8] Regifercam had struggled to cope with the ensuing increase in traffic, which had continued to follow this route even after the civil war in Nigeria came to an end.

The bank showed itself open to consider involvement in the funding of the line's rehabilitation. The Cameroonian agency for implementation of railway projects was already undertaking a technical study of a potential realignment (as opposed to less fully-fledged upgrading possibilities), so it was agreed that the bank would provide funds for consultants to carry out a study of the project's economic viability. This was, however, only a small item in the loan package. Other more substantial components were urgent investments such as the reconstruction of the Japoma Bridge, the relaying of 52.5 kilometres of track, and the purchase of rolling stock.

While the US$5.2 million of the bank's first railway loan were a welcome injection of funds for the railway company, it paled in comparison with the type of investment Cameroon railways had attracted in the previous decade. Indeed, after independence (1960), the government had 'moved heaven and earth to get providers of funds' for the long-held aspiration of extending the railway network northwards.[9] These efforts crystalised in the construction of an additional 628 kilometres of railroad between Yaounde and Ngaoundere,

---

6   Albert Dikoumé, 'Les Transports au Cameroun de 1884 à 1975'.
7   Commissariat Général d'Information (CGI), *Chemin de Fer Transcamerounais,* Yaoundé, 1965; International Bank for Reconstruction and Development (IBRD), *Appraisal of a Railway Project – Federal Republic of Cameroon,* Washington, D.C., 1970.
8   Phillipe Decraene, 'Le Chemin de Fer Transcamerounais Facteur de Développement et d'Unification', *Le Monde Diplomatique,* September 1971, p. 7.
9   European Development Fund (EDF), *Cameroon 1960–1975,* Brussels, 1975, p. 13.

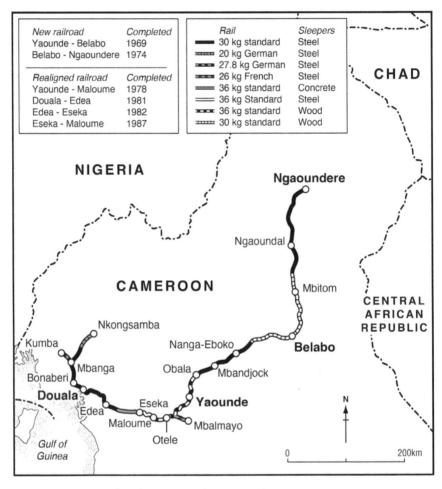

Map 8.1. Cameroon's railway network circa 1974.
(Source: World Bank, Cameroun Fourth Railway Project – Staff Appraisal Report, Washington D.C., 1979.)

which began in October 1964 and would cost some US$93.9 million. With the TAZARA project, this was one of the rare new investments in railways of the early postcolonial era.[10] The Transcamerounais, as the line was baptised, was

10   Richard Bullock, *Off Track: Subsaharan African Railways*, Washington, 2009, p. 5.
      Financed by China, the TAZARA (Tanzania–Zambia Railway Authority) project
      involved the construction of linking the port of Dar es Salaam to the Zambian town
      of Kapiri Mposhi. See: Jamie Monson, *Africa's Freedom Railway*, Bloomington, 2011.

made possible by grants and concessional loans from the European Development Fund (EDF), which contributed more than half of the funds, as well as French and US sources. An autonomous railway agency, the Office du Chemin de Fer du Transcamerounais (OCFT), oversaw the work undertaken by the Italo-German consortium between the firms Cogefar and Hochtief that won the bid for the construction contract. The first phase finished in May 1969 with the opening of traffic from Yaounde to Belabo. The line from Belabo to the railhead Ngaoundere was completed in February 1974.

The new railway's political significance was prominent from the start.[11] When construction began, President Ahidjo emphasised its potential to create 'closer ties and unity between our inhabitants'. In this view, the Transcamerounais was 'an essential foundation stone for the building of our nation', an especially useful one for political leaders who not only lacked anticolonial credentials but had embraced nationalism only in recent years.[12] In spite of repeated claims to the contrary, the national framework overshadowed the project's regional dimension, particularly the improved access to the sea for Chad and Central African Republic that derived from the project.[13] More broadly, the project was celebrated as *'le grand événement'* and a 'a great adventure'.[14] The European funders' emotions were particularly charged, perhaps not surprisingly, given the gargantuan budget of the 'Transcam', as it became popularly known, in comparison to their other investments in African railways in the 1960s and 1970s.[15] Consider the EDF coordinator's speech for the inauguration in Ngaoundéré, in which he harked

---

The construction of Transgabonais began later and, unlike the Transcamerounais and the TAZARA, was more narrowly conceived as a mining railway. See: Roland Pourtier, 'Les Chemins de Fer en Afrique Subsaharienne, entre Passé Révolu et Recompositions Incertaines', *Belgeo*, 2, 2007, pp. 1–15.

[11]   Adrian Hewitt, 'The European Development Fund as a Development Agent: Some Results of EDF Aid to Cameroon', *Overseas Development Institute Review*, 2, 1979, pp. 41–56; Veronique Dimier, *The Invention of a European Development Aid Bureaucracy: Recycling Empire*, New York, 2014, pp. 137–39.

[12]   CGI, *Chemin de Fer*, 3; Achille Mbembe, 'Le Cameroun après la Mort d'Ahmadou Ahidjo', *Politique Africaine*, 37, 1990, pp. 117–22.

[13]   Dimier, *Invention*, p. 128.

[14]   Pierre Billard, 'On Construit des Chemins de Fer au Cameroun', *Revue de Géographie Alpine*, 54:4, 1966, pp. 611–20, at p. 615, (EDF), *Cameroon 1960–1975*, p. 13.

[15]   EDF aid allocation to Cameroon's railways (EUA 64.5 million) dwarfed the sums invested in other countries' railways networks (Congo–Brazzaville 19.6 million, Côte d'Ivoire–Burkina Faso 18.2 million and Togo 14.7 million) in the 1958–1978 period. See: Hewitt, 'The European Development Fund as a Development Agent', p. 49.

back to his time as a colonial official and quoted his fellow Corsican Napoléon, and which the national press found 'brilliant and spiritual'.[16] As he put it, the new railway was "only prestigious because it was beautiful and full of hope".[17] Other international funders were equally delighted to be associated with the project (Photo 8.1). As of one of the USAID staffers, looking back on his involvement four decades later, reminded me, "it was a fairly sexy project in that it received a lot of attention ... It was also fun."[18]

Photo 8.1.
European Commission's President Ortoli and Cameroon's Minister of Planning Maïkano watching track-laying operations in the vicinity of Ngaoundéré, July 1973. (Source: © Ortoli family.)

Such a large-scale investment, with the money, time and energy it required and the accompanying prestige at stake, was bound to generate the kind of hard-to-reverse commitments that Albert Hirschman had dissected so lucidly in his coetaneous *Development Projects Observed*.[19] The paradox was that, while the new railway construction was being celebrated, the older existing line could not hide its fragility. As a USAID manager put it, 'within the promise [of the Transcamerounais]', there was 'a weak spot'.[20] That the construction of the new railroad called for the realignment of the old one did not come as a surprise to

16 'Deux Réalisations Grandioses Fêtées dans l'Enthousiasme', *Cameroon Tribune*, 11 December 1974.
17 Jacques Ferrandi, 'Inauguration à Ngaoundéré', *Le Courrier*, 30, 1975, pp. 16–17, at p. 17.
18 Interview, Washington, D.C., 28 April 2017.
19 Albert O. Hirschman, *Development Projects Observed*, Washington, D.C., 1967.
20 John Swenson, 'Le *Transcamerounais* Vu par un Américain', *Courrier de l'Association*, 17, 1973, pp. 48–52, at p. 52.

those who had promoted the Transcamerounais. In fact, one of the conditions of the EDF's financial commitment in 1964 had been that the Cameroon government should upgrade, with its own resources, the original Douala–Yaounde stretch of the railway. That this was a highly unrealistic condition in the national economy's pre-oil era hardly seemed to matter. The words of Luc Towa-Fotso, the OCFT's secretary general, capture well the ways in which both projects were intertwined: 'Admittedly, Cameroon, like the neighbouring countries relying on the Transcamerounais railway, will only get the full benefits of the heavy investments made in the Yaounde–Ngaoundere railroad when the old section Douala–Yaoundé is entirely renovated.'[21]

In the aftermath of the UK's accession to the European Community, British critics of European aid would denounce the circularity of the argument justifying both these projects. While 'the existence of the Yaoundé–Douala railway was itself a major reason for adopting the railway option [in the Yaounde–Ngaoundere section] in the first place', it had been subsequently argued that the poor performance of the new line could only be remedied by addressing the 'deterioration of the Yaounde–Douala railway to which it connects'.[22] But such Overseas Development Institute-sponsored assessments were made with the benefit of hindsight. The planning for the Transcamerounais had been carried out when the end of the 'golden era' of African railways was not quite within sight. By this 'golden era' shorthand, specialists designate the period that began after the end of the Second World War, when this mode of transport benefited from abundant and often highly skilled human resources, ease of access to finance and steady growth in traffic.[23] It was only in the 1980s that the combined effects of economic crisis and road competition led to a reckoning that the times of plenty were over.[24]

The vision behind the 'Transcam' and the financial calculus that informed the project were premised on the primacy of railways. The all-season road network inherited from the colonial era was extremely limited. Even Douala and Yaounde, the country's two main cities, had an only partially paved road connection (Douala–Edea, 90 of the total 260 kilometres) on which circulation during the rainy season was highly disrupted. In the north of the country, where

---

21 Luc Towa-Fotso, 'Apres le Deuxieme Troncon Entrée en Service en 1974 la Refection de la Portion Douala–Yaoundé', *Le Courrier*, 28, 1974, pp. 47–49.

22 Hewitt, 'The European Development Fund as a Development Agent', pp. 51–52.

23 François Dupré la Tour, 'Cent-vingt Ans de Chemins de Fer en Afrique Noire Francophone: De la Construction aux Privatisations', *Revue Generale des Chemins de Fer*, 7–8, 1998, pp. 135–51, at p. 143.

24 Michel Baranger, 'Afrique Intertropicale: L'Avenir du Rail', *Le Rail et le Monde*, 46, 1987, pp. 28–29.

there was no prospect of railway coverage, the construction of new paved roads was explicitly co-ordinated with the railway project and these roads were seen as the railway's *'prolongements routiers* (road extensions)'.[25]

> At the time of the decision to build the railway, there was no clear highway alternative. The railroad had been surveyed; hence the extension, unlike some alternative highway projects, was ready to be undertaken. It is always difficult to argue that some nebulous alternative is better than what is being proposed in concrete detail.[26]

What Hirschman wrote about the construction of the Kuru–Maiduguri railway extension in Nigeria (1958–1964) applies well to the Transcamerounais project. By the time plans for the upgrading of the Douala–Yaounde old railway began to take shape, highway alternatives were becoming less and less nebulous.

Planning for the Douala–Yaoundé Realignment

When the World Bank and the Cameroon government began negotiating what became the First Railway Project, transport planning was the responsibility of the Ministry of Planning, which underwent several restructurings and name changes in the 1960s and 1970s. The country was then in the midst of its second five-year plan (1966–1971). In spite of the public prominence of indicative planning exercises in the French tradition, the Ministry was at the time portrayed as failing to perform essential tasks in a satisfactory manner, when not neglecting them altogether.[27] 'Who studies the programmes of public investment ...? Two or three high-level technical experts cannot suffice', we read in the sombre diagnostic of a long-serving technical advisor.[28] A Ministry of Transport only came into being in 1970. It subsequently struggled to live up to its missions in policy formulation and in the co-ordination and review of investment proposals. By the end of the decade, the bank's assessment was

25 Ferrandi, 'Inauguration', 17.
26 Albert O. Hirschman, *Exit, Voice and Loyalty: Responses to Decline in Firms, Organisations and States*, Cambridge, 1970, p. 129 at fn. 1.
27 Philippe Hugon and Olivier Sudrie, 'La Crise de la Planification Africaine: Diagnostic et Remèdes', *Tiers-Monde*, 28:110, 1987, pp. 407–34.
28 Gerard Winter, 'Note sur la Planification du Developpement au Cameroun', Yaoundé, 1968, p. 2 <http://horizon.documentation.ird.fr/exl-doc/pleins_textes/pleins_textes_5/b_fdi_04–05/04042.pdf> [Accessed 27 April 2021].

damning: the Ministry of Transport had 'neither the qualified staff nor the authority to perform its functions adequately'.[29]

Other actors were going to prove important in this and successive railway projects. Created in 1962 by presidential decree, the OCFT was conceived as an implementation agency for the Transcamerounais project. During the construction of the Yaounde–Ngaoundere line, it had distinguished itself for high professional and technical standards. Heavily staffed with expatriate personnel, it was an enclave of the French office for overseas railways within the Cameroon administration.[30] Regifercam (the railway company) dated back to the post-war period, when the French colonial authorities decided to grant autonomy to the existing railway networks whose finances and management had up until then been controlled from the metropolitan centre.[31] Independence marked the beginning of the gradual 'Africanisation' of the company's management, but this proved elusive. In 1969, Regifercam employed about 3,100 people, including 41 French technical assistants holding key posts.[32] The first Cameroonian president-general manager was appointed only in 1975 and he continued to work closely with a French deputy. A programme training young Cameroonian engineers and administrators and placing them alongside expatriate managers as 'national counterparts' had mixed results and failed to achieve the levels of Africanisation expected. During the 1970s, the company kept finding it hard to attract and retain qualified, competent Cameroonian staff in positions of responsibility. By the end of the decade, the company still employed 37 French technical assistants.[33]

The renovation required in the Douala–Yaounde section of the Transcamerounais surfaced as a potential bone of contention from the early negotiations of the World Bank's First Railway Project in 1969. The

29   World Bank, *Cameroun Fourth Railway Project – Staff Appraisal Report*, Washington, D.C., 1979.
30   With the independence of most French territories in Africa, the former Office Central des Chemins de Fer de la France d'Outremer (OFERFOM) changed its name to Office Central des Chemins de Fer d'Outremer (OFEROM). In 1975, it was revamped, and renamed once more, as Office de Coopération pour les Chemins de Fer et les Matériels d'Équipement (OFERMAT).
31   Dupré la Tour, 'Cent-vingt Ans', pp. 143–44; Edy-Claude Okalla Bana, 'Les Entreprises Françaises de Travaux Publics Face au Développement Économique de l'Outre-Mer: La Mise en Place du Réseau Ferré au Cameroun', *Outre-Mers*, 98, 2011, pp. 275–98, at pp. 278–79.
32   IBRD, *Appraisal of a Railway Project*, pp. 6–7.
33   Operations Evaluation Department (OED), *Cameroon Second and Third Railway Projects – Performance Audit Report*, Washington, D.C., 1980, p. 12.

- 2 -

5.   In addition, you will review the progress of the following
highway feasibility studies carried out by Ingeroute and Lamarre Valois:

          Douala   -   Pont du Nkam

          Garoua   -   Mora

6.   You will furthermore briefly discuss with the Government the
          the improvement to the
progress of the realignment study of the central railway line (Douala -
          the Consultants OCCR - SOFRERAIL.
Yaounde) undertaken by Office Transcamerounais.

7.   Upon your return to Abidjan you will prepare a report on your
findings and recommendations concerning items 2, 3 and 4. For items 5
and 6 you will be expected to write a separate report.

Photo 8.2. De la Renaudière to Delapierre, 'Cameroon –
Identification of highway projects & supervision of ongoing
studies – Terms of Reference', 11 February 1972.
(Source: World Bank Group Archives.)

correspondence of the following years between the bank and various counterparts, including Regifercam, OCFT, the Cameroonian government and the
consultants entrusted with the economic study of realignment options (led by
Sofrerail, the French railways' engineering outfit) allows us to reconstruct the
contours of the discussion.[34] There was a shared consensus on the deficiencies
of the existing railroad. Even the most cautious participants in these discussions
conceded that a realignment of the entire line to rectify its steep gradients and
sharp curves would be necessary eventually. The issue, then, was when and how
the realignment should be undertaken. In determining 'the optimum timing'
(including a possible phasing) of realignment works, calculations of when the
existing line would become saturated became crucial. The estimate of this point
of in time, in turn, depended on traffic forecasts, which concerned not only
tonnage to be carried in any given year but also the seasonality of traffic, i.e.
its concentration in specific months. Early on, the bank's caution contrasted

---

[34] Archival work took place during two visits to Washington, D.C. in November
      2017 and December 2018. Unless otherwise specified, sources are from the First
      and Second Railway Projects correspondence: Railroads Project – Cameroon –
      Correspondence vols. 1–3, Folders 1607852–54, WBGA; and Railway Project II
      – Correspondence vols. 1–7, Folders 30222208–30222213, WBGA.

with the keener approach of the railway company and the government. The archive contains subtle signs of the reticence underlying the bank's stance. When reviewing the draft of instructions to staff traveling on an April 1972 mission to Cameroon, for example, their Transportation Department manager substituted 'the study of the improvement to the central railway line' for 'the realignment study of the central railway line' (Photo 8.2). At this early stage, thus, there was a clear willingness on the part of bank managers to give serious consideration to solutions that did not necessarily involve a realignment in the near future.

By June 1972, the consultants began to informally share preliminary conclusions with the bank and Regifercam.[35] It appeared to be a case of offering the bitter with the sweet. Their estimates initially pointed to 1980 as the year when existing line capacity would reach its limits. On the other hand, they hinted at a probable recommendation to go ahead without delay with the total realignment of the line, based on the substantial operating and maintenance savings this would produce. Predictably, Regifercam questioned the estimate of the saturation point, pushing for a considerably earlier date, whereas the World Bank argued against any recommendation to proceed with the realignment earlier than 1979.[36] These two contrasting positions hardened alongside the various iterations of the report: an interim report in July 1972, a draft final report in November 1972 plus an addendum in January 1973, and the final report in September 1973. All the actors involved met repeatedly in Cameroon over the course of Bank missions to the country, in Paris, where the consultants were based and both the bank and the OCFT had an office, and in Washington D.C., which the railway company's assistant managing director visited in February 1974 and where bank staff and Cameroon government representatives met every year during bank's annual meetings.

The bank took nine months to communicate to the Cameroonian government its official response to the consultants' final report. It expressed several important reservations: they found the report's traffic forecasts too high and they questioned the assumptions made in calculating the concentration of traffic on peak months; they found that the determination of the least costly option to meet the demand was premised on a flawed comparison of rail/road alternatives; and they pointed out a series of deficiencies in the assessment of

---

[35] Letter from Brechot to Oursin, 'Railway Project – Back-to-Office Report', 29 June 1972, WBGA.

[36] Letter from Brechot, De Gryse and du Parc to Oursin, 'Discussion of Consultants' Draft Final Report Concerning the Realignment of the Douala–Yaoundé Railway Line – Combined Back-to-Office and Full Report', 1 December 1972, WBGA.

the realignment's economic and financial return as well as the analysis of the relevant costs of opportunity.

Significantly, the bank's official response to the report was sent on 27 June 1974, only two weeks before a meeting called by the government to gauge the readiness of donors to fund the realignment, a meeting that had been scheduled months earlier and in which the bank itself was taking part. As early as November 1972, the Cameroonian government had intimated to the bank their intention to cast the net wide in their search for donors interested in financing the realignment works. Indeed, as the OCFT was quick to advertise through the European–African Association's newsletter, the outcome of the July 1974 meeting with donors was a Western German and French commitment to fund a first phase of the realignment project (the Otele–Yaounde section).[37] While the concessional terms in which these funds were offered undermined the bank's argument that the realignment project's estimated economic rate of return (8 per cent) was not high enough, the decision to split the project into smaller components was a sign of the fundraising difficulties that lay ahead.

Part of the rationale behind the German and French support for the realignment was the possibility to redeploy the work teams and equipment that had been engaged in building the northernmost segment of the Transcamerounais (Goyoum [north of Belabo]–Ngaoundere), whose completion was imminent. This was a possibility of which the bank staff were fully aware, as it had been discussed internally by the engineers involved in preparations for the Second Railway Project. In proposing a negotiation strategy to their boss at the bank's Division of Port's and Railways in February 1973, they noted: 'It has been argued that advantage should be taken of the availability of competent contracting and supervisory staff after completion of the *Transcamerounais* scheduled for 1974. This indeed may result in savings (mobilisation costs etc.) but these savings would probably be more than offset by the loss resulting from premature investment.'[38]

The bank soon found itself under pressure. Formally, the government could not go ahead with the realignment of the Otele–Yaounde section, as the loan agreement for the First Railway Project included an explicit commitment not to undertake the realignment unless the government and the bank were satisfied that the investment was economically and financially sound. Other donors, who had repeatedly approached the bank in the preceding two years about co-financing arrangements for the realignment, probed the bank's decision to disregard the

37   Towa-Fotso, 'Apres le Deuxieme Troncon', p. 49.
38   Letter from Brechot, De Gryse and Du Parc to Oursin, 'A Proposed Strategy for a Second Railway Project', 14 February 1973, WBGA.

consultants' recommendation. In a letter to their colleague at the bank's Paris office, who had informed them of the French government's complaints about their position in this matter, the division chiefs for Western Africa took pains in setting the record straight: 'The Bank, at no time has taken the position that it is unwilling to finance the realignment of the Douala–Yaounde leg of the Transcameroon Railway.' They had simply stated that they could not commit to finance these works unless a complementary study on road/rail competition was completed.[39]

Realignment as a 'Corridor' Matter

A study on road/rail competition in the Douala–Yaounde link had been included in the Second Railway Project package, which was negotiated and approved during the period when the bank was still grappling with its response to the economic study of realignment. It was in this context that the word 'corridor' made its first appearance in connection with the bank's investments in Cameroon's transport infrastructure. This part of the transport routes that converged in the port of Douala was the section that had highest density of freight and passenger traffic in the country. Not only did it link Douala to Cameroon's capital and second largest city, it also was one of the main routes through which cargo to and from Chad and Central African Republic gained access to the sea. From the outset, the framing in terms of corridor was understood to bring to the foreground 'a complex transport coordination problem' that pitted 'road construction' against 'railway realignment'.[40] In this case, the relationship between these two modes of transport was the core policy issue at the heart of the notion of corridor. The need for the new study was premised on the view that the previous one 'did not go deep enough into problems of least-cost solution to the long-term question of capacity on the Douala–Yaounde corridor'.[41] However, insufficient loan funds meant that this and other items had to be transferred to a Third Railway Project, so the chapter opened by this study did not end for another four years.

The preparation and the undertaking of the new study run parallel to the planning and works of the Otele–Yaounde realignment, for which German, French and Canadian financial contributions had been confirmed. This commitment had obvious implications for the study, which could no longer

---

39 Letter from Steckhan and Brandreth to Carriere, 'Transcameroon Railway (Douala–Yaoundé)', 13 December 1974, WBGA.

40 IBRD, *Appraisal of a Second Railway Project – Cameroon*, Washington, D.C., 1974, pp. ii, 6.

41 IBRD, *Appraisal of a Second Railway Project*, pp. iv–v.

treat the realignment of this section as an option to be assessed but as a given. Moreover, these three countries' financial backing of works in that portion of the railway generated a momentum towards further commitments. Indeed, in early 1975, the Minister of Planning contacted the bank's vice-president for Western Africa to appeal to the bank's 'willingness to associate themselves to the already formed group [of funders]', so that the government could 'forge ahead, as fast as possible, towards our final objective', which was no other than the realignment of the entire line.[42] As the bank's lead in the railway projects noted in a memo to one of the Western Africa division chiefs: 'The Minister's letter...puts us in a difficult position. On the one hand, we and the Government should await the results of the rail/road study...before undertaking any works on the Douala–Yaoundé transport corridor. On the other hand, we more or less gave no objection in June 1974 to the Otélé–Yaoundé section being carried out.'[43]

The bank could do little but to urge that the corridor study should get under way and emphasise the importance of subordinating all investments to the study's conclusions. To speed up the process, in April 1975 the bank agreed to retain the same consultants that had conducted the first economic study on the realignment.[44]

The logic of postponing further investment decisions until the completion of the new study was anyhow hard to impose. The government, Regifercam and, less directly, the OCFT and the construction contractors kept pushing for potential lenders to agree to further phases of realignment and were successful, particularly in the case of a very receptive German government. After a visit to Frankfurt in July 1975, one of the Bank's financial analysts reported that the German development bank, Kreditanstalt für Wiederaufbau (KfW), felt 'committed to the realignment of the entire Douala–Yaounde section' and that 'the financial constraints of both KfW and Cameroon' were the main reason for the slow pace of implementation.[45] Bank managers, in turn, were not open-minded about what the implications of the corridor study could be. In a memo of November 1975, they stated clearly that 'it is increasingly unlikely that we shall contribute to the realignment project'.[46]

42   Letter from Maikano Abdoulaye to Chaufournier, 7 February 1975, WBGA.
43   Letter from Johnson to Steckhan, 'Cameroon Railways', 24 February 1975, WBGA.
44   Letter from Bayon to Johnson, 'Compte Rendu des Reunions du 19 Mars 1975 a Bruxelles a/s Rélignement Douala-Yaoundé', 2 April 1975, WBGA.
45   Letter from Apitz to Brandreth, 'Second Douala Port Project and Proposed Douala-Yaoundé realignment', 9 July 1975, WBGA.
46   Letter from Agueh de la Renaudiere to Chaufournier, 'Cameroon – Status of Implementation and Preparation of our Railway Projects', 3 November 1975, WBGA.

For close to a year after the choice of consultants was made, much energy was spent in reaching an agreement on the terms of their remit. Even the profile of the team of consultants was subject to considerable discussion, as the bank detected 'a lack of balance in favour of railway [expertise]'.[47] The impasse was reflected on a gap of 13 months (from November 1975 to December 1976) without a bank supervision mission. Once the consultants finally got to work, they were able to produce an interim report. Regifercam received it in July 1976 and sent copies of it to the bank in August. In the following months, bank staff, including railway and highway engineers and financial analysts, reviewed the report and travelled to Paris to discuss it with the consultants. However, to the Regifercam managers' exasperation, they declared that the members of a mission to Cameroon in December 1976 were 'still not in a position to discuss [the report]'. In a wire to Washington, the mission staff informed their bosses that the 'railway is very embarrassed about delays purportedly caused by the Bank in finalising this study'. By that stage, the consultants had already produced a draft final report without allowing for the bank, the railway company, or the government's comments to be incorporated. Eventually, it was agreed that the consultants would prepare an addendum to respond to the bank's and Regifercam's comments.

Once the bank had communicated their observations about the interim report to Regifercam, the company shared with the bank the draft final report and the two parties reviewed the consultants' addendum. Only after the new year could they sit down to discuss their respective positions. When they did, predictably, their observations went in opposite directions: whereas the bank found the forecasts of timber traffic too optimistic, Regifercam thought the study had underestimated the beneficial impact realignment would have on accidents. They agreed on asking the consultants to rectify both aspects in the final report.[48]

Beyond such technical requests for rectification, whose implications were not likely to bring about any surprises, both parties seemed to have already drawn their own conclusions. The Western Africa Region economist in charge of railway projects informed the bank's representative in Yaoundé in early January of how their 'highly confidential' review suggested that 'realignment [is] not economically viable but minor improvements to railway probably

47 Letter from Brandreth to Regifercam, outgoing wire, 26 January 1976, WBGA.
48 Letter from Dick to Brandreth, 'Second Railway Project – Douala–Yaoundé Corridor Study – Back to Office and Full Report', 24 February 1977, WBGA.

are'.[49] Sensing the bank's continued reticence on this score and knowing
that the government had by then received assurances of German support for
realigning a new section (Douala–Edea), Regifercam reoriented their requests
to the bank towards the purchase of new rolling stock. To complicate matters
more, an announcement by the Cameroonian president seemed to undermine
the relevance of the planning exercise itself. In a speech that had purportedly
'caught even the relevant ministers by surprise', President Ahidjo made public
the government's intention to construct a four-lane autoroute between Douala
and Yaounde.[50] Confirmation that Gauff, a German firm, had been hired to
undertake engineering studies for this future highway and was considering
constructing a stretch of it with its own funds caused alarm among bank staff.[51]

The next step was a three-day 'co-donors meeting' held in Paris in March
1977.[52] This larger meeting was preceded by further 'technical discussions'
among the consultants Sofrerail, the Cameroon delegation and the bank. This
restricted forum was the opportunity for Regifercam to confirm its intention
to go ahead with the realignment of Douala–Edea, for which the consultants'
analysis showed acceptable rates of return. The bank explained that they would
only be able to participate in the financing of this investment under certain
conditions. Some of the conditions concerned the complementary future road
investments, including the autoroute the president had recently 'decreed' be
built. The Cameroon delegation stated that such conditions would be 'difficult
to meet' and the discussions ended without reaching 'a meeting of minds'.[53]
Eventually, the meeting with the larger pool of potential funders led to 'an overall
accord in principle' on future railway investments and on each of the parties'
respective financial contributions. The bank's proposed participation was, in the

49 Letter from Dick to Palein, 'Cameroon Corridor Study', telex, 4 January 1977,
    WBGA.
50 Letter from Dick to Brandreth, op. cit., 24 February 1977, WBGA.
51 Letter from Palein to Steckhan, 'Progress Report from Cameroon', telex, 7 February
    1977, WBGA.
52 The Cameroon delegation was led by the Minister of Transport and included a
    Ministry of Economy and Planning director, Regifercam's president and his French
    assistant director and the OCFT's managing director, also French. Potential
    funders present at the table were Germany (four delegates), France (six), European
    Community (three), US (two), Canada (two), World Bank (two) and the Arab
    Bank for Economic Development in Africa (one).
53 Letter from Dick to Brandreth, 'Cameroon Second Railway Project: Co-donors'
    Meeting – Back to Office and Full Report', 11 April 1977, WBGA.

view of its own staff, 'marginal' but deemed sufficient to give them 'leverage'.[54] The bank staff were also satisfied to obtain a commitment to supplementary analysis by Sofrerail of the proposed infrastructure investment plan, in light of various new factors that had not been considered in the original study, including the autoroute project.

The Path from 'Partial' to 'Non-Involvement'

In May 1977, when the final report on the Douala–Yaounde Corridor study reached them, the bank staff reviewing it could not but be disappointed. Traffic forecasts used in the draft version, which as far as the bank was concerned had been 'the most significant cause of dispute', had not been changed. The staff's take was openly cynical: 'the consultants have managed to squeeze slightly higher rates out of the packages favoured by Regifercam (presumably a coincidence)'. However, there was solace in that the report supported the bank's stance against the Edea–Makak realignment. In any case, arriving after the April donors meeting as it had, the report was a non-event. The supplementary study followed soon after and this time the bank was pleased to read that 'the high cost of autoroute construction renders this economically unacceptable' and that 'a self-financing toll autoroute is an untenable proposition between Douala and Yaounde'.[55]

In spite of its unequivocal conclusions, Sofrerail's supplementary study did not put an end to what bank staff now called 'the road/rail controversy'.[56] Speculation and rumours kept feeding uncertainties surrounding the prospect of a new autoroute. While French opposition to the project seemed strong, the German Ministry for Economic Cooperation remained rather supportive. In discussions with the bank, the Cameroon government showed itself 'unwilling to modify [the engineering survey contractor Gauff's] terms of reference to include a more modest concept', such as the paved two-lane road on the existing alignment advocated by Sofrerail.[57] More alarmingly from the bank's point of view, everything seemed to be up for grabs again on the railway side of things. During the 1977 bank annual meetings in D.C., the Cameroonian

54 Letter from Dick to Brandreth, ibid., 11 April 1977, WBGA.
55 Letter from Dick to Brandreth, 'Douala-Yaoundé Corridor Study – Supplementary Study'. 28 June 1977, WBGA.
56 Letter from Eigen to Steckhan, 'Discussions with BMZ/KfW in Bonn', 28 July 1977, WBGA.
57 Letter from Dick to files, 'Douala-Yaoundé Road Construction', 7 October 1977, WBGA.

delegation was 'non-committal' about the investment package agreed in Paris a few months earlier and 'adamant' that the realignment of the Eseka–Maloume section be discussed.[58]

In November 1977, only a few weeks after the tense discussions of the annual meetings, the Minister of Economy and Planning sent a new letter 'to clarify from now on the Cameroon government's position'. The conciliatory tone seemed to be aimed at securing the bank's green light for the realignment of the Douala–Edea section. With regards to the prospects of the realignment of remaining sections and the autoroute project, the minister reassured the bank that 'our constant policy had never led us to envisage overinvesting but, on the contrary, to modulate such investments with regards to our needs and our possibilities'.[59] The bank took this as outright acceptance of its own position.[60]

When commitments for the Douala–Edea realignment were firmed up, the bank was no longer among the funders.[61] The bank's Fourth Railway Project focused instead on the construction of new railway facilities in both Douala and Yaounde and on technical assistance to improve Regifercam's management and operational performance. Yet, one of the covenants contained in this loan agreement referred to the railway realignment. The government thereby agreed to pursue a closer study of all possible improvement alternatives to completely realigning the Edea–Maloume section and committed itself not to make any capital investments in this section unless their 'economic justification' had been established.[62] By the time the new railway loan was approved in June 1979, the bank had also prevailed upon the government to drop the idea of a Douala–Yaounde autoroute and to redefine the terms of reference of the project's contractors, so that the economic feasibility and detailed engineering of a two-lane paved road would be studied instead.[63]

58 Letter from Calvo to Palein, 'Annual Meeting', telex, 14 October 1977, WBGA.
59 Letter from Minister of Economy and Planning to Chef de Division, 4 November 1977, WBGA.
60 Letter from Apitz to Brandreth, 'Second and Third Railway Projects Supervision – Preparation of the Fourth Railway Project – Back-to-Office report', 8 December 1977, WBGA.
61 Nor did the bank finance the rolling stock about which Regifercam had approached them back in early 1977, as the Canadians showed themselves more willing to cover that particular investment: see letter from Apitz to Brandreth, op. cit., 8 December 1977, WBGA.
62 Fourth Railway Project, Staff Appraisal, p. 52, WBGA.
63 Fourth Highway Project, Staff Appraisal Report, p. 5, WBGA.

Thus, as in the previous phase, when construction works for the realignment of the Douala–Edea portion began in December 1978, uncertainty surrounded the fate of the remaining sections. In spite of the bank's continued objections to the project, the government continued to seek out potential funders. Consider the presidential speech for the opening in June 1979 of the new Japoma railway bridge, a project whose completion arrived almost a decade after the bank had first agreed to partially fund it. While the occasion was framed as a celebration of international co-operation, the president did not miss the opportunity to remind Cameroon's partners of the priority projects still in need of support:

> The government will not spare any efforts to obtain funding for the last section Edéa–Maloumé as soon as reasonably possible, so that the works can begin quickly. Only this way will we eliminate the bottleneck that hinders the optimal performance of our transport system and will Cameroon have at its disposal a heavy-duty route ready to play its role fully as the backbone of our transport system.[64]

In the end, the realignment of the remaining section of old railway was carried out in two stages. The first one, from Edea to Eseka, began in 1981 and opened for traffic *sans tambours ni trompettes* [without fanfare]' in December 1982.[65] The most technically challenging and expensive part (Eseka–Maloume), which included an 'infernal' elevation gain of 350 metres within 19 kilometres as the crow flies, was left for last. It comprised building four spectacular viaducts and excavating three long tunnels. The much-awaited completion took place in 1987, by which time the country's economic prospects had taken a drastic turn for the worse.[66] Years of annual deficits and underinvestment followed for Regifercam,

---

[64]   Letter from Rabeharisoa to Chaufournier, 'Inauguration of Japoma Railroad Bridge', 27 June 1979, WBGA; See also: 'Un Nouveau Pont à Japoma', *Le Rail et le Monde*, 7:9, 1979.

[65]   Michel Baranger, 'Transcam: Plus que 25km', *Le Rail et le Monde*, 24, 1983, pp. 48–50.

[66]   'Infernal' is the adjective chosen by Daniel Vincent, who was then the European Commission's division chief for general infrastructure and industry. It is interesting that even within the European Economic Community, which remained a constant funder throughout the whole realignment process, there was already in 1974 a clear sense that the more technically and financially demanding sections to be rebuilt 'weighed' heavily on those involved in the project. See Daniel Vincent, 'La politique du F.E.D. en matière de cooperation ferroviaire', *Le Courrier*, 28, 1974, pp. 43–46. The sense of exhaustion when the final works approached completion is apparent in the title that the editors of *Le Rail et le Monde*, the French periodical devoted to

whose privatisation was agreed by the government and its financiers in 1994. It finally materialised in 1999 through a 30-year concession agreement with a consortium led by the French multinational Bollore.

In sum, the complete realignment ended up being a much longer, tortuous and expensive affair than could have been anticipated in the early 1970s, when planning for it had begun. Carrying it out took roughly as long as the construction of the original Douala–Yaounde line – and it cost almost twice as much as the construction of the new Yaounde–Belabo–Ngaoundere railroad.[67] Throughout this period, the World Bank stood firm in their stance of not supporting the project, while taking active part in various other transport investments in the country. These included one of nine lots in which the construction of a paved Douala–Yaounde road was divided, a project that took place from 1980 to 1983.

Running the Clock Down?

The plan to realign the Douala–Yaounde railway raised a series of complex questions and presented the different parties involved with various dilemmas. The two studies commissioned by Regifercam at the behest of the bank were conceived to inform decisions on the timing and modalities of the rehabilitation of the existing network. The agreement to conduct the first study committed the Cameroon government to a deferred timetable. The study opened a process that included the drafting of the terms of reference, the international call for bids, and the selection of consultants. Once the consultants were selected, the study itself would involve months of both in-country and distance work. Similarly, the second study committed the government to wait for its results. These studies entailed as one of their most immediate effects the postponement of realignment.

For the bank, the delay seems to have been welcome. Their '*petit projet ferro-viaire*', as the OCFT dismissively referred to the First Railway Project, had given the bank a say in the government's investment policy.[68] Its small size notwithstanding, the terms of that first loan explicitly subjected future decisions on realignment to the bank being satisfied that they constituted sound investments.

---

international railway co-operation, chose for the issue they devoted to the project: 'Transcamerounais: the end of the tunnel'. See: Michel Baranger, 'Transcamerounais: Le Bout du Tunnel en 1986', *Le Rail et le Monde, 33,* 1985, pp. 6–11.

67   Dupré la Tour, 'Cent-vingt Ans', p. 140.

68   Office du Chemin de Fer Transcamerounais (OCFT); 'La Revision de la Voie Ferrée Douala-Yaoundé', 25 September 1972, Revision de la Ligne Doula/Yaoundé – Dossiers, Fol. 581571, WBGA.

From the preliminary discussions of the consultants' findings, well before the final report, they knew that the cost–benefit analysis was going to generate what were by their standards low economic rates of return. As far as they were concerned, it was an investment that could wait. From the point of view of the Cameroonian parties, the old line was a major hindrance to the railway company's operations and the investment was justified and urgent. They had been led to assume that if the consultants' recommendations were favourable, the bank would follow through with a financial contribution towards realignment. As we saw, they were up for a disappointment. Although the report recommended to proceed with the investment, it also placed the point of saturation of existing line in 1980. The bank could latch on to this to argue that any earlier investment would be premature.

There was an acute awareness of the potential dilatory effects of technical studies when the bank and the government negotiated the Second Railway Project (Photo 8.3). Firstly, the difficulties involved in securing the bank's board of executive directors' approval of a loan were not to be underestimated. Going through the motions of the bank's bureaucratic procedures to reach the stage of the presentation to the board, from the 'issues paper' and the 'yellow cover' president's report to the 'green cover' documents for the loan committee and the negotiations with the government, could take up to ten months when things went as planned.[69] Secondly, it was fresh in everyone's minds that, for the preceding study on the economic viability of the realignment, the bank had taken nine months to respond to the consultants' final report. The government therefore voiced its reservations about the new 'corridor' study proposed by the bank, 'fearing that [on the basis of this further study] the Bank might not finance the realignment'. The bank offered assurances that 'the study can be completed within a year of commencement and this ... would still leave time to complete the realignment before traffic constraints on the existing line reach an unacceptable level'.[70] At the bank's insistence, the study thus became one of the items in the new railway project.

---

[69] Sympathetic bank staff could make efforts to 'compress' the typical schedule to seven months, as they offered doing for Cameroon's Third Railway Project. See: Memo from Agueh to Files, 'Cameroon – Third Railway Project – Decision Memorandum', 18 December 1975.

[70] Letter from Steckhan and Brandreth to Carriere, 'Transcameroon Railway (Douala–Yaoundé)', 13 December 1974, WBGA; See also: IBRD, *Appraisal of a Railway Project – Federal Republic of Cameroon*, pp. 6–7; Similarly, the project appraisal document stated that that, even 'allowing for construction lead time', a decision

Loan budgeting shortages resulting from currency exchange dynamics slowed down the launch of the corridor study. Although a decision was taken to entrust it to the previous consultants to expedite the process, it was only in July 1976, more than two years after the agreement, that the consultants produced an interim report. It is not hard to understand the railway company's frustration when, five months later, a bank mission to Douala informed them that they were not in a position to discuss the report. When those discussions finally took place in February 1977, the transport economist leading the banks's team showed full awareness of the effects that all that waiting was having on their relations with the borrowers. When discussing the options that the bank faced in an upcoming donors meeting, he wrote: '[Our] non-involvement [in the financing of realignment] could have a serious adverse effect on the Bank's influence on the Cameroon transport sector. The Bank initiated the consultants' study, this study has been patiently awaited for two years, and complete dissociation of the Bank from railway investment associated with its conclusions would be incomprehensible to the Cameroon government.'[71]

Yet that was exactly what ended up happening. As we have seen, an initial agreement in principle to contribute alongside other donors to the realignment of the Douala–Edea section, then under discussion, soon came to nothing.

As much as the rhythms of work within various bureaucracies ranging from the railway company to the relevant ministries and funding agencies were oriented towards short- and long-term planning, the converse relationship also obtained. 'Planning itself takes time', Simone Abram has recently reminded us.[72] In Cameroon, throughout the 1970s, this obvious but often neglected fact served well the bank in its efforts to either prevent or slow down investments that they deemed premature. There were certainly clear limits to this strategy. When the bank distanced itself from the consultants' recommendations in both the economic study of realignment and in the corridor study, there was an inevitable fallout. At those points, the clauses contained in the loans that required bank approval did not count for much and the government was able to forge ahead and secure commitments from other donors to realign first Yaounde–Otele–Maloume and later Douala–Edea. The bank's overestimation of its ability to exert control over events was costly in particular instances. For example, track of the old line renewed as late as November 1976 was taken out of use in April 1978, when the realigned

on 'either railway realignment or road improvement' would be 'unnecessary before 1976', see: IBRD, *Appraisal of a Second Railway Project – Cameroon*, p. 6.

71   Letter from Dick to Brandreth, 'Second Railway Project – Douala–Yaoundé Corridor Study – Back-to-Office and Full Report', 24 February 1977, WBGA.

72   Simone Abram, 'The Time it Takes: Temporalities of Planning', Journal of the Royal Anthropological Institute, special issue, 2014, pp. 12947 at p. 145.

Photo 8.3. Loan signing for Cameroon's Second Railways Project; seated from right to left World Bank's Vice-President Chaufournier (Western Africa Region) and Cameroon's Ambassador Tchoungui, Washington, D.C., 18 September 1974. (Source: © Edwin Huffman/World Bank. Licence: CC BY NC-SA 4.0.)

Yaounde–Otele section was completed (Map 8.1). Although the track from the renewed sections was salvaged and repurposed by the railway company for other projects, the expense of the ballast and the labour required for the relaying of the track looked wasteful. The bank's financial analyst, who, as Figure 8.1 shows, devoted considerable attention to this matter, concluded that 'with the benefit of hindsight, it might have been anticipated that ... the extent of benefits from track relaying were very uncertain'.[73] As the bank's staff acknowledged, such a blatant case of mistiming was 'partly due to weaknesses in the Bank's relationship with the borrower'.[74] Such glitches aside, in a matter of months after each of the fallouts resulting from the bank's response to the two studies, both parties made a point of patching their differences up and, as the rhetoric of international finance diplomacy would have it, find ways of 'concentrat[ing] on areas where government and Bank can develop enlarged co-operation and avoid confrontation'.[75]

[73] World Bank, *Cameroon Second and Third Railway Projects – Project Completion Report,* Washington, D.C., 1979, p. 45.
[74] World Bank, *Cameroon Second and Third Railway Projects,* p. 44.
[75] Letter from Calvo to Palein, 'Annual Meeting', telex, 14 October 1977, WBGA.

Critical Steps in Realignment/Track relaying

Date	-----Realignment-----	-------Relaying-------
Jan 74	OCCR/SOFRERAIL Study – Final Report received	
Jan 74		Rail, etc. bid documents to Bank
May 74		Rail II negotiations
June 74		Rail II Board Presentation
June 74		Rail II Rail bids received
July 3, 74		Bank accepted bids
July 74	Co-donor meeting – expression of interest by several parti- cipants in financing Yaoundé- Otele realignment. Bank takes position realignment not justified	
Sept 74		Regifercam strongly expressed wish to use rails on existing Yaoundé-Otele track – Bank agreed
Jan 75	Invitation to review bid documents – Yaoundé-Otele (first formal notification of decision to realign)	
May 75		Rail relaying commenced
Nov 76		Rail relaying finished
April 78	Realigned Yaoundé-Otele opened	

Figure 8.1. Critical steps in track relaying/realignment of Yaoundé–Otele section. (Source: World Bank Group Archives.)

Ultimately, the factor that seems to have influenced most the timing and the pace of realignment was the presence in Cameroon of Cogefar-Hochtief, the tried and tested contractor that had built the Yaounde–Ngaoundere line. As it turned out, the various phases of the realignment ended up being scheduled so as to ensure the Italo-German consortium kept getting steady contracts without significant periods of idleness. Resorting to these contractors mitigated the uncertainties surrounding the engineering challenges of the realignment works themselves. This was presented as both a matter of lower cost, given the installation savings, and of quality. But, equally decisively if not more, retaining the same contractor – while complying with the motions of international bidding procedures – was for the Cameroon government also key in addressing the uncertainties surrounding the supply of finance. The choice of contractor was indeed far from immaterial to the co-funders involved in both the construction of the new line to Ngaoundere and the realignment of the old line.[76] The tying of aid to contracts for companies from the European Economic Community member countries was at the time a requirement for the EDF and, in fact, the Transcamerounais was a pioneering project in relaxing these restrictions to make US firms eligible bidders.[77] A similar logic applied to the position of the OCFT as the supervisor of railway projects. Large projects such as the successive phases of realignment were what justified the OCFT's continuous existence; it was also a crucial consideration behind France's financial support at various points.

Conclusion

It was only in the 1990s and the 2000s that the term 'corridor' became fashionable to refer to certain approaches to planning, building and managing transport infrastructure in the African continent and beyond, although even

---

[76] According to Hewitt, the Transcamerounais project benefited from 'the surplus capacity civil engineering sector of the Italian economy'. Cogefar was 'prepared to offer relatively cheap but highly skilled labour and expertise and to bid aggressively for the works contracts', see: Hewitt, 'The European Development Fund as a development agent', p. 52. Most grants and loans for Cameroonian railways were tied aid. Referring specifically to the realignment, a USAID officer recalled "difficult issues surrounding the transparency and fairness of the procurement arrangements for the various aspects of the project ...The European donors were inclined to be cavalier about these issues": Frederick Gilbert, Deputy Regional Development Officer, USAID Cameroon (1976–1980), *Foreign Affairs Oral History*, 1997, p. 135 <https://adst.org/wp-content/uploads/2013/12/Gilbert-Frederick-E.pdf> [Accessed 27 April 2021].

[77] Dimier, *Invention*, 64.

then it remained 'a geographical object waiting for a definition'.[78] This chapter has documented the earlier usage of the term with a significantly different emphasis from the ones it acquired later. Throughout the 1970s, the World Bank proposed that the transport links between Cameroon's two largest cities be conceived as a corridor. By this they meant adopting an approach that compared the costs and benefits of various combinations of investments in railway and road infrastructure as a basis for strategic decision-making. What had begun as a study of the economic returns of a railway investment morphed into an assessment of the relative merits of alternative modes of transport, which the bank managers ultimately thought should encourage the government to take a more cautious investment strategy and one that privileged roads over railways. Yet, the vision behind the 'corridor study' proposed by the bank was not without inconsistencies.

The design of these transport infrastructure projects in Cameroon had been done along modal lines, with separate loans for ports, highways and railways. In fact, it was only much later, in the 1990s, that the bank's loans to Cameroon adopted the more encompassing 'transport sector' denomination. Furthermore, in these projects of the 1970s, the arena for co-ordination of intermodal investments that the bank itself had agreed to was one dominated by railway professionals. Indeed, the commissioner of the corridor study was the railway company – and, according to such far from neutral legal arrangements, it was the company that would have to return the money they had borrowed from the bank.[79] It was also small wonder that railway expertise would be overrepresented in consultant teams led by a railway engineering contractor; or that the consultants' recommendations for the corridor ended up being sympathetic to the investment packages favoured by the railway company.

That corridor irrupted as the watchword for a technical problematisation of rail–road competition in Cameroon at this particular time also reflected a global swing of the pendulum in favour of roads. Indeed, the 1970s was the decade when road transport became 'the right mode'.[80] This gradual dominance was long in the making and was decisively strengthened by the standardisation of shipping

[78] Benjamin Steck, 'Preface', in Jérôme Lombard, *Le Monde des Transports Sénégalais*, Marseille, 2015, p. 9. See also Nugent and Lamarque, in this volume.
[79] Laura Bear, 'Speculations on Infrastructure: From Colonial Public Works to a Post-Colonial Global Asset Class on the Indian Railways 1840–2017', *Economy & Society*, 49:1, 2020, pp. 45–70.
[80] International Road Union (IRU), 'Seven Decades: Driving Road Transport', *IRU Factsheet*, 2018, p. 2 <www.iru.org/system/files/factsheet-tir-seven-decades-driving-road-transport.pdf> [Accessed 27 April 2021].

containers. The process certainly had many specific histories. In Nigeria, a case that became paradigmatic because it caught Albert Hirschman's imagination and was the spark that inspired some of his most celebrated work, the triumph of road transport was already palpable by the mid-1960s.[81] In Cameroon, because of the limitations of the road network and the foreign and national backing of railways, the pendulum swung later but the swing was equally pronounced. As in numerous other contexts, road transport eventually developed a powerful political platform that found its reflection in government policies premised on the road's superior competitiveness. As if to atone for the sense of repeated deferral that surrounded the entire realignment project, a 1980 evaluation of the bank's railway lending to the country ended on a positive note: 'Regifercam is at least fortunate in having time to prepare for the increased competitive situation [that would derive from the completion of the Douala–Yaounde paved road in 1983].'[82] Yet, what unfolded in later years seems instead to instantiate Hirschman's point about the Nigerian railways. In both cases, road competition seems to have provided 'the railways not so much with a spur for good performance as with a special kind of latitude for poor performance'.[83]

The present offers a suggestive vantage point from which to look back on the 1970s. While the twenty-first century opened with announcements of an imminent 'rail renaissance'[84] in the African continent, its substance, momentum and durability have been variously assessed. Certainly, the enthusiastic tone of the early 2010s has given way to more circumspect views.[85] Yet, a number of new railroads have been completed in recent years and construction of others is ongoing. In Cameroon, the government published an ambitious Railway Master Plan (RMP) in 2012. The investments designated as short- and mid-term are gargantuan. It is the new construction projects to be undertaken that have captured most of the media attention, even though they remain to this day distant possibilities.[86] The RMP also comprises a substantial but less conspicuous package for rehabilitation of the existing network, within which the renovation

---

81   Albert Hirschman, *Exit, Voice and Loyalty*.
82   World Bank, *Cameroon Second and Third Railway Projects*, p. 13.
83   Hirschman, *Development Projects Observed*, pp. 147–48.
84   Neil Ford, 'Africa's Rail Renaissance', *African Business*, June 2004, pp. 22–23.
85   'Puffed Out; Railways in Africa', *The Economist*, 42, 2016, p. 419; Vincent Defait, 'En Afrique, le Train Revient au Cœur des Grands Projets du Continent', *Le Monde*, 5 October 2016.
86   Rousseau-Joël Foute, 'Transport Ferroviaire: L'Incontournable Modernisation', *Cameroon Tribune*, 19 June 2013; Paul Eboa, 'Projets à Réaliser à Moyen Terme: Une Dizaine de Tronçons dans le Pipe', *Cameroon Tribune*, 28 April 2016.

of the northernmost section of the existing line (Pangar–Ngaoundéré) is the largest project.

In the aftermath of the country's most lethal railway accident on 21 October 2016 (82 deaths and nearly 600 injured) and faced with a pronounced decline in freight volume, the concessionary company Camrail (Regifercam's successor) has been questioned in recent years. While the concession does not expire until 2034, the government itself commissioned an audit of the company's performance in 2017. However, the auditors' recommendations have neither been made public nor acted upon. In ways that both resemble and differ from the situation in the 1970s, many railway professionals in Cameroon today see the present as a period of uncertainty and confusion. Some of this uncertainty and confusion refers specifically to what the best ways of ensuring the long-term durability of railway infrastructure might be, a question that occupied all those who took an active interest in the Douala–Yaounde realignment. A greater policy focus on intermodal co-ordination and competition might be in the cards. In this, the coming decade may echo the 1970s.

Bibliography

Abram, Simone, 'The Time It Takes: Temporalities of Planning', *Journal of the Royal Anthropological Institute*, special issue, 2014, pp. 129–47.

Baranger, Michel, 'Afrique Intertropicale: L'Avenir du Rail', *Le Rail et le Monde*, 46, 1987, pp. 28–29.

— 'Transcam: Plus que 25km', *Le Rail et le Monde*, 24, 1983, pp. 48–50.

— 'Transcamerounais: Le Bout du Tunnel en 1986', *Le Rail et le Monde, 33,* 1985, pp. 6–11.

Bear, Laura, 'Speculations on Infrastructure: From Colonial Public Works to a Post-Colonial Global Asset Class on the Indian Railways 1840–2017', *Economy & Society,* 49:1, 2020, pp. 45–70.

Billard, Pierre, 'On Construit des Chemins de Fer au Cameroun', *Revue de Géographie Alpine*, 54:4, 1966, pp. 611–20.

Bullock, Richard, *Off Track: Subsaharan African Railways*, Washington, 2009.

Cameroon Tribune, 'Deux Réalisations Grandioses Fêtées dans l'Enthousiasme', *Cameroon Tribune*, 11 December 1974.

Commissariat Général d'Information, *Chemin de Fer Transcamerounais*, Yaoundé, 1965.

Decraene, Phillipe, 'Le chemin de Fer Transcamerounais Facteur de Développement et d'Unification', *Le Monde Diplomatique*, September, 1971, p. 7.

Defait, Vincent, 'En Afrique, le Train Revient au Cœur des Grands Projets du Continent', *Le Monde,* 5 October 2016.

Dikoumé, Albert, 'Les Transports au Cameroun de 1884 à 1975', unpublished PhD thesis, École des Hautes Études en Sciences Sociales, 1982.

Dimier, Veronique, *The Invention of a European Development Aid Bureaucracy: Recycling Empire*, New York, 2014.

Dupré la Tour, François, 'Cent-Vingt Ans de Chemins de Fer en Afrique Noire Francophone: De la Construction aux Privatisations', *Revue Generale des Chemins de Fer*, 7–8, 1998, pp. 135–51.

Eboa, Paul, 'Projets à Réaliser à Moyen Terme: Une Dizaine de Tronçons dans le Pipe', *Cameroon Tribune*, 28 April 2016.

Economist, 'Puffed out; Railways in Africa', *The Economist*, 42, 2016, 419.

European Development Fund (EDF), *Cameroon 1960–1975*, Brussels, 1975.

Ferrandi, Jacques, 'Inauguration à Ngaoundéré', *Le Courrier*, 30, 1975, pp. 16–17.

Ford, Neil, 'Africa's Rail Renaissance', *African Business*, June 2004, pp. 22–23.

Foreign Affairs Oral History, Frederick Gilbert Interview, 1997 <https://adst.org/wp-content/uploads/2013/12/Gilbert-Frederick-E.pdf> [Accessed 27 April 2021].

Foute, Rousseau-Joël, 'Transport Ferroviaire: L'Incontournable Modernisation', *Cameroon Tribune*, 19 June 2013.

Hewitt, Adrian, 'The European Development Fund as a Development Agent: Some Results of EDF Aid to Cameroon', *Overseas Development Institute Review*, 2, 1979, pp. 41–56.

Hirschman, Albert O., *Development Projects Observed*, Washington D.C., 1967.

— *Exit, Voice and Loyalty: Responses to Decline in Firms, Organisations and States*, Cambridge, 1970.

Howe, Cymene, *et al.*, 'Paradoxical Infrastructures: Ruins, Retrofit, and Risk', *Science, Technology and Human Values*, 41:3, 2016, pp. 547–65.

Hugon, Philippe and Sudrie, Olivier, 'La Crise de la Planification Africaine: Diagnostic et Remèdes', *Tiers-Monde*, 28:110, 1987, pp. 407–34.

International Bank for Reconstruction and Development, *Appraisal of a Railway Project – Federal Republic of Cameroon*, Washington D.C., 1970.

— *Appraisal of a Second Railway Project –Cameroon*, Washington D.C., 1974.

International Road Union, 'Seven Decades: Driving Road Transport', *IRU Factsheet*, 2018, p .2 <www.iru.org/system/files/factsheet-tir-seven-decades-driving-road-transport.pdf> [Accessed 27 April 2021].

Mbembe, Achille, 'Le Cameroun après la Mort d'Ahmadou Ahidjo', *Politique Africaine*, 37, 1990, pp. 117–22.

Monson, Jamie, *Africa's Freedom Railway*, Bloomington, 2011.

Okalla Bana, Edy-Claude, 'Les Entreprises Françaises de Travaux Publics Face au Développement Economique de l'Outre-Mer: La Mise en Place du Réseau Ferré au Cameroun', *Outre-Mers*, 98, 2011, pp. 275–98.

Operations Evaluation Department, *Cameroon Second and Third Railway Projects – Performance Audit Report*, Washington D.C., 1980.

Pourtier, Roland, 'Les Chemins de Fer en Afrique Subsaharienne, entre Passé Révolu et Recompositions Incertaines', *Belgeo*, 2, 2007, pp. 1–15.

Samuel, Boris 'Planifier en Afrique', *Politique Africaine*, 145, 2017, pp. 5–26.

Steck, Benjamin, 'Preface', in Jérôme Lombard, *Le Monde des Transports Sénégalais*, Marseille, 2015.

Swenson, John, 'Le *Transcamerounais* Vu par un Américain', *Courrier de l'Association*, 17, 1973, pp. 48–52.

Towa-Fotso, Luc, 'Apres le Deuxieme Troncon Entrée en Service en 1974 la Refection de la Portion Douala–Yaoundé', *Le Courrier*, 28, 1974, pp. 47–49.

Vincent, Daniel, 'La politique du F.E.D. en Matière de Cooperation Ferroviaire', *Le Courrier*, 28, 1974, pp. 43–46.

Winter, Gerard, 'Note sur la Planification du Developpement au Cameroun', Yaoundé, 1968, <http://horizon.documentation.ird.fr/exl-doc/pleins_textes/pleins_textes_5/b_fdi_04-05/04042.pdf> [Accessed 27 April 2021].

World Bank, *Cameroun Fourth Railway Project – Staff Appraisal Report*, Washington D.C., 1979.

— *Cameroun Second and Third Railway Projects – Project Completion Report*, Washington D.C., 1979

World Bank Group Archive, Railroads Project – Cameroon – Correspondence vols. 1–3, Folders 1607852–54.

— Railway Project II – Correspondence vols. 1–7, Folders 30222208–30222213.

CHAPTER 9

When is a Corridor Just a Road? Understanding Thwarted Ambitions Along the Abidjan–Lagos Corridor

PAUL NUGENT

When you reach border, immigration officer dey
Him go bluff you, waste your time
Change him pants
Some dey comb dem hair
Den tidy dem table
Den dem pull dem chair
Before him go know say you dey there
If you no talk quick
Him go go for shit
Him go shit, come-back
And you talk to am
Then you surprise when him
Shock for you
Him go say you no go cross
You no go cross today
Na that time dem go start dem
Power Show.[1]

Introduction

To ask what is a transport corridor is not to pose an entirely facetious question. Most analysis proceeds on the assumption that we can infer what a corridor is from 'its' effects rather than by trying to define any intrinsic attributes. But there are countless roads that are not regarded as corridors, while almost all of the corridors are effectively labels placed upon routes that already existed – and

---

[1]   Fela Kuti, 'Power Show' from the album *Original Sufferhead*, 1981.

often for a very long time.[2] One possible basis for a distinction might be that along designated corridors the roads are widened and the surfaces improved – processes of upgrading that are often associated with the interpolation of toll-booths – but this is not necessarily the case. In fact, there are stretches along all the main corridors in Africa that are severely potholed and in far worse shape than other national roads – as we will see below. So what serves to transform a mere road into something that is constitutive of a corridor? At the most fundamental level, a corridor exists when governments, donors and planners think it does, or should, exist. This obviously imparts a large measure of circularity to the exercise. But two other considerations that most analysts would regard as essential may instil a greater measure of rigour: firstly, whether a route connects two or more places that represent centres of particular importance – because of some combination of demography, strategic positioning or the location of natural resources – and, secondly, whether it carries unusually high levels of traffic. The Abidjan–Lagos Corridor (ALCo) evidently meets the first condition, given that the corridor links no fewer than five capital cities, namely Abidjan, Accra, Lomé, Cotonou and Lagos. However, the status of the second criterion is much more debatable. Whereas long-distance trucking along some of Africa's other transport corridors – such as along the Northern Corridor in East Africa – is highly visible, this can hardly be said of ALCo. Although there are passenger vehicles that regularly ply the route, there is relatively little evidence of serious trucking. Revealingly, unlike in Southern and East Africa there are no real trucking companies that make their business from using the corridor on a sustained basis. At best one might say that ALCo is a developmental idea that is still under development.

In this chapter, I seek to make sense of this baffling state of affairs. First of all, in probing some possible historical reasons, I pose the question of where the rationale for this particular corridor emanated from and how it has evolved over time. Secondly, I seek to identify why there remains such a mismatch today between the official discourse surrounding ALCo and what actually unfolds along the route. This requires us to be alert to the nuances of space and scale, both of which play out in significant ways along sections of the corridor. Comparing corridor dynamics is something that can yield fruitful insights. Although ALCo exhibits a number of peculiarities – and might be said to occupy one end of a corridor spectrum – it does throw up some lessons that have a more general application.

---

2   The same would hold *mutatis mutandis* for railways.

The Why and the When of the Abidjan–Lagos Corridor

Whether it emanates from mainstream economists or transport specialists, the literature on transport corridors tends to be at once technical and highly presentist. But a recent report from the Asian Development Bank factors in a much older history of transport corridors in South Asia, viewed through the prism of Mughal trade routes, the interventions of the East India Company and colonial railways – all of which (it is claimed) had a demonstrable impact on the regions through which they passed.[3] These deeper histories are arguably well-worth excavating for different regions of Africa as well (see Soi in this volume). Between what is now Côte d'Ivoire and western Nigeria there is a string of coastal ports that have been in existence for a very long time. Although there was some trade and migration between the coastal settlements during the era of the trans-Atlantic slave trade, the routes followed a broadly north–south orientation. Trading communities in the interior typically kept their options open, so that slaves and ivory would pass in one direction and cowries and manufactured goods in the other, depending on a number of factors that were operational at any given time: most notably, the level of physical security along the trade routes and the prevailing prices at the various ports.[4] Some of these routes from the interior to the coast provided the precedent for colonial roads and railways. In interesting ways, the Asante great roads remain etched into the contemporary landscape and some have subsequently been rebranded as corridors. But as for the littoral itself, the underlying pattern was one of active competition between coastal ports, which has an obvious echo in the present. The interpolation of colonial borders was associated with a contradictory double manoeuvre: that is, states constructed better roads along the coast to facilitate the export of cash crops and communications with the capital city – which was always located on the coast – but they also imposed taxes and restrictions on much of the trade that traversed borders. The net result was that coastal infrastructure was the composite of separate segments of road that had been constructed at different times to serve colonial, and later national, rather than regional or continental ends.

In the mid-1970s, during the oil boom, the eastern segment of the coastal route became famous as the means by which migrants entered Nigeria. The actual crossings remained as gruelling as ever, as immortalised in Fela Kuti's

---

3   World Bank, *The Web of Transport Corridors in South Asia*, Washington, D.C., 2018, pp. 27–48.

4   Paul Nugent, *Boundaries, Communities and State-Making in West Africa: The Centrality of the Margins*, Cambridge, 2019, ch. 2.

scathing lyrics in 'Power Show' which highlighted the capricious exercise of power by officials at Nigerian border posts.[5] The instrumentalisation of borders was graphically illustrated in 1983 when around a million Ghanaians found themselves stranded at the Seme border with Benin as they attempted to leave Nigeria in advance of the deadline set by the authorities. 'Ghana Must Go!' was the slogan, but the practical difficulty was that the border between Ghana and Togo was closed because of ongoing tensions between their governments over smuggling and allegations of subversion. Although Nigerian leaders liked to think of themselves as the driver of regional integration processes, following the foundation of the Economic Community of West African States (ECOWAS) in 1975, the country also had an interest in seeking to preserve rather hard borders – in large part because the oil boom afforded abundant opportunities for smuggling to and from Benin which had cemented its position as an entrepôt state. In short, there were successive stretches of road between Abidjan and Lagos, but there was no corridor in a meaningful sense.

Curiously, the origins of ALCo reside not in the effort to foster economic interdependence, but rather in the playing out of responses to the HIV/AIDS pandemic. One of the comparative insights that had emerged from the mapping of infection rates across Africa was that the prevalence was especially high along trucking routes. The risky sexual behaviour of truckers was thought to correlate with the lengthy administrative delays at border crossings. In the 1990s, the UNAIDS West Africa Initiative made the link explicit and in 2000 the decision was taken to target this particular route for a public health intervention.[6] In 2002, the Abidjan–Lagos Corridor Organisation (ALCO) was formally inaugurated as an inter-governmental agency. Two years later, the International Development Agency (IDA) provided US$16.6 million of funding to pilot work aimed at 'improving access to HIV/AIDS prevention, treatment, care and social support services for target populations'; 'enhancing regional capacity and co-operation to deal with HIV/AIDS'; and finally 'improving the flow of commercial and passenger traffic along the corridor'.[7] The initiative specif-

5   Fela Kuti, 'Power Show' from the album *Original Sufferhead*, 1981.
6   Indicatively perhaps, the prevalence rates did not seem overly high by comparison with other routes in Eastern and Southern Africa. See: Deepa Chakrapani and Catherine Gwin, *An Independent Evaluation of the World Bank's Support of Regional Programs: Case Study of the West Africa HIV/AIDS Project for the Abidjan-Lagos Corridor*, Washington, D.C., 2006, p. 1 <http://documents.worldbank.org/curated/en/277671468204835498/pdf/392960AFR0W1AF1agos1Transp01PUBLIC1.pdf> [Accessed 27 April 2021].
7   Chakrapani and Gwin, *Independent Evaluation*, p. 3.

ically targeted truck drivers, sex workers and borderlanders as segments of the population that were considered hard to reach through existing HIV/AIDS initiatives. An interim report of 2006 makes clear that there were many reasons why the initiative received the backing of governments. They clearly saw it as a means of levering additional funding for their individual HIV/AIDS-prevention programmes. But the report also noted that the governments of Ghana and Benin saw the programme as a means of bringing about greater inter-govern-mental co-operation and so giving regional integration a much-needed shot in the arm.[8] The net result was that the programme began to range well beyond a narrow engagement with public health issues. Hence the report observed that: 'There is general stakeholder agreement that (a) countries on both sides of the border need to agree on ways to harmonise border control procedures or at least reduce the time taken at borders, and (b) truckers and transporters need to be educated on documentation needed to cross the various borders.'[9]

In a rather sideways manner, therefore, the idea of ALCo as an instrument of regional integration was born. Although HIV/AIDS prevention remained a component of the package, it occupied a less prominent position as the immediate crisis passed. The corridor was increasingly justified in terms of the positive economic effects that it would generate. This was bound up with the observation that a thick belt of urban development along the littoral lent itself to the kind of agglomeration effects that the World Bank has recently posited.[10] In 2014, a treaty was signed in Yamoussoukro by the leaders of the five states concerned. This ostensibly reinvented ALCo as a development corridor – although confus-ingly it has continued to be referred to simply as the Abidjan–Lagos Corridor. Since 2014, two new elements have been added to the mix. The first is a hugely ambitious plan for infrastructural development along the length of the corridor. In 2012 the African Union's Programme for Infrastructure Development in Africa (PIDA) had already adopted ALCo as one of its 16 flagship programmes. The current plan outlined in *One Road, One Vision* is for a six-lane highway running the 1,022 kilometres between Abidjan and Lagos with one-stop border posts (OSBPs),

---

8   Chakrapani and Gwin, *Independent Evaluation*, p. 5.
9   Chakrapani and Gwin, *Independent Evaluation*, p .5.
10 World Bank, *World Development Report, 2009: Reshaping Economic Geography*, Washington, D.C., 2009. The corridor is said to bring together a population of 30 million, which is projected to increase to more than 65 million by 2040. See: ECOWAS Commission, *Abidjan–Lagos Corridor: One Road, One Vision* [henceforth *One Road, One Vision*], Abuja, 2017, p. 25 <http://aid.nepad.org/m_ assets/uploads/document/1509234122244212809.pdf> [Accessed 27 April 2021].

described as joint border posts, interpolated at each of the four border crossings.[11] In line with the notion that ALCo would generate spillover effects well beyond the road itself, public information materials project, albeit in leaden prose, an optimistic vision of the future:

> The Abidjan–Lagos corridor cannot be reduced to the simple construction of a motorway. First, it is a trade and transport corridor, that is to say a coordinated set of multimodal transport and logistics infrastructures and services that facilitate trade and transport flows between the main centers of economic activity. Then, the corridor, thanks to the spatial planning dimension, by which it can fulfil a territory Development function, will allow the opening of the landlocked countries and the deployment of sector-specific policies (industry, agriculture, energy, environment, ICT, tourism, Etc.) in the regional community, thus becoming an economic corridor.[12]

The second innovation has been the decision to establish an ALCO Management Authority (ALCoMA) as a supranational body operating under an ECOWAS mandate and enjoying a separate legal and financial status. The importance of beefing up the organisational side of the operation amounts to recognition of the fact that ALCO has struggled to persuade member states to deliver on two other elements that are crucial to the success of the corridor. The first is consistent implementation of ECOWAS agreements relating to freedom of trade. The second is the harmonisation of transportation, phytosanitary and sanitary regulations, and the removal of a range of non-tariff barriers (NTBs).[13] At the time of writing, it remains to be seen whether ALCoMA will be able play a more proactive role in eliciting co-operation between agencies operating in different countries.

11 Program for Infrastructure Development in Africa, 'Abidjan–Lagos Corridor Highway' <www.au-pida.org/view-project/2002/> [Accessed 19 March 2021]. There have already been some delays. Although construction was supposed to start in 2018, the project is still waiting for the feasibility studies to be completed. The project has support from the European Union (EU) and the African Development Bank (ABD).
12 ECOWAS, *One Road, One Vision*, p. 26.
13 A report by UNCTAD refers to Non-Tariff Measures (NTMs) that consist in part of regulations designed to protect health and the environment 'and NTBs with an intent to distort trade such as quotas'. See: UNCTAD, *Regional Integration and Non-Tariff Measures in the Economic Community of West African States (ECOWAS)*, Geneva, 2018, p. vii.

So Who Uses the Thing?

I will now look more closely at the level of correspondence between the way ALCo is depicted and what actually happens on the ground. Although it ought to be straightforward to get a fix on the corridor, in reality there is very little hard evidence to draw upon. The supporting data exists in fragments and mostly at a country level. The only real information for the corridor as a whole arises out of the collection of data on roadblocks and bribes by the now defunct West Africa Trade Hub and other data relating to border crossing and port dwell times. The problem is compounded by the fact that the various organisations that have been seeking to sell the idea of a development corridor have deployed statistics in a confusing manner. ALCO's own information states that: 'Around 27 million travellers, many of whom are traders and 140,000 truckers, each year use this service, which is lined with harbors, agro-industries, bus stations, major regional markets, places of transit for goods, border areas and parks. used vehicle sales. It concentrates 65 per cent of the economic activities of the region.'[14]

Leaving aside the truckers, the figure for travellers would average 18,493 people crossing each of the four sets of border crossings per day, which is patently not the case. One can only presume that this is aggregated immigration data for the countries as a whole. Again, it is not clear where the figure of 140,000 truckers emanates from. There are certainly not that many trucks using the route on a regular basis, but if it is an aggregate of all the trucks crossing the corridor in a year, this would amount to a daily average of 384 across the length of the corridor. This is certainly possible, but it may also reflect some double- and triple-counting. Again, it is difficult to assess the claim about the economic contribution of the corridor. Adding Lagos to the equation bulks up the numbers considerably, but the economy of the metropolis does not revolve primarily around the existence of the corridor. It seems likely that that these figures also factor in the trade conducted through the five ports of Abidjan, Tema, Lomé, Cotonou and Apapa. These lie along the corridor and are counted by ALCO as part of its infrastructure. But the ports are primarily intended to service a different set of corridors leading to the Sahelian countries.

There is a case, of course, for seeing the big picture here. Hence Theo Notteboom writes that:

> A transport corridor is very often viewed as a point-to-point connection. In reality, individual transport corridors are mostly part of extensive transport

---

[14] www.corridor-wa.org/index.php/en/presentation-alco [Accessed 19 March 2021].

and logistics networks consisting of a range of corridors, each with specific characteristics in terms of scale, transport modes used, price and service quality. The future development of transport corridors will therefore have to be assessed ever more from a network perspective.[15]

Indeed, *One Road, One Vision* itself refers to the complementarity between ALCo and the north–south corridors running from the ports to the landlocked Sahelian states.[16] But if one seeks to understand what difference ALCo itself makes, it is rather misleading to factor in the ports unless it can be shown that their existence contributes to economic activity on the stretch between Abidjan and Lagos. As things stand, investments in the ports are being made almost as if ALCo does not exist. Because the ports are in direct competition with one another, it is important to recognise that there are vested interests in ensuring that goods do *not* travel along the corridor. For example, if transit freight is landed at Tema and then moved sideways across the border to Togo and Benin before being transported northwards, this presents a problem. The port authorities in Lomé and Cotonou would feel that their operations were being undercut, but equally the authorities responsible for the Tema–Ouagadougou Corridor in Ghana would consider that they were losing business. As Ghana lays out plans for a whole series of new corridor routes to the Sahel, including a railway running close to the Togo border, the push to gain a greater share of the transit trade from a rather low base (see Byiers and Woolfrey, this volume) is only likely to increase. The tacit understanding, therefore, is that goods entering through the port of a given country will be channelled onto road and rail within that country before exiting into Burkina Faso or Mali. And this is perhaps one reason why governments have been so schizophrenic in their approach to ALCo. While they cherish the notion that they are furthering the cause of regional integration, the investments that they need to justify, and then to protect it, mean that they have relatively little interest in removing many of the practical obstacles to the free flow of goods along an east–west axis. Despite persistent lobbying, economic actors and lobby groups like the Borderless Alliance struggle to convince governments to translate formal commitments into action.

---

[15]   Theo Notteboom, 'Strategies and Future Development of Transport Corridors', in Alix Yann (ed.), *Les Corridors de Transport*, Caens, 2012, no page <www.faq-logistique.com/EMS-Livre-Corridors-Transport-18-Strategies-Future-Develoment. htm> [Accessed 19 March 2021].

[16]   ECOWAS, *One Road, One Vision*, p. 27.

In order to secure a better grasp of what the dynamics of the corridor look like, one would ideally want fine-grained data on the number of vehicles and people making use of it. As things stand, such data does not exist, at least in the public domain.[17] On the face of things, there does not seem to be great pressure on the corridor. For example, one does not encounter the long queues of heavy-goods vehicles that used to be a feature of the Northern Corridor between Kenya and Uganda. One rough estimate from those working at the Kraké–Seme border in 2017 was that a total of around 200 vehicles a day crossed in either direction.[18] By contrast, Malaba handles around 1,000 and Busia another 500 trucks. At the border crossings themselves, there are vehicles lined up along the route at Aflao and around Seme, but this reflects the lack of proper parking facilities rather than the pressure of volume per se. Although there are buses and private vehicles that ply the route on a daily basis, one does not witness acute strain on the immigration services at any of the four crossing points either. On the face of it, therefore, the visible evidence would suggest that the corridor is under-utilised.

At least when it comes to trade, one can cross-check this data against ECOWAS trade statistics. According to *One Road, One Vision*, more than 90 per cent of intra-regional trade is carried by road.[19] The ECOWAS trade statistics furnish data on the trade between particular countries, but they also offer some clues as to the direction and nature of the flows. Two points clearly emerge. The first is that between 2011 and 2016, at a time when the dollar value of intra-regional trade for all of ECOWAS actually declined, the picture for members of the ALCo was not significantly better: it only increased for Benin, while the value of trade was essentially static for Nigeria and Côte d'Ivoire, declined for Togo and fell precipitously for Ghana. Only 5 per cent of Nigerian exports were directed to ECOWAS countries and nearly half of that was accounted for by Côte d'Ivoire (Table 9.1).

Given that half of the latter's oil has come from Nigeria by sea, this would imply that the transportation of other Nigerian goods by road is rather limited.[20] Conversely, the statistics reveal a marked decline in the value of Ivorian goods

---

[17]   Revealingly, repeated efforts to secure information from Ghana customs officials about the number of vehicles crossing through the Aflao have drawn a blank.

[18]   Interview, Kraké border post, 22 August 2017; When I had the opportunity to ask the head of the Nigerian side of the newly-opened OSBP at Seme in 2018 he said he was unaware of the number.

[19]   ECOWAS, *One Road, One Vision*, p. 22.

[20]   Logistics Capacity Assessment, 'Côte d'Ivoire Fuel' <https://dlca.logcluster.org/pages/releaseview.action;jsessionid=1234892089338EA50A738A649067E0F5?pageId=853596> [Accessed 19 March 2021].

imported into Nigeria, the bulk of which was presumably transported by road
(e.g. kola nuts). Hence one can reasonably conclude that the two ends of the
corridor are not closely connected with one another. Ghana, which currently
boasts the third largest economy, ought to capture a significant amount of
regional trade. Over the same period, Ghana exported less to Nigeria than
Côte d'Ivoire, but was the second largest importer of goods from Nigeria. But
again, the value of the goods was rather modest. This is reflected in the limited
number of trucks with Ghana number plates that can be seen around Seme – or,
for that matter, Nigerian vehicles at the Aflao border crossing. At the Kraké–
Seme border, interviews in 2017 revealed a relatively limited range of goods that
originated in Ghana – that is some plastic goods, cosmetics and kola nuts – and
virtually nothing from Côte d'Ivoire.[21]

Table 9.1. Exports from countries on Abidjan–Lagos Corridor (US$).

Country	Total exports	ECOWAS exports	Two top recipients of exports
Cote d'Ivoire	12,311,780,008	3,253,472,623	Nig: 1,347,720,420
2011	13,621,083,378	3,437,243,069	Bur: 423,559,719
2016			Nig: 764,530,162
			Gha: 942,949,113
Ghana	17,969,004,595	5,906,372,283	Tog: 4,394,205,500
2011	12,919,721,309	1,362,848,820	Bur: 500,427,359
2016			Mal: 407,841,529
			Bur: 317,967,973
Nigeria	126,716,069,468	3,603,478,741	CI: 1,810,075,928
2011	72,952,353,155	3,687,410,495	Gha: 896,496,101
2016			CI: 1,805,920,385
			Gha: 673,357,606
Benin	390,819,131	115,349,344	Nig: 46,352,999
2011	791,526,649	165,449,291	Gha: 18,644,483
2016			Niger: 58,246,760
			Nig: 43,738,676
Togo	625,314,495	991,695,250	Gha: 127,836,814
2011	582,099,457	1,011,829,371	Bur: 126,466,068
2016			Bur: 126,999,156
			Gha: 107,924,377

Source: ECOWAS, 'Exports', <www.ecowas.int/23749-2/> [Accessed 19 March 2021].

---

21   Interview Kraké border post, 22 August 2017.

The second very striking finding is that states have tended to trade most with their immediate neighbours. This is amply demonstrated by the relationship between Ghana and Togo, although the exports of Ghana have fluctuated widely by year. The Sahelian countries have loomed disproportionately large for the ALCo countries. This is very clear in the case of Ghana where 53 per cent of the value of exports in 2016 was accounted for by Mali and Burkina Faso – a figure that does not take into account the transit trade. The entrepôt states of Benin and Togo are a specific variant because they depend on the Sahelian trade, but also rely on trade to their larger neighbours, namely Nigeria and Ghana respectively. The volume of the trade between Benin and Nigeria is clearly much greater than the official statistics would imply because of the continuing vitality of contraband economy. According to one estimate, as much as 75 per cent of GDP in Benin is accounted for by informal cross-border trade.[22] What all of this would tend to indicate is two things: firstly, that the overall volume of trade conducted along the length of the corridor is limited and, secondly, that the corridor actually functions as a series of segments rather than as an integrated whole.

This is apparent when one zooms in to consider the behaviour of small-scale traders. Prior to the closure of the borders in March 2021 in order to reduce the spread of COVID-19, there was a vigorous trade concentrated on Lomé. Every day, busloads of traders from Abidjan and Kumasi arrived at Aflao and crossed on foot to buy goods at Asigamé (or the Grand Marché). The mostly female traders bought goods in Lomé (still largely textiles) before making the return journey the following day.[23] They did not consider going any further than Lomé because what little profit they make would be eroded by the rigours of crossing another border. The same logic played out in the fish trade. The fish markets in Lomé draw much of their supply from traders who come from as far as western Ghana. A recent study describes what is essentially a relay system in which, say, dried fish from Ada will be transported as far as Aflao, then moved across the border in smaller quantities by motorcycle or carts, and then picked up by other traders from Togo and Benin.[24] It makes no economic sense for any trader to seek to transport the goods across multiple borders. In the case of manufactured goods, there is a tendency to sell to

<hr />

[22]   UNCTAD, *Regional Integration*, p. 4.
[23]   I have interviewed many of these traders. I have both met them as they left and rejoined the buses in Aflao and have traced them to hotels in Lomé that cater specifically to Ivorian traders.
[24]   Faridath Aboudou, *et al.*, *Study on the Specific Problems of Women Traders on the Abidjan–Lagos Corridor*, Dakar, 2017, section 8.2.

the neighbouring countries, but very few enterprises exploit the corridor as a whole. The exception is cement, over which the Nigerian empire of Dangote has established a firm grip within the regional market. Despite rapid urban growth in West Africa, there is fierce competition for market share between Dangote and factories in each of the countries concerned. A common sight along the corridor in recent years has been convoys of Dangote lorries that transport Nigerian cement in vehicles bearing Ghana number plates. Whereas Ghana removed its controls on imported cement, Nigeria remains a *de facto* protected market for Dangote. In this case, one could reasonably argue that the corridor and the removal of tariff barriers is reflected in the movement of cement, but it is all in one direction and it is an exception to the rule. In most cases, those who produce manufactured products sell their goods in neighbouring countries, but do not venture much further.

This begs the obvious question of why there is not more traffic along the length of the corridor. The simple answer resides in the many disincentives that manufacturers, traders and transporters encounter when they try to cross multiple borders. The first of these relate to the persistence of a multiplicity of restrictions on trade. Along with other regional economic communities (RECs), ECOWAS has been on a five-step path to full economic integration.[25] With the coming into force of the Common External Tariff (CET) in 2015, it is supposedly transitioning from a free trade area (FTA) into a fully-fledged customs union (stage three). But the common market, which would involve the creation of common policies relating to agriculture, communications, energy and so on, is still in the planning – alongside the monetary union. To some extent, this programme has been superseded by the inauguration of the African Continental Free Trade Area (AfCFTA), although the latter still depends on the architecture of the RECs. A further source of difficulty is that the Francophone countries also belong to UEMOA (Union Economique et Monétaire Ouest Africaine), which has been seeking to move towards its own customs union. Despite attempts to harmonise regulations, discrepancies abound, for example with respect to rules of origin. Under the ECOWAS Trade Liberalisation Scheme (ETLS), which came into effect in 2003, there needs to be 60 per cent local content and value added to the tune of at least 30 per cent of the price of processed goods in order for them to qualify for exemption from tariffs. Although there is now agreement on

---

[25] The five steps derive from the Abuja Treaty on trade liberalisation. See: United Nations Economic Commission for Africa, *Progress Report on Regional Integration Efforts in Africa Towards the Promotion of Intra-African Trade*, Addis Ababa, 2005, p. 3.

the 30 per cent rule, the Francophone states often calculate the value added differently.[26] This becomes a very real issue when customs officials at the border choose to question whether a consignment of goods should actually be exempt from duty. Whether the duty is eventually paid, or the goods pass through after lengthy delays, this creates a strong element of uncertainty and risk for economic operators. Although AfCFTA has addressed rules of origin explicitly, it is likely that some of the underlying issues of non-compliance will remain because of vested interests that cluster at the national level.

Along the corridor, there is a strong sense that Nigeria is the country where there is by far the greatest risk associated with trying to despatch goods across border. Despite the fact that the country ostensibly has the most to gain from opening up the regional market, and hence from ALCo itself, Nigerian leaders have focused much more on protecting the domestic market and shielding the vested interests that are encrusted around it. It is striking that while Nigeria accounted for 44.6 per cent of intra-regional exports in 2015, it accounted for a mere 14 per cent of intra-regional imports – which is substantially lower than Ghana and Côte d'Ivoire which were responsible for 25.7 per cent and 18.4 per cent of the total respectively.[27] Nigeria is the country that is primarily responsible for a proliferation of NTBs. It has imposed import bans on 24 categories of commodities, including goods produced by fellow ECOWAS member states.[28] Nigeria also operates a series of import levies, for example on rice, which are justified with reference to the need to protect local producers from external competition. The Buhari regime has been particularly susceptible to national interest arguments based on the imperative to reduce food prices and to defend jobs. In 2017, it banned the import of tomato paste, powder and concentrate in a consumer-ready form, increased duties on other tomato concentrate and imposed an import levy at US$1,500 per tonne, after the largest manufacturer threatened to relocate its operations to China.[29] This is significant because tinned tomatoes were one of the items that neighbouring countries had managed to sell to Nigeria with some success. Rice is another commodity that is defined as strategic, with the government professing to be

26   UNCTAD, *Regional Integration*, pp. 24–25.
27   UNCTAD, *Regional Integration*, p. 3 (fig. 2).
28   Erik von Uexkull and Lulu Shui, *Implementing the ECOWAS Common External Tariff*, Africa Trade Practice Working Paper Series, 5, 2014, p. 13; Nigerian Ministry of Finance, Import Prohibition List, 2015.
29   EPA Monitoring, 'Nigerian Government Adopts Trade Measures against Tomato Imports', 15 May 2017 <http://epamonitoring.net/nigerian-government-adopts-trade-measures-against-tomato-imports/> [Accessed 19 March 2021].

promoting national self-sufficiency. In August 2019, the government closed the
Seme border without any warning as part of its attempts to deal with increased
rice smuggling from Benin.[30] Despite repeated promises to revisit the issue,
the border remained closed in the early months of 2020 when the COVID-19
pandemic intervened – which justified closing all the borders indefinitely. At
the end of 2020, Buhari announced the reopening of the borders, allegedly
after the intercession of none other than Aliko Dangote, whose cement had
been blocked from the Benin market.[31] However, as of March 2021 little traffic
was passing the border legally, while the corridor remained effectively closed.
To make matters worse, the Benin government decided in June that goods
transiting to Nigeria needed to pay duty, ostensibly on the basis that rules of
origin were being flouted.[32] It was widely believed that this was really an act of
revenge aimed specifically at Nigeria. The protectionist impulse in Nigeria also
throws up a major disincentive to manufacturers in neighbouring countries
that might otherwise attempt to compete in the largest market of all.

There have also been numerous other anomalies in the way duties have
been applied. In principle, goods produced within an ECOWAS country
should enjoy free and equal access to other countries in the region under the
principles of the FTA. There are inevitably questions about the compliance
with provisions for a minimum of 60 per cent local content, but in most cases
the formal procedure is straightforward.[33] Manufacturers simply need to file an
application for accreditation under the ECOWAS Trade Liberalisation Scheme
(ETLS) through a national committee, and provide supporting evidence. On

---

30   Felix Onuah, 'Nigeria Closes Part of Border with Benin to Check Rice Smuggling',
      29 August 2019 <www.reuters.com/article/instant-article/idUKL5N25O5SP>
      [Accessed 19 March 2021].

31   Nicholas Norbook and Ruth Olourounbi, 'Nigeria: President Buhari Opens Land
      Border at Seme, Illela, Maigatari and Mfun', 16 December 2020[Accessed 19 March 2021]. Another Dangote business,
      Dangote Farms, was involved in rice production and was a beneficiary of the initial
      closure. Matthieu Millecamps 'The Benin–Nigeria Border Is Officially Open Again,
      but Smuggling Is on the Rise', 18 January 2021 <www.theafricareport.com/59504/
      the-benin-nigeria-border-is-officially-open-again-but-smuggling-is-on-the-rise/>
      [Accessed 19 March 2021].

32   Trucks that could not cross to Nigeria became stuck in Benin or at the Ghana border.
      Interview with freight forwarders in Aflao and Benin, and direct observation at
      Aflao, June 2021. The matter remained unresolved as of the end of July.

33   See ECOWAS Trade Liberalisation Scheme (ETLS) <www.etls.ecowas.int/>.

approval of the company and the product, the HS code reflects ETLS accreditation and the list of companies is even searchable on the ECOWAS website.[34] But there have been complaints about Nigerian customs officials refusing to accept the certification of imported goods and insisting on levying duties at the border. Hence ETLS accredited companies that produce iron goods have effectively been blocked from the Nigerian market.[35] The delays and uncertainty have served to deter manufacturers from trying to export goods to Nigeria – which is almost certainly the intended effect.

Secondly, a major source of grievance for manufacturers has been the transit fees, tolls and other levies that are imposed on vehicles that seek to move along the corridor. In 2017, one Ivorian manufacturer of plastic bottles and caps estimated that the cost of moving a truck from Abidjan to Cotonou was as much as CFA Francs 915,000, or the equivalent of €1,390.00.[36] Of that total, CFA Francs 830,000 was attributable to transit fees. By contrast, a truck that travelled from Abidjan to Ouagadougou would incur a total cost of CFA Francs 158,650 or €241.15. In addition, to those that are required to be discharged by the central government, local authorities and transport unions in Benin often impose their own fees upon trucks – as happens along many of Africa's transport corridors. All of this makes it uneconomic for businesses to make full use of ALCo: every border that is traversed simply multiplies the operating expenses.

Thirdly, a major constraint on the free flow of vehicles along ALCo has been the proliferation of weigh stations and roadblocks. Different standards are laid down by UEMOA and ECOWAS, which causes considerable confusion because the Francophone countries have a foot in both organisations. There have also been problems arising from the sequencing of efforts at convergence. In 2014 Benin sought to apply the newly agreed ECOWAS limit whereas its neighbours did not. This created months of confusion as large numbers of vehicles became stuck in that country. The roadblocks, which have proliferated in the name of police, gendarmes, customs and immigration, have contributed to delays, but are also associated with blatant extortion. This affects the transporters, but also impacts especially on the profit margins of small-scale traders.

---

[34] See ELTS <www.etls.ecowas.int/approved-products/>. UEMOA has a parallel process which applies only between the Francophone member states.

[35] Interview, Kraké border post, 22 August 2017.

[36] Kouadio Sey, 'Obstacles to Free Movement of Goods within UEMOA and ECOWAS', Borderless Alliance Conference, Ouagadougou, 10–12 May 2017 <http://borderlesswa.com/sites/default/files/BA2017/Kouadio%20Sey%20_English.pdf> [Accessed 19 March 2021].

Those who travel between Abidjan and Lomé complain of being fleeced by Ghanaian and Togolese officials along the route.[37] A recurring theme during interviews with fish sellers in 2019 was the money that had routinely to be paid to border officials. An intriguing pattern is that while officials often demand token bribes from their own nationals, they charge 'foreigners' more depending on where they have come from. A trader in Togo, who buys used plastic bottles in Ghana, explained that the worst thing she could do was to show her Benin documentation, remarking that: "If you show your Benin ID card, you are dead: they will tax you more!"[38]

A survey of the difficulties faced by traders in foodstuffs found that the greatest complaint (mentioned by 83 per cent of respondents) was harassment on the road.[39] The problem has been identified many times, most recently by an ECOWAS Task Force, but the results of lobbying have been patchy. Whereas Togo and Benin have removed almost all of the roadblocks, Ghana and Nigeria have not dealt with the issue. The newly elected Akuffo-Addo government in Ghana publicly pledged to remove all but a couple of customs barriers by September 2017. But a year later, very little had changed. The promises of President Buhari have similarly come to nothing. The stretch of road from Seme to Badagry is in a league all of its own. During a Borderless fact-finding caravan in which I participated, the bus passed through 19 check-points in 21 minutes (at speed only because we were travelling in a quasi-official vehicle that was waved through the obstacle course) – controls that were manned by competing branches of immigration, customs and police. The case for maintaining the checkpoints in the face of constant complaints from travellers and transporters is typically made on grounds of security and crime prevention. These effectively trump arguments about the need to facilitate trade and freedom of movement. Part of the reason for the heavy customs presence is that Nigerian import restrictions on items such as rice have created enormous incentives to smuggle.

And, finally, there are the chronic delays that impacts on the traffic along the borders. The state of the roads is a relatively minor part of the problem. Most of the corridor is single-track, although there are stretches of two-lane highway in Benin and Ghana. The roads themselves are in a reasonable state (79 per cent are defined as good and 12 per cent as average) with the exception of the

---

37   Interview with Ivorian traders, Aflao, 25 August 2017.
38   Interview with trader at Kodome market, Lomé, 21 March 2019.
39   Abdou, *et al*, *Study*, Table 16 (no page given).

Nigerian section of the corridor, which is in a severely degraded condition.[40] The real bottlenecks have occurred at the border crossings themselves. In 2011/2012, trucks travelling eastwards along the corridor would spend an average of no fewer than 205 hours at the four border crossings, with the Togo–Benin and Benin border posts representing the greatest bottlenecks (Table 9.2).

There are many different reasons for this. Some arise directly from the duplication of bureaucratic procedures. Part of the problem also relates to the difficulties of sharing data, when agencies are using systems that speak to each other imperfectly and when officials struggle with either English or French. The opening of OSBPs along the corridor was intended to tackle the issue, but the facilities that were built at Kraké-Seme and Noepe-Akanu stood empty for years because of the lack of agreement on the fundamentals. These were finally opened for business towards the end of 2018, while a third is planned for Sanveecondji-Hillacondji at the border between Togo and Benin. If the evidence for East Africa is anything to go by, there is a reasonable chance that these will assist in harmonising procedures and reducing delays.[41] But much still hinges on a willingness to implement agreements and align the information technologies. In the last couple of years, the processing times at the borders have improved, with the total average delay for a truck travelling eastwards along the corridor being reduced to 68 hours in 2016/2017. However, there is a long way to go to match the operations of the functioning OSBPs in East Africa. The delays at the Ghana/Côte d'Ivoire and Togo/Benin borders are especially acute, as Table 9.2 indicates. This cannot really be attributed to the challenge of dealing with high volumes of traffic. The bottlenecks lie within the implementation of regulations at the border. Needless to say, slowing things down – or facilitating speedier passage – creates abundant opportunities for rent-seeking on the part of border officials. As things stand, the OSBPs that have been completed stand more or less unused with expensive equipment left to rot.

40   ECOWAS, *One Road, One Vision*, p. 16.
41   Paul Nugent and Isabella Soi, 'One-stop Border Posts in East Africa: State Encounters of the Fourth Kind', *Journal of Eastern African Studies*, 14:3, 2020, p. 9.

Table 9.2. Border crossing times for trucks in hours, 2010–2017.

Crossing Point	2010/11	2011/12	2012/13	2013/14	2014/15	2015/16	2016/17
Noé (CI) to Elubo (Gh)	37	36	30	34	30	21	21
Elubo to Noé	14	25	38	32	23	11	14
Aflao (Gh) to Lomé (Tog)	41	33	19	22	16	13	16
Lomé to Aflao	65	36	23	42	19	11	9
Sanveecondji (Tog) to Hillacondji (Ben)	13	75	34	30	28	20	22
Hillacondji to Sanveecondji	10	22	4	7	6	5	4
Kraké (Ben) to Seme (Nig)	15	61	45	24	38	32	9
Seme to Krake	28	86	87	63	31	27	14

Source: Abidjan–Lagos Corridor Organisation.

By Way of a Conclusion: The Disappearing Corridor

The Abidjan–Lagos Corridor presents us with something of a paradox. The case for making substantial infrastructural investments is that ALCo is the 'lung' or the 'beating heart' of West Africa where most of the commerce of the region is transacted. But this is not reflected in the volume of traffic on the road or, more tellingly, in the ECOWAS trade statistics. And when governments invest in expansion of the ports, their focus is on maximising traffic along the north–south corridors to the Sahel. This means that governments in practice seek to retard the flow of goods along ALCo itself. The corridor does link no fewer than five capital cities, and many smaller urban centres. The vision that is increasingly articulated concerning the potential advantages of urbanism, in a context where the corridor provides the connective tissue, is certainly worthy of closer attention. But at the moment, using the corridor is prohibitively expensive for most businesses. Selling manufactured goods across one border is sustainable, but beyond that it often becomes financially perilous. In reality, the corridor as an economic space is constituted by two other sets of actors. The first is made up of countless smaller traders who deploy a system of relays to move fish, agricultural goods and other consumer items between markets in border regions that are often closely connected to each other. In so doing, they avoid much of the financial burden that comes with crossing multiple borders in a single journey. And the second is made up of the smugglers who are able to carve out a living by exploiting the differences in pricing and availability on either side of a particular border. Here the ironies abound. The first of these groups receives little treatment in the documents that justify ALCo as a target of investment, while the activities of the second provide the justification for ratcheting up surveillance and control measures that defeat the very purpose of the corridor. This is captured perfectly in the opening of an OSBP at Kraké-Seme, with a great deal of fanfare, only to be followed by the Nigerian decision to unilaterally close the border in August 2019. Maybe the dynamic will change in the coming years but, as things stand, ALCo remains a bundle of unresolved contradictions. Although the five member states formally rank the development of the east–west corridor as their foremost priority, their actions have so far demonstrated a rather weak commitment to the corridor in practice. The closure of land borders as a response to COVID-19, which unleashed none of the anguish that was witnessed in East and Southern Africa, has merely underlined how under-utilised ALCo really is. Although small traders were disadvantaged, larger manufacturers and transporters were remarkably accepting about the *de facto* closure of the entire corridor. Because the only real complaints issued from borderlanders, who could be dismissed as hardened smugglers, governments (especially that of Ghana) almost seemed to prefer this state of affairs. The disjuncture between the lofty rhetoric about the corridor and its practical disappearance could not have been greater than over 2020–2021. One is left wondering what Fela would have made of the ongoing 'powershow'.

Bibliography

Aboudou, Faridath, *et al.*, *Study on the Specific Problems of Women Traders on the Abidjan–Lagos Corridor*, Dakar, 2017.
Chakrapani, Deepa and Gwin, Catherine, *An Independent Evaluation of the World Bank's Support of Regional Programs: Case Study of the West Africa HIV/AIDS Project for the Abidjan–Lagos Corridor*, Washington D.C., 2006 <http://documents.worldbank.org/curated/en/277671468204835498/pdf/392960AFR0W1AF1agos1Transp01PUBLIC1.pdf>.
ECOWAS Commission, *Abidjan–Lagos Corridor: One Road, One Vision*, Abuja, 2017 <http://aid.nepad.org/m_assets/uploads/document/1509234122244212809.pdf>.
— 'Exports' <www.ecowas.int/23749-2/> [Accessed 19 March 2021].
EPA Monitoring, 'Nigerian Government Adopts Trade Measures against Tomato Imports', 15 May 2017 <http://epamonitoring.net/nigerian-government-adopts-trade-measures-against-tomato-imports/> [Accessed 19 March 2021].
Logistics Capacity Assessment, 'Côte d'Ivoire Fuel' <https://dlca.logcluster.org/

pages/releaseview.action;jsessionid=1234892089338EA50A738A649067E0F5?p
ageId=853596> [Accessed 19 March 2021].

Millecamps, Matthieu, 'The Benin–Nigeria Border is Officially Open Again, but
Smuggling Is on the Rise', 18 January 2021 <www.theafricareport.com/59504/
the-benin-nigeria-border-is-officially-open-again-but-smuggling-is-on-the-rise/>
[Accessed 19 March 2021]

Norbook, Nicholas and Olourounbi, Ruth, 'Nigeria, President Buhari Opens Land
Border at Seme, Illela, Maigatari and Mfun', 16 December 2020[Accessed 19 March 2021].

Notteboom, Theo, 'Strategies and Future Development of Transport Corridors', in Yann,
Alix, (ed.), *Les Corridors de Transport*, Caens, 2012, pp. 289–312 <www.faq-logis-
tique.com/EMS-Livre-Corridors-Transport-18-Strategies-Future-Develment.htm>.

Nugent, Paul, *Boundaries, Communities and State-Making in West Africa: The Centrality
of the Margins*, Cambridge, 2019.

Nugent, Paul and Soi, Isabella, 'One-Stop Border Posts in East Africa: State Encounters
of the Fourth Kind', *Journal of Eastern African Studies*, 14:3, 2020, pp. 433–54.

Onuah, Felix, 'Nigeria Closes Part of Border with Benin to Check Rice Smuggling',
29 August 2019 <www.reuters.com/article/instant-article/idUKL5N25O5SP>
[Accessed 19 March 2021].

Program for Infrastructure Development in Africa, 'Abidjan–Lagos Corridor Highway'
<www.au-pida.org/view-project/2002/ [Accessed 19 March 2021].

Sey, Kouadio, 'Obstacles to Free Movement of Goods within UEMOA and ECOWAS',
Borderless Alliance Conference, Ouagadougou, 10–12 May 2017 <http://border-
lesswa.com/sites/default/files/BA2017/Kouadio%20Sey%20_English.pdf>
[Accessed 19 March 2021].

von Uexkull, Erik and Shui, Lulu, *Implementing the ECOWAS Common External Tariff*,
Africa Trade Practice Working Paper Series, 5, 2014.

UNCTAD, *Regional Integration and Non-Tariff Measures in the Economic Community
of West African States (ECOWAS)*, Geneva, 2018.

United Nations Economic Commission for Africa, *Progress Report on Regional Integration
Efforts in Africa Towards the Promotion of Intra-African Trade*, Addis Ababa, 2005.

World Bank, *The Web of Transport Corridors in South Asia*, Washington D.C., 2018.

— *World Development Report, 2009: Reshaping Economic Geography*, Washington D.C.,
2009.

CHAPTER 10

The Jealousy of Roads:
Construction, Circulation and Competition
on East Africa's Transport Corridors

HUGH LAMARQUE

Nothing is more usual, among states which have made some advances in commerce, than to look on the progress of their neighbours with a suspicious eye, to consider all trading states as their rivals, and to suppose that it is impossible for any of them to flourish, but at their expense.[1]

Introduction

This chapter investigates some of the more abstract questions about transport corridors and geopolitics: *How is corridor development shaped by competition? Under what conditions is trading infrastructure that spans multiple states mutually beneficial? When, and for whom, is a trading corridor a threat?* In approaching these questions, I draw on interview material with officials, corridor users and freight forwarders from across East Africa, supplemented by news reports, government documents, and by my own observations travelling the region in the passenger seats of freight vehicles between 2017 and 2019.

Rwanda's capital city, Kigali, stands at a critical junction in East Africa's road network – a nodal point where importers and exporters make a choice about their route to the coast (see Maps 10.1 and 10.2). Heading north, freight vehicles embark on the 1,660-kilometre Northern Corridor, crossing two international borders through Uganda and Kenya to the port of Mombasa. Heading southeast, they travel the 1420-kilometre Central Corridor to the Tanzanian port of Dar es Salaam. Both routes have undergone significant changes in recent years

---

[1] David Hume, 'Of the Jealousy of Trade', *Walker's Hibernian Magazine, or Compendium of Entertaining Knowledge*, May 1785–December 1811, pp. 623–25.

– with much more scheduled to follow – and decisions made in Kigali offer a valuable lens into their different characteristics.

A great many groups are involved in planning, building, using and benefitting from East Africa's transport corridors, and their divergent interests complicate analysis of the politics underlying their competition. In approaching the topic, it is important to note that corridor competitiveness is not the same thing as corridor attractiveness from the perspective of road and rail users. This distinction is valuable and can often be overlooked. Corridors compete not only to be used, but also to be funded and built. A second, related distinction is drawn between groups that generate revenue from corridor access and those for which access is an expenditure. Dominating the first category are entrepreneurial elites, very often embedded in state institutions, who play a significant role in shaping East Africa's corridor development. These gatekeepers pursue a fine balancing act between maximising the circulation of people and goods along a corridor and maximising the revenue that can be extracted from them: activities that are inherently in tension. The monopolising spirit of elites involved in infrastructure development has prompted a dialectical relationship between the Central and Northern Corridors, with changes to either one giving rise to changes in the other. The process does not always sit comfortably with the needs of importers, drivers and passengers.

Approaching transport corridors in this manner brings regional geo-politics to the forefront of analysis. The distribution of gatekeeping revenue among groups involved in the development of transport infrastructure has become a central feature of state power in the region, where large-scale transport infrastructure informs election campaigning, coalition formation and international disputes.[2] An official discourse of complementarity among states in the regional economic community masks a contentious decision-making process that must account for potentially damaging path dependencies, collective action and sequencing problems, and high-risk strategies for first-movers. What follows proceeds in four sections: a theoretical background, a timeline of developments along the Northern and Central Corridors, empirical comparisons of movements and shipments in each case, and an analysis of their competition.

---

[2]   See: Michael Bratton and Mwangi S. Kimenyi, 'Voting in Kenya: Putting Ethnicity in Perspective', *Journal of Eastern African Studies*, 2:2, 2008, pp. 272–89; Nic Cheeseman, Gabrielle Lynch and Justin Willis, 'Decentralisation in Kenya: the Governance of Governors', *The Journal of Modern African Studies*, 54:1, 2016, pp. 1–35.

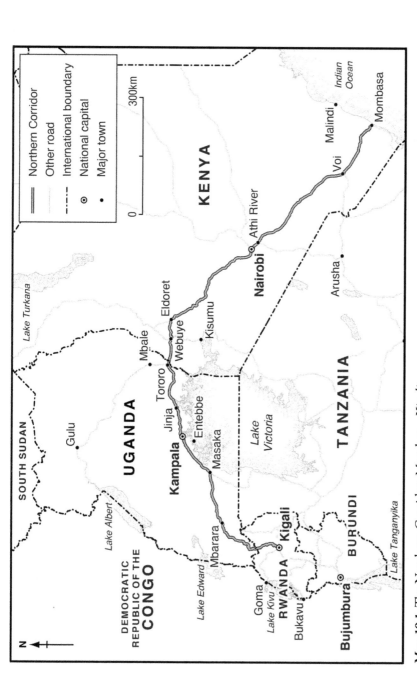

Map 10.1. The Northern Corridor, Mombasa–Kigali. (Source: Author.)

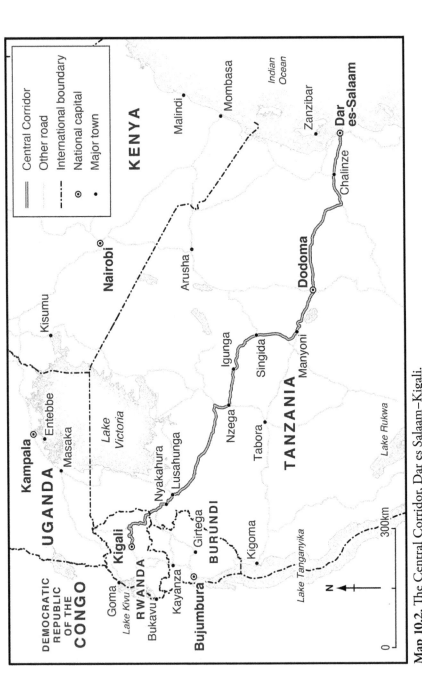

Map 10.2. The Central Corridor, Dar es Salaam–Kigali.
(Source: Author.)

Competition or Complementarity?

The term 'transport corridor' is used here in a straightforward descriptive sense, referring to overland transport infrastructure, connecting large urban centres, containing at least one seaport, and spanning at least one international border.[3] As in the maps above, they very often involve a central artery, with smaller off-shoots extending from them. The overall effect resembles a river basin, with tributaries joining a core pathway – though notably in this case the flow of goods and people moves in both directions. Transport corridors can become essential avenues for international trade, often involving road, rail and other modes of transport simultaneously.[4]

The subject of corridor competition has given rise to a growing literature that investigates infrastructural strategies and best practices, corridor co-ordination, the interaction of gateway ports and corridors, and corridor attractiveness.[5] While productivity rests on proximity to 'markets, customers, competitors, supporting industries, and governments', competition between corridors is most often understood in terms of the expansion of seaport capacity and the efficiency of transport operations.[6] This chapter takes a different approach, exploring concepts in classical political economy to offer a framework for understanding the geopolitical repercussions when corridors compete.

Writing on competition between states in industrialising Europe, David Hume observes how the logic of war and the logic of trade become blurred at

3   Cf. Jean-Paul Rodrique, 'The Geography of Global Supply Chains: Evidence from Third-Party Logistics', *Journal of Supply Chain Management*, 48:3, 2012, pp. 15–23; Fraser & Notteboom, 2010; Albie Hope and John Cox, *Development Corridors*, London, 2015.

4   Hope and Cox, *Development*; Pradeep Srivastava, *Regional Corridors Development in Regional Cooperation*, *Asian Development Bank Economics Working Paper Series*, 258, Washington, D.C., 2011.

5   Theo Notteboom, 'Strategies and Future Development of Transport Corridors', *Les Corridors de Transport*, 2012, pp. 289–311; John Arnold, *et al.*, *Best Practices in Corridor Management*, No. 45128, pp. 1–51, Washington, D.C., 2005; Martijn R. Van Der Horst and Peter W. De Langen, 'Coordination in Hinterland Transport Chains: A Major Challenge for the Seaport Community', *Maritime Economics & Logistics*, 10:1–2, 2008, pp. 108–129; Notteboom & Rodrigue, 2005; Fraser & Notteboom, 2014.

6   Wim Naudé, *The Financial Crisis of 2008 and the Developing Countries*, No. 2009/01 WIDER Discussion Paper, Helsinki, 2009; Monios & Lambert, 2013.

the level of government decision-making.[7] This is not a natural development, he argues, since war produces a winner at the expense of a loser, while the natural state of trade is one of mutual benefit. What Hume calls the jealousy of trade arises when commercial success becomes a matter of political and military survival.[8] It is grounded in the political influence of a powerful mercantile class, combined with a misconception among elites about the threat posed by thriving neighbours. Hume considers the jealousy of trade to be a corruption of thinking that, in the most extreme cases, brings Hobbesian jealousy of state into the realm of economic exchange and makes the balance of military power inseparable from the balance of economic power.[9]

Writing in the same period, Jean-Francois Mélon reasons that, among states with distinct manufacturing specialities, trade rests on necessity, produces mutual reciprocity, and may act as a stabilising force in geopolitics.[10] Once one state becomes more diversified in its manufacturing, it gains the power to deprive its neighbours of goods without suffering in return. This behaviour can amount to a case for war on the part of those who are cut out of the supply chain.[11] Even where all the states involved are effectively self-sufficient, the instability lingers. Trade is pursued not out of absolute necessity, but for 'profit, economic growth and luxury'.[12] It can be used as leverage in order to maximise each of these ends, or else as a political tool to punish rivals. In this context, what makes trade warlike is the jealousy among sellers looking for new markets and increased profits. This mercantile jealousy, Adam Smith writes, 'inflames, and is itself inflamed by the violence of national animosity'.[13] From the moment that merchants become the trusted councillors of the governing elite, he argues, their expert council teaches the state the jealousy of trade.[14]

Some are more vulnerable to the jealousy of trade than others. According to Hume, the only states that should fear the improvements and industry of their neighbours are those who 'flourish only by being the brokers, the factors, and

7   Hume, 'Jealousy of Trade'; Istvan Hont, *Jealousy of Trade: International Competition and the Nation-state in Historical Perspective*, Cambridge, 2005.
8   Hont, *Jealousy of Trade*, p. 7.
9   Hont, *Jealousy of Trade*, p. 8.
10   Bindon & Mélon, 1738.
11   Hont, *Jealousy of Trade*, p. 31.
12   Hont, *Jealousy of Trade*, p. 31.
13   Adam Smith, *The Wealth of Nations: An Inquiry into the Nature and Causes of the Wealth of Nations*, Petersfield, 1776 [2010], IV.iii 2.13.
14   Smith, *Wealth of Nations*, IV.iii 2.13; Hont, *Jealousy of Trade*, p. 55.

carriers of others'.[15] It is natural, Hume argues, for states of this nature to be apprehensive about their neighbours, who may at any moment 'take into their own hands the management of their affairs', depriving brokering states of their source of revenue.[16]

In order to apply these concepts to contemporary events, it is necessary to introduce the divergent interests of actors representing the state. I draw on a literature in political and sociological theory that regards the state as an arena of power rather than an agent in its own right.[17] Competition within this arena forces trade-offs that economic institutions do not have to make, balancing the interests of politicians, civil servants, voters, and powerful non-state actors.[18] Add to this the pressures of distributing gatekeeping revenue and the difficulty of predicting the impact of government investment on trade flows, and corridor development becomes shrouded in conflicting motivations, economic uncertainty and political risk.[19]

These theoretical discussions resonate with contemporary accounts of geopolitics in the East African Community (EAC). The idea of economic equilibrium as a substitute for military equilibrium is a common feature in high-level meetings at the EAC and is echoed in the language of its fourth 'pillar' on political federation.[20] Hume's call for regional collaboration is reflected in the public statements of national leaders, who, in public at least, continue to stress the complementary nature of infrastructure linking East African territories.[21]

[15]   Hume, 'Jealousy of Trade', p. 2.

[16]   Hume, 'Jealousy of Trade', p. 2.

[17]   See Mann, 1984; Abrams, 1988.

[18]   Terry M. Moe, 'Political Institutions: The Neglected Side of the Story', *Journal of Law, Economics & Organisation*, 6, 1990, pp. 213–53.

[19]   See also: Jean-Paul Rodrigue, 'Transportation and the geographical and functional integration of global production networks', *Growth and Change*, 37:4, 2006, pp. 510–25.

[20]   East African Community, 'EAC Integration Pillars' <www.eac.int/integration-pillars> [Accessed 12 November 2019].

[21]   For example, when Kenya's President Uhuru Kenyatta was asked about the impact of a Uganda decision to circumvent Kenya and export oil through Tanzania, he responded: "I have always said that my view of our region is a region not in competition with itself but complementing each other with a view of competing with the rest of the world. I do not see the central corridor as a threat to our northern corridor. I don't see it as a threat at all'. Kenyatta, 2016, quoted in: 'In his Own Words – President Kenyatta's Take on Issues of the Day": *Capital FM*, Nairobi), 20 June 2016 <www.capitalfm.co.ke/news/2016/06/in-his-own-words-president-kenyattas-take-on-issues-of-the-day/> [Accessed 27 April 2021].

The infiltration of the merchant class into state decision-making can be seen in the rise of public–private partnerships and in accusations of the illegal manipulation of tenders.[22] Meanwhile, the language of fierce nationalism pervades news reports on the development of the Northern and Central Corridors.[23]

Transport Corridor Development in East Africa

Following the collapse of the formal economic community between Kenya, Uganda and Tanzania in 1977, large-scale infrastructural projects in East Africa were put on hold, international highways degraded, and railways went into systematic decline. It was not until the mid-1990s that a formalised economic partnership was revived in the form of the EAC, with a secretariat in Arusha, Tanzania. In 2004, a protocol for the new customs union was ratified, followed by an EAC Customs Management Law that replaced the East African Customs Act of 1960.[24] New common import tariffs to the region were enforced in March 2005. In September 2006, the governments of Burundi, DRC, Rwanda and Uganda formed the Central Corridor Transit Transport Facilitation Agency (TTFA). One year later, in 2007, the Northern Corridor Transit and Transport Agreement (NCTTA), a treaty originally signed in 1985, was significantly revised and resubscribed to by the governments of Burundi, DRC, Kenya, Rwanda and Uganda. The years that followed mark a new phase of large-scale infrastructural investments in East Africa. In railway, road and port developments, the results have been dramatic, and transit times for containers passing from the ports to cities in the hinterland have fallen by as much as 80 per cent.[25]

Similar large-scale infrastructural investments can be seen across the continent. Observers have attributed this shift in priorities to a range of factors; notably high commodity prices, recent technological developments, pushes for greater regional integration, and a drive for more neoliberal modes of governance.[26] A recent surge in competitive general and presidential elections has

---

22 These groups were commonly nicknamed 'Tenderpreneurs'.
23 Frictions over corridor investments are routinely described in militaristic language; see, for example: 'Magufuli Meets Kenyatta to Discuss Trade Row', 23 February 2018.
24 David Booth, *et al.*, *East African Prospects; An Update on the Political Economy of Kenya, Rwanda, Tanzania and Uganda*, ODI Report, Nairobi, 2014.
25 'Dar es Salaam Port Increases Rwanda, Domestic Cargo', *Tanzania Daily News*, Dar es Salaam, 2 December 2016.
26 Ulf Engel and Paul Nugent, 'Introduction: The Spatial Turn in African Studies', in *Respacing Africa*, Leiden, 2009, pp. 1–9.

also played a significant role, as governing parties use large-scale infrastructural investments as flagship policies with visible results. Individual projects, even when funded and constructed separately, do not exist in isolation. They form part of larger infrastructural systems – in this case the ambitious corridor initiatives connecting ports in Dar es Salaam and Mombasa with cities throughout East and Central Africa. These systems, in turn, are being constructed in the context of one another.

Timeline of Major Developments

The Northern and Central Corridors consist of thousands of kilometres of road and rail, with each section in a state of perpetual degradation, repair and replacement. A comprehensive overview of every amendment, tariff change, resurfacing, added ring road, flyover, or bridge, is beyond the scope of what is possible here. Instead, I draw on a series of interviews with Kenyan, Ugandan, Rwandan and Tanzanian stakeholders conducted between 2017 and 2019. Those interviewed include freight forwarders, transporters, logistics managers, clearance agents, dock workers, dry port operators, journalists and representatives of shipping lines, trading associations and government agencies. In early 2019 I travelled the length of the Northern Corridor in the passenger seat of a large freight vehicle, and draw further material from this extended, four-day 'interview' with the driver and with the various corridor users we encountered along the way. I asked interviewees to recount the key flashpoints in corridor development that have occurred over the past 20 years. These accounts have been compiled into a timeline below. Supplementing interview material, I make a heavy use of the accounts circulating in newspaper print media from across the region, drawing on over 400 articles in total. Although these sources contain information on which many East Africans base their own opinions about infrastructural developments, I acknowledge that newspaper accounts are not always reliable, especially when it comes to statistical data. I make use of these sources for facts and figures only in cases where I have been able to triangulate the material through interview accounts and other sources. Nevertheless, the repeated narrative accounts circulating in national and regional press serve as a valuable thermometer for popular sentiment on international competition. Rather than map every change in the development of the two corridors, the purpose here is to identify the decisions, incidents and infrastructures that stakeholders consider central to competition between the rival routes.

In May 2005, the train ferry MV *Kabalega*, operated by the Uganda Railways Corporation, collided with the passenger ferry MV *Kaawa* on Lake Victoria.[27] Both vessels were rendered unserviceable, severing containerised trade across the lake between Mwanza (Tanzania) and Port Bell (Uganda). The ports declined significantly, with the result that Ugandan access to Dar es Salaam became restricted to road connections via Kigali in Rwanda. The distance and expense involved in the route gave the Kenyan port of Mombasa close to a total monopoly of Uganda maritime trade.[28]

Three years later, in January 2008, widespread violence rocked Kenya in the aftermath of a fiercely contested general election.[29] The event paralysed regional trade and left the hinterland states suspicious of an overreliance on goods transiting Kenya. Political instability in Kenya triggered a fuel shortage throughout the Great Lakes Region, pushing up prices and resulting in significant political backlash against governments in the hinterland.[30] Key sections of the Northern Corridor around Kisumu in western Kenya and Nakuru in the Rift Valley were impassable in the immediate aftermath of the election, and widespread insecurity saw freight vehicles hijacked and their containers stolen. Importers were left out of pocket by over US$US40 million, with insurance voided and compensation unforthcoming.[31]

These events set the stage for the respective development of the Northern and Central Corridors in the years since. Ugandan importers, suspicious of an over-reliance on routes through Kenya, looked to make greater use of Tanzania as a 'back door' – insurance against similar disruptions in the future.[32] In spite of the greater distances involved circumnavigating Lake Victoria, Ugandans began using the southern route more frequently to trade in coffee, motor vehicles, wheat, building materials and fuel. Both corridors suffered from poor quality infrastructure, limited logistical services, costly bureaucratic procedures and a

---

27 'Uganda Now Moving to Revive Transport and Trade on Lake Victoria', *The East African*, Nairobi, 15 November 2018.

28 'Will Uhuru Kenyatta Mediate Uganda, Rwanda Row?', *The East African*, 12 March 2019.

29 'Will Economy Survive Kenya's Post-Election Fears?' *The Monitor*, 25 October 2017.

30 'Ugandan Traders Turn to Dar Port as Kenya Polls Close In', *The Monitor*, 23 June 2017.

31 'Ugandan Traders on Edge Over Kenya Election Results', *The East African*, 12 August 2017.

32 Kampala-Dar es Salaam: Another Route Uganda Should Consider?, *The Monitor*, 8 March 2017.

host of non-tariff barriers to trade.[33] When Rwanda and Burundi joined the EAC in 2009, the Central Corridor through Tanzania proved a more natural, shorter and less bureaucratic route to the sea for the new members than transiting goods through Uganda to the Kenyan port of Mombasa. Freight transiting Rwanda to Dar es Salaam began to steadily grow in volume.

This situation endured, with periodic infrastructural improvements along each route, until July 2014, when a single customs territory (SCT) along the Northern Corridor was put into effect by the presidents of Kenya, Uganda and Rwanda.[34] The SCT was accompanied by an agreement to construct a standard gauge railway (SGR) along the route, the first phase of which would link Mombasa with Nairobi. At its inception, the line was intended to continue across Kenya to Kisumu in west of the country, where it would link up with a line constructed in Uganda connecting it to Kampala, then Kigali, and ultimately as far as Juba in South Sudan and Kisangani in DRC. Funding for the first phase was secured from the Chinese Export Import (EXIM) Bank, a build-operate-transfer agreement was negotiated with the China Road and Bridge Company (CRBC), and construction began in 2016.

The rush of developments on the Northern Corridor in 2015–2016 coincided with the election of President Magufuli in Tanzania. Magufuli stood on a staunchly nationalist platform and, within a year of inauguration, Tanzania had refused to implement EAC Economic Partnership Agreements (EPAs) and introduced protectionist policies on commodities including fertiliser, paper, cement, sugar and furniture.[35] Tanzania began a US$593 million renovation of the port of Dar es Salaam, adding new berths and increasing container storage capacity.[36] Simultaneously, the Tanzanian government began work planning its own SGR, and construction began on the first phase – 300 kilometres from Dar es Salaam to Morogoro.[37] The railway deal was signed between state-owned Reli Assets Holding Company Ltd (RAHCO) and the Turkish firm Yapi Merkezi, in joint venture

---

[33] 'Bribery, Red Tape Still Dog Trade on Central Corridor', *The New Times*, 27 February 2018.

[34] 'EAC Trade, Free Movement of Goods Machinery Starts', *Tanzania Daily News*, 6 November 2018.

[35] 'Tanzania Keeps Walking a Thin Line on EAC Deals', *The Citizen*, 14 September 2016.

[36] 'Congrats TPA for Reaching Out to Potential Customers', *Tanzania Daily News*, 18 October 2016.

[37] 'Standard Gauge Railway Tenders Announced', *Tanzania Daily News*, 9 November 2016.

with Portugal's Mota-Engil Engenharia e Construção Africa.[38] Among Magufuli's
early commitments as president was to raise the national budget allocation for
developmental and infrastructural projects from 26 per cent to 40 per cent.[39]

In 2016, with Phase I of Kenya's SGR well under construction, the grand
designs of Kenyan authorities were hit by two simultaneous setbacks. First,
Rwanda withdrew entirely from the Northern Corridor SGR project, citing cost
concerns and the possibility of a more affordable line connecting the Rwandan
capital Kigali to Dar es Salaam port via Isaka in Tanzania.[40] Almost simultaneously, Uganda withdrew from a joint oil pipeline scheme with Kenya in
favour of a route south through Tanga port in Tanzania. Uganda authorities
stalled the initial construction of the country's own SGR from Kampala to
the Kenyan border.[41] This was justified by parliamentary accusations that the
US$2.3 billion price tag for the line had been inflated, and by a report from
the engineering procurement and construction contractor CHEC that certain
aspects of the project were unnecessary.[42] Ugandan authorities turned instead
to the rehabilitation of the metre gauge connecting Kampala with Port Bell, and
set about renovating the facilities for cross-lake trade.[43] By mid-2017, Uganda
and Tanzania had signed a memorandum of understanding on joint ministerial co-operation and improvements of ports, inland waterways and railway
transport.[44] As Phase I of the Kenyan SGR was launched, not a single kilometre
of the Ugandan line had been laid. Trade between Kenya and Uganda stagnated
at approximately US$280 million in the 2016–2017 period.[45]

---

[38] 'SGR Construction Means Big Business to Local Firms', *Tanzania Daily News*, 7
February 2017.

[39] 'Magufuli's Signature Projects get More Funding', *The East African*, 19 December
2016.

[40] Estimates suggested the Isaka connection would cost Rwanda up to US$200 million
less than connecting to the Northern Corridor.

[41] 'Uganda Government Puts SGR on Hold Over Unresolved Issues', *The Monitor*,
30 October 2018; 'Uganda, Tanzania Oil Pipeline Deal Unlocks More Funding
Options', *The East African*, 27 May 2017.

[42] 'Uganda May Join Dar as Kenya Weighs Options of Extending SGR to Malaba',
The East African, 21 May 2017.

[43] 'Kampala Upbeat with Dar Port, Central Railway Line Facelift', *Tanzania Daily
News*, 6 June 2018.

[44] 'Port Bell to Kampala Line due to Reopen', *The Observer*, 23 April 2018.

[45] 'The Good, the Bad and the Ugly of Kenya's SGR Cargo', *The Nation*, 30 October
2018; 'Kenya, Uganda to Upgrade the Suam Border Crossing', *The East African*, 27
August 2017.

On 1 June 2017, the Kenyan SGR passenger service opened to the public. A freight service came into operation later in the year, rapidly scaling up the number of services per day. With low-cost passenger services accompanied by port regulations that required up to 40 per cent of all containerised goods to exit the port by rail, the train has radically changed the transport landscape in Kenya. The line has since been extended to link up with large inland container depots (ICDs) at Naivasha in the Rift Valley north of Nairobi. These developments have not been without controversy, and have exacerbated a political rift between central government in Nairobi and municipal authorities in Mombasa. Coastal residents accuse the government of shifting the most lucrative elements of the port – the handling, clearance and storage of goods – to the heartlands of the governing elite. The economy of the port town has suffered, particularly those working in the public transport and freight haulage industries.

President Kenyatta has tended to dismiss these concerns as the inevitable repercussions of what are otherwise grand improvements in the country's capacity to trade. Combined with the construction of a series of large new berths at Mombasa capable of housing Panamax-sized vessels, the expansion of port capacity through an additional container terminal, and the streamlining of clearance through a single-window system, the container throughput of the port has surpassed one million TEUs (twenty-foot equivalent units) per year, growing at a rate of approximately 10 per cent annually since 2014.[46] In August 2017, two months after Tanzania began upgrading its Nyahua–Chanya road and its Chalinze Expressway to a six-lane carriage way, Kenya signed a binding agreement with Betchel International (US) to design, build and operate a new expressway connecting Mombasa and Nairobi.[47]

The second half of 2017 was marked by two Kenyan elections, the first in August and the second in October, following a ruling from the Kenyan Supreme Court that nullified the first result. Although both elections were conducted peacefully, the economic uncertainty surrounding them caused serious disruption of supply chains along the Northern Corridor and importers in the hinterland were reluctant to continue operations until the political situation had been resolved.[48] Interviewees frequently offered this disruption as further justification

---

[46] Growth of TEU capacity, ODI Report.

[47] 'Tanzania: Kuwait Grants Tz 109 billion for Central Corridor Road Project', *Tanzania Daily News*, 22 March 2017.

[48] 'Uganda on High Alert as Kenya, Rwanda go to polls', *The Monitor*, 30 July 2017.

for Ugandan and Rwandan authorities' efforts to diversify their access to the sea, and to increase their use of the Central Corridor.[49]

2018 compounded the Kenyan vision of a united East Africa linked by rail to the port of Mombasa. In March 2018, Rwanda and Tanzania agreed on an electric SGR with an open tender, and Rwanda began construction of the line east of Kigali.[50] Part of the negotiation included the simultaneous reduction in road user charges, already synchronised between Tanzania and Rwanda, which fell to approximately US$150 per freight vehicle.[51] Uganda was given land to construct its own ICD in Mwanza, Tanzania, and the Uganda Railway Corporation, the Tanzania Ports Authority, the Tanzania Railways Corporation and the Marine Services determined a tariff rate of US$60–70 per 20 foot containers crossing the lake (significantly less expensive than the cost of road transport).[52] In June 2018, a 900-tonne capacity cargo ship landed at Port Bell from Mwanza for the first time since the collision of the MV *Kabalega* and the MV *Kaawa* in 2005.[53] According to the World Food Programme (WFP), the route across the lake cut transit time from Kampala to Dar es Salaam by approximately 50 per cent, and costs by 40 per cent.[54]

Kenya quickly struck back, offering Uganda a significant land holding to construct an ICD in Naivasha.[55] The intention was to incentivise Ugandan authorities to stay true to their original commitments on the Northern Corridor SGR. Kenyan authorities remain concerned about the prospect of a Uganda–Tanzania railway agreement, with upgraded railways connecting Dar es Salaam to Mwanza, and Port Bell to Kampala. With Uganda accounting for over 80 per cent of all transit cargo passing through Mombasa, a competing railway linking Kampala to the Tanzanian port and offering as little as four-day shipping times constitutes a very real threat to Kenyan interests.[56] The situation was escalated

49 'Is Kagame Looking for an Alternative Route to the Sea?', *The Monitor*, 11 March 2019.
50 'Rosier Future as Rwanda Gets Star Borrower Ratings', *The East African*, 2 June 2018.
51 'DRC, Uganda Engaged on Road User Fee', *Tanzania Daily News*, 1 March 2018.
52 'Port Bell to Kampala Rail Line due to Re-open', *The Observer*, 23 April 2018.
53 'Uganda Focuses on Old Railway', *The East African*, 3 November 2018.
54 'Optimism High on Re-Opened Mwanza-Port Bell Route', *Tanzania Daily News*, 14 August 2018.
55 'A Shot in the Arm for Kenya's Railway Project as Uganda Buys Into the Deal', *The East African*, 30 March 2019.
56 'Cargo Destined to Uganda to Take Four Days From Dar Port', *East African Business Week*, 22 February 2018.

further by Tanzanian plans to introduce an international tea auction in Dar es Salaam, aiming to rival the Kenyan monopoly in Mombasa.[57]

In 2019, deteriorating diplomatic relations between Rwanda and Uganda radically altered the playing field for international trade along the transport corridors. On 27 February 2019, Rwandan authorities closed their two largest border posts with Uganda, severing freight trade with its northern neighbour. Thirty-seven Kenyan vehicles were left stranded, and it was only after a period of absolute disruption to the Northern Corridor that trade between Rwanda and Kenya resumed.[58] Trade between Rwanda and Uganda remains on hold. The details of the closure are disputed and tied into historical enmities between Ugandan and Rwandan elites.[59] Uganda has publicly accused Rwanda of introducing trade barriers, while Rwandan importers have, for most commodities, been forced to pivot their operations south where they had not done so already.[60]

In April 2019, Kenyatta returned from China having failed to secure a US$3.6 billion loan required for Phase III of the Northern Corridor SGR, intended to connect Naivasha with the town of Kisumu close to the Uganda border. The government of Kenya was instead given US$400 million to upgrade the metre line that spans the same route. The extension of the line has struggled for two principal reasons. First, China's EXIM bank has voiced concerns about the debt burden involved and in Kenya's capacity to pay.[61] This situation was not helped by financial mismanagement scandals and negative press surrounding Phase I of the line. The second reason is the increasing uncertainty about the possibility of extending the line beyond the Kenyan border into Uganda. Feasibility studies suggest the cost of Phase III, linking Naivasha over five hundred kilometres to the western Kenyan town of Kisumu, is unjustifiable unless it gives access to the Ugandan capital Kampala in the short to medium term.[62] This is not guaranteed, as Ugandan authorities have lowered the priority of developing the SGR on their side of the border in favour of relaunching trade across Lake Victoria to Tanzania.

---

57 'Will Uhuru's Visits Reconcile Uneasy Neighbours Rwanda and Uganda', *The East African*, 17 March 2019.

58 Ibid.

59 'Sibling Rivalry Turns Ugly', *Africa Confidential*, 60:6, 22 March 2019.

60 'Uganda, Rwanda Better Off Together Than Divided', *The Monitor*, 10 March 2019.

61 'Regional Countries Have Accumulated $651.8 Million in Development Loans', *The East African*, 12 August 2018.

62 More critical analysis suggests the line is not viable if it fails to extend the full distance to Bujumbura in Burundi, see: 'Kenya Finds Going Tough With Its Regional Partners', *The Nation*, 2 August 2016.

Two Ports, Two Roads, Two Railways

Table 10.1. Timeline of Northern and Central Corridor developments.

Year	Event
2000 (signed in 2009)	Treaty establishing the East African Community (EAC) (originally Uganda, Tanzania and Kenya) comes into effect.
2004	Protocol for a new East African customs union is ratified by Uganda, Kenya and Tanzania
2005	Common import tariffs come into effect throughout the EAC.
	The collision of MV *Kabalega* and MV *Kaawa* effectively halts trade between Uganda and Tanzania across Lake Victoria.
2006	The Central Corridor Transit Transport Facilitation Agency (TTFA) is launched.
2007	The Northern Corridor Transit and Transport Agreement (NCTTA) is revised and renewed.
2008	A major disruption to international trade results from the violent aftermath of the 2007 Kenyan elections.
2009	Rwanda and Burundi join the EAC.
2013	President Uhuru Kenyatta elected in Kenya.
	Kenya, Uganda and Rwanda institute a Single Customs Area.
2015	The EAC Elimination of Non-Tariff Barriers to Trade Bill is signed, but implementation remains patchy.
	President John Magufuli elected in Tanzania.
	Tanzania pushes a protectionist economic agenda regarding key commodities.
2016	Construction begins on Phase I of the Northern Corridor SGR, linking Mombasa to Nairobi.
	Rwanda withdraws from the Northern Corridor SGR.
	Uganda withdraws from an oil pipeline project with Kenya in favour of a route through Tanzania.
	Ugandan authorities assert that they will not begin construction of the SGR to the Kenyan border until the Kenyan SGR is guaranteed to reach the western Kenyan town of Kisumu.
March 2017	The government of Kuwait releases a US$47 million loan to Tanzania to being construction on a Nyahua–Chanya highway along the Central Corridor.
August 2017	The government of Kenya signs a binding agreement with Betchel International (US) to design, build and operate an expressway linking Mombasa and Nairobi.

2017	Construction begins on Phase I of the Central Corridor SGR, linking Dar es Salaam with Morogoro.
	The Kenyan SGR launches between Mombasa and Nairobi.
	President Uhuru Kenyatta is re-elected in October after a disputed August poll. Political uncertainty stalls trade.
2018	Rwanda and Tanzania agree on electric SGR with an open tender.
	Rwanda and Tanzania reduce road fees in each other's favour.
	Uganda is given land to construct ICD in Mwanza, Tanzania
	A 900-tonne freight ship lands in Port Bell (Uganda) from Mwanza (Tanzania) for the first time in over a decade.
	Kenya offers Uganda land in Naivasha to construct a large inland container depot.
2019	Rwanda closes its two largest border posts with Uganda, restricting Northern Corridor trade.
	The Chinese EXIM bank refuses to loan Kenya the money required for Phase III of the SGR, linking ICDs in Naivasha with Kisumu in the west of the country.

Source: Author.

The timeline in Table 10.1 shows a clear pattern in which developments to either one of East Africa's two largest transport corridors prompts changes to the other. Beyond the headline events recounted here, a similar pattern can be seen in the more mundane developments along each route, with greater seaport container capacity, more dry ports, more paved highways, and other incremental improvements mirroring each other in the two cases.

Considering the extensive developments that have occurred over the past 20 years, the question arises whether one corridor has outcompeted the other. This cannot be answered at the domestic level of the coastal states, since Mombasa and Dar es Salaam remain subject to autarchic polices regarding port traffic.[63] It is only once goods transit out of (or enter in from outside of) Tanzania and Kenya that real competition begins.[64] Since importers in the Rwandan capital make regular use of seaports at both Mombasa and Dar es Salaam, Kigali a practical site to illustrate different dimensions of corridor competition along the

---

[63] This situation may change if the Kenyan Ports Authority continues with a plan to construct a large inland container terminal in Taita Taevta on the Tanzania border, which would 'bring competition to the doorstep of the neighbouring country'; see: 'East Africa Ports in Fresh Push to Attract Shipping Lines', *The East African*, 15 January 2018.

[64] See also Hoyle & Charlier, 1988.

two roads. As a starting point for comparison, I make use of seven factors that determine competition between the trading corridors: distance from gateway to market, cost from gateway to market, transit time in days, relative logistics performance index scores, political stability, security issues and environmental conditions – looking at each from the perspective of road and railway users.[65]

Corridor Attractiveness: Distance, Expense, Speed, Bureaucracy and Security

Examining the Northern and Central Corridors from the position of importers and exporters in Kigali, many of the key metrics of corridor attractiveness favour Dar es Salaam over Mombasa. Detailed statistical analyses of freight on each route can be found through the annual reports of the respective transport corridor authorities.[66] Underlying these statistics is the fact that the Tanzanian port is approximately 220 kilometres closer over land than its Kenyan rival. Furthermore, the Northern Corridor journey involves crossing two borders, choke-points in which system failures, extortion and long queues are all significant risks. Border concerns feature prominently in the complaints of freight forwarders, despite the introduction of one stop border posts at Busia (Kenya)–Busia (Uganda), at Gatuna (Rwanda)–Katuna (Uganda).[67] The additional distance through Kenya and Uganda is reflected in transportation costs, which were approximately 20 per cent higher on shipments from Mombasa than Dar es Salaam in early 2019.[68] Although freight forwarders with whom I spoke tended to be cautiously optimistic about the prospects of the railway improving shipping in the medium to long term, the introduction of Phases I and II of the Kenyan SGR, which transfers containers directly from the coast to Nairobi and Naivasha, was not considered to have made a significant difference to the expense or the time taken to deliver containers to the hinterland.

[65] The index scores are an interactive benchmarking tool implemented by the World Bank: see <https://lpi.worldbank.org/> [Accessed 1 November 2019]; see Pelletier & Alix 2011.

[66] Northern Corridor Transport Observatory (NCTO), *Annual Report 2018*, Nairobi, 2019; Central Corridor Transport Observatory (CCTO), *Annual Report 2017*, Dar es Salaam, 2018.

[67] 'Who Will Gain Most from Busia Joint Border Post', *The Monitor*, 28 February 2018.

[68] Interview, Freight Logistics Manager, Kigali, 17 March 2019; See also: NCTO, *Annual Report*; CCTO, *Annual Report*.

Over 70 per cent of Rwandan maritime trade passes through Dar es Salaam, strongly suggesting that time and cost remain the fundamental determinants of corridor attractiveness.[69] Nevertheless, it is worth noting that averaging gateway to market costs and timings can be misleading in East Africa, where the duration and expense of shipments vary enormously depending on the nature of the cargo, drivers' experience, vehicle quality and the cost of fuel.[70] Importers with whom I spoke tended to be dismissive of statistics claiming one route to be superior to the other and stressed that the major improvements were down to reduced clearance time rather than transport time.[71] They emphasised the fact that it is only recently that the overall time taken from a container at the port to reach Rwanda could be counted in days, rather than weeks, and the difference of a few days between shipping times was secondary to reliability. They also noted that, given Tanzania's protectionist policies on certain commodities, they were left with no choice but to look to Mombasa for the import of goods such as fertiliser and paper.

Whether the corridors perform efficiently or otherwise depends in large part on the skill, networks and prior knowledge of the transporters and freight forwarders involved with each shipment. Although performance indexes are available through the corridor authorities, the way in which informal networking overcomes institutional inertia is extremely difficult to capture and even harder to institute through policy.[72] Different companies have radically different experiences of the roads and, according to interviewees, there is little to separate them in logistical terms, except the fact, mentioned above, that the Northern Corridor involves two border crossings. Even this was not always cited as a reason to favour the Tanzanian route, since it affords opportunities as well as potential delays. Importers bringing goods to Kigali from Dar es Salaam were not always assured of a backload, and often return to the port with empty containers. This was much less likely for vehicles transiting Uganda on the Northern Corridor, which could pick up goods from Kampala on their way back to Kenya.

[69]   'Relief as Tanzania Ports Authority Open Liaison Office in Kigali', *The New Times*, 15 August 2016.

[70]   For a detailed analysis of expenditure on the corridors, see: Andreas Eberhard-Ruiz and Linda Calabrese, *Would More Trade Facilitation Lead to Lower Transport Cost in the East African Community?* ODI Briefing Paper, London, 2017; Andreas Eberhard-Ruiz and Linda Calabrese, *Trade Facilitation, Transport Costs and the Price of Trucking Services in East Africa*, ODI Briefing Paper, London, 2017.

[71]   See also NCTTCA, 2019; Eberhard-Ruiz and Calabrese, *Trade Facilitation, Transport Costs*.

[72]   Monios & Lambert, 2013.

Political stability is tied closely to issues of security on both corridors. The aftermath of the 2007 Kenyan election remains fresh in the minds of importers and freight forwarders throughout the region, and interviewees spoke of a difficult period and of unpaid debts owed to transporters who lost vehicles and consignments. Kenyan elections since have triggered a great deal of anxiety for those involved in the transit trade. Outside of Nairobi, the 2007/2008 crisis centred on the Rift Valley west of Naivasha, and in Kisumu in the country's west – both of which lie in the path of the Northern Corridor. Drivers still consider these areas dangerous and try to limit their time on roads there, especially after dark. Stories of banditry on the Rift Valley's steeper climbs – in which slow-moving trucks become a target – circulate widely throughout the East African transport network.

In Tanzania, by contrast, the election of John Magufuli and his emphasis on national security is seen by many to have had a stabilising effect. Rather than concerns surrounding political dissidents, protests and electoral violence, drivers and importers were more concerned with what they perceive to be increasing xenophobia in the Tanzanian population and in the attitudes of state representatives.[73] Importers in Rwanda consistently complained that, while Tanzania has the biggest trucking fleet in the region, Tanzanian drivers and their assistants tended to lack the same level of professionalism and training as those from elsewhere. They felt pressured to make use of Tanzanian transporters since they were less likely to encounter harassment from officials and from other drivers. Off the roads, interviewees also cited well-publicised examples of goods disappearing in Dar es Salaam port as a reason to be cautious of trade through Tanzania.[74]

In terms of environmental conditions, drivers did not consider the roads dissimilar. Both consist of two lanes of tarmac in relatively good repair, although with some sections degrading faster than others.[75] The chief concern in both cases was that, lacking a central divide and with a poorly enforced speed limit, the road produced a very high number of head-on collisions. According to figures from Kenya's National Transport and Safety Authority and Tanzania's Central Corridor Transport Observatory, thousands of lives are lost on the

---

[73] 'Why Mombasa Remains Port of Choice for Uganda Even When Crisis Strikes', *The East African*, 25 August 2017.

[74] In 2016, the Rwandan company Mineral Supply African Ltd and another shipper, Trading Services Logistics (TSL), lost minerals worth US$2 million in Dar es Salaam port. See: 'Regional Traders Continue to Face Hurdles on Central Corridor', *The New Times*, 27 July 2016.

[75] NCTTCA, 2019.

corridors each year.[76] Hillslopes in both corridors were considered highly dangerous, especially where they lacked climbing lanes or where climbing lanes were misused by drivers. Stretches of each road that saw freight vehicles travelling through urban neighbourhoods were particularly disliked by drivers due to the prevalence of 14-seat Matatu minibuses, which were considered notorious for causing collisions.

Path Dependencies, Network Effects, First Movers and Speculation

Corridor competition extends beyond importer and exporter convenience, reflecting the fact that corridors have two distinct categories of stakeholder: those who extract revenue from access to the corridor, and those for whom corridor access is an expenditure. Corridors compete not only to be used, but also to be built, a process that can conflict with the metrics of corridor attractiveness discussed above. In East Africa, government sponsorship is essential to the development of large-scale infrastructure, commonly involving presidential interventions. Presidents Kenyatta, Museveni, Magufuli and Kagame have all had a direct hand in shaping the Northern and Central Corridors; signing off on key initiatives, negotiating in multinational forums and inaugurating new services.

For states developing transport corridor infrastructure, the extension of routes into the hinterland is subject to a network effect, in which the value of the service increases with the number of people using it.[77] This incentivises coastal states to push for extensions to the corridors linked to their ports. The process often involves more than one mode of transportation, and the use of dry ports to fight for markets further inland.[78] This requires a different approach to the norm for infrastructure development in the region, which has tended to be fragmented, relatively uncoordinated, and to have a predominantly national focus.[79]

The decision by Kenyan authorities to develop the Northern Corridor, furnishing the route with a standard gauge railway, large inland container depots and modern highways, was based on the idea that increasing circulation and creating stronger trade partnerships with states in the African interior was in

[76] 'Alarm Over Increased Road Crashes', *The Nation*, 14 May 2017; See also: NCTTCA, 2019; CCTO, *Annual Report*.
[77] Naudé, *The Financial Crisis of 2008*; Piet Buys, Uwe Deichmann, and David Wheeler, *Road Network Upgrading and Overland Trade Expansion in Sub-Saharan Africa*, Washington, D.C., 2006.
[78] See Hoyle & Charlier, 1988.
[79] Naudé, *The Financial Crisis of 2008*.

Kenya's best interest. The project involves a high degree of path dependency, due to a combination of high setup costs, learning effects, co-ordination efforts and adaptive expectations.[80] Uganda and Rwanda are differently incentivised: as hinterland states, their best interest lies in diversifying access to the sea, especially considering Kenya's reputation as an unreliable trading partner in times of political unrest.

The asymmetry of incentives between coastal and hinterland states creates collective action problems in infrastructure development. Commitments, especially long-term ones, are not always credible.[81] Elsewhere, hinterland access regimes have been given the autonomy required to counter some of these problems.[82] In East Africa, the corridor authorities have struggled in this regard. Resolutions are not always implemented, and national and EAC regulations are not always harmonised.[83] The construction of the Northern Corridor SGR is a clear example of the risks involved. In the absence of effective third-party enforcement, the project required a high degree of speculation on the part of government authorities in Kenya. Estimates have suggested the line will only become viable after it is extended beyond Uganda into Rwanda, Burundi and DRC, while its passenger service is likely to be permanently subsidised by freight on the line.

Rwanda's withdrawal from the Northern Corridor SGR in favour of a joint venture with Tanzania was not as concerning to Kenyan authorities as the prospect of losing the country's effective monopoly on Uganda's access to the coast. Simultaneously, Uganda's decision to delay construction on its SGR line to the Kenyan border until the Kenyan line to Kisumu is complete, on the back of its withdrawal from a shared oil pipeline, were both serious setbacks to Kenyan interests in the hinterland.[84] If Uganda were to construct an SGR linking Kampala with Dar es Salaam via Lake Victoria, one interviewee suggested it would constitute the biggest humiliation in President Kenyatta's career.[85]

---

80   See also Martin, 2000.

81   Naudé, *The Financial Crisis of 2008*.

82   Peter W. De Langen and Ariane Chouly, 'Hinterland Access Regimes in Seaports', *European Journal of Transport and Infrastructure Research*, 4:4, 2004, pp. 361–80.

83   See, for example, 'Ugandan Traders Ask Tanzania to Harmonise Cargo Transit Fees', *The Monitor*, 15 December 2016; 'Is it Time the EAC Walks the Integration Talk', *The New Times*, 28 July 2016.

84   'East Africa's Joint Mega Railway Project at the Crossroads', *The East African*, 28 January 2019.

85   Interview, Journalist, Nairobi, 10 January 2019.

These events raise an important question: under what conditions is moving first in corridor infrastructural development a disadvantage at the level of inter-state competition? Interviewees suggested that Kenya may suffer as a result of its early enthusiasm for large-scale, multilateral corridor projects. The Tanzanian SGR was planned in the aftermath of Kenya's, and authorities responsible for it have learnt lessons from their neighbours to the north. Estimates for the Tanzanian SGR, with funding secured through the Turkish EXIM bank and not the Chinese EXIM bank, have been significantly lower than the Kenyan line, despite the former being electrified and the latter running on diesel.[86] The decision to opt for an open tender stands in obvious contrast to Kenya's closed arrangements with the Chinese Road and Bridge Company (CRBC).[87] The comparisons have already attracted negative press towards the Kenyan project, while the appeal of the Tanzanian alternative was enough to sway Rwandan authorities into switching sides.

Gatekeepers, Geopolitics and the Jealousy of Infrastructure

The states described up to this point should not be seen as unitary, autonomous actors.[88] Even where presidential interventions serve to launch new initiatives, corridor development is subject to complicated internal negotiations among rival ministries and stakeholders, and external negotiation with donors, lenders, construction firms, operators and special interest groups. The overarching agenda may be to facilitate trade, but decisions remain contentious due to limited funds, conflicting priorities and secondary agendas.

States in East Africa are under particular pressure to provide an attractive entrepreneurial culture capable of drawing in mobile international capital. To indicate the scale involved, Tanzania's Finance Minister, Dr Phillip Mpango, estimated over US$20 billion of private funds would be needed in the country's five-year development plan from 2016 to 2021, while estimates of the regional investment in scheduled transport infrastructure upgrades range up to US$100 billion.[89] In 2017, Kenyan authorities announced a US$3.6 billion price tag for five of its key road projects – with the addition that tolling would be key

---

[86] 'Turkish Involvement in Railway Project Time', *The Citizen*, 25 January 2017.
[87] 'Rwanda, Tanzania Agree on Electric SGR, Opt for Open Tender', *The East African*, 18 March 2018.
[88] See Abrams 1988
[89] 'Private Sector Key to Devt Plan Success – Mpango', *Tanzania Daily News*, 6 February 2017.

to the projects' financial success.[90] The use of public–private partnerships is strongly encouraged in regional agreements, and article 128 of the Treaty for the Establishment of the EAC emphasises strengthening private sector involvement as a key partner in EAC integration.[91] The result is the significant influence of private sector actors in state-sanctioned roles, reminiscent of the rise of mercantile elites in the early discussions of Smith and Hume.[92]

One of the key attractions for private sector actors involved in the development of transport infrastructure is the potential to extract revenue available to gatekeepers of the trading route. Transport corridors embody the interface between the national and the international – and provide a wealth of what Cooper would consider 'gatekeeping' revenue, in transit fees, container storage, warehousing, loading and unloading, parking, parking security, cleaning fees, fuel costs, road tariffs and demurrage, among others.[93] All of these sources of revenue come under threat when hinterlands overlap and alternative routes open up through separate territories. When influenced by gatekeeper elites, the logic of the corridor is to maximise circulation, maximise particular forms of revenue extraction, and to minimise competition.

Does this logic result, as the managing director of Maersk Line East Africa has argued, in 'healthy competition' between the two corridors, 'both fighting for position in terms of some of the swing countries that could export or import cargo through either corridor'?[94] The case offers up a mixed picture over the last 20 years. On the one hand, rapid developments have occurred along each route, often mirroring those along the other, and have dramatically reduced the port-to-market time for containerised goods. Nevertheless, the tension between revenue extraction and trade facilitation is evident in the frustration of importers and corridor users in both cases. The majority of importers, drivers and freight

90 'Region Plans to Charge for Use of Major Highways', *The East African*, 30 March 2017.

91 'East Africa Private Sector Feted for Integration Efforts', *The East African*, 31 March 2018; 'New Thrust for Efforts to Improve Trade, Investments in East Africa', *Tanzania Daily News*, 16 April 2019.

92 Peter Hall, Markus Hesse, and Markus Jean-Paul, 'Reexploring the interface between economic and transport geography', *Environment and Planning A*, 38, 2006, pp. 1401–08.

93 Frederick Cooper, *Africa Since 1940: The Past of the Present*, Cambridge, 2002; 'KPA Evacuates Cargo at its Nairobi Inland Container Terminal', *The East African*, 3 July 2018.

94 Steve Felder, Managing Director, Maersk East Africa, Quoted in 'Central Corridor Performs Badly in First Quarter of this Year', *The Citizen*, 29 June 2017.

forwarders with whom I spoke were suspicious of the large-scale corridor development projects, especially the upgrading of metre gauge railways to a standard gauge. Many would have preferred the investment to have targeted upgrading the road network with a four-lane highway and spoke cynically about the opportunities for personal profit afforded by both railways and by the privately owned ICDs that they serve. The removal of non-tariff barriers along the route was described by one interviewee as a 'game of whack-a-mole', in which new fees emerged as quickly as others were done away with.[95]

Perhaps a greater indictment of healthy competition between the two corridors can be found in the breakdown of diplomatic relations between Rwanda and Uganda in early 2019. The situation has its roots in complex personal disputes and historical conflict dating back to the 1990s.[96] Nevertheless, it has been manifested in the weaponisation of the Rwanda–Uganda border, the severance of trade between the two states, and a push by Rwandan authorities to minimise reliance on the Northern Corridor for the import and export of essential goods. Although Kenyan vehicles are allowed in and out of Rwanda at present, drivers speak of a great deal of uncertainty each time they reach the border post. The East African Business Council (EABC) has complained openly about the unresolved issues, and Kenya's President Kenyatta has repeatedly toured the Great Lakes pushing for trade assurances and for resolution to the dispute.[97]

This is the point at which Hume's jealousy of trade finds a strong parallel in contemporary events. The development of transport corridors constitutes an investment in brokering revenue, rather than manufacturing revenue, making states especially vulnerable to the aggressive manoeuvring of their neighbours. Uganda's decision to renege on its commitments to extend developments begun at great expense in Kenya, Rwanda's choice to sever trade relations with Uganda and to suspend joint infrastructural commitments, and Tanzania's choice not to implement EPAs and to roll out protectionist policies on essential commodities, all speak to the precariousness of the situation. Print media have framed events in militaristic language, with the situation between Rwanda and Uganda, as well as between Kenya and Tanzania, being described as 'trade wars' where the

---

95   One example is the $40 transit stickers introduced for containers in Tanzania in 2016. See: 'Removal of NTBs Paying Dividends Despite New Setbacks', *The New Times*, 11 August 2016.

96   'Sibling Rivalry Turns Ugly', *Africa Confidential*, 60:6, 22 March 2019.

97   'Why Kenya is Threatened by Uganda-Rwanda Standoff', *The Exchange*, 13 March 2019; 'Will Uhuru's Visits Reconcile Uneasy Neighbours Rwanda and Uganda', *The East African*, 17 March 2019.

cities of Nairobi, Kampala, Kigali and Dar es Salaam are involved in a 'game of check-mating'.[98]

The threats involved in the geopolitics of infrastructure extend beyond the economic damage that can be exerted on regional rivals. The distribution of gatekeeping revenue, infrastructural contracts, and the political capital that accompanies improvements to local infrastructure, all form central components in political coalition building in East Africa. The capacity for neighbouring states to undermine all three and potentially to saddle neighbours with heavy debt burdens based on projects that are no longer economically viable, equips them with an existential threat to the governing elites across their borders.

Conclusion

This chapter has focused on the geo-political competition underlying transport corridor development in East Africa. The events and initiatives analysed here were identified by a range of corridor stakeholders interviewed between 2017 and 2019 as key flashpoints for competition. Looking closely at the timeline of developments since 2000, several central observations can be made.

The first is the continuity with the past. The rise and fall of the first East African Community between 1967 and 1977 was driven by many of the same dynamics that exist in the region today. Despite significant infrastructural and technological changes, the underlying structural conditions of the region remain the same as those identified in previous studies now decades old.[99] Two seaports – Dar es Salaam and Mombasa – dominate trade flows in and out of East Africa. The hinterland access regimes extending out from them do not compete at the domestic level between Tanzania and Kenya. Fierce competition for cargo begins once they reach the landlocked states of Rwanda, Uganda, Burundi, South Sudan and DRC. This dynamic produces different incentives for the coastal and hinterland states when it comes to corridor development. While Kenyan and Tanzanian authorities look to monopolise trade flows through 'their' corridor, the states further inland look to diversify their access to the sea.

Second is the accelerating rate of competition. Since 2010, the infrastructural development of the Central and Northern Corridors has progressed rapidly and come to resemble an arms race, with developments along one route being quickly matched by the other. The picture is more complicated than a simple

---

98 'Magufuli Meets Kenyatta to Discuss Trade Row', *The Daily Nation*, 23 February 2018; 'A Shot in the Arm for Kenya's Railway Project as Uganda Buys into the Deal', *The East African*, 30 March 2019.

99 See, for example, Hoyle & Charlier, 1988.

dialectic in which the corridors continually become more attractive to road users, importers and exporters. Recent disruption resulting from the global pandemic, which began shortly after the fieldwork for this chapter, is unlikely to alter this trajectory in the mid-long term. The development of the two corridors is being driven both by the logic of trade facilitation (measured in TEU throughput per year and the time taken for a container to move from seaports to hinterland markets), and by the logic of revenue extraction, in which both public and private sector actors seek to re-co-operate some of the expense of costly corridor development investments through formal and informal fees and tariffs.

Third is the geo-political tension provoked by corridor development. Recent years have highlighted some of the dangers of moving first and relying on neighbouring states to stay true to their earlier commitments. Considering that coalitions and political campaigns are built on the success or failure of grand projects, the stakes are raised with each perceived success or failure. A development such as the Kenyan SGR is both extremely costly and path dependent, especially considering that its long-term viability depends on significant extensions into the hinterland. Uganda's decision to de-prioritise linking up its own railway with the Kenyan line and focus on developing trade across Lake Victoria to Tanzania has frustrated Kenyan authorities and highlighted the heavy debt burden that phase I and II of the Kenyan SGR project have incurred. Tanzania and Rwanda were able to learn lessons from the Kenyan experience and apply them to their own SGR project. Meanwhile, Rwanda's closing of its northern border to Ugandan traders, and Tanzania's decision not to implement regional EPAs, highlight the fragility of corridor initiatives; as one interviewee remarked "even among siblings, the nation comes first".

Bibliography

Abrams, Philip, 'Notes on the Difficulty of Studying the State', *Journal of Historical Sociology*, 1.1, 1988, pp. 58–89.

Africa Confidential, 'Sibling Rivalry Turns Ugly', *Africa Confidential*, 60:6, 22 March 2019.

Alix, Yann, and Jean-François Pelletier, 'Territoires enclavées et opportunités de marché: analyse des performances logistiques des corridors de transport en Afrique subsaharienne', *Revue Organisations & Territoires*, 2011, 20.1, pp. 41–52.

Arnold, John, *et al.*, *Best Practices in Corridor Management*, No. 45128, pp. 1–51, Washington D.C., 2005.

Booth, David, *et al.*, *East African Prospects; An Update on the Political Economy of Kenya, Rwanda, Tanzania and Uganda*, ODI Report, Nairobi, 2014.

Bratton, Michael and Kimenyi, Mwangi S., 'Voting in Kenya: Putting Ethnicity in Perspective', *Journal of Eastern African Studies*, 2:2, 2008, pp. 272–89.

Buys, Piet, Deichmann, Uwe and Wheeler, David, *Road Network Upgrading and Overland Trade Expansion in Sub-Saharan Africa*, Washington D.C., 2006.

Capital FM, 'In his Own Words – President Kenyatta's Take on Issues of the Day', *Capital FM*, 20 June 2016 <www.capitalfm.co.ke/news/2016/06/in-his-own-words-president-kenyattas-take-on-issues-of-the-day/> [Accessed 27 April 2021].

Central Corridor Transport Observatory, *Annual Report 2017*, Dar es Salaam, 2018.

Cheeseman, Nic, Lynch, Gabrielle and Willis, Justin, 'Decentralisation in Kenya: the Governance of Governors', *The Journal of Modern African Studies*, 54:1, 2016, pp. 1–35.

Citizen, 'Central Corridor Performs Badly in First Quarter of this Year', *The Citizen*, 29 June 2017.

— 'Tanzania Keeps Walking a Thin Line on EAC Deals', *The Citizen*, 14 September 2016.

— 'Turkish Involvement in Railway Project Time', *The Citizen*, 25 January 2017.

Cooper, Frederick, *Africa Since 1940: The Past of the Present*, Cambridge, 2002.

De Langen, Peter W. and Chouly, Ariane, 'Hinterland Access Regimes in Seaports', *European Journal of Transport and Infrastructure Research*, 4:4, 2004, pp. 361–80.

East African, 'East Africa's Joint Mega Railway Project at the Crossroads', *The East African*, 28 January 2019.

— 'East Africa Ports in Fresh Push to Attract Shipping Lines', *The East African*, 15 January 2018.

— 'East Africa Private Sector Feted for Integration Efforts', *The East African*, 31 March 2018.

— 'Kenya, Uganda to Upgrade the Suam Border Crossing', *The East African*, 27 August 2017.

— 'KPA Evacuates Cargo at its Nairobi Inland Container Terminal', *The East African*, 3 July 2018.

— 'Magufuli's Signature Projects get More Funding', *The East African*, 19 December 2016.

— 'Region Plans to Charge for Use of Major Highways', *The East African*, 30 March 2017.

— 'Regional Countries Have Accumulated US$651.8 Million in Development Loans', *The East African*, 12 August 2018.

— 'Rosier Future as Rwanda Gets Star Borrower Ratings', *The East African*, 2 June 2018.

— 'Rwanda, Tanzania Agree on Electric SGR, Opt for Open Tender', *The East African*, 18 March 2018.

— 'A Shot in the Arm for Kenya's Railway Project as Uganda Buys Into the Deal', *The East African*, 30 March 2019.

— 'Uganda Focuses on Old Railway', *The East African*, 3 November 2018.

— 'Uganda May Join Dar as Kenya Weighs Options of Extending SGR to Malaba', *The East African*, 21 May 2017.

— 'Uganda, Tanzania Oil Pipeline Deal Unlocks More Funding Options', *The East African*, 27 May 2017.

— 'Ugandan Traders on Edge Over Kenya Election Results', *The East African*, 12 August 2017.

— 'Why Mombasa Remains Port of Choice for Uganda Even When Crisis Strikes', *The East African*, 25 August 2017.

— 'Will Uhuru's Visits Reconcile Uneasy Neighbours Rwanda and Uganda', *The East African*, 17 March 2019.

East African Business Week, Uganda, Kampala, 'Cargo Destined to Uganda to Take Four Days From Dar Port', *East African Business Week*, 22 February 2018.

East African Community, 'EAC Integration Pillars', <https://www.eac.int/integration-pillars> [Accessed 12 November 2019].

Eberhard-Ruiz, Andreas and Calabrese, Linda, *Trade Facilitation, Transport Costs and the Price of Trucking Services in East Africa*, ODI Briefing Paper, London, 2017.

—*Would More Trade Facilitation Lead to Lower Transport Cost in the East African Community?* ODI Briefing Paper, London, 2017.

Engel, Ulf and Nugent, Paul, 'Introduction: The Spatial Turn in African Studies', in *Respacing Africa*, Leiden, 2009, pp. 1–9.

Exchange, Tanzania, Dar es Salaam, 'Why Kenya is Threatened by Uganda–Rwanda Standoff', *The Exchange*, 13 March 2019.

Fraser, Darren, and Theo Notteboom, 'Gateway and Hinterland Dynamics: The case of the Southern African container seaport system', *African Journal of Business Management,* 6.44, 2012: pp. 10807–25.

Fraser, Darren, and Theo Notteboom, 'A strategic appraisal of the attractiveness of seaport-based transport corridors: the Southern African case', *Journal of Transport Geography,* 36, 2014, pp. 53–68.

Hall, Peter, Hesse, Markus, and Jean-Paul, Markus, 'Reexploring the Interface between Economic and Transport Geography', *Environment and Planning A,* 38, 2006, pp. 1401–08.

Hont, Istvan, *Jealousy of Trade: International Competition and the Nation-State in Historical Perspective*, Cambridge, 2005.

Hope, Albie and Cox, John, *Development Corridors,* London, 2015.

Hoyle, Brian, and Jacques Charlier, 'Inter-port competition in developing countries: an East African case study', *Journal of Transport Geography*, 3.2, 1995, pp. 87–103.

Hume, David, 'Of the Jealousy of Trade', *Walker's Hibernian Magazine, or Compendium of Entertaining Knowledge*, May 1785–December 1811, pp. 623–25.

Mann, Michael, 'The autonomous power of the state: its origins, mechanisms and results', *European Journal of Sociology,* 25.2, 1984, pp. 185–213.

Moe, Terry M., 'Political Institutions: The Neglected Side of the Story', *Journal of Law, Economics, & Organisation*, 6, 1990, pp. 213–53.

Monios, Jason, and Bruce Lambert, 'The Heartland Intermodal Corridor: public private partnerships and the transformation of institutional settings', *Journal of Transport Geography,* 27, 2013, pp. 36–45.

Monitor, 'Is Kagame Looking for an Alternative Route to the Sea?', *The Monitor*, 11 March 2019.

— 'Kampala-Dar es Salaam: Another Route Uganda Should Consider?', *The Monitor*, 8 March 2017.

— 'Uganda Government Puts SGR on Hold Over Unresolved Issues', *The Monitor*, 30 October 2018.

— 'Uganda on High Alert as Kenya, Rwanda go to polls', *The Monitor*, 30 July 2017.

— 'Uganda, Rwanda Better Off Together Than Divided', *The Monitor*, 10 March 2019.

— 'Ugandan Traders Ask Tanzania to Harmonise Cargo Transit Fees', *The Monitor*, 15 December 2016.

— 'Ugandan Traders Turn to Dar Port as Kenya Polls Close In', *The Monitor*, 23 June 2017.

— 'Who Will Gain Most from Busia Joint Border Post', *The Monitor*, 28 February 2018.

Nation, 'Alarm Over Increased Road Crashes', *The Nation*, 14 May 2017.

— 'The Good, the Bad and the Ugly of Kenya's SGR Cargo', *The Nation*, 30 October 2018.

— Kenya Finds Going Tough With Its Regional Partners', *The Nation*, 2 August 2016.

Naudé, Wim, *The Financial Crisis of 2008 and the Developing Countries*, No. 2009/01 WIDER Discussion Paper, Helsinki, 2009.

New Times, 'Bribery, Red Tape Still Dog Trade on Central Corridor', *The New Times*, 27 February 2018.

— 'Is it Time the EAC Walks the Integration Talk', *The New Times*, 28 July 2016.

— 'Regional Traders Continue to Face Hurdles on Central Corridor', *The New Times*, 27 July 2016.

— 'Relief as Tanzania Ports Authority Open Liaison Office in Kigali', *The New Times*, 15 August 2016.

— 'Removal of NTBs Paying Dividends Despite New Setbacks', *The New Times*, 11 August 2016.

Northern Corridor Transport Observatory, *Annual Report 2018*, Nairobi, 2019.

Notteboom, Theo, 'Strategies and Future Development of Transport Corridors', *Les Corridors de Transport*, 2012, pp. 289–311.

Nugent, Paul, 'Africa's re-enchantment with big infrastructure: White elephants dancing in virtuous circles?', in *Extractive industries and changing state dynamics in Africa*, Abingdon, 2018, 22–40.

Observer, Kampala, Uganda, 'Port Bell to Kampala Line due to Reopen', *The Observer*, 23 April 2018.

Rodrique, Jean-Paul, 'The Geography of Global Supply Chains: Evidence from Third-Party Logistics', *Journal of Supply Chain Management*, 48:3, 2012, pp. 15–23.

— 'Transportation and the Geographical and Functional Integration of Global Production Networks', *Growth and Change*, 37:4, 2006, pp. 510–525.

Smith, Adam, *The Wealth of Nations: An Inquiry into the Nature and Causes of the Wealth of Nations*, Petersfield, 1776 (2010).

Tanzania Daily News, 'DRC, Uganda Engaged on Road User Fee', *Tanzania Daily News*, 1 March 2018.

— 'Congrats TPA for Reaching Out to Potential Customers', *Tanzania Daily News*, 18 October 2016.

— 'Dar es Salaam Port increases Rwanda, Domestic Cargo', *Tanzania Daily News*, 2 December 2016.
— 'EAC Trade, Free Movement of Goods Machinery Starts', *Tanzania Daily News*, 6 November 2018.
— 'Kampala Upbeat with Dar Port, Central Railway Line Facelift', *Tanzania Daily News*, 6 June 2018.
— 'New Thrust for Efforts to Improve Trade, Investments in East Africa', *Tanzania Daily News*, 16 April 2019.
— 'Optimism High on Re-Opened Mwanza-Port Bell Route', *Tanzania Daily News*, 14 August 2018.
— 'Private Sector Key to Devt Plan Success – Mpango', *Tanzania Daily News*, 6 February 2017.
— 'SGR Construction Means Big Business to Local Firms', *Tanzania Daily News*, 7 February 2017.
— 'Standard Gauge Railway Tenders Announced', *Tanzania Daily News*, 9 November 2016.
— 'Tanzania: Kuwait Grants Tz 109 billion for Central Corridor Road Project', *Tanzania Daily News*, 22 March 2017.
Van Der Horst, Martijn R. and De Langen, Peter W., 'Coordination in Hinterland Transport Chains: A Major Challenge for the Seaport Community', *Maritime Economics & Logistics*, 10:1–2, 2008, pp. 108–129.

CHAPTER 11

Following the Tracks:
Chinese Development Finance and the
Addis–Djibouti Railway Corridor

YUNNAN CHEN

Introduction

The ubiquity of Chinese capital is visible across the Addis Ababa skyline: from glossy skyscrapers and airport terminals to the new modern light rail that glides through Meskel Square. Ethiopia has been a major beneficiary of China's 'going out' in Africa, which has seen growing flows of trade, investment, as well as aid and development finance between the two regions. After Angola, Ethiopia is the second largest African recipient of Chinese loans, much of which is channelled into supporting the country's infrastructure and industrial development strategy. In turn, Ethiopia has sought to emulate the East Asian development experience, developing its industrial capacity and investing heavily in infrastructure connectivity to engender economic transformation through export-oriented growth. China has become an instrumental partner, in providing both technology and financing for Ethiopian ambitions. In turn, Ethiopia and its position in the Horn of Africa has become another chain-link in the expansion of China's Belt and Road Initiative and its maritime trade corridors.

Within this salient relationship, one sector that has received major attention is transport – specifically, railways. As well as the Addis Ababa Light Rail Transit project, the new Chinese-built Addis–Djibouti line (or Ethio-Djibouti Railway) has become a flagship project in the twenty-first century Maritime Silk Road, in Sino-Ethiopian co-operation, and in the Ethiopian government's ambitions for economic modernisation. Commencing commercial operation in January 2018, the railway is the first constructed in Ethiopia since the French-built *Chemin de Fer* over a century ago, and is notably the first electrified railway in Africa. Under the government of the Ethiopian People 's Revolutionary Democratic Front (EPRDF), and the leadership of former premier, Meles Zenawi (in power from 1995 until his death in 2012), railway development was one part of a wider industrial strategy that sought to use infrastructure investment to foster the development of regional economic corridors from Ethiopia's manufacturing centres, to key seaports in Djibouti, and the Addis Djibouti line was to be the first of a broader national network that would also connect industrial hubs in Mekele in the north and Hawassa in the south-west. By lowering the economic and transaction costs of logistics through infrastructure investment, the government hoped to foster industrial zone development along these railway corridors. In turn, this boost to export sectors would generate much-needed foreign exchange that would repay the borrowing for infrastructure investment, and in the longer term, to the structural transformation of the economy.

Symbolically, the Addis–Djibouti railway (ADR) carries a special significance in the China–Africa relationship, as the first Chinese railway project in Africa since the Tanzania–Zambia (TAZARA) railway, built in the 1970s with Chinese aid. Belt and Road Initiative discourse has also enfolded the Horn and East African regions, making them strategically valuable in Chinese foreign and economic policy. In Kenya, China Road and Bridge Construction Company (CRBC), supported by China's Eximbank, has constructed two phases of a standard gauge railway from Mombasa to Nairobi, initially planned to extend to Naivasha and to the Ugandan border.[1]

In the African context, however, railways have also been historically associated with the colonisation of Western powers into African states.[2] This has been reflected in the extractive design of colonial railway, which tends to connect inland resources to ports and colonial metropoles, rather than improving regional connections.[3] The Addis–Djibouti railway follows this model, but with the design of boosting the integration of Ethiopian manufacturing into global supply chains. It is notable for its genesis and development as an Ethiopian initiative; however its long-term sustainability and financial viability remains under question. Initial operation, which remains under Chinese management, has proved problematic, including technical challenges relating to its electrification, local social impacts and the spillover impacts of sub-regional security

---

[1]   These sections extending towards the Ugandan border have proved a challenge for the Kenyan government, as Chinese finance has not been forthcoming since the completion of the section to Naivasha and, as of 2019, plans for funding the SGR's extension with China Eximbank have stalled indefinitely.

[2]   T. W. Roberts, 'Republicanism, Railway Imperialism, and the French Empire in Africa, 1879–1889', *The Historical Journal*, 54:2, 2011, pp. 401–20.

[3]   Remi Jedwab, Edward Kerby and Alexander Moradi, 'History, path dependence and development: Evidence from colonial railways, settlers and cities in Kenya', *The Economic Journal* 127.603 (2017): 1467–94.

challenges. The case highlights not only the risks and costs to foreign debt financed infrastructure, but also the importance of developing domestic capacity in order to manage it, and ensure its long-term sustainability.

The Rationale for Railway

The expansion of Chinese railway technology into Africa, and the ever-encompassing Belt and Road Initiative could hold huge potential for African structural transformation. Chinese development finance has become an important means of filling the wider infrastructure investment gap in African economies, which the African Development Bank estimates to be in the range of US$68–108 billion annually.[4] Within this, the transport sector is recognised as a key sector for regional connectivity and in fostering economic agglomeration. While the impacts of infrastructure on growth are well-documented, particularly in the impact of road in contribution to economic development, railway development in Africa has generally been more problematic.[5] Unlike road transport, railway systems depend on both the base infrastructure and also an operator for full service. Operation and maintenance require far more intensive systems of management, as well as capital-intensive maintenance, all of which are a challenge in countries where governance and capacity is weak.[6]

However, the potential of railway lies in its contribution to industrial and urban development and in serving logistical needs – a key constraint for African industries and particularly manufacturing. For rapidly urbanising African centres and nascent industrial hubs, rail can serve as a lower-cost option for freight transportation compared to trucking; railways also serve as a more sustainable, less polluting transport option for passenger travel. The African Development Bank's (AfDB) 2015 report on rail also notes its potential to spur the growth of complementary industries, including food, retail and in maintenance of rolling stock, and due to its interlinked nature with other core industries such as steel and energy. As such, 'railways should be seen as a component part of a wider

4   African Development Bank (ADB), 'Africa's 3 Infrastructure: Great Potential but Little Impact on Inclusive Growth', in *Africa Economic Outlook,* Abidjan, 2018.
5   See: César Calderón and Luis Servén. *Infrastructure, Growth, and Inequality: An Overview*, Policy Research Working Paper, Washington, D.C., 2014; César Calderón and Luis Servén, *The Effects of Infrastructure Development on Growth and Income Distribution*, Washington, D.C., 2004, p. 270; Christian Volpe Martincus, Jerónimo Carballo and Ana Cusolito, 'Roads, Exports and Employment: Evidence from a Developing Country', *Journal of Development Economics*, 125, 2017, pp. 21–39.
6   ADB, *Rail Infrastructure in Africa: Financing Policy Options*, Abidjan, 2015.

industrial development plan'.[7] More recently in 2020, the AfDB funded part of a feasibility study (a total of around US$1.2 million) into the development of an Ethiopia–Sudan railway link connecting Addis Ababa to the Sudanese port of Khartoum, in line with the economic development plan of both states, as well as the broader goal of fostering regional integration.[8]

The Dragon in the Horn of Africa

While much of China's engagement in Africa has been viewed through the lens of resource exploitation and Chinese demand for African commodity imports, Chinese capital has also been flowing into Africa in the form of investment and lending. Chinese state financing has supported the construction of large swathes of infrastructure across Africa and the developing world and Chinese construction contractors, often winners of World Bank construction projects, have been responsible for many more.[9]

This rise in Chinese infrastructure lending during the 2000s accelerated after the global financial crisis, at a time when major Western lenders were unable and/or unwilling to support large infrastructure projects in Africa, despite the infrastructure gap. In China, industrial overcapacity at home and the lure of untapped markets abroad have also pushed investors and firms overseas.[10] Simultaneously, China's foreign economic policy has encouraged and supported Chinese (usually state-owned) companies in 'going out' through preferential incentives and benefits, as well as through its policy banks, China's Eximbank and China's Development Bank, which offer favourable and quick loans to governments conditional on the procurement of Chinese goods.

7   ADB, *Rail Infrastructure in Africa*, 99.
8   AfDB, 'Ethiopia: The African Development Bank Gives $1.2 Million for Ethiopia-Sudan Railway Study', *African Development Bank* <www.afdb.org/en/news-and-events/press-releases/ethiopia-african-development-bank-gives-12-million-ethiopia-sudan-railway-study-36099> [Accessed 1 May 2021].
9   Vivien Foster and Cecilia Briceno-Garmendia, *Africa's Infrastructure: A Time for Transformation*, Washington, D.C., 2010 <https://openknowledge.worldbank.org/handle/10986/2692>; Jamie Farrell, *How Do Chinese Contractors Perform in Africa? Evidence from World Bank Projects*, SAIS China Africa Research Initiative Working Paper, Washington, D.C., 2016.
10   See: Deborah Brautigam, Tang Xiaoyang and Ying Xia, 'What Kinds of Chinese "Geese" Are Flying to Africa? Evidence from Chinese Manufacturing Firms', *Journal of African Economies*, 27: supplement 1, 2018, pp. i29–51.

Much of this has been channelled through the Forum of China–Africa Cooperation (FOCAC) political initiative, the triannual summit that serves as a platform for bilateral meetings and engagement. The more recent Belt and Road Initiative (BRI) is the latest emanation of this policy impulse. While the BRI's mission aims to foster economic connectivity across the Eurasian 'belt' and maritime routes – partly through investments in transportation and communication infrastructure – it also serves Chinese domestic economic needs, by offshoring domestic excess capacity. Though many African projects' inception pre-dates the official Belt and Road discourse, both the Light Rail and ADR, the Kenyan SGR, the new Chinese naval/logistics base in Djibouti, and commercial port investments have all been folded into the BRI.

Elsewhere, Chinese companies bringing Chinese high-speed rail technology are competing against European and Japanese firms to construct lines in Southeast Asia and North Africa.[11] Rail technology has been designated a key strategic sector. Having developed through foreign technology transfer and deliberate government support, Chinese rail exports – and the 'supply-chain export' of its manufacturing chain that international railway projects allow – are now a key opportunity to offshore Chinese domestic overcapacity. Beyond Ethiopia and Kenya, Chinese firms have competed for railway contractors in Nigeria, where Chinese finance and firms are constructing a new line from coastal Lagos to the northern provincial capital of Kano; in Angola, Chinese firms constructed the Benguela railway line; and has also financed locomotive purchases in Zambia.[12]

Chinese companies and financing have also attracted their share of criticism. Compared to traditional infrastructure financing from multilateral development banks, Chinese loans do not mandate the same kind of open competition as World Bank or other multilateral development bank (MDB) financing. Infrastructure finance guarantees are instead tied directly to procurement of Chinese goods and services. Chinese loans are often characterised as 'no-strings attached', as they lack the same kind of conditionality over environmental and social protections that MDB or Western financing dictates, generating concerns over their

---

[11] Agatha Kratz and Dragan Pavlićević, 'Norm-Making, Norm-Taking or Norm-Shifting? A Case Study of Sino-Japanese Competition in the Jakarta-Bandung High-Speed Rail Project', *Third World Quarterly*, 40:6, 2019, pp. 1–22; Michelle Ker, *China's High Speed Rail Diplomacy*, Staff Research Report: US–China Economic and Security Review Commission, Washington, D.C., 2017; Uwe Wissenbach and Yuan Wang, *Local Politics Meets Chinese Engineers: A Study of the Chinese-Built Standard Gauge Railway Project in Kenya'*, Policy Brief: China Africa Research Initiative, Washington, D.C., 2016.

[12] Based on SAIS-CARI data.

environmental impacts in the context of weak governance and institutions.[13] Labour relations have also been a source of controversy, as local employment and treatment of labour has been a source of unrest in Chinese resource and construction sector projects.[14]

Beyond environmental sustainability, Chinese-financed projects and infrastructure also face long-term project sustainability issues. For example, the decline of the Tazara railroad after the departure of Chinese engineers, despite efforts in skills training, showed the failure in long-term knowledge transfer and in the self-dependence principles that Chinese aid purported to represent.[15] The current surge of Chinese infrastructure projects presents similar risks but also opportunities to correct these earlier failures.

Ethiopia's Industrial Ambitions

Like the industrialising Asian economies in the 1980s and 1990s, Ethiopia's leadership under the Ethiopian People's Revolutionary Democratic Front (EPRDF) shares characteristics of a 'developmental state': an assertive central state with a strong orientation towards economic growth and poverty reduction.[16] Under the late prime minister, Meles Zenawi (1995–2012), Ethiopia consciously borrowed and mimicked Chinese and other Asian newly industrialised economies' strategies, attracting FDI in targeted export-industries, as well as leveraging capital from both traditional aid donors and alternative 'rising powers' like China.[17]

---

[13] Frauke Urban, Johan Nordensvard, Giuseppina Siciliano, and Bingqin Li, 'Chinese Overseas Hydropower Dams and Social Sustainability: The Bui Dam in Ghana and the Kamchay Dam in Cambodia: Chinese Overseas Hydropower Dams', *Asia & the Pacific Policy Studies*, 2:3, 2015, pp. 573–89.

[14] Ching Kwan Lee, *The Specter of Global China: Politics, Labor, and Foreign Investment in Africa*, Chicago, 2017.

[15] Jamie Monson and Liu Haifang, 'Railway Time: Technology Transfer And The Role Of Chinese Experts In The History Of TAZARA', in Terje Oestigaard, Mayke Kaag, Kjell Havnevik and Ton Dietz (eds), *African Engagements*, Leiden, 2011, pp. 226–51.

[16] Christopher Clapham, 'The Ethiopian Developmental State', *Third World Quarterly*, 39:6, 2018, 1151–65; Toni Weis, 'Ethiopia's Vanguard Capitalists', *Foreign Affairs*, 26 May 2016 <www.foreignaffairs.com/articles/ethiopia/2016-05-26/ethiopias-vanguard-capitalists> [Accessed 27 April 2021].

[17] Fantu Cheru, 'Emerging Southern Powers and New Forms of South–South Cooperation: Ethiopia's Strategic Engagement with China and India', *Third World Quarterly*, 37:4, 2016, pp. 592–610.

Infrastructure is a crucial component of the government's long-term development strategy, and an integral part of Ethiopia's Growth and Transformation Plans (GTP I and II), which aim to structurally transform the economy from an agrarian base to an industrial and manufacturing powerhouse in the region. Railways are only one part of a wider industrial strategy that seeks to use infrastructure investment to facilitate economic corridors in an export-led growth model. By lowering the economic and transaction costs of logistics, Ethiopia seeks to facilitate industrial zone development and its export and manufacturing sectors, in turn promoting the long-term structural transformation of the economy towards higher value sectors. Priority industries have been targeted for export promotion, including cut flowers, textiles and leather.[18]

Borrowing from Chinese and Asian successes in industrial zone development, Ethiopia has also heavily invested in developing industrial zones across the country. One, the Eastern Oriental Zone, was the first Chinese state-sponsored zone to be constructed, from 2006–2007. Since then, other zones have been constructed by GOE, including around Bole airport in Addis Ababa, and in some cases with Chinese contractors, such as Havassa and Dire Dawa, south and east of the capital. Further industrial parks are planned in Adama, Mekele and Kombolcha, all cities along (planned) railway corridors.[19] A total of 17 integrated agro-industrial parks are also planned across four different states, targeting the development of its agricultural sector.

This focus on railway infrastructure is also connected to the concept of 'transit-oriented development' (TOD), which the GOE has also applied to its urban railway projects, namely the Chinese-built Light Rail Transit in the Addis Ababa centre. Urban and cross-national railways stimulate investment through raising land values and defining industrial and commercial development corridors, which include the numerous industrial zones.[20] The capital intensiveness of railways makes them difficult to justify financially, however, as many

---

[18] Deborah Brautigam, Toni Weis and Xiaoyang Tang, 'Latent Advantage, Complex Challenges: Industrial Policy and Chinese Linkages in Ethiopia's Leather Sector', *China Economic Review*, 48, 2018, pp. 158–69.

[19] A report by Fudan SIRPA notes that ten industrial parks are planned. In 2016, Havasa and Bole Lemi will be completed. In 2017, the three parks of Mekele, Kombolcha and Adama will be implemented. In addition, there are Kilinto, Dire Dawa, Bahir Dar, Jimma and the five parks in the airport's airport logistics park are scheduled to be completed by 2019. Take the Hawasa Industrial Park as an example. As of July 2017, the foreign exchange earning capacity was US$15 million.

[20] Mentioned by several interviewees at the Ethiopian Railway Corporation: 22/5/18a; 22/05/18b; 26/06/18; 17/1/19.

Ethiopian emphasised during interviews; it was not the 'financial' returns but the broader benefits to the economy that made it rational.

Railway Development in Ethiopia

Ethiopia is no stranger to railways. The Addis–Djibouti corridor was originally the site of a narrow-gauge railway, built by the French in 1897, which led to the emergence and development of Dire Dawa, Ethiopia's second largest city. From 1981 to 2004, this was run by La Compagnie du Chemin de Fer Djibouto-Ethiopien (CDE), which was jointly owned 50:50 by the governments of Djibouti and Ethiopia. However, by the 2000s, the rail was in disrepair and out of service in tracts, due to lack of infrastructure maintenance, poor management and the competition of road trucking alternatives.[21]

The aftermath of the Ethiopia–Eritrean war changed the calculus, making the Djibouti port connection a veritable lifeline for now-landlocked Ethiopia, and revitalised the national necessity of railway. Driven by Prime Minister Meles Zenawi, in the early 2000s the government created a Technical Advisory Group under the Ministry of Transport and Communications. The group laid out a master plan for nine railway lines across the country, a total network of 5,060 kilometres of track.[22] Of this, the Addis–Djibouti line was considered a priority, while the second to be tendered was the section from Awash to Mekele, the northern regional capital. The drive for railway was not only motivated by economic necessity, but also as a means for political and social cohesion.[23] Out of these plans, the Ethiopian Railway Corporation (ERC) was created in 2007 and tasked with managing the future development of the network.

The GOE turned to several international partners, particularly the Agence du Developpement Français (AFD) during this period, who agreed to fund the rehabilitation of the railway. However, in the wake of the financial crisis, the AFD was unable to extend sovereign concessional loans to the project that would have attracted private investment for a new concession.[24] The European Commission in 2009 also offered €50 million in development aid to finance its refurbishment, but the final sum was far too low – '50 million is a peanut' quipped one respondent

---

21 Arthur Foch, 'The Paradox of the Djibouti-Ethiopia Railway Concession Failure', *Proparco's Magazine*, 9, 2011, pp. 18–22.
22 310518a, Ministry of Transport.
23 220518b, ERC.
24 Foch, 'The Paradox'; Dipti Ranjan Mohapatra, 'An Economic Analysis of the Djibouti–Ethiopia railway Project', *European Academic Research*, 3:10, 2016, pp. 11376–400.

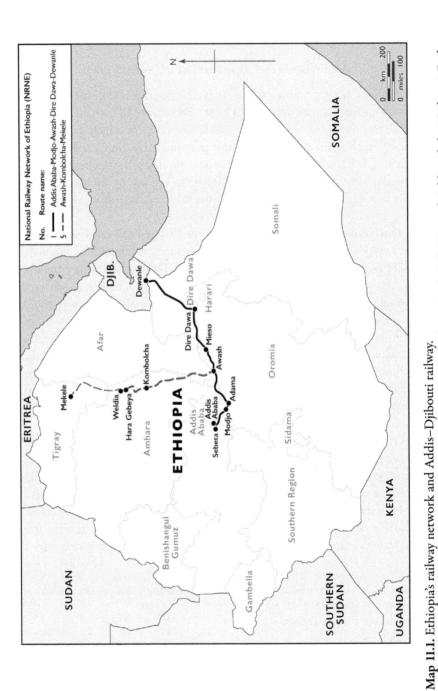

Map 11.1. Ethiopia's railway network and Addis–Djibouti railway.
(**Source:** Wikipedia open source database <https://commons.wikimedia.org/.wiki/File:Map_of_Addis_Ababa–Djibouti_Railway.png>.)

at the ERC.[25] After multiple delays and conflicts with the contractor, the refurbishment was eventually abandoned around 2011. Meanwhile, the old CDE company was retrenched, with most of the staff absorbed into the state-owned Metals and Engineering Technology Company (METEC).[26]

Around this time, Ethiopia had already begun negotiations with new partners for an electrified railway line. Both Brazil and India showed interest, and Indian consultants were also involved in initial pre-feasibility studies. However, it was Chinese contractors and Chinese financing that won the contract. Through a series of high-level bilateral talks, China negotiated not only a proposal for the new railway but also pledges for a new industrial sugar plant at Kuraz and the Grand Ethiopian Renaissance Dam transmission line. Chinese contractors offered a modern railway with a completely new standard-gauge width track, based on Chinese technology and design, and China Eximbank would guarantee the funds.[27]

Railway Projects in Ethiopia

Of the nine originally planned major national routes, two have been constructed as of writing: the Addis–Djibouti line and the Awash–Weldiya Line, while a further extension from Weldiya to Mekele has stalled (see Map 11.1). This section details the technical design, specifications and the chronology behind the projects.

The Addis–Djibouti Standard Gauge Railway

The ADR is considered a 'lifeline': the corridor forms a backbone that connects landlocked Ethiopia to the major regional port in Djibouti. The ADR is intended to substitute for the single, poorly maintained road from Addis Adaba, which currently channels the majority of Ethiopia's import and exports.[28] The total length is 656 kilometres standard gauge railway, of which 115 kilometres

---

25 220518b, ERC.

26 While the old CDE workshop and assets remain, both in Addis Ababa and in Dire Dawa (having now been absorbed into METEC property), they have been largely abandoned and are not functional. The old CDE workshop in Dire Dawa (which the author visited), is now preserved largely as a museum. The CDE reportedly still runs a local freight service between Dire Dawa and Djibouti twice a week, though this could not be confirmed.

27 12062018 MOFEC; 24 May 2018, Ministry of Finance.

28 Infrastructure Consortium for Africa, *Briefing Memorandum: The Djibouti–Ethiopia Railway*, no place of publication, 2007.

are double-track between Addis Ababa and Adama and single-track until its endpoint in Nagad, Djibouti. Like the Kenyan Madaraka express, the ADR is built according to the Chinese standard gauge model for Chinese rolling stock, according to Chinese Class 2 standards with Chinese CTCS signalling and communications systems. Notably, unlike the Kenyan railway, which uses diesel locomotives, the Addis–Djibouti rail has the added feature of being electrified along the entire route.[29]

Financing for both the ADR's construction and the power transmission lines were provided by China's Eximbank in two separate packages. Project construction was financed through a US$2.49 billion commercial loan, which covers 70 per cent of the total US$3.49 billion construction project cost. The Ethiopian government, notably, divided the construction contract into two sections, from Addis Ababa to Mieso and from Mieso to Dewele at the border with Djibouti, in order to foster competition and faster completion. As contractor for the Addis light rail transit project, CREC was a competitive choice for the Addis–Mieso section, with the idea that the railway would eventually be linked to the urban LRT. Meanwhile CCECC won the eastern section from Mieso to the Djiboutian border.

Contracts were signed at the end of 2011, and construction began in 2012. After winning the Ethiopian contract, CCECC promptly crossed over the border to lobby the government of Djibouti for the Djiboutian segment of the contract as well, also facilitating China Eximbank for financing.[30] A separate loan package for rolling stock procurement was arranged with the China North Industries Group (Norinco), who later signed a contract with Ethiopia's METEC to assemble wagons domestically.

Ethiopia already had a bilateral commitment with China to finance a railway on the provision that Chinese contractors would be awarded its construction. However, a conflict arose regarding the Ethiopian government's representative. Originally, the ADR project was going to be supervised by SweRoad, the same consultant who supervised the construction of the LRT on behalf of the Ethiopian government. However, under pressure from Chinese financiers, the contract with SweRoad was severed and replaced with a Chinese company, the CIECC, instead.[31]

---

29 220518c, ERC.
30 A loan of around US$500 million (based on SAIS-CARI data collection efforts).
31 Africa Intelligence, 'Ethiopia: SweRoad Wants to Be Compensated', *The Indian Ocean Newsletter*, 18 January 2013 <www.africaintelligence.com/ion/business-circles/2013/01/18/sweroad-wants-to-be-compensated,107940602-art> [Accessed 27 April 2021].

Implementation of the project was also complicated by inter-governmental negotiations with Djibouti over joint management as well as immigration issues, delaying construction. In January 2017, Ethiopia and Djibouti signed an agreement to create a joint venture company, the Ethio–Djibouti Railway, to manage the new trunk line. The negotiation of this was lengthy due to the issue of ownership shares, as Djibouti would face a diminished share compared to the 50:50 split they enjoyed in the concession for the old CDE railway. The final agreement took much of a year, and was a compromise of 75:25 in favour of Ethiopia.

Other Railway Projects

The Addis Ababa Light Rail Transit Project (LRT)

The Addis Ababa Light Rail Transit (LRT) project was the first rail sector project to be contracted, constructed and commissioned. The project was awarded to China Railway Engineering Company No. 2 Bureau (CREC) in 2009, and the Ethiopian government's representative was Swedish transport consultant SweRoad. Financing came in the form of a $475 million loan from China's Eximbank to the ERC, signed in 2011. The loan was set at a commercial rate, with a 23-year tenor and three-year grace period. Construction began in early 2012 and was completed in 2015. Since its completion, a three-year contract for the management and operation (M&O) of the LRT has been awarded to a Chinese consortium between contractor CREC and Shenzhen Metro – the latter's first overseas venture. During this M&O contract, the project was expected to transition to build local capacity with the goal to be solely under Ethiopian management. As of early 2019, the M&O contract had been extended by one year to August 2019.

The Awash–Kombolcha–Hara Gebeya/Weldiya Railway

The Awash–Weldiya line is the second national network line to be tendered, and forms the first of two sections that connects the ADR to Mekele in the north. The Awash–Kombolcha–Weldiya (AKH) was contracted to Turkish construction giant Yapi Merkezi, while the Weldiya–Mekele segment was contracted to Chinese Communications Construction Company (CCCC). The Turkish-built section began construction in 2014 and is close to completion, though staff on the project estimate the railway will not be operational until

2020 at the earliest. However, work on the northern section under CCCC has stalled due to lack of financing.[32]

After winning the construction contract in 2013, Yapi Merkezi played a significant role in facilitating a US$300 million loan from the Turkish Eximbank as well as subsequent financing from European partners, including Credit Suisse, who supported the project with a total US$1.1 billion loan. Notably, the AKH railway follows European technical and social standards, and European financiers exercised much more stringent requirements for social impact management schemes for displaced communities along the route. However, aspects of railway design have had to accommodate to the Chinese ADR. Beyond its standard gauge, specifications for tunnels and curvatures of the route were altered to accommodate larger Chinese locomotives.

A key technological divergence between the projects are the signalling systems employed between the two railways, which reflect the differences in European and Chinese standards. This presents a logistical challenge for the AKH's integration with the main ADR trunk line, first in terms of the hardware to integrate the sections of rail track and of onboard equipment for the Chinese locomotives, and second the technical and management training for staff to operate between the two lines. Ensuring cross-compatibility between the two systems will also require additional funding, a perennial challenge to Ethiopia's cash-strapped railway corporation. A further, major challenge is the financing and construction of corresponding transmission lines to power the AKH–ADR line. One respondent noted that, "even if we install everything, we cannot test it because there is no power supply".[33]

Railway and Ethiopia's Industrial Ambitions

The industrial export ambitions of Ethiopia's leadership, combined with the constraints of its landlocked geography and dependence on the entrepôt of Djibouti, has made the Addis–Djibouti Corridor an essential component of its industrialisation strategy. Djibouti has also been a major recipient

---

[32] China Eximbank has yet to disburse funds for the CCCC project, despite the project being tendered on the basis of the loan, and construction to date has proceeded using Ethiopian Birr (ETB). ERC representatives state that Eximbank refused to disburse finance for a second railway until the first Chinese railway (ADR) was shown to be successful. This chapter does not delve into the northern project's issue, but it does illustrate the wider financial constraints the Ethiopian government faces in its infrastructure ambitions.

[33] 170119a, Addis Ababa.

of Chinese infrastructure financing in the region, and forms an important strategic Belt and Road partner in the region: as well as being the site of a new multi-purpose free trade zone, Djibouti is also the site of the first Chinese 'naval base' in Africa.

The Doraleh Multipurpose Port (DMP) which opened in May 2017 was constructed by CCECC, the same contractor as the railway, with a loan from China Eximbank. At a project cost of US\$590 million for Phase 1 and Phase 2, it has the capacity to handle 8.8 million tons of goods per year. In contrast to Kenyan ports and other major African ports, the Djibouti Doraleh Container Terminal (which Djibouti holds the status of primary shareholder) has a higher than average efficiency for the region, with a crane productivity of 37 moves per crane hour. Ethiopia revenue and customs also has an internal dry port located at Modjo, between Awash and Addis Ababa where containers from the railway would be offloaded. These complementary infrastructures are also essential to the eventual functioning and economic feasibility of the Addis–Djibouti railway.

According to a 2018 UNCTAD report, the volume of road freight transportation between Addis and Djibouti was 1,000 trucks per day, which includes 350 fuel tankers and 500 container vehicles on average. The capacity of a cargo train of 3,500–4,000 tons of freight would be equivalent to between 100–200 truckloads. At current volumes of cargo, the report estimates a need for 11 trains and 50 wagons moving daily. As of early 2019, the number of trains moving daily between Addis and Djibouti was four (two daily in each direction), as the ERC and EDR company sought to start slowly and increase gradually.

Table 11.1. Railway projects constructed in Ethiopia.

Project	Addis Ababa Light Rail Transit	Addis–Djibouti/Ethio-Djibouti Railway (EDR)	Awash–Kombombla–Hara Gebeya/Weldiya Railway (AKH)
Specifications	Two electrified lines: north–south connecting Menelik Square to Kality; (16.9 km) east–west line from Ayat to Torhailoch (17.35 km)	656 km total length electrified standard gauge railway Double track 107 km; single track 549 km Chinese Class 2 standard CTCS Signalling systems	392 km total length electrified standard gauge railway, single track European Class 1 ERMTS Level 2 Signalling system.
Contractor	China Railway Engineering Company (CREC) No. 2 bureau China Railway Eryuan Engineering (design) Employers Rep: Sweroad O&M: CREC & Shenzhen Metro Company	China Railway Engineering Company (CREC) No. 2 bureau China Civil Engineering Construction Company (CCECC) Norinco (locomotive supplier) Employers Rep: CIECC O&M: CREC & CCECC	Yapi Merkezi & Yapiray Bombardier Molinari (equipment suppliers) Employer's Rep: Systra MD O&M: N/A

Financing	US$475 million 85 per cent China Eximbank	Total cost US$4.5 billion China Eximbank loan of US$2.49 billion, in three tranches, signed 2013 (Libor 6 m + 3), 15-year tenor, six-year grace period. Tenor renegotiated to 30 years in 2018.	Total cost US$1.7 billion Turkish Eximbank loan of US$300 million, estimated rates between 7–12 per cent, 15-year tenor. Credit Suisse loan of US$1.1 billion, in two tranches of US$700 million and US$400 million. Terms unverified. Other financiers include Swedish Exportkreditdamnden, Danish Eksport Kredit Fonden; Swiss Export Risk Insurance
Status	Commercial operation since 2015 Daily capacity of 120,000 passengers.	Construction completed 2016 Commercial operation since January 2018 One passenger train every other day (Addis/Djibouti) Four freight trains every day (from mid-2018)	Phase I 95 per cent completion, Phase II initiating. Reading for testing/operation in 2020/3021

Source: Author.

Operational Challenges

Construction of the Addis–Djibouti railway was completed in early 2016. However, it was not until January 2018 that it finally opened to commercial operation. Though it earned recognition as the first contemporary railway constructed in Sub-Saharan Africa, the implementation and operation of the railway has faced a number of operational challenges in the years following its completion. These include technical challenges, low uptake and last-mile issues and security challenges and local impacts.

Technical Challenges

Electrification and power supply have been a major issue in the commission and operation of the railway in its first year. The Ethiopian government intended the ADR project to run on 'clean' energy from Ethiopia's abundant hydropower resources, and pushed hard for the railway to be electrified along the entire route. This choice itself was a point of contention – Chinese contractors as well as American bidders initially submitted tenders for diesel-fuelled railway systems (as is the case in Kenya's SGR) but this was a point of no-compromise for Ethiopian decision-makers. However, the added complication of constructing the power transmission system and linking it to the physical railway infrastructure was an added obstacle, as power failures delayed the railway during the testing phase, and delayed the railway's commission by a year, despite the project being physically complete.

Technical issues with the power supply have also been problematic for the railway during its first months of operation. Since commercial operations began, power problems due to overvoltage issues in the stretch between Dire Dawa and Djibouti has caused repeated service interruptions, and is a challenge to the Ethiopian Railway Company's technical capacity.[34] While the long-term environmental and economic rationale for electrification holds, in the short and medium-term it has been a major obstacle to operation.

Last-mile and Uptake

Compared to the neighbouring Chinese-built SGR in Kenya, the Ethiopian railway's service uptake in its first year has been relatively weak, in both passenger and freight numbers. While railway freight volumes have been rising – the EDR

---

[34] Though lessening in frequency, this is a technical problem where surges in the electrical grid (due to Ethiopia's export of power to its neighbours) lead to overvoltage in the railway transmission line, akin to blowing a fuse.

company estimates that around a total of 800,000 tonnes were transported in 2018 using the railway – less than 1 per cent of this was export goods.[35] Part of this is due to the last-mile costs of the railway: construction of railway links to the major industrial zones were not part of the initial trunk line construction contract and are still being finalised. The construction of the Modjo dry port (which serves as an inland point where goods can be transported and stored, mitigating long wait times or hold-up at the port) was completed in 2018, the same year that the railway began commercial operation. However the added logistics costs of having to transport to Modjo, and the additional transaction costs of stevedoring and freight forwarding, has made export firms understandably reticent to use railway to ship cargo over trucking, which, despite higher overall costs and time, allows greater flexibility over time, and perhaps reliability.

Some of these last-mile costs are also due to political economy factors: the monopoly of the state-owned Ethiopian Shipping and Logistics Service Enterprise (ESLSE) has a monopoly over stevedoring and freight forwarding services; road freight is also 'dominated' by a small number of Ethiopian companies with vested interests against railway competition.[36]

Social and Security Challenges

While the railway has been relatively low profile in terms of its environmental impacts compared to neighbouring Kenya, where environmental and wildlife concerns were a major issue in the construction phase, the Ethiopian railway has suffered from problems of local social impacts in its operation phase, and in turn been impacted by them. The problem of animal collisions along the track in the remote Somali regions on the unfenced railway line has been a hindrance to the railway, which is subsequently unable to run at full design speed. As well as contributing to local grievances against the railway project, it is a major cost to the ERC, which have had to regularly compensate local farmers and establish frameworks to report and manage compensation for such incidents.[37]

More worryingly, ethnic clashes between Afar and Somali groups in the eastern parts of the country have negatively hampered the operation and uptake of the railway in its debut year. While these are not directly caused

35   Interview, Addis Ababa, January 2019.
36   Foch, 'The Paradox'.
37   *The Economist* (2018) reports on the perverse incentives for camel owners generated by the policy of compensating livestock killed in collisions on the ADR, as the compensation price is set too high above market value. This has led to incidents involving droves of camels killed on the tracks.

by the railway's construction, the railway has become a flashpoint for existing social grievances and inter-ethnic tensions in the region, as a representation of a federal project and perceived to have little benefit for the local communities that it bypasses. Collisions with livestock have also contributed to these resentments. There have been reports of multiple instances where the railway and road were blockaded by local protestors: in one case the passenger train was held up overnight, with all passengers forced to remain on board until local representatives were able to negotiate with protesting groups for their safe release. This has had an unambiguously detrimental impact on the railway's uptake and its reputation: despite improvements in passenger numbers in mid-2018 and a doubling of freight trains by the third quarter, numbers had fallen by the end of the first year due to stoppages caused by security issues.

Implications for African Agency

Despite the challenges highlighted above, many of which were results of decisions made by Ethiopian actors, the Addis–Djibouti railway is notable in its representation of a case of an African borrower that has been able to exercise significant agency vis-a-vis its Chinese partners. At each design and construction stage, Ethiopian decision-makers made conscious trade-offs with respect to financing and implementation.

Overwhelmingly, many of these decisions were governed by political considerations. One ERC respondent even described the pressure of completing the railways on time to meet the GTP Phase as "a pressure point". This prioritisation of speed above all else motivated strategic decisions such as the division of the Addis–Djibouti and Awash–Mekele lines into dual segments, introducing competition between contractors. This decision incentivised the firms' lower-cost bids during the tender process – one factor that contributed to the ADR's substantially lower total project cost compared to the Kenyan SGR.[38]

However, prioritising speed came with other costs. One major weakness has been the lacklustre efforts at technology transfer and capacity building during the project construction phase. One ERC respondent noted that they "tried to voice needs during the approval process". The lack of institutional and technical capacity was a huge disadvantage in bargaining or pressuring external partners.[39] In contrast, ERC respondents noted a much stronger emphasis on skill training

---

[38]   150119a, CCECC.
[39]   220518, ERC.

during the construction of the Turkish phase of the project, showing they had learned the second time around from their experiences with Chinese contractors.

There are several areas where Ethiopia's elite exercised agency and made conscious choices within the constraints of technological specifications. Electrification for the line is also a distinctive feature that the Ethiopian government strongly pushed, though this has not been without challenges, as detailed previously. The absence of fencing for large sections of the Addis to Djibouti route is another example of this. Although fencing is standard design in China's railways, the ERC was motivated by considerations both for cost-saving and for not cutting through local communities. This choice has, as noted, generated major operational problems with livestock collisions, forcing limits on train speed and generating local grievances, and illustrates some of the challenges in transplanting foreign technological systems and practices into new contexts. The unintended consequences it has generated also demonstrates the need for new legal and regulatory frameworks.

These challenges highlight the political will and ambition within Ethiopia's governmental institutions, but also the weakness of capacity in terms of evaluating and managing large-scale infrastructure projects. In the design and negotiations over the railway, lack of technical capacity has been a hindering factor for Ethiopia. A long-term meta-challenge for Ethiopia's railway institutions will be the development of a managerial infrastructure and a body of technical expertise to accommodate the different technologies that it has absorbed, and to eventually integrate those technologies. Long-run operation requires the parallel development of regulations, protocols and operating procedures. By not relying solely on Chinese material technology, Ethiopia is better positioned to be less dependent on China for this aspect. However, it now faces the challenge of integrating two foreign systems while developing its own indigenous standards, and will still depend heavily on the intervention and management of Chinese operating firms in the meantime.

The Dragon's Gold: Finance and Debt Issues

Compared to private sector commercial financing, the major advantage to Chinese loans has been financial flexibility in the post-construction phase. One ERC respondent noted the Chinese were more "flexible" and "willing to support you".[40] In Ethiopia's case, the government has struggled to repay external debts due to the ongoing shortage of foreign reserves. Poor export performance and years of internal instability left the country by 2018 with dollar reserves

---

[40]   240119, ERC.

worth only one to two months of imports. The shortage has also made many railway-related expenditures unaffordable including spare parts, locomotives and management fees for the railway's O&M.[41] On the Eximbank loans itself, after the expiration of the grace period, Ethiopia has reportedly struggled to repay the interest, let alone principal, on the commercial loans. The IMF in 2018 classed the country as 'at high risk' of debt distress.[42]

On this, China appears to have been remarkably lenient. Ethiopia was able to default on its loan repayments to China for one year, which was mutually agreed upon and came with no penalty. Additionally, in late 2018 after high-level bilateral talks and via the FOCAC platform, the original SGR loan terms were renegotiated from a 15- to 30-year tenor, or repayment period.[43] On the part of the contractors, the SOEs have had to swallow their costs: the optics of the Belt and Road demands that the projects continue to run, even if the Ethiopian state cannot pay for them.

The political advantages that Chinese financing entails have been a boon for cash-strapped Ethiopia, but it has perverse implications for the balance of power between the ERC and its Chinese contractors. While the ERC finds itself dissatisfied with aspects of the railway's quality and management, it has limited bargaining power *vis-à-vis* the companies. On the ADR, due to delayed O&M contract payments, ERC staff found themselves regularly surrounded by CREC and CCECC staff pressuring them for payment; they also made several concessions to assuage contractors. The manager of the light rail notes that it took two years to pressure the contractor to provide resources for a new maintenance workshop, and even then it was only made possible by pulling political strings, negotiating and involving the Chinese economic counsellor's office.

As debt sustainability becomes increasingly salient, the Ethiopian government has sought other options. Under Prime Minister Abiy Ahmed, there has also been an effort to diversify away from Chinese debt financing, towards public–private partnerships, encouraging private sector involvement in railways. China's Eximbank has also shown greater risk aversion to further railway lending, given the huge losses that have come out of lending to the project. The extension of the Awash line to Mekele was contracted to China Communications Construction Company (CCCC); however China Eximbank funding for the project has not

---

41   310119, Kality.
42   International Monetary Fund, *The Federal Democratic Republic of Ethiopia 2018 Article IV Consultation-Press Release; Staff Report; and Statement by the Executive Director for The Federal Democratic Republic of Ethiopia*, Country Reports: Article IV Consultation, Washington, D.C., 2018.
43   170119, ERC.

been so forthcoming, and it is unlikely until confidence is restored in the performance of the Addis–Djibouti line.

Conclusion

The Addis–Djibouti Railway reflects the opportunities and challenges for African governments who seek to leverage Chinese development finance, and the resources that Chinese partners can provide in terms of infrastructure development resources. Chinese finance has been a valuable resource for Ethiopia's infrastructure and industrial development, which implicitly reflects the African developmental state's conscious mimicry of the Asian development model. However, choosing Chinese finance has not been without problems for the African state. Despite decisive leadership and a strategic developmental vision, Ethiopia has suffered in the undertaking of the project due to challenges of technical capacity and in prioritisation of political goals in the railway's construction, at the expense of more diligent evaluation of its technical and economic feasibility. The challenges that have emerged from its operation have tested the Ethiopian Railway Company, as well as the managerial capacity of the Chinese contractors tasked with running the railway as a business. Ensuring the transfer of skills and embedded knowledge from the Chinese contractors to local staff, and moving away from dependence on Chinese contractors, will be a long-term objective and challenge.

For the time being, there is little appetite on both sides for further railway finance. The financial burden of the railway's debt finance has strained the capacity of Ethiopia's cash-strapped government to repay, but the case also illustrates the other side of the 'debt-trap' narrative: while Chinese lending has contributed to higher debt, as a partner it has also shown much-needed flexibility in the face of Ethiopia's repayment struggles. For China, Ethiopia remains a key strategic partner, even if, in the railway sector, the light at the end of the tunnel seems dim.

Bibliography

African Development Bank (ADB), *Rail Infrastructure in Africa: Financing Policy Options*, Abidjan, 2015.

— 'Africa's 3 Infrastructure: Great Potential but Little Impact on Inclusive Growth', in *Africa Economic Outlook,* Abidjan, 2018.

— 'Ethiopia: The African Development Bank Gives $1.2 Million for Ethiopia-Sudan Railway Study', *African Development Bank* <www.afdb.org/en/news-and-events/

press-releases/ethiopia-african-development-bank-gives-12-million-ethiopia-sudan-railway-study-36099> [Accessed 1 May 2021].

Africa Intelligence, 'Ethiopia: SweRoad Wants to Be Compensated', *The Indian Ocean Newsletter*, 18 January 2013 <www.africaintelligence.com/ion/business-circles/2013/01/18/sweroad-wants-to-be-compensated,107940602-art> [Accessed 27 April 2021].

Brautigam, Deborah, Weis, Toni and Tang, Xiaoyang, 'Latent Advantage, Complex Challenges: Industrial Policy and Chinese Linkages in Ethiopia's Leather Sector', *China Economic Review*, 48, 2018, pp. 158–69.

Brautigam, Deborah, Xiaoyang, Tang and Xia, Ying, 'What Kinds of Chinese "Geese" Are Flying to Africa? Evidence from Chinese Manufacturing Firms', *Journal of African Economies*, 27: supplement_1, 2018, pp. i29–51.

Calderón, César and Servén, Luis, *The Effects of Infrastructure Development on Growth and Income Distribution*, Washington DC, 2004.

— *Infrastructure, Growth, and Inequality: An Overview*, Policy Research Working Paper, Washington D.C., 2014.

Cheru, Fantu, 'Emerging Southern Powers and New Forms of South–South Cooperation: Ethiopia's Strategic Engagement with China and India', *Third World Quarterly*, 37:4, 2016, pp. 592–610.

Clapham, Christopher, 'The Ethiopian Developmental State', *Third World Quarterly*, 39:6, 2018, pp. 1151–65.

Farrell, Jamie, *How Do Chinese Contractors Perform in Africa? Evidence from World Bank Projects*', SAIS China Africa Research Initiative Working Paper, Washington D.C., 2016.

Foch, 'The Paradox of the Djibouti–Ethiopia Railway Concession Failure', *Proparco's Magazine*, 9, 2011, pp. 18–22.

Foster, Vivien and Briceno-Garmendia, Cecilia, *Africa's Infrastructure : A Time for Transformation*, Washington D.C., 2010 <https://openknowledge.worldbank.org/handle/10986/2692>.

Infrastructure Consortium for Africa, *Briefing Memorandum: The Djibouti–Ethiopia Railway*, no place of publication, 2007.

International Monetary Fund, *The Federal Democratic Republic of Ethiopia 2018 Article IV Consultation-Press Release; Staff Report; and Statement by the Executive Director for the Federal Democratic Republic of Ethiopia*, Country Reports: Article IV Consultation, Washington D.C., 2018.

Jedwab, Remi, Edward Kerby, and Alexander Moradi, 'History, path dependence and development: Evidence from colonial railways, settlers and cities in Kenya', *The Economic Journal*, 127.603 (2017): 1467–94.

Ker, Michelle, *China's High Speed Rail Diplomacy*, Staff Research Report: US–China Economic and Security Review Commission, Washington D.C., 2017.

Kratz, Agatha and Pavlićević, Dragan, 'Norm-Making, Norm-Taking or Norm-Shifting? A Case Study of Sino-Japanese Competition in the Jakarta-Bandung High-Speed Rail Project', *Third World Quarterly*, 40:6, 2019, pp. 1–22.

Lee, Ching Kwan, *The Specter of Global China: Politics, Labor, and Foreign Investment in Africa*, Chicago, 2017.

Martincus, Christian Volpe, Carballo, Jerónimo and Cusolito, Ana, 'Roads, Exports and Employment: Evidence from a Developing Country', *Journal of Development Economics*, 125, 2017, pp. 21–39.

Mohapatra, Dipti Ranjan, 'An Economic Analysis of the Djibouti–Ethiopia Railway Project', *European Academic Research*, 3:10, 2016, pp. 11376–400.

Monson, Jamie and Haifang, Liu, 'Railway Time: Technology Transfer and the Role of Chinese Experts in the History of TAZARA', in Terje Oestigaard, Mayke Kaag, Kjell Havnevik and Ton Dietz (eds), *African Engagements*, Leiden, 2011, pp. 226–51.

Roberts, T. W., 'Republicanism, Railway Imperialism, and the French Empire in Africa, 1879–1889', *The Historical Journal*, 54:2, 2011, pp. 401–20.

Urban, Frauke, *et al.*, 'Chinese Overseas Hydropower Dams and Social Sustainability: The Bui Dam in Ghana and the Kamchay Dam in Cambodia: Chinese Overseas Hydropower Dams', *Asia & the Pacific Policy Studies*, 2:3, 2015, pp. 573–89.

Weis, Toni, 'Ethiopia's Vanguard Capitalists', *Foreign Affairs*, 26 May 2016 <www.foreignaffairs.com/articles/ethiopia/2016-05-26/ethiopias-vanguard-capitalists> [Accessed 27 April 2021].

Wissenbach, Uwe and Wang, Yuan, *Local Politics Meets Chinese Engineers: A Study of the Chinese-Built Standard Gauge Railway Project in Kenya'*, Policy Brief: China Africa Research Initiative, Washington D.C., 2016.

CHAPTER 12

Corridors of Opportunity?
African Infrastructure and the Market
Expansion of Chinese Companies

ELISA GAMBINO

Introduction

In May 2019, I was conducting observations at a Belt and Road Initiative (BRI) business fair in Beijing, when I heard a curious exchange between the secretary general of a Chinese government-affiliated BRI think-tank and the director of a private maritime investment fund. Upon meeting for the first time, the pair began discussing their respective jobs and their involvement in BRI. To my surprise the think-tank secretary general, a BRI 'veteran', used the Mandarin term for BRI – 一带一路, *yi dai yi lu* – as an 'activity', asking whether the director of the investment fund was 'belt-and-roading'.[1] After that conversation, I began noticing that, differently from what I had observed during my previous fieldwork trip to Beijing in 2018, this formulation, whereby the BRI is something that is 'done', an 'activity' (or even a 'profession'), had become part of the vocabulary of state officials and business people alike. As the BRI continues to make headlines and to be the subject of lively scholarly and policy debates, this vignette speaks to the fact that, although no consensus has been reached on what BRI actually is, what it encompasses, and, in turn, what the implications of being (or not being) part of it are, the BRI is something 'to be done'.

In a recent *Diplomat* commentary, Jiang echoed this sentiment, stating that '[t]he BRI is nowadays like a growing adolescent during puberty. It genuinely aims to do things, but rarely contemplate[s] the "why" and "how"'.[2] The fog surrounding the BRI has not, however, hindered its expansion. Since the then

---

1   你做一带一路吗? *ni zuo yi dai yi lu ma?*
2   Yuan Jiang, 'The Continuing Mystery of the Belt and Road', *The Diplomat*, 6 March 2021 <http://bit.ly/2OVhQXW> [Accessed 13 March 2021].

called One Belt One Road – the literal translation of the Chinese *yi dai yi lu* – was first presented by President Xi in 2013, the BRI has gone from a Eurasian corridor to a global initiative expected to enhance policy, infrastructure, trade, finance and people-to-people connectivity. When BRI guidelines were published by the Chinese National Development and Reform Commission in 2015,[3] this initiative encompassed the Silk Road Economic Belt[4] – a system of land-based infrastructure to recreate the Tang Dynasty's Silk Road – and the Twenty-First Century Maritime Silk Road[5] – a maritime connectivity initiative aimed to increase links between China, South East Asian nations and India. It was only in 2017, during the BRI Forum, that the African continent was referred to as the 'natural' extension of the BRI and was formally included in this initiative, with East Africa's coast as the mooring point.[6]

Since then, an increasing number of African infrastructure initiatives, including transport corridors, have been labelled as being part of the BRI. Among the African transport corridors discussed in this volume, the Northern Corridor, connecting Mombasa port in Kenya to Uganda and Rwanda (see Lamarque in this volume), and the Addis Ababa–Djibouti Corridor, connecting Ethiopia to Djibouti (see Chen in this volume), were included under the BRI umbrella in 2019.[7] The bundling of African transport corridors into BRI comes at a time when Sino-African engagement in infrastructural development has prompted a rapidly expanding body of literature.[8] Indeed,

---

3   National Development and Reform Commission, 'Vision and Actions on Jointly Building Silk Road Economic Belt and 21st-Century Maritime Silk Road', National Development and Reform Commission, 2015 <https://bit.ly/2CRNJuI> [Accessed 25 June 2018].

4   丝绸之路经济带 – *sichou zhi lu jingji dai.*

5   21世纪海上丝绸之路 – *er shiyi shiji haishang sichou zhi lu.*

6   Belt and Road Forum, '第二届'一带一路'国际合作高峰论坛圆桌峰会联合公报 *Di Er Jie 'Yi Dai Yi Lu' Guoji Hezuo Gaofeng Luntan Yuanzhuo Fenghui Lianhe Gongbao* (Joint Communique of the Leaders' Roundtable of the Second Belt and Road Forum for International Cooperation]', *Xinhua News*, 2019 <https://bit.ly/2VCuqM9> [Accessed 27 January 2020].

7   Belt and Road Forum.

8   See among many others Chris Alden, Cobus van Staden, and Yu-Shan Wu, 'The Flawed Debate around Africa's China Debt and the Overlooked Agency of African Leaders', *Quartz Africa*, 2018 <http://bit.ly/2OgmpJi> [Accessed 06 December 2019]; Giles Mohan and May Tan-Mullins, 'The Geopolitics of South-South Infrastructure Development: Chinese-Financed Energy Projects in the Global South', *Urban Studies* 56:7, 2019, pp. 1368–85; Folashadé Soulé-Kohndou, 'Bureaucratic Agency and Power Asymmetry in Benin-China Relations', in Chris

the process of *respacing*[9] Africa through the development of infrastructure, unfolding since the late twentieth century, coincided with a push towards internationalisation of Chinese companies. Already at the end of the 1990s, the Chinese government had published a set of guidelines under the 'going out policy'[10] for companies to access financial incentives in the form of preferential lines of credit, access to preferential foreign exchange rates and trade insurances to support their overseas expansion.[11]

In the aftermath of the 2007/2008 financial crisis, as overseas demand for Chinese goods declined, the reduction in exports posed a severe risk to the profitability of many businesses, particularly in the manufacturing and construction sectors.[12] The Chinese government introduced a stimulus package which encompassed a broad programme of development of the national infrastructure systems.[13] However, this was not enough to mitigate the overcapacity crisis in the construction sector.[14] To avoid economic stagnation and debt crises,

Alden and Marcus Power (eds), *New Directions in Africa-China Studies*, London, 2019, pp. 189–204; Yuan Wang and Uwe Wissenbach, 'Clientelism at Work? A Case Study of Kenyan Standard Gauge Railway Project', *Economic History of Developing Regions*, 3, 2019, pp. 280–99; Ian Taylor and Tim Zajontz, 'In a Fix: Africa's Place in the Belt and Road Initiative and the Reproduction of Dependency', *South African Journal of International Affairs* 81, 2020, pp. 1–19; Pádraig R. Carmody, Ian Taylor and Tim Zajontz, 'China's Spatial Fix and 'Debt Diplomacy' in Africa: Constraining Belt or Road to Economic Transformation?', *Canadian Journal of African Studies*, 2021, pp. 1–21; Ian Taylor, 'Kenya's New Lunatic Express: The Standard Gauge Railway', *African Studies Quarterly*, 19:3–4, 2020, pp. 29–52; Xiao Han and Michael Webber, 'From Chinese Dam Building in Africa to the Belt and Road Initiative: Assembling Infrastructure Projects and Their Linkages', *Political Geography*, 77, 2020, pp. 1–12; Tom Goodfellow and Zhengli Huang, '"Contingent Infrastructure and the Dilution of 'Chineseness'": Reframing Roads and Rail in Kampala and Addis Ababa', *Environment and Planning A: Economy and Space*, 2020, pp. 1–20.

9   Ulf Engel and Paul Nugent, 'The Spatial Turn in African Studies', in Ulf Engel and Paul Nugent (eds), *Respacing Africa*, Leiden, 2009, pp. 1–9.
10   走出去政策 – *zou chu qu zhengce*.
11   Barry Naughton, *The Chinese Economy: Transition and Growth*, London, 2007.
12   Taylor and Zajontz, 'In a Fix: Africa's Place in the Belt and Road Initiative and the Reproduction of Dependency'.
13   Nicholas R. Lardy, *Sustaining China's Economic Growth After the Global Financial Crisis*, Washington, D.C., 2012, p. 129.
14   Ngai-Ling Sum, 'The Intertwined Geopolitics and Geoeconomics of Hopes/ Fears: China's Triple Economic Bubbles and the 'One Belt One Road' Imaginary', *Territory, Politics, Governance*, 7:4, 2019, pp. 528–52.

companies were told to 'turn the challenge into an opportunity by "moving out" this overcapacity'.[15] Former Deputy Foreign Minister He Yafei suggested that new clients and markets should be found overseas and Chinese companies were encouraged to 'closely study the investment environment abroad' and 'act without delay' as 'a "win–win" future awaits'.[16] The renewed push towards internationalisation to sustain the recovery of the national economy relied upon 'exporting' overcapacity beyond Chinese borders.[17]

Meanwhile, the promotion of the principle that infrastructure needs to be built, upgraded and rendered more efficient to decrease transportation costs and increase African states' ability to deliver economic and social development continues to dominate international discourse and to be promoted by international organisations.[18] On the African continent, the push towards regional and

[15] Yafei He, 'China's Overcapacity Crisis Can Spur Growth through Overseas Expansion', *South China Morning Post*, 7 January 2014.

[16] Ibid. It should be noted that the Chinese political economy is characterised by an apparent dichotomy between state oversight and operational autonomy of Chinese state-owned companies, particularly overseas. See for instance Thierry Pairault, 'Les Entreprises Chinoises Sous la Tutelle Directe du Gouvernement Illustrées par Leur Investissement en Afrique [Chinese Enterprises under Direct Supervision as Shown by Their Direct Investment in Africa]', *Économie Politique de l'Asie*, 13:1, 2013; Kjeld Erik Brødsgaard, '"Fragmented Authoritarianism" or "Integrated Fragmentation"?', in Kjeld Erik Brødsgaard (ed.), *Chinese Politics as Fragmented Authoritarianism*, London, 2017, pp. 38–55. Although the geo-political significance of African infrastructure to the Chinese state should not be overlooked, Chinese companies operating overseas have increasingly gained autonomy with regards to decision-making processes for the participation to international tenders for infrastructure projects not financed by Chinese actors. Many scholars have underlined the fragmented nature of Chinese governance in relations to Sino-African engagement, thus demystifying Fishman's 'China Inc'. narrative. Ted C. Fishman, *China Inc.: The Relentless Rise of the Next Great Superpower*, 2nd ed., New York, 2006. See among others: Katy N. Lam, *Chinese State-Owned Enterprises in West Africa*, London, 2017; Ian Taylor and Yuhua Xiao, 'A Case of Mistaken Identity: "China Inc". and Its "Imperialism" in Sub-Saharan Africa', *Asian Politics & Policy* 1:4, 2009, pp. 709–25; Deborah Brautigam, Xiaoyang Tang, and Xia Ying, *What Kinds of Chinese 'Geese' Are Flying to Africa? Evidence from Chinese Manufacturing Firms*, Washington, 2018.

[17] Sum, 'The Intertwined Geopolitics and Geoeconomics of Hopes/ Fears: China's Triple Economic Bubbles and the 'One Belt One Road' Imaginary'.

[18] Ulrikke Wethal, 'Building Africa's Infrastructure: Reinstating History in Infrastructure Debates', *Forum for Development Studies*, 43:3, 2019, pp. 473–99; Paul Nugent, 'Africa's Re-Enchantment with Big Infrastructure: White Elephants and

continental integration[19] has played a key role in repositioning infrastructure at the centre of African developmental agendas.[20] That of the African Union (AU), for instance, aims to 'connect Africa with world-class infrastructure'[21] and the African Development Bank (AfDB) estimates a current 'financing gap' of US$68–108 billion a year to reach this goal.[22] In other words, the conjunction of the growing demand for infrastructure in Africa and the necessity to address China's over-accumulation crisis through the 'moving out' of overcapacity created the conditions for the proliferation of Chinese participation to Africa's infrastructure, including transport corridors.

Nonetheless, increased engagement also meant more scrutiny. The sustainability of China–Africa engagement has been questioned by political leaders, civil society organisations and the public well beyond Africa. Debt sustainability concerns have emerged as African governments' debt to China increases, and security concerns grow in parallel with the increase in risk assessment mechanisms. Thus, this chapter aims to explore Chinese interests in African transport corridors, suggesting that participation in Africa's transport corridor development is prompting Chinese companies in related and unrelated sectors to venture along corridor routes to expand their businesses. To do so, I will first discuss the two main vehicles for China–Africa engagement, namely the FOCAC and the BRI. In this section, I will first underscore China's own experience in infrastructure construction and transport corridor development, to then investigate the inclusion of African transport corridors in the BRI and FOCAC. In the second section, I will explore the challenges to the sustainability of Chinese engagement in African transport corridors, focusing on Chinese loan conditionalities and security presence. Lastly, in the conclusion, I will reflect on the key findings.

Dancing in Virtuous Circles?', in Jon Schubert, Ulf Engel and Elisio Macamo (eds), *Extractive Industries and Changing State Dynamics in Africa*, London, 2018, pp. 22–40; Didier Péclard, Antoine Kernen and Guive Khan-Mohammad, 'États d'Émergence: Le Gouvernement de la Croissance et du Développement en Afrique', *Critique Internationale*, 89, 2020, pp. 9–27.

19 See Daniel C. Bach, *Regionalism in Africa: Genealogies, Institutions and Trans-State Networks*, London, 2016.

20 Nugent, 'Africa's Re-Enchantment with Big Infrastructure: White Elephants Dancing in Virtuous Circles?'.

21 African Union, *Agenda 2063: The Africa We Want*, Addis Ababa, 2015.

22 AfDB, *Africa's Infrastructure: Great Potential But Little Impact on Inclusive Growth*, Abidjan, 2018.

Channelling Sino–African Engagement

The first time China formally engaged with African nations continent-wide was in 1955 at the Bandung Asian–African Conference in Indonesia.[23] Starting from ideology-driven engagement in the 1950s, China's foreign policy for Africa has evolved into engagement mainly driven by pragmatism, as China has attempted to assume a leading role among developing countries. The economic growth of China drove the leadership of many African, Asian and Latin American states to increasingly look to China as a possible strategic partner, and economic engagement assumed a central role in China–Africa relations. As early as the 1990s, growing China–Africa engagement brought to light the need for an international forum to facilitate multilateral co-operation. Moving away from bilateral coordination was deemed necessary to address the concerns of asymmetric power between China and single African nations, as well as to channel Chinese engagement towards initiatives aimed at continental integration.

On the one hand, continental integration has been at the centre of Africa's developmental agenda since the early independence period. Already in 1963, the Organisation of African Unity was established to safeguard the continent's political independence and secure its economic development. Africa's integration agenda was then relaunched through the Lagos Plan (1980), which proposed the consolidation of African countries into regional economic communities (RECs). The RECs are envisioned to operate as building blocks for wider forms of integration, such as the AU's Agenda 2063 mentioned earlier. On the other hand, China's limited experience in multilateral co-operation was already recognised as a challenge to China–Africa engagement in the last decade of the twentieth century.[24] Therefore, several African leaders suggested the formation of a platform for engagement with China, referring to other

---

[23] Delegates from 29 Asian and African countries participated in the Bandung conference held in Indonesia, and in this setting what Chinese scholars consider Zhou Enlai's 'Five Principles for Peaceful Coexistence' were brought as the base of Chinese foreign policy. These principles, namely mutual respect for territorial integrity and sovereignty, non-aggression, non-interference in internal affairs, equality and mutual benefit and peaceful coexistence still guide, at least rhetorically, Chinese foreign policy and are said to be the basis of China's African policies of 2006 and 2015. See Bruce Larkin, *China and Africa, 1949–1970: The Foreign Policy of the People's Republic of China*, Berkeley, 1971, p. 17.

[24] Chris Alden, *China in Africa*, London, 2007, p. 27; Anna Samson, 'A "Friendly Elephant" in the Room? The Strategic Foundations of China's Multilateral Engagement in Asia', *Security Challenges*, 8:3, 2012 pp. 57–82; Henning Melber, 'Europe and China in Sub-Saharan Africa: Which Opportunities for Whom?', in

multilateral platforms such as the European Union–Africa Summit or the Tokyo International Conference of African Development.[25] Within China, scholars also called for the government to further their efforts in providing a platform and a framework for Sino-African engagement.[26] These factors, together with Chinese companies' requests for support in entering African markets and the pressure caused by African nations establishing diplomatic relations with Taiwan,[27] all contributed to the creation of the Forum on China Africa Cooperation (FOCAC).[28]

Since its formation, FOCAC has served several purposes.[29] First, it has been a platform to evaluate the evolution of the relations between China and African nations and put China–Africa co-operation initiatives on public display. Second, FOCAC offers the opportunity to set the agenda for the next three years, defining both Chinese and African nations' key projects and diplomatic agendas. Third, in addition to ministerial meetings attended by government officials, FOCAC offers officials and businesspeople several opportunities to carry out detailed discussions over future plans in the many FOCAC thematic sub-sessions. Although financial commitments witnessed a substantial increase – jumping from US\$5 billion in 2000 to US\$60 billion in investment in 2018 – FOCAC commitments have also reflected the evolving nature of China–Africa engagement. Table 12.1 summarises the key commitments made by China to African counterparts between 2006 and 2018.

Xing Li and Abdulkadir Osman Farah (eds), *China–Africa Relations in an Era of Great Transformations*, Farnham, 2013, pp. 107–26.

25   Guimei Yao, '中非合作论坛及其对中非经贸合作的影响 *Zhongfei hezuo luntan ji qi dui zhongfei jingji hezuo de yingxiang* [Forum on China-Africa Cooperation and Its Impact on China-Africa Economic Cooperation]', in Gongyuan Chen (ed.), 中国与非洲新型战略伙伴关系探索 *Zhongguo yu feizhou xinxing zhanlue huoban guanxi tansuo* [Exploration of the New Strategic Partnership between China and Africa], Beijing, 2007, p. 263.

26   Fei Gao, '当前非洲形势和中非关系 *Dangqian feizhou xingshi he zhongfei guanxi*' [Current Situation in Africa and China-Africa Relations], 西亚非洲 *Xiya feizhou* (West Asia and Africa), 1, 1998, pp. 1–3.

27   Sven Grimm, *The Forum on China-Africa Cooperation (FOCAC) – Political Rationale and Functioning*, Stellenbosch, 2012.

28   中非合作论坛 – *zhong fei hezuo luntan*.

29   Ian Taylor, *The Forum on China-Africa Cooperation (FOCAC)*, London, 2010.

Table 12.1. Key FOCAC financial commitments.

2006	2009	2012	2015	2018
Double aid to Africa by 2009	US$10 billion in concessional loans	US$20 billion investment	US$60 billion investment in different forms:	US$60 billion in investment in different forms:
Debt cancellation: matured interest-free loans to governments	US$1 billion for African small and medium size enterprises	China–Africa Development Fund (established in 2006) received a budget of US$5 billion	– US$35 billion in concessional loans and export credits*	– US$20 billion new credit lines
US$5 billion investment in different forms	Debt cancellation: interest-free loans due to mature by the end of 2009		– US$5 billion in grants	– US$15 billion in grants, interest free and concessional loans
China–Africa Development Fund US$1 billion			– US$5 billion to the China–Africa Development Fund	– US$10 billion for a fund for development finance
			– US$5 billion in loans to African small- and mid-sized firms	– US$5 billion to finance imports from Africa
			– US$10 billion for the enhancement industrial capacity	– US$10 billion from Chinese companies
			$60 million towards peace and security over five years	China–Africa Peace and Security Fund under BRI

* Concessional loans (援外优惠贷款 – *yuanwai youhui daikuan*) are one of the two preferential loan types that the Chinese government provides through China Export Import Bank (China Exim Bank), together with preferential buyer's credit (优惠买方信贷 – *youhui maifang xindai*) – a type of export credit. Typically, concessional loans are fixed interest rate (2–3 per cent) loans with long-term maturity (usually 15–20 years) and requires an inter-governmental agreement. Preferential buyer's credit does not require an inter-governmental agreement, and it refers to a loan covering up to 85 per cent of the total cost of a project implemented by a Chinese company; its interest rates are similar to those of concessional loans.

Sources: Ministry of Foreign Affairs of the PRC, *Forum on China–Africa Cooperation Johannesburg Action Plan (2016–2018)* (Beijing: Ministry of Foreign Affairs of the PRC, 2015; Ministry of Foreign Affairs of the PRC, *Forum on China–Africa Cooperation Beijing Action Plan (2013–2015* (Beijing: Ministry of Foreign Affairs of the PRC, 2012); Ministry of Foreign Affairs of the PRC, *Forum on China–Africa Cooperation Beijing Action Plan (2019–2021)* (Beijing: Ministry of Foreign Affairs of the PRC, 2018; Ministry of Foreign Affairs of the PRC, *Forum on China–Africa Cooperation Addis Ababa Action Plan (2004–2006)* (Beijing: Ministry of Foreign Affairs of the PRC, 2003; Ministry of Foreign Affairs of the PRC, *Forum on China–Africa Cooperation Beijing Action Plan (2007–2009)* (Beijing: Ministry of Foreign Affairs of the PRC, 2006; Ministry of Foreign Affairs of the PRC, *Forum on China–Africa Cooperation Sharm El Sheik Action Plan (2010–2012)* (Beijing: Ministry of Foreign Affairs of the PRC, 2009.

During the 2006 FOCAC China also pledged to donate a US$200 million building purposed to host the headquarters of the AU. The official publications that resulted from the 2006 FOCAC directly mention the AU parliament for the first time, reiterating support to pan–African initiatives already displayed in the China's Africa Policy (2006) published earlier the same year.[30] During the 2015 FOCAC, Chinese President Xi discussed the need for a comprehensive strategic partnership between China and Africa, and the need to align FOCAC commitments to the AU's Agenda 2063, which already shared the objective of enhancing connectivity. Notwithstanding the rhetorical alignment of FOCAC objectives with the African regional and continental integration agenda, African national governments and RECs continue to drive the push for connectivity (see Cissokho in this volume). The rhetorical emphasis on partnership would suggest support for African integration initiatives, particularly when several Chinese political figures, including Chinese President Xi Jinping and the Minister for Foreign Affairs Wang Yi, have expressed support for the importance of an African goal of connectivity and integration.[31] According to the AfDB, Chinese engagement has been focusing on projects that involve single countries, instead of regional projects involving multiple countries. The Africa Growing Together Fund jointly managed by the People's Bank of China and the AfDB was supposed to be a response to this claim,[32] but little efforts were made in directing these funds to multilateral projects.

After the financial crisis of 2007/2008, as funding from countries belonging to the Organisation for Economic Cooperation and Development (OECD) and Bretton Woods institutions decreased and the demand for infrastructural investment in the African continent continued to increase, China began to fill the gap. Between 2010 and 2018, the African transport sector alone recorded a total of US$37.4 billion commitments from Chinese lenders.[33] Simultaneously, Chinese construction companies' revenues from projects in Africa grew from US$28 billion in 2009 to US$54.7 billion in 2015, the highest ever.[34] The infrastructure financing trend, together with the grouping of many transport infrastructure projects – and the corridors they belong to – under the BRI umbrella,

---

30   For the full policy paper see Ministry of Foreign Affairs of the PRC, *China's African Policy*, Beijing, 2006 <https://bit.ly/2xiXfEH> [Accessed 27 April 2021].

31   Yi Wang, *Wang Yi: Pan-Africanism Is the Direction for Africa and in Tune with the Times*, Beijing, 2014.

32   AfDB, *AfDB Announces US$2 Billion Fund with China*, Abidjan, 2014.

33   China Africa Research Initiative (CARI), 'CARI Loan Database', Washington, 2021 <http://bit.ly/2P6wgCb> [Accessed 20 January 2021].

34   Ibid.

underlines the relevance of connective infrastructure to Chinese actors. Indeed, the strong focus on infrastructure connectivity of BRI is rooted in China's own experience of developing transport corridors.

Between 1992 and 2011, China used 8.5 per cent of its yearly gross domestic product (GDP) for the development of its national infrastructure system.[35] The high spending is underpinned by China's infrastructure-driven development model. In China, infrastructural investments were first directed towards established economic hubs (for instance Shanghai or Chongqing), and then to emerging economic ones (such as Kunming or Xiamen).[36] Nonetheless, the Chinese experience with infrastructure development is not linear and faces several sustainability challenges both nationally and internationally, and I will return to this point soon.[37] China's infrastructure development process culminated in the creation of national transport corridors to supply coal – the main source of China's energy for the past 50 years – and other natural resources to the eastern part of the country, where most of industrial and financial activities are located. Nationally, China's focus on the construction of transport corridors is motivated by the asymmetrical distribution of natural resources and production activities across the territory. Since the 1970s, coal has been transported across China through interregional transport infrastructure systems, known as coal corridors.[38]

In 2009, China became a coal importer, and the necessity to import from Russia and Mongolia arose,[39] culminating in the development of the China–Mongolia–Russia economic corridor in 2016. The China–Mongolia–Russia economic corridor is one of the six proposed corridors under the umbrella of the BRI.[40] At this initial stage, the BRI was envisioned to address the Asian 'infra-

---

[35] Yougang Chen, Stefan Matzinger, and Jonathan Woetzel, *Chinese Infrastructure: The Big Picture*, Hong Kong, 2013.

[36] Abhijit Banerjee, Esther Duflo and Nancy Qian, *On the Road: Access to Transportation Infrastructure and Economic Growth in China*, Boston, 2012.

[37] Xiaoyang Tang, 'Co-Evolutionary Pragmatism: Re-Examine "China Model" and Its Impact on Developing Countries', *Journal of Contemporary China*, 29:126, 2020, pp. 853–70.

[38] Shengkui Chen, Zengrang Xu, and Lei Shen, '中国省际煤炭资源流动的时空演变及驱动力 *Zhongguo sheng ji meitan ziyuan liudong de zhi kong yanhua ji qudong ji* (Spatial-Temporal Processes and Driving Forces of Interprovincial Coal Flows in China]', 地理学报 *Dili xuebao* (Acta Geographica Sinica], 63:6, 2008, pp. 603–12.

[39] Hongyan Yu, 'China Becomes a Net Coal Importer in 2009', *China Daily*, 23 February 2010.

[40] Crossing Central Asia, the BRI also envisions the development of the 'New Eurasia Land Bridge', a railway link through Russia and Kazakhstan towards Europe and

structural gap'. Through several refinements, the BRI has gone from a corridor initiative to promote the development of Asian connective infrastructure to a global initiative encompassing projects in a diverse array of sectors, from infrastructure to education. For instance, in January 2015, Lin Yifu, Honorary Dean of Peking University National School of Development suggested that African markets could bring significant opportunities to Chinese companies' internationalisation journey, and should therefore be part of BRI.[41] In the same month, Special Envoy to the AU Zhang Ming met with Nkosazana Dlamini-Zuma, then Chairperson of the AU Commission to sign a memorandum of understanding concerning the development of infrastructure networks across the continent.[42] Then, during the 2017 BRI Forum, the African continent was formally included in the BRI and, in 2018, the BRI was integrated in the FOCAC agenda, giving China yet another opportunity to showcase the opportunities BRI could bring to African nations, particularly in the infrastructure sector.

In Kenya, the port of Lamu stands out as a recent addition to the BRI maritime portfolio. Lamu port – currently under construction – is financed by the Kenyan government and is being built by China Road Bridge Corporation, a subsidiary of the Chinese state-owned enterprise (SOE) China Communication Construction Company. This SOE is no stranger to the Kenyan construction market. In May 2017, China Road Bridge Corporation completed the construction of the 478 kilometres standard gauge railway (SGR) between the capital Nairobi and the

the 'China–Central Asia–West Asia Economic Corridor' linking China to the Central Asian republics, Iran and Turkey. In South Asia, the BRI umbrella covers the 'China–Indochina Peninsula Economic Corridor', expected to connect China to South East Asian nations. The 'China–Bangladesh–India–Myanmar Economic Corridor' is currently the slowest-moving BRI project in the region, due to the security concerns among India and China, which have both attempted to retain their sphere of influence in South Asia though bilateral investment or cross-border infrastructure funding. See Christian Wagner, 'The Role of India and China in South Asia', *Strategic Analysis*, 40:4, 2016, pp. 307–20. Lastly, the 'China–Pakistan Economic Corridor', expected to run from the western Chinese province of Xinjiang to Gwadar port in Pakistan is also facing security challenges, as Gwadar port poses a threat to India's influence in the Bay of Bengal. See David Brewster, 'Is India "Losing" the Bay of Bengal?', *The Interpreter*, 19 March 2014.

41 Yifu Lin, '林毅夫：'一带一路'需要加上'一洲' *Lin Yifu: 'yi dai yi lu' xuyao jia shang 'yi zhou'* (Lin Yifu: The 'Belt and Road Initiative' Needs to Add 'One Continent'], *China Observer*, 2015.

42 He Xiao, 'African Agenda 2063 with the Belt and Road Initiative', in Cai Fang and Peter Nolan (eds), *Routledge Handbook of the Belt and Road*, London, 2019, pp. 425–30.

country's biggest port, Mombasa.[43] It should be highlighted that the contract for the construction of Lamu port was signed in 2013, the same year the BRI was first presented, while the loan for the construction of the Nairobi–Mombasa SGR was agreed between China Exim bank and the government of Kenya in 2014, when Kenya was not yet part of the BRI. Yet, during the BRI Forum of 2019, both Lamu port and the Nairobi–Mombasa SGR were included under the BRI umbrella, together with the broader corridor initiatives they belong to.[44] The Lamu Port–South Sudan–Ethiopia Transport (LAPSSET) Corridor, which encompasses Lamu port, is now considered one of the 'key strategic corridors' of the BRI even though it was initiated and designed by the governments of the three African countries it is envisioned to connect. Similar examples of pre-existing corridors that were relabelled BRI can be found in the Horn of Africa – such as the Djibouti–Addis Ababa Railway discussed in this volume by Chen – and in South East Asia.

Bundling African transport corridors into the BRI can serve several purposes. The BRI is a global initiative that would require capital-intensive investment over a long period of time. Through the inclusion of pre-existing projects in the BRI it is possible to continue its expansion and begin to address the investment sustainability concerns. Moreover, the BRI provides a platform to showcase connectivity projects and attract further investment for other components of the corridors, such as operation contracts, special economic zones (SEZs), or urban development projects.[45] The BRI label thus serves its purpose of accelerating the quest for funding, either from other Chinese actors, national or international investors. Nonetheless, an increased spotlight can also throw into relief the many concerns surrounding Chinese-sponsored infrastructure projects. Some of these concerns were addressed by President Xi during the 2018 FOCAC meeting in Beijing.

At this meeting, in addition to a pledge of US$60 billion in different forms, the forum orbited around issues arising in China–Africa engagement. First, debt sustainability was at the centre of discussions. Even though China pledged the same amount as in 2015, the composition of these financial commitments stands

---

[43]   Uwe Wissenbach and Wang Yuan, *African Politics Meets Chinese Engineers: The Chinese-Built Standard Gauge Railway Project in Kenya and East Africa*, Washington, 2017; Taylor, 'Kenya's New Lunatic Express: The Standard Gauge Railway'.

[44]   Belt and Road Forum, '第二届'一带一路'国际合作高峰论坛圆桌峰会联合公报 *Di er jie 'yi dai yi lu' guoji hezuo gaofeng luntan yuanzhuo fenghui lianhe gongbao* [Joint Communique of the Leaders' Roundtable of the Second Belt and Road Forum for International Cooperation]'.

[45]   Interview, Chinese scholar, Beijing, 25 May 2019.

out.[46] Overall, preferential and concessional lending decreased, while interest-free loans increased. The pledge also included US$10 billion, which should be invested by Chinese companies directly, reducing the government's commitments to US$50 billion. Second, Xi Jinping also reiterated the (at least rhetorical) importance of the non-interference principle guiding Chinese foreign policy.[47] This was a way to address the critiques received from the West, concerned that China's first foreign military base overseas in Djibouti was the beginning of China's military expansion. The formulation of the non-interference foreign policy principle, however, predates the rapid increase of Chinese engagement overseas and the country's growing prominence in the international sphere, raising questions about its contemporary significance.[48]

Infrastructural Engagement 'with Chinese Characteristics'

Chinese funding is marketed as having 'no-strings attached', as the official narrative suggests that loans from Chinese financial institutions do not require conditionality. In this sense, Chinese loans are portrayed as being in stark contrast to Western lending, which typically relies on conditionalities of 'good governance', environmental protection and ethical labour practices. Yet, although Chinese loans might be portrayed as being without conditionality, 'China attaches commercial conditions to its loans',[49] thus relying on 'loan-debt contractuality'.[50] The loan frameworks not only vary according to the funder, but are also tailored *ad hoc* for each project. For instance, the case of the

---

[46] Deborah Brautigam, 'China's FOCAC Financial Package for Africa 2018: Four Facts', CARI, 3 September 2018.

[47] Ministry of Foreign Affairs of the PRC, 'China's Initiation of the Five Principles of Peaceful Coexistence', Beijing: Ministry of Foreign Affairs of the PRC, 2000 <https://bit.ly/3g1lVm6> [Accessed 12 May 2019].

[48] Chris Alden, 'China and Africa: The Relationship Matures', *Strategic Analysis*, 36:5, 2012, pp. 701–07; Chris Alden, 'Beijing's Security Plans beyond Djibouti and the Horn', *Italian Institute for International Political Studies*, 28 September 2018<www.ispionline.it/en/pubblicazione/beijings-security-plans-beyond-djibouti-and-horn-21278> [Accessed 27 April 2021]; Zheng Chen, 'China Debates the Non-Interference Principle', *The Chinese Journal of International Politics*, 9:3, 2016, pp. 349–74.

[49] Mohan and Tan-Mullins, 'The Geopolitics of South-South Infrastructure Development: Chinese-Financed Energy Projects in the Global South', p. 1373.

[50] Sum, 'The Intertwined Geopolitics and Geoeconomics of Hopes/ Fears: China's Triple Economic Bubbles and the 'One Belt One Road' Imaginary', p. 27.

resource-for-infrastructure (RFI) agreement signed between the Angolan government and China Exim bank in 2004 to finance the post-conflict reconstruction of the infrastructure system offers a good example. The RFI framework allows governments to access financing for the development of infrastructure 'without ...having to produce sufficient revenues to support its financing',[51] but instead pledging to provide resources for the repayment.

China's deal with Angola was inspired by the 1978 agreement between China and Japan, when Japanese companies developed transport and power infrastructure in China in exchange for oil.[52] The agreement with Angola required a fixed price for oil to be exported to China, but when oil prices dropped during the financial crisis of 2007/2008, the Angolan government was forced to borrow again in order not to default on the US$2 billion loan,[53] further adding to the national debt. Similarly, a 2010 RFI loan agreement between the Ghanaian government and China Development Bank amounting to US$3 billion was renegotiated in light of fluctuating oil prices.[54] From Mohan and Tan-Mullins' analysis, it emerges that the loan conditions 'meant that China remained relatively insulated from the risk of non-payment'[55] while succeeding in entering the Ghanaian oil market, speaking to the long-term outlook often associated with Chinese engagement in Africa.[56]

Similarly, risk associated with funding infrastructure is also mitigated through the stipulation of conditionalities with regards to the acquisition or hiring of Chinese goods and services.[57] Indeed, the majority of Chinese loans require the signing party to contract a Chinese construction company without any public

51   Havard Halland, et al., Resource Financed Infrastructure, Washington, 2014, p. 31.
52   Deborah Brautigam, China in Africa: What Can Western Donors Learn?, Oslo, 2011.
53   Kevin Acker, Deborah Brautigam, and Yufan Huang, Debt Relief with Chinese Characteristics, Washington, 2020.
54   Mohan and Tan-Mullins, 'The Geopolitics of South-South Infrastructure Development: Chinese-Financed Energy Projects in the Global South'.
55   Ibid, p. 1378.
56   Thierry Pairault, 'Examining the Importance of the New Silk Roads for Africa and for Global Governance', in Maria A Carrai, Jean-Christophe Defraigne and Jan Wouters (eds), The Belt and Road Initiative and Global Governance, Cheltenham, 2020, pp. 155–80.
57   See for instance Michael Mitchell, Omoruyi Ehizuelen and Hodan Osman Abdi, 'Sustaining China–Africa Relations: Slotting Africa into China's One Belt, One Road Initiative Makes Economic Sense', Asian Journal of Comparative Politics, 3:4, 2018, pp. 285–310.

tendering processes. For instance, China Exim Bank loans are contingent on at least 50 per cent of the contract content – such as machineries, materials, or goods – to be Chinese.[58] Between 2010 and 2017, Chinese actors have funded one-fifth of infrastructure projects in Africa and have constructed one-third of them.[59] It is estimated that 89 per cent of projects with Chinese funding also have a Chinese contractor, with decision-making processes taking place behind closed doors.[60]

Chinese contractors are often chosen through private decision-making among Chinese ministries and the China International Cooperation Development Agency (CICDA) in Beijing.[61] CICDA replaced the State Aid Department in 2018, yet the channelling processes for infrastructure sponsoring overseas – and foreign aid more generally – have not evolved greatly since the mid-1990s. In 1995, then Chinese Minister for Trade Wu Yi formalised new guidelines for foreign aid – which also includes concessional loans for infrastructure development – based on the principle that financing should be channelled through already consolidated aid processes.[62] Although only slight changes have taken place in the decision-making processes for overseas infrastructure development, the modalities of engagement have evolved greatly in the past decades, prompting growing alarm over the sustainability of China–Africa infrastructure development.

In Tanzania, former President Magufuli's policy shift lead to the Bagamoyo port project being suspended indefinitely. The government of the previous president, Jakaya Kikwete – who was born in Bagamoyo– and Chinese port operation giant China Merchants Port had signed a US$10 billion framework

---

58 Deborah Brautigam, 'Aid "With Chinese Characteristics": Chinese Foreign Aid and Development Finance Meet the OECD-DAC Aid Regime', *Journal of International Development*, 23:5, 2011, pp. 752–64; Lucy Jane Corkin, 'Chinese Construction Companies in Angola: A Local Linkages Perspective', *Resources Policy*, 37:4, 2012, pp. 475–83.

59 Deloitte, *Africa Construction Trends Report 2018*, Nairobi, 2019.

60 Jonathan E. Hillman, 'The Belt and Road's Barriers to Participation', *Center for Strategic and International Studies*, 2018 <http://bit.ly/2GGoquo> [Accessed 22 March 2019]; Suisheng Zhao, 'China's African Relations and the Balance with Western Powers', in Jing Men and Benjamin Barton (eds), *China and the European Union in Africa*, Farnham, 2011, pp. 61–80.

61 Interview, Chinese scholar, Beijing, 12 July 2018; Interview, Senior Representative of Chinese state actor, Beijing, 27 July 2018.

62 Deborah Brautigam, 'Aid "With Chinese Characteristics": Chinese Foreign Aid and Development Finance Meet the OECD-DAC Aid Regime', p. 752.

agreement in 2013.[63] Bagamoyo port was expected to address the congestion of the first Tanzanian port, Dar es Salaam, but it was stalled in 2016 following the election of former President Magufuli.[64] His concerns revolved around the unfavourable contract conditions, given that China Merchants Port was rumoured to have set the condition of 99 years for the port operation concession.[65] The long concession period was seen as an attempt to reduce the government's sovereignty over Tanzanian assets, as the Chinese company was believed to have set this condition to eventually take control of the port.

In summary, lack of transparency and accountability are a recurring critique of the 'no-strings attached' engagement. For example, in 2018 a newspaper article suggested that Mombasa port had been agreed as guarantee in case the government of Kenya defaulted on the loan repayment,[66] which resulted in public discontent and demands for accountability.[67] Kenyan President Kenyatta stated he would publish the contract of the Nairobi–Mombasa SGR to put rumours to rest, yet no contract has been released. Against this background, ongoing debates among African elites, business people and civil society organisations are centred on the evaluation of whether the infrastructure being constructed reflects the needs and demands of African countries.

Debt Sustainability Concerns and African Transport Corridors

African governments' debt to Chinese state actors was estimated to be between US$72billion and US$7100 billion in 2017, amounting to 20 per cent of their total stock of debt, compared to US$66 billion owed to the World Bank.[68] With regards to infrastructure, Chinese lending to African nations increased significantly over the last decade. Between 2003 and 2011, Chinese policy banks

[63] Tairo Apolinari, 'Tanzania Surrenders Bagamoyo Port Project to Chinese Firm', *The EastAfrican*, 3 October 2017.
[64] Interview, Senior Manager of Chinese state-owned company, Hong Kong, 31 May 2019.
[65] The Citizen, 'How the Dream for a Port in Bagamoyo Became Elusive', *The Citizen*, 9 June 2019.
[66] Paul Wafula, 'Chinese Firm Withholds Key Detail in SGR Deal Review', *Daily Nation*, 10 December 2018.
[67] Edwin Okoth, 'SGR Pact with China a Risk to Kenyan Sovereignty, Assets', *Daily Nation*, 13 January 2019.
[68] Jubilee Debt Campaign, *Africa's Growing Debt Crisis: Who Is the Debt Owed To?*, London, 2018, pp. 7–8.

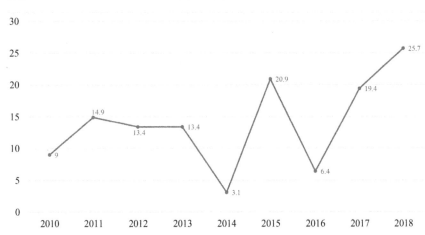

Figure 12.1. China's commitments to fund African Infrastructure (2010–2018) in US$ billion.
(Sources: ICA, Infrastructure Financing Trends in Africa – 2010, Abidjan: ICA, 2011; ICA, Infrastructure Financing Trends in Africa – 2011, Abidjan: ICA, 2012; ICA, Infrastructure Financing Trends in Africa – 2012, Abidjan: ICA, 2013; ICA, Infrastructure Financing Trends in Africa – 2013, Abidjan: ICA, 2014; ICA, Infrastructure Financing Trends in Africa – 2014, Abidjan: ICA, 2015; ICA, Infrastructure Financing Trends in Africa – 2015, Abidjan: ICA, 2016; ICA, Infrastructure Financing Trends in Africa – 2016, Abidjan: ICA, 2017; ICA, Infrastructure Financing Trends in Africa – 2017, Abidjan: ICA, 2018; ICA, Infrastructure Financing Trends in Africa – 2018, Abidjan: ICA, 2018.)

offered loans and credit lines to 43 African countries for a total of US$52.8 billion, most of which was devoted to infrastructure construction, often implemented by Chinese contractors.[69] In 2018, African governments remained the main funders of infrastructure projects, funding around 22.8 per cent of 480 infrastructure projects valued at US$50 million or more, while funding from Chinese sources increased to 20.4 per cent from 18.9 per cent in 2017.[70] The Infrastructure Consortium for Africa highlights an increase in Chinese funding from US$19.4 billion in 2017 to US$25.4 billion in 2018.[71] Figure 12.1 shows

---

69 Deborah Brautigam and Kevin Gallagher, 'Bartering Globalisation: China's Commodity-Backed Finance in Africa and Latin America', *Global Policy*, 5:3, 2014, p. 348.
70 Deloitte, *Africa Construction Trends Report 2018*.
71 Infrastructure Consortium for Africa (ICA), *Infrastructure Financing Trends in Africa – 2018*, Abidjan, 2018, p. 48.

the trends in Chinese commitments to fund infrastructure projects in Africa between 2010 and 2018, which have shown a substantial increase in 2015, 2017 and 2018.

The sustainability of Chinese loans and the nature of their conditionalities are being questioned by political leaders, civil society organisations and the public across African nations, China and the West. In Washington, the long-standing narrative of the 'China Threat'[72] was considerably fuelled by the Trump administration, which labelled Chinese lending practices 'debt trap diplomacy'. This suggests that Chinese loans are aimed to 'trap' borrowing countries in unrepayable loan agreements and to then appropriate infrastructure upon default.[73] The 'debt trap' narrative builds upon the case of the Hambantota Port in Sri Lanka, where, upon default of loan repayments, the Chinese state-owned China Merchants Ports obtained the concession of the port and surrounding land for 99 years.[74] Nevertheless, through the analysis of loan data, scholars have suggested that Chinese financiers have been turning to debt relief programmes – such as debt restructuring or cancellation – as opposed to asset seizures.[75] Thus, the political narrative constructed around the case of Hambantota is hardly convincing, as this case represents an exception rather than a model being replicated elsewhere.

What instead captures the attention in regard to the case of Hambantota port is its multi-sector model, as the port was envisioned to follow the Port+Park+City[76] model. This engagement blueprint is inspired by the experience of Shekou industrial zone in the 1970s, which is considered the

[72] For further details on the origins and development of the 'China Threat' narrative see Herbert Yee and Ian Storey, *China Threat*, Hoboken, 2013; in China-Africa studies see Deborah Brautigam, 'A Critical Look at Chinese 'Debt-Trap Diplomacy': The Rise of a Meme', *Area Development and Policy*, 5:1, 2020, pp. 1–14; and Stacey Links, 'Ascertaining Agency Africa and the Belt and Road Initiative', in Florian Schneider (ed.), *Global Perspectives on China's Belt and Road Initiative*, Amsterdam, 2021, pp. 113–39.

[73] Brahma Chellaney, 'China's Debt-Trap Diplomacy', *Project Syndicate*, 2017 <http://bit.ly/3pJR7uK> [Accessed 18 November 2020].

[74] Maria Abi-Habib, 'How China Got Sri Lanka to Cough Up a Port', *The New York Times*, 25 June 2018; Jonathan E. Hillman, 'Game of Loans: Sri Lanka', in Jonathan E Hillman (ed.), *The Emperor's New Road: China and the Project of the Century*, New Haven, 2020, pp. 151–70.

[75] Acker, Brautigam, and Huang, 'Debt Relief with Chinese Characteristics'; Deborah Brautigam, Yufan Huang and Kevin Acker, *Risky Business: New Data on Chinese Loans and Africa's Debt Problem*, Washington, 2020.

[76] 港口+园区+城市 *gangkou + yuanqu + chengshi*.

first 'seed' of the Shenzhen SEZ, which is now often hailed as the 'template' of the so-called 'China Model' of development.[77] Now also an official blueprint of the BRI, the Port+Park+City Model encourages Chinese actors to not only participate in port construction, but also to develop a network of related infrastructure surrounding the port, specifically SEZs.[78] This understanding of transport corridors (see Nugent and Lamarque in this volume) resembles the latest characterisation of the BRI umbrella discussed earlier. The now suspended Bagamoyo port project was envisioned to include a SEZ funded by the Omani Sovereign Fund, while the Kenyan government is currently accepting privately initiated investment proposals[79] for the concession of operations of Lamu port. In the latter, China Merchants Port is negotiating the development of Lamu metropolis and a SEZ as envisioned under the LAPSSET corridor masterplan.[80] The sustainability of China Merchants Port's investment offer for Lamu operations relies on securing different contracts under evaluation by Kenyan state actors.

First, there is a concessional contract for Lamu port operations of 50 years, which is deemed to be double what the Kenyan Ports Authority considers the life of the physical infrastructure of a port. Second, there is the design and development of Lamu city. Third, land is to be allocated for the creation of a SEZ. Simultaneously, China Merchants Port is rumoured to have requested a contract for Mombasa port expansion, which echoes the concerns raised around the rumoured collateralisation of Mombasa port as part of Nairobi–Mombasa SGR contract discussed earlier.[81] The negotiation of sustainable financing agreements continues to remain a priority.[82] In Kenya, total debt to Chinese lenders amounts

[77]   Xiangming Chen, '4. The BRI and Development', *Regional Studies Policy Impact Books*, 2:2, 2020, pp. 61–78.
[78]   Belt and Road Initiative Portal, "一带一路'建设海上合作设想 *Yi dai yi lu jianshe haishang hezuo shexiang* [Vision for Maritime Cooperation Under the Belt and Road Initiative]', Belt and Road Initiative Portal, 2017 <http://bit.ly/2GFPQAr> [Accessed 25 June 2020].
[79]   These differ from public tenders in that they are unsolicited.
[80]   Gediminas Lesutis, 'How to Understand a Development Corridor? The Case of Lamu Port–South Sudan–Ethiopia-Transport Corridor in Kenya', *Area*, November 2019, pp. 1–9.
[81]   Interview, official of state corporation, Lamu, 24 February 2019; Interview, senior official of state corporation, Mombasa, 26 March 2019; Interview, officer of state authority, Nairobi, 28 March 2019.
[82]   Thierry Pairault, 'Djibouti's Chinese Debt', *The China Africa Project*, 31 July 2020; Chris Alden and Lu Jiang, 'Brave New World: Debt, Industrialisation and Security

to about 30 per cent of these governments' total debt.[83] Even considering recent debt restructuring initiatives in light of the COVID-19 pandemic,[84] concerns remain over whether any of the Chinese-funded projects are at risk of default on loan repayment.

China's Security Presence Along African Transport Corridors

Initial analysis of overseas engagement suggested that Chinese companies undertake projects in countries considered 'risky' by other financiers, such as Western firms or international organisations.[85] Yet, this trend does not mean that all Chinese actors have a higher appetite for risk. Instead, the increase in economic interests in African nations led to the realisation that the Chinese internationalisation journey might be at risk due to political and economic shocks. During the early stages of the 'going out' process, the limited international expertise of Chinese companies pushed abroad by the government meant that excessive risks were being taken.[86] Risk assessment mechanisms have been a focal point of project evaluation in recent years, showing that more attention is paid to the debt sustainability issues. This also derives from the negotiation trajectories of African partners and Chinese companies, the latter of which are aware of possible risks posed by highly-publicised projects, such as those

---

in China–Africa Relations', *International Affairs*, 95:3, 2019, pp. 641–57; Taylor, 'Kenya's New Lunatic Express: The Standard Gauge Railway'; Carmody, Taylor and Zajontz, 'China's Spatial Fix and 'Debt Diplomacy' in Africa: Constraining Belt or Road to Economic Transformation?'.

83 Jubilee Debt Campaign, 'Africa's Growing Debt Crisis: Who Is the Debt Owed To?'; Constant Munda, 'Public Debt Repayment Hits Sh1trn for First Time', *Business Daily*, 22 February 2021; Alden and Jiang, 'Brave New World: Debt, Industrialisation and Security in China–Africa Relations'. In Kenya, the government's debt rose substantially in light of the expiration of grace periods in December 2020: see Business Daily, 'Payment of External Debt Nearly Doubles in 6 Months to Dec', *Business Daily*, 12 March 2021.

84 CARI, 'Debt Relief Dashboard', *CARI*, 2021 <http://bit.ly/3lkWTBS> [Accessed 12 March 2021].

85 Bala Ramasamy, Matthew Yeung and Sylvie Laforet, 'China's Outward Foreign Direct Investment: Location Choice and Firm Ownership', *Journal of World Business*, 47, 2012, pp. 17–25.

86 Katy N. Lam, *Chinese State-Owned Enterprises in West Africa*, p. 17.

under the BRI umbrella.[87] At the same time, Chinese companies are increasingly embedded in the socio-economic environment of the host country.[88] In 2017 alone, Chinese firms established 3,400 companies in Africa, most of which are in Zambia, Nigeria, Ethiopia, Kenya, South Africa, Ghana, Uganda and Angola.[89] This signals that companies' roles are evolving, perhaps moving away from dependency on Chinese financing for their business expansion.

When Chinese engagement with Africa nations began increasing at the end of the twenty-first century, Chinese companies were 'flying the flag of non-interference', and they had little capacity to be involved in security.[90] Chinese internationalisation processes carried on as if no security risks were present. This approach, however, changed due to Chinese companies' increasing economic interests and the growing numbers of Chinese citizens living and working on the African continent. The turning point occurred during the Arab Spring in 2011, when China needed to evacuate over 35,000 Chinese nationals from Libya. Due to China's then weak security capabilities in the region, they had to rely on Greek ships to complete the rescue mission.[91] Unable to protect its citizens and their businesses, China's security strategy shifted.[92] Not surprisingly, during the FOCAC of 2012, China made its first security commitments to African counterparts, announcing further financial assistance. During the 2018 FOCAC, President Xi announced the establishment of the China–Africa Peace and Security Fund, which encompasses 50 security assistance programmes under BRI, and the first China–Africa Peace and Security Forum took place in 2019, suggesting that security is gaining a prominent role in China–Africa engagement.

---

87   Kejin Zhao, "'一带一路'不应回避的十大问题 *Yi dai yi bu' bu ying huibi de shi da wenti* [Ten Issues That Cannot Be Overlooked in the Belt and Road Initiative]', 鳳凰 *Fenghuang* (Phoenix), 2015 <http://bit.ly/2OSV9nz> [Accessed 25 September 2020].

88   Elisa Gambino, 'La Participation Chinoise dans le Développement des Infrastructures de Transport au Kenya: Une Transformation des Géométries du Pouvoir? (Chinese Participation in Kenyan Transport Infrastructure: Reshaping Power-Geometries?)', *Critique Internationale*, 89, 2020, pp. 95–114.

89   Interview, Director of investment fund, Beijing, 18 May 2019; Interview, Manager of Risk Management Company, Nairobi, 5 July 2019; Lam, *Chinese State-Owned Enterprises in West Africa*, pp. 61–63. Ministry of Commerce of the PRC, '中国对外投资发展报告 *Zhongguo dui wai touzi fazhan baogao* [Report on the Development of China's Outward Investment]', Beijing: Ministry of Commerce of the PRC, 2018, p. 68.

90   Alden, 'China and Africa: The Relationship Matures', p. 704.

91   Alden, 'Beijing's Security Plans beyond Djibouti and the Horn'.

92   Alden, "China and Africa: The Relationship Matures'.

The most notable example of Chinese presence in African security is the presence of the first overseas military base of the People's Liberation Army Navy (PLAN) in Djibouti. Negotiations concluded in 2016, but this military base had long been in the making. In 2008, China had joined anti-piracy missions in the Gulf of Aden, and the PLAN had been surprisingly public about the need for an overseas base to support their anti-piracy missions.[93] Once the Chinese military base in Djibouti became a reality, the debate around the use of overseas ports for Chinese military purposes intensified. Chinese maritime investment began to be associated with the so-called 'String of Pearls Strategy', which refers to the creation of a Chinese maritime network across the Indian Ocean with the final goal of becoming a maritime power.[94] According to this line of enquiry, China is seeking to increase its influence in the Indian Ocean through the expansion of its dual-use port network, but evidence of Chinese militarised maritime expansion remains highly questionable.[95] China's increasing focus on security should not be seen merely through the lens of securitisation, but as an attempt to support Chinese companies' further internationalisation. Indeed, even more vital to the market expansion and capital growth of Chinese companies – a path underpinned by the development–security nexus – is the engagement of Chinese security companies in African nations.

Although security along African transport corridor routes is only discussed with regards to coastlines, the surge in risk assessment practices has resulted in the further presence of Chinese companies in the field of risk mitigation, shifting to a more active approach in addressing security issues that pose a risk to the economic development of Chinese businesses. The expansion of the BRI umbrella to African transport corridors signifies that security services will be required along corridor routes. These security services range from static guards deployed to protect construction sites, manufacturing plants, residential compounds or people, to security in hostile environments, for instance anti-piracy. In the

---

[93] Susanne Kamerling and Frans-Paul Van Der Putten, 'An Overseas Naval Presence without Overseas Bases: China's Counter-Piracy Operation in the Gulf of Aden', *Journal of Current Chinese Affairs*, 40:4, 2011, pp. 119–46.

[94] David Brewster, 'Silk Roads and Strings of Pearls: The Strategic Geography of China's New Pathways in the Indian Ocean', *Geopolitics*, 22:2, 2017, pp. 269–91.

[95] Dual-use refers to a type of port design which makes the port viable for both commercial and military purposes, usually associated with deep-water ports. Toshi Yoshihara and James R. Holmes, *Red Star Over the Pacific: China's Rise and the Challenge to U.S. Maritime Strategy*, Annapolis, 2010; Devin Thorne and Ben Spevack, *Harboured Ambitions: How China's Port Investments Are Strategically Reshaping the Indo-Pacific*, Washington, 2017.

Horn of Africa, the Chinese maritime security company Hua Xin Zhong An is widely employed on commercial ships.[96] Nearby, on the coastal land of Kenya, where the threat of Somali terrorist group al-Shabaab persists, the Chinese SOEs building the LAPSSET corridor component at Lamu port employ former Chinese People's Liberation Army personnel as heads of security, in charge of training Kenyan security contractors and watching over the construction site perimeters through security cameras.[97] Employing former members of the military or the police is a common practice in the security industry worldwide, but until 2010 Chinese national laws required chief executive officers of Chinese security companies to be former People's Liberation Army or police members.[98] New security markets also mean new opportunities to engage in the intelligence field. Most of the services offered by Chinese intelligence firms are in the public security sphere, such as facial recognition or traffic control programmes deployed in collaboration with governments. In 2018, the Zimbabwean government and the Chinese intelligence company CloudWalk signed a strategic partnership for a country-wide facial recognition programme.[99] In 2015, Huawei installed the 'Safe City' system made of 1,800 cameras and 200 traffic surveillance systems in Nairobi.

The spatial expansion and business development of Chinese contractors in a specific country leads to more companies in the same, related, or unrelated industry also venturing into the same country to expand their businesses. The case of China–Djibouti engagement offers insights into the interconnectedness amongst Chinese actors in different, yet interrelated, sectors. In addition to hosting the first PLAN overseas military base, Djibouti–China engagement in the infrastructural sector has prompted reflections on the sustainability of the debt accumulated,[100] but has also prompted a series of new engagements in other sectors. Currently, it is estimated that Djibouti's debt to Chinese lenders is over 70 per cent of the country's GDP,[101] as Chinese financing for infrastructure – such as the expansion of the Goubet Salt port, the Addis–Djibouti Railway

---

[96]   Hua Xin Zhong An (Beijing) Security Services, 华信中安(北京) 保安服务 – *hua xin zhong an (Beijing) baoan fuwu*. See Alessandro Arduino, *The Footprint of Chinese Private Security Companies in Africa*, Washington, 2020.

[97]   Interview, employee of Chinese SOE, Lamu, 25 February 2019.

[98]   Arduino, *The Footprint of Chinese Private Security Companies in Africa*.

[99]   Hongpei Zhang, 'Chinese Facial ID Tech to Land in Africa', *Global Times*, 17 May 2018.

[100] Pairault, 'Djibouti's Chinese Debt'.

[101] Mordechai Chaziza, 'China Consolidates Its Commercial Foothold in Djibouti', *The Diplomat*, 26 January 2021.

and the Doraleh Port – amounts to a total of US$936 million.[102] Nevertheless, this comes as Djibouti and China have established a strategic partnership to strengthen economic relations through an array of projects.[103] These not only revolved around transport infrastructure quickly folded under the BRI umbrella, but also on the development of related projects, such as a SEZ and a pipeline to transport oil to the port of Djibouti. In December 2020, China Merchants Port signed a US$350 million deal with the Djibouti state-owned Great Horn Investment Holding for the development of a Port+Park+City project on the model of the abovementioned Shekou in Shenzhen.[104]

In other words, the networks among Chinese companies and their relations with state actors – what Lam refers to as 'Chinese embeddedness'[105] – are vital. This suggests that the relationship between state support in the form of financial incentives and Chinese companies' operations abroad is central to their spatial expansion. As Chinese companies expand their businesses along African transport corridors – and BRI routes – the services of other Chinese companies, such as security and intelligence firms, will be needed, thus suggesting a similar 'going out' path to that of their clients. This engagement pattern, as shown in this chapter, is increasingly taking place along the routes of African transport corridors.[106]

[102] CARI, 'CARI Loan Database'.

[103] Xinhua News, 'China, Djibouti Agree to Establish Strategic Partnership', *Xinhua News*, 23 November 2017.

[104] Jevans Nyabiage, 'China Merchants Signs US$350 Million Deal for Shekou-Style Revamp of Djibouti Port', *South China Morning Post*, 5 January 2021.

[105] Lam, *Chinese State-Owned Enterprises in West Africa*, p. 6.

[106] See for instance Arduino, *The Footprint of Chinese Private Security Companies in Africa*; Donghoon Hahn and Keun Lee, 'Chinese Business Groups: Their Origins and Development', in Sea-Jin Chang (ed.), *Business Groups in East Asia: Financial Crisis, Restructuring, and New Growth*, Oxford, 2006, pp. 207–31; Jun Zhao, 'Ownership Structure and Corporate Diversification Strategies of Chinese Business Groups', *Management Research Review* 33:12, 2010, pp. 1101–12; Lucy Jane Corkin, 'Chinese Construction Companies in Angola: A Local Linkages Perspective'; Haifang Liu, 'Associations as Social Capital of 'New Chinese Migrants' in Africa: Empirical Investigations of Ghana, Zimbabwe, Tanzania and South Africa', in Scarlett Cornelissen and Yoichi Mine (eds), *Migration and Agency in a Globalising World*, London, 2018, pp. 69–90; Lam, *Chinese State-Owned Enterprises in West Africa*.

Conclusion

The growing participation of Chinese actors in the elaboration of African transport corridors can be traced to the intersection of the push towards the internationalisation of Chinese companies and the increasing demand for infrastructure funding across the African continent. Chinese contractors and funding bodies are furthering their presence in Africa through channels such as the FOCAC or the BRI, but they are not shielded from challenges and critiques. Here, I specifically discussed the questionable financial sustainability of Chinese funding for Africa's infrastructure and the growing Chinese security engagement along African transport corridors. On the one hand, debt to Chinese financiers continues to pose sustainability challenges even in light of shifting negotiation trajectories of African governments. On the other hand, the increased expansion of Chinese contractors on transport corridor routes suggests that companies in related and unrelated sectors will follow.

I have also highlighted that, even when African transport corridors are being grouped under the BRI umbrella, China is not setting the agenda for corridor development. Indeed, the corridors agenda had already been adopted by African actors – at the continental level, such as the AU and the AfDB, and at the government level, as the Kenyan and Djiboutian cases exemplified – before Chinese actors became major players in Africa's infrastructural development. This means that Chinese actors engage in segments of African transport corridors rather than in the agenda setting and governance of said corridors. Yet, African transport corridors can be neatly folded into the BR I, pointing to their relevance to Chinese actors. Through Chinese partner companies and business groups ranging from contractors to third-sector services already operating in the African countries involved in corridor development, other Chinese companies can identify possible clients with the goal of expanding their overseas businesses.

Bibliography

Abi-Habib, Maria, 'How China Got Sri Lanka to Cough Up a Port', *The New York Times*, 25 June 2018.

Acker, Kevin, Brautigam, Deborah and Huang, Yufan, *Debt Relief with Chinese Characteristics*, Washington, 2020.

AfDB, *AfDB Announces US$2 Billion Fund with China*, Abidjan, 2014.

— *Africa's Infrastructure: Great Potential But Little Impact on Inclusive Growth*, Abidjan, 2018.

African Union Commission, *Agenda 2063*, Addis Ababa, 2015.

Alden, Chris, *China in Africa*, London, 2007.

— 'Beijing's Security Plans beyond Djibouti and the Horn', *Italian Institute for*

International Political Studies, 28 September 2018 <www.ispionline.it/en/pubbli-cazione/beijings-security-plans-beyond-djibouti-and-horn-21278> [Accessed 27 April 2021].

— 'China and Africa: The Relationship Matures', *Strategic Analysis*, 36:5, 2012, pp. 701–07.

Alden, Chris and Lu Jiang, 'Brave New World: Debt, Industrialization and Security in China–Africa Relations', *International Affairs*, 95:3, 2019, pp. 641–57.

Alden, Chris, van Staden, Cobus, and Wu, Yu-Shan, 'The Flawed Debate around Africa's China Debt and the Overlooked Agency of African Leaders', *Quartz Africa*, 2018 <http://bit.ly/2OgmpJi> [Accessed 27 April 2021].

Apolinari, Tairo, 'Tanzania Surrenders Bagamoyo Port Project to Chinese Firm', *The EastAfrican*, 3 October 2017.

Arduino, Alessandro, *The Footprint of Chinese Private Security Companies in Africa*, Washington D.C., 2020.

Bach, Daniel C., *Regionalism in Africa: Genealogies, Institutions and Trans-State Networks*, London, 2016.

Banerjee, Abhijit, Duflo, Esther and Qian, Nancy, *On the Road: Access to Transportation Infrastructure and Economic Growth in China*, Boston, 2012.

Belt and Road Forum, '第二届'一带一路'国际合作高峰论坛圆桌峰会联合公报 *Di Er Jie 'Yi Dai Yi Lu' Guoji Hezuo Gaofeng Luntan Yuanzhuo Fenghui Lianhe Gongbao* (Joint Communique of the Leaders' Roundtable of the Second Belt and Road Forum for International Cooperation]', *Xinhua News*, 2019 <https://bit.ly/2VCuqM9> [Accessed 27 January 2020].

Brautigam, Deborah, *China in Africa: What Can Western Donors Learn?*, Oslo, 2011.

— 'A Critical Look at Chinese "Debt-Trap Diplomacy": The Rise of a Meme', *Area Development and Policy*, 5:1, 2020, pp. 1–14.

— 'Aid "With Chinese Characteristics": Chinese Foreign Aid and Development Finance Meet the OECD-DAC Aid Regime', *Journal of International Development*, 23:5, 2011, 752–64.

— 'China's FOCAC Financial Package for Africa 2018: Four Facts', CARI, 3 September 2018.

Brautigam, Deborah and Gallagher, Kevin, 'Bartering Globalization: China's Commodity-Backed Finance in Africa and Latin America', *Global Policy*, 5:3, 2014, pp. 346–52.

Brautigam, Deborah, Tang, Xiaoyang, and Ying, Xia, *What Kinds of Chinese 'Geese' Are Flying to Africa? Evidence from Chinese Manufacturing Firms,* Washington, 2018.

Brautigam, Deborah, Huang, Yufan and Acker, Kevin, *Risky Business: New Data on Chinese Loans and Africa's Debt Problem*, Washington, 2020.

Brewster, David, 'Is India "Losing" the Bay of Bengal?', *The Interpreter*, 19 March 2014.

— 'Silk Roads and Strings of Pearls: The Strategic Geography of China's New Pathways in the Indian Ocean', *Geopolitics*, 22:2, 2017, pp. 269–91.

Brødsgaard, Kjeld Erik, '"Fragmented Authoritarianism" or "Integrated Fragmentation"?', in Kjeld Erik Brødsgaard (ed.), *Chinese Politics as Fragmented Authoritarianism*, London, 2017, pp. 38–55.

Business Daily, 'Payment of External Debt Nearly Doubles in 6 Months to Dec', *Business Daily*, 12 March 2021.

CARI, 'Debt Relief Dashboard', *CARI*, 2021 <http://bit.ly/3lkWTBS> [Accessed 12 March 2021].

Carmody, Pádraig R., Taylor, Ian and Zajontz, Tim, 'China's Spatial Fix and 'Debt Diplomacy' in Africa: Constraining Belt or Road to Economic Transformation?', *Canadian Journal of African Studies*, 2021, pp. 1–21.

Chaziza, Mordechai, 'China Consolidates Its Commercial Foothold in Djibouti', *The Diplomat*, 26 January 2021.

Chellaney, Brahma, 'China's Debt-Trap Diplomacy', *Project Syndicate*, 2017 <http://bit.ly/3pJR7uK> [Accessed 18 November 2020].

Chen, Shengkui, Xu, Zengrang, and Shen, Lei, '中国省际煤炭资源流动的时空演变及驱动力 *Zhongguo sheng ji meitan ziyuan liudong de zhi kong yanhua ji qudong ji* (Spatial-Temporal Processes and Driving Forces of Interprovincial Coal Flows in China)', 地理学报 *Dili xuebao, Acta Geographica Sinica)* 63:6, 2008, pp. 603–12.

Chen, Xiangming, '4. The BRI and Development', *Regional Studies Policy Impact Books*, 2:2, 2020, pp. 61–78.

Chen, Yougag, Matzinger, Stefan and Woetzel, Jonathan, *Chinese Infrastructure: The Big Picture*, Hong Kong, 2013.

Chen, Zheng, 'China Debates the Non-Interference Principle', *The Chinese Journal of International Politics*, 9:3, 2016, pp. 349–74.

China Africa Research Initiative, 'CARI Contract Database', 2019 <https://bit.ly/2xbzL4c> [Accessed 27 April 2021].

— 'CARI Loan Database', 2019 <http://bit.ly/2P6wgCb> [Accessed 27 April 2021].

Citizen, 'How the Dream for a Port in Bagamoyo Became Elusive', *The Citizen*, 9 June 2019.

Constantinescu, Cristina and Ruta, Michele, *How Old Is the Belt and Road Initiative?*, Washington D.C., 2018.

Corkin, Lucy Jane, 'Chinese Construction Companies in Angola: A Local Linkages Perspective', *Resources Policy*, 37:4, 2012, pp. 475–83.

Deloitte, *Africa Construction Trends Report 2018*, Nairobi, 2019.

Engel, Ulf and Nugent, Paul, 'The Spatial Turn in African Studies', in Ulf Engel and Paul Nugent (eds), *Respacing Africa*, Leiden, 2009, pp. 1–9.

Fishman, Ted C., *China Inc.: The Relentless Rise of the Next Great Superpower*, 2nd ed., New York, 2006.

Gambino, Elisa, 'La Participation Chinoise dans le Développement des Infrastructures de Transport au Kenya: Une Transformation des Géométries du Pouvoir? (Chinese Participation in Kenyan Transport Infrastructure: Reshaping Power-Geometries?)', *Critique Internationale*, 89, 2020, pp. 95–114.

Gao, Fei, '当前非洲形势和中非关系 *Dangqian Feizhou Xingshi He Zhong Fei Guanxi*', 西亚非洲 *Xiya Feizhou (West Asia and Africa)* 1, Beijing, 1998: pp. 1–3.

Goodfellow, Tom and Huang, Zhengli, '"Contingent Infrastructure and the Dilution of 'Chineseness'": Reframing Roads and Rail in Kampala and Addis Ababa', *Environment and Planning A: Economy and Space*, 2020, pp. 1–20.

Grimm, Sven, *The Forum on China–Africa Cooperation (FOCAC) – Political Rationale and Functioning*, Stellenbosch, 2012.

Halland, Havard, *et al.*, *Resource Financed Infrastructure*, Washington D.C., 2014.

Hahn, Donghoon and Lee, Keun, 'Chinese Business Groups: Their Origins and Development', in Sea-Jin Chang (ed.), *Business Groups in East Asia: Financial Crisis, Restructuring, and New Growth*, Oxford, 2006, pp. 207–31.

Han, Xiao and Webber, Michael, 'From Chinese Dam Building in Africa to the Belt and Road Initiative: Assembling Infrastructure Projects and Their Linkages', *Political Geography*, 77, 2020, pp. 1–12.

He, Yafei, 'China's Overcapacity Crisis Can Spur Growth through Overseas Expansion', *South China Morning Post*, 7 January 2014.

Hillman, Jonathan E., 'Game of Loans: Sri Lanka', in Jonathan E Hillman (ed.), *The Emperor's New Road: China and the Project of the Century*, New Haven, 2020, pp. 151–70.

— 'The Belt and Road's Barriers to Participation', *Reconnecting Asia*, Center for Strategic and International Studies, 2018 <http://bit.ly/2GGoquo> [Accessed 27 April 2021].

Infrastructure Consortium for Africa, *Infrastructure Financing Trends in Africa – 2018*, Abidjan, 2019.

Jiang, Yuan, 'The Continuing Mystery of the Belt and Road', *The Diplomat*, 6 March 2021 <http://bit.ly/2OVhQXW> [Accessed 13 March 2021]

Jubilee Debt Campaign, *Africa's Growing Debt Crisis: Who Is the Debt Owed To?*, London, 2018.

Kamerling, Susanne and Van Der Putten, Frans-Paul, 'An Overseas Naval Presence without Overseas Bases: China's Counter-Piracy Operation in the Gulf of Aden', *Journal of Current Chinese Affairs*, 40:4, 2011, pp. 119–46.

Lam, Katy N., *Chinese State-Owned Enterprises in West Africa*, London, 2017.

Lardy, Nicholas R., *Sustaining China's Economic Growth After the Global Financial Crisis*, Washington, D.C., 2012, p. 129.

Larkin, Bruce, *China and Africa, 1949–1970: The Foreign Policy of the People's Republic of China*, Berkeley, 1971.

Lesutis, Gediminas, 'How to Understand a Development Corridor? The Case of Lamu Port–South Sudan–Ethiopia-Transport Corridor in Kenya', *Area*, November 2019, pp. 1–9.

Li, Anshan, *et al.*, *The Forum on China–Africa Cooperation: From a Sustainable Perspective*, Beijing, 2012.

Lin, Yifu, '林毅夫: '一带一路'需要加上'一洲' *Lin Yifu: 'yi dai yi lu' xuyao jia shang 'yi zhou'* (Lin Yifu: The 'Belt and Road Initiative' Needs to Add 'One Continent')', *China Observer*, 2015 <https://bit.ly/2Uz6h9p> [Accessed 27 April 2021].

Links, Stacey, 'Ascertaining Agency Africa and the Belt and Road Initiative', in Florian

Schneider (ed.), *Global Perspectives on China's Belt and Road Initiative*, Amsterdam, 2021, pp. 113–39.

Liu, Haifang, 'Associations as Social Capital of 'New Chinese Migrants' in Africa: Empirical Investigations of Ghana, Zimbabwe, Tanzania and South Africa', in Scarlett Cornelissen and Yoichi Mine (eds), *Migration and Agency in a Globalising World*, London, 2018, pp. 69–90.

Melber, Henning, 'Europe and China in Sub-Saharan Africa: Which Opportunities for Whom?', in *China–Africa Relations in an Era of Great Transformations*, ed. Xing Li and Abdulkadir Osman Farah, Farnham, 2013, pp. 107–26.

Ministry of Commerce of the PRC, '中国对外投资发展报告 *Zhongguo dui wai touzi fazhan baogao* (Report on the Development of China's Outward Investment)', Beijing, 2018.

Ministry of Foreign Affairs of the PRC, *China's African Policy*, Beijing, 2006 <https://bit.ly/2xiXfEH> [Accessed 27 April 2021].

— *Forum on China–Africa Cooperation Beijing Action Plan (2019–2021)*, *Ministry of Foreign Affairs of the PRC*, Beijing, 5 September 2018, no page given.

— 'China's Initiation of the Five Principles of Peaceful Coexistence', Beijing: Ministry of Foreign Affairs of the PRC, 2000 <https://bit.ly/3g1lVm6> [Accessed 12 May 2019].

Mitchell, Michael, Ehizuelen, Omoruyi and Abdi, Hodan Osman, 'Sustaining China–Africa Relations: Slotting Africa into China's One Belt, One Road Initiative Makes Economic Sense', *Asian Journal of Comparative Politics*, 3:4, 2018, pp. 285–310

Mohan, Giles and Tan-Mullins, May, 'The Geopolitics of South-South Infrastructure Development: Chinese-Financed Energy Projects in the Global South', *Urban Studies* 56:7, 2019, pp. 1368–85.

Munda, Constant, 'Public Debt Repayment Hits Sh1trn for First Time', *Business Daily*, 22 February 2021.

National Development and Reform Commission, 'Vision and Actions on Jointly Building Silk Road Economic Belt and 21st-Century Maritime Silk Road', National Development and Reform Commission, 2015 <https://bit.ly/2CRNJuI> [Accessed 25 June 2018].

Naughton, Barry, *The Chinese Economy: Transition and Growth*, London, 2007.

Nugent, Paul, 'Africa's Re-Enchantment with Big Infrastructure: White Elephants Dancing in Virtuous Circles?', in Jon Schubert, Ulf Engel and Elisio Macamo (eds), *Extractive Industries and Changing State Dynamics in Africa*, London, 2018, pp. 22–40.

Nyabiage, Jevans, 'China Merchants Signs US$350 Million Deal for Shekou-Style Revamp of Djibouti Port', *South China Morning Post*, 5 January 2021.

Okoth, Edwin, 'SGR Pact with China a Risk to Kenyan Sovereignty, Assets', *Daily Nation*, 13 January 2019.

Pairault, Thierry, 'Djibouti's Chinese Debt', *The China Africa Project*, 31 July 2020.

— 'Examining the Importance of the New Silk Roads for Africa and for Global

Governance', in Maria A Carrai, Jean-Christophe Defraigne and Jan Wouters (eds), *The Belt and Road Initiative and Global Governance*, Cheltenham, 2020, pp. 155–80.

— 'Les Entreprises Chinoises Sous la Tutelle Directe du Gouvernement Illustrées par Leur Investissement en Afrique [Chinese Enterprises under Direct Supervision as Shown by Their Direct Investment in Africa]', *Économie Politique de l'Asie*, 13:1, 2013.

Péclard, Didier, Kernen, Antoine and Khan-Mohammad, Guive, 'États d'Émergence: Le Gouvernement de la Croissance et du Développement en Afrique', *Critique Internationale*, 89, 2020, pp. 9–27.

Ramasamy, Bala, Yeung, Matthew and Laforet, Sylvie, 'China's Outward Foreign Direct Investment: Location Choice and Firm Ownership', *Journal of World Business*, 47, 2012, pp. 17–25.

Ruta, Michelle, *et al.*, *Belt and Road Economics: Opportunities and Risks of Transport Corridors*, Washington D.C., 2019.

Samson, Anna, 'A "Friendly Elephant" in the Room? The Strategic Foundations of China's Multilateral Engagement in Asia', *Security Challenges* 8:3, 2012, pp. 57–82.

Soulé-Kohndou, Folashadé, 'Bureaucratic Agency and Power Asymmetry in Benin-China Relations', in Chris Alden and Marcus Power (eds), *New Directions in Africa-China Studies*, London, 2019, pp. 189–204.

Sum, Ngai-Ling, 'The Intertwined Geopolitics and Geoeconomics of Hopes/ Fears: China's Triple Economic Bubbles and the "One Belt One Road" Imaginary', *Territory, Politics, Governance*, 7:4, 2019, pp. 528–52.

Sun, Yuan, Jayaram, Kartik and Kassiri, Omid, 'Dance of the Lions and Dragons', *McKinsey Global Institute*, 2017, p. 43 <https://mck.co/39tUQV6> [Accessed 27 April 2021].

Tang, Xiaoyang, 'Co-Evolutionary Pragmatism: Re-Examine "China Model" and Its Impact on Developing Countries', *Journal of Contemporary China*, 29:126, 2020, pp. 853–70.

Taylor, Ian, *The Forum on China-Africa Cooperation (FOCAC)*, London, 2010.

— 'Kenya's New Lunatic Express: The Standard Gauge Railway', *African Studies Quarterly*, 19:3–4, 2020, pp. 29–52.

Taylor, Ian and Xiao, Yuhua, 'A Case of Mistaken Identity: "China Inc". and Its "Imperialism" in Sub-Saharan Africa', *Asian Politics & Policy* 1:4, 2009, pp. 709–25.

Taylor, Ian and Zajontz, Tim, 'In a Fix: Africa's Place in the Belt and Road Initiative and the Reproduction of Dependency', *South African Journal of International Affairs*, 81, 2020, pp. 1–19.

Thorne, Devin and Spevack, Ben, *Harboured Ambitions: How China's Port Investments Are Strategically Reshaping the Indo-Pacific*, Washington D.C., 2017.

Wafula, Paul, 'Chinese Firm Withholds Key Detail in SGR Deal Review', *Daily Nation*, 10 December 2018.

Wagner, Christian, 'The Role of India and China in South Asia', *Strategic Analysis*, 40:4, 2016, pp. 307–20.

Wang, Yi, *Wang Yi: Pan-Africanism Is the Direction for Africa and in Tune with the Times*, Beijing, 2014.

Wang, Yuan and Wissenbach, Uwe, 'Clientelism at Work? A Case Study of Kenyan Standard Gauge Railway Project', *Economic History of Developing Regions*, 3, 2019, pp. 280–99.

Wethal, Ulrikke, 'Building Africa's Infrastructure: Reinstating History in Infrastructure Debates', *Forum for Development Studies*, 43:3, 2019, pp. 473–99.

Wissenbach, Uwe and Yuan, Wang, *African Politics Meets Chinese Engineers: The Chinese-Built Standard Gauge Railway Project in Kenya and East Africa*, Washington, 2017.

Xiao, He, 'African Agenda 2063 with the Belt and Road Initiative', in Cai Fang and Peter Nolan (eds), *Routledge Handbook of the Belt and Road*, London, 2019, pp. 425–30.

Xinhua News, 'China, Djibouti Agree to Establish Strategic Partnership', *Xinhua News*, 23 November 2017

Yao, Guimei, '中非合作论坛及其对中非经贸合作的影响 *Zhong fei hezuo luntan ji qi dui zhong fei jingji hezuo de yingxiang* [Forum on China-Africa Cooperation and Its Impact on China-Africa Economic Cooperation]', in Gongyuan Chen (ed.), 中国与非洲新型战略伙伴关系探索 *Zhongguo yu feixhou xinxing zhanlue huoban guanxi tansuo* [Exploration of the New Strategic Partnership between China and Africa], Beijing, 2007, p. 263.

Yee, Herbert and Storey, Ian, *China Threat*, Hoboken, 2013.

Yoshihara, Toshi and Holmes, James R., *Red Star Over the Pacific: China's Rise and the Challenge to U.S. Maritime Strategy*, Annapolis, 2010.

Yu, Hongyan, 'China Becomes a Net Coal Importer in 2009', *China Daily*, 23 February 2010.

Zhang, Hongpei, 'Chinese Facial ID Tech to Land in Africa', *Global Times*, 17 May 2018.

Zhao, Jun, 'Ownership Structure and Corporate Diversification Strategies of Chinese Business Groups', *Management Research Review* 33:12, 2010, pp. 1101–12.

Zhao, Kejin, '"一带一路"不应回避的十大问题 *'Yi dai yi bu' bu ying huibi de shi da wenti* [Ten Issues That Cannot Be Overlooked in the Belt and Road Initiative]', 凤凰 *Fenghuang* (Phoenix), 2015 <http://bit.ly/2OSV9nz> [Accessed 25 September 2020].

Zhao, Suisheng, 'China's African Relations and the Balance with Western Powers', in Jing Men and Benjamin Barton (eds), *China and the European Union in Africa*, Farnham, 2011, pp. 61–80.

Index

Lightning Source UK Ltd.
Milton Keynes UK
UKHW021643271022
411196UK00008B/1206